Kalahari Hunter-Gatherers

Kalahari Hunter-Gatherers

Studies of the !Kung San and Their Neighbors

Edited by Richard B. Lee and Irven DeVore

Harvard University Press

Cambridge, Massachusetts, and London, England

Library of Congress Cataloging in Publication Data

Main entry under title:

Kalahari hunter-gatherers.

  Bibliography: p.
  Includes index.
  1. Bushmen—Addresses, essays, lectures. I. Lee, Richard B. II. DeVore,
Irven.
DT764.B8K3   301.29'6   75-28320
ISBN 0-674-49980-8 (cloth)
ISBN 0-674-49985-9 (paper)

To future generations of San in a Free Africa

Acknowledgments

Although over a hundred articles on the San have been published by the members of the Kalahari Research Group since its founding in 1963, this work is the first book-length account of our research. The authors and editors take this opportunity to thank the many colleagues, fellow scientists, and citizens who have given us valuable advice and encouragement over the years. The roster includes friends not only in Botswana and other parts of Africa, but in the United States, Canada, England, Belgium, Australia, and Japan. Rather than list them all, we offer a collective expression of gratitude.

The National Science Foundation generously funded our initial fieldwork in Bechuanaland in 1963 to 1965. For the second and third phases of our work (1967 to 1973) the National Institute of Mental Health provided sustained financial support. To the NIMH and to Projects Director Lorraine Torres we offer a special vote of thanks. In recent years the Wenner-Gren Foundation for Anthropological Research, New York, and the Canada Council, Ottawa, have provided invaluable assistance for specific projects.

The San research project has enjoyed good working relations with the government of the Republic of Botswana since 1966. We wish to thank the officials of the government and the people of the country for welcoming us in their midst. Thanks also to the Honorable Dr. Quett Masire, Vice President of the Republic of Botswana, for his continuing interest in our project.

Finally, we thank the San people themselves for their unfailing hospitality (after their own fashion) toward more than a dozen researchers over as many years. We have all come to appreciate their cheerfulness in the face of adversity, their peculiar sense of humor, and their fierce egalitarianism.

Contents

x

Maps

Figures

Tables

Illustrations

Contents

Foreword

Sherwood L. Washburn

The San (Bushman) project is an ideal demonstration of what the science of anthropology can do. Over a number of years a wide variety of specialists have brought their various techniques and talents to bear on the interpretation of the behavior of a small group of people. The attempt has been made to understand a way of life, not some limited segment of human behavior. A remarkable number of productive young scientists has been involved in the studies, and this has enriched the work at every stage. Clearly, DeVore and Lee deserve much commendation for engineering such an imaginative project.

The importance of the San comes from the fundamental role which hunting has played in human history. Large-brained humans (*Homo erectus* and subsequent forms) supported themselves by hunting and gathering for at least a million years prior to the advent of agriculture. It is probable that men of the genus *Australopithecus* (using the term in the widest possible sense) hunted for some millions of years before that, and it may well be that it was the complex of weapons-hunting-bipedalism which accounts for the evolutionary origin of man. However that may be, for a period of at least a million years, men have hunted large animals, and hunting has been of major importance in human economies. Before the onset of agriculture man had evolved into his present form, and all the basic patterns of human behavior had appeared: language, complex social life, arts, complex technology. It was during this span of about 99 percent of the duration of the genus *Homo* that hunting was a major factor in the adaptation of man. If we are to understand the origin of man, we must understand man the hunter and woman the gatherer.

The contemporary peoples who still rely on hunting, or did so until very recently, give evidence which will help in understanding human history. They show complexity and diversity, adaptations to a very wide variety of environmental opportunities. The human gathering-hunting ways are based on language, technology, social patterns, and, especially, reciprocity. The whole pattern is far removed from anything seen in the carnivores. To hunt as a dog does, a human mother would have to carry an infant while running a two-minute mile! Further, as Lee has shown, reciprocity between humans demands some measure of technical complexity. Useful amounts of items such as vegetables cannot be carried without using some container, and larger animals must be disjointed and cut into portions before they can be transported. The human complexity of the hunting life is described in the following chapters.

Today people tend to regard the San as a small relic population. Science has been so dominated by Europeans with European problems in mind that it comes as a surprise to many that only a few thousand years ago San ancestors may have greatly outnumbered Europeans. Before agriculture and during the last advance of the Ice Age, approximately half of the area occupied by man was in Africa. If the habitat of the ancestral San was East and South Africa, then something on the order of one-sixth of the people in the world lived in that area. There can be no precision in figures of this kind, but some attempt to see the numbers of mankind in their relation to the world as it was then is necessary if extreme ethnocentrism is to be avoided. For example, in traditional physical anthropology, enormous efforts have been devoted to trying to determine whether Neanderthals were directly ancestral to Europeans, and no comparable effort was made to understand what was happening to most of the people in most of the world. From an evolutionary point of view, it is likely that until very recently San ancestors were far more numerous and important in human evolution than European populations—limited as the latter were by glacial advances, winters, and geographical isolation.

Three findings come from the San project which seem to be of particular importance to those interested in human evolution. The first is the complexity of the human hunting adaptation: hunting is not one simple way of life, and human hunting is not similar to the hunting of any other mammal. This poses major problems for the archaeologist who must seek clues to many different ways of life, some probably not closely paralleled by any known in recent times. Second is that this way of life is relatively easy except in time of crisis. Deeply embedded in our intellectual tradition is the idea that surplus time makes technical advance possible. Yet the San have much time. The roots of civilization lie not in time, but in the social organization of advancing technology. Thirdly, the San are living longer than might be expected from the usual generalizations of the length of life of early man. The discrepancy between their ages and the ages assigned to early skeletons seemed hard to reconcile, but I think the solution is that skeletons of known age in the great collections are largely from medical schools. They came from people who were not only old, but paupers—people who had been mistreated by society for many years. These diseased, long-edentulous skeletons have been the guide for estimates of age, and primitive man did not age according to the pattern of the modern ghetto.

Thus, even in estimates of the age of skeletons, there may be deep social biases, and the findings of the San project may help us to see some of the world's problems more clearly.

Note on Orthography

The San languages are characterized by click sounds produced with an ingressive air stream when the tongue is drawn sharply away from various points of articulation on the roof of the mouth. The four clicks used in !Kung and /Gwi appear as follows:

/	Dental click as in */Xai/xai, /Du/da.* (In spoken English this sound denotes a mild reproach, written *tsk, tsk.*)
≠	Alveolar click as *≠To//gana, ≠Ton!a.*
!	Alveopalatal click as in *!Kung, /Ti!kai.*
//	Lateral click as in *≠To//gana, //Gun//geni.* (In spoken English, this sound is used in some dialects to urge on a horse.)

Other features of the San orthography which should be noted include:

˜	nasalization as in */twã*
—	pressing as in *ma̲a̲*
’	glottal stop as in *ts’i*
”	glottal flap as in */”xai*

For the nonlinguist, San words may be pronounced by simply dropping the click, for example, for *≠To//gana* read *Togana* and for */Ti!kai* read *Tikai.*

Hunter testing a hollow tree for water

The nature of anthropology is rapidly changing. The past ten years have witnessed the radical shrinkage of the world's viable tribal and band societies. This has been accompanied by a corresponding expansion of commercial and governmental interests into the arctic, desert, and jungle hinterlands of the world where traditional societies have successfully persisted. While the future of anthropology lies with the study of these processes of development (and underdevelopment), the traditional task of the discipline—to record the ways of life of people—still has an important role to play.

3

Since 1963 a group of us has been studying the !Kung, a San- or Bushman-speaking people in the Republic of Botswana. What started out as a two-man field study has grown to include twelve long-term and again as many short-term investigations covering a spectrum of research from folklore to cardiology. Our overall goal has been to develop as complete a picture as possible of the hunting and gathering way of life, an adaptation that was, until ten thousand years ago, a human universal. We view this work as a contribution to the understanding of the evolution of human behavior and society. In particular, we dedicate this work to future generations of San.

In a sense, this book is a sequel to our earlier work, *Man the Hunter* (Lee and DeVore, eds., 1968). Many of the field workers have followed leads presented in the earlier volume, and all of us have been aware of the urgency of further study of this rapidly disappearing way of life.

Although the scope of our studies has been considerable, four major groups of research problems can be distinguished: ecology and social change, population and health, child development, and the cognitive world. We have been concerned primarily with the adaptive basis of San society. Under this heading comes studies of subsistence ecology and spatial organization (Lee), hunting behavior and settlement patterns (Yellen), and the plant and animal resource base (Yellen and Lee). Tanaka presents a comparative perspective on the /Gwi and //Gana San of the Central Kalahari, while Guenther focuses on the highly acculturated San of the Ghanzi farms.

Demographic research was carried out by Nancy Howell in the Dobe Area and by Henry Harpending over a wide range of northern San populations. Medical and nutritional research by a number of investigators is reported by Truswell and Hansen.

A third group of problems concerns the study of childhood. Draper examined childrearing practices in relation to subsistence economy and Konner has concentrated on the ethology of infant development. Shostak's life-history materials explore the psychosocial development of the !Kung in the words of the people themselves.

4

The cognitive world of the !Kung is approached from several directions. Katz has studied the ritual healing dance of the !Kung as a process of socialization and growth, while Biesele has collected a rich corpus of !Kung myth, folklore, and cosmology. Blurton Jones and Konner examined the !Kungs' knowledge of animal behavior as an adaptive system of ideas for the effective utilization of resources.

Each of these studies contributes in its way to a dozen or more specialties in anthropology and related fields. What these diverse projects have in common is a shared theoretical orientation that can be broadly defined as ecological, ethological, and evolutionary. All of the project workers have sought to relate their data to the basic adaptive strategies of the hunting and gathering way of life.

Throughout the book, a series of questions crops up again and again. It may be useful to list some of these at the outset.

Ecology and demography. What do the people do for a living? How do they allocate their time and energy? How does the hunting and gathering way of life affect reproduction, fertility, and mortality? How long do people live? How do people distribute themselves with reference to resources? How do they find spouses in a sparsely populated land? How are groups structured and maintained? Are group spaces defined and defended? And what is the range of variation observed among various San groups?

Medicine and nutrition. How hard or easy is it to make a living? How is this reflected in nutritional status of children and adults? What is the incidence of stress-related conditions such as heart disease?

Ethnoarchaeology. In light of the continuing controversy over the importance of hunting in human evolution, how important is hunting in the economy of the !Kung? How can the study of a contemporary hunting people help us to interpret prehistoric living floors?

Child development. How does growing up in a hunting society differ from growing up in an agricultural or industrial society? What is the effect on the infant of such features as constant handling and skin contact, demand feeding and long nursing? How does the developing !Kung infant compare with the North American or British infant in the appearance of behavioral landmarks? How does life in a hunting and gathering society affect the learning of adult sex roles? And how does sex-role differentiation change when the !Kung shift from nomadic to sedentary life?

Cognitive world. How do the !Kung conceive of themselves in relation to other tribes? How do they account for the human, plant, and animal reality around them? How do they meet the crises of life: illness, separation, and death? What resources in terms of special

knowledge and skills do they bring to the struggle for existence? And
how are these passed on from generation to generation? What does
the world look like if you are a !Kung hunter-gatherer?

Who Are the San?

The San are the hunting and gathering people of southern Africa
who live south of the Congo-Zambezi watershed. For three hundred
years they have been called "Bushmen," a term given them by the
Dutch settlers in the Cape of Good Hope. Recently, African scholars
have complained that "Bushman" is a term of derogation with racist
overtones and have suggested that "San" be adopted as a more digni-
fied and respectful term of reference (Wilson and Thompson 1969).
San means "aborigines," or "settlers proper" in the Cape Hottentot
dialect (Hahn 1881). They called the "Bushmen" the "Sanqua"
(Sonqua), and the term San was used by Isaac Schapera in the title
of his classic, *The Khoisan Peoples of South Africa* (1930).

The San have lived in southern Africa for at least 11,000 years
(Clark 1970). Some authorities suggest an even deeper time connection, relating recent San peoples to the Florisbad fossil finds of
40,000 years ago (Tobias 1956b, 1962b). Archaeological evidence
of the Wilton and Smithfield cultures are generally thought to be
produced by San peoples, and some Wilton materials have been
associated with San in historic times (Mason 1962).

In precolonial times, the San peoples covered the whole of
southern Africa from the Zambezi Valley to the Cape. Their numbers in 1650 can be roughly estimated at 150–300,000 people. The
arrival of the Dutch in 1652 led to a precipitous decline in San numbers. The San were almost entirely wiped out south of the Orange
River by 1850 as a result of a systematic Dutch extermination cam-
paign (Moodie 1839). We have no way of knowing how many were
killed and how many were carried off into slavery by the Dutch
(S. Marks 1972). Peoples of San origin who have completely lost
their language and culture now form a significant porportion of the
"colored" population of the Republic of South Africa (Marais 1939).

Long before the European invasion, in the eastern half of the subcontinent, San came into contact with Bantu-speaking pastoralists.
Here the warfare was on a much smaller scale than with the Europeans. Over the centuries, the San have been assimilated through
intermarriage into the general African population. It is believed that
the click sounds in several southern Bantu languages (Zulu, Xhosa,
Swazi) represent a borrowing from the San. These sounds have been

made familiar to westerners through Miriam Makeba's "Click Song" (Makeba is a Xhosa speaker).

6

The Dutch extermination and Bantu assimilation reduced the numbers of surviving San to an estimated 45–55,000 by 1955 (Tobias 1956a, Lee 1965). Since then their numbers appear to be increasing. Today San people are found primarily in the Kalahari Desert and its environs in Botswana, Namibia (South West Africa), and Angola. An additional few hundred may still be found in Zambia, Rhodesia, and the Republic of South Africa. The estimated population of 50,000 in the mid-1970s is divided by country roughly as follows: Botswana (60 percent); Namibia (30 percent); Angola (8 percent); all other countries (2 percent).

R. Lee examining the debris of an old campfire

San and Hottentot

Historically and culturally, these two peoples are closely related. The nature of their relationship, however, continues to puzzle scholars. The Hottentots share with the San a number of distinctive physical traits that suggest a common ancestry. The Hottentots, however, are pastoralists, not hunter-gatherers, and their social and political organization resembles that of tribal stock-raising peoples elsewhere in Africa (Schapera 1956; Carstens 1966).

The language problem is especially puzzling. Both Hottentot and San languages possess the clicks and other phonetic similarities, but at the level of morphology and grammar Hottentot and several of the San languages are quite dissimilar (Westphal 1963).

Although a great deal of linguistic work remains to be done, it is conceivable that all of the "Khoisan" languages may be ultimately related. It is clear that San and Hottentot have coexisted as neighbors for centuries in southern Africa.

San Language and Ethnic Groups

Westphal (1963) has made a major contribution to the unravelling of San language history. He demonstrated first a basic division of the many San tongues into two groups: those related to Hottentot (the Tshu-Khwe group) and those not related to Hottentot (the Bush group). It should be emphasized that speakers of both language groups practice a hunting and gathering way of life. In fact, one of the most isolated study groups, the /Gwi (see Tanaka), are Tshu-Khwe speakers.

Westphal further subdivided the Bush group into Bush A, Bush B, Bush C, and Bush D. Bush A is the language spoken by the !Kung, our main study group. The !Kung have a cultural and linguistic unity from southern Angola to central Botswana, an area of 600,000 km² The other three Bush languages include !Xo (Bush B), of southern Botswana, and two remnant languages spoken by a few survivors in the Republic of South Africa. Recently, Anthony Traill has done additional work on the southern San languages (Bush B and C). He has demonstrated that these two languages have a common ancestor and are representative of the formerly widespread Cape Bushmen languages (Traill 1973).

In light of Traill's work, the older classification of Dorothea Bleek (1929) into Northern, Central, and Southern deserves to be reinstated. The major San languages are set out in the accompanying table.

The San are not dying out as a race, despite the frequent predictions of their demise by learned authorities. Our data on San groups in western Botswana indicate a growing population. However, assimilation into Tswana groups does appear to be reducing San numbers in eastern Botswana.

The San are turning with increasing frequency to economic alternatives other than hunting and gathering. All over Botswana, San families work on the cattle posts of well-to-do stock raisers. The nature of the work relationship combines feudal and capitalist elements. Workers receive payment in rations, clothing, and livestock; and in some cases they receive cash wages. In the areas of Botswana and Namibia where white ranchers have settled, San often work for (low) wages or live as squatters on outlying holdings. Near Chum!kwe, Namibia, the South African government has established a station for settling the San and incorporating them into the apartheid system. About one thousand San have been settled since 1960. In several parts of Botswana, San have set up independent communities based on agriculture, cash game hunting and wage labor (see Lee 1965).

From the turn of the century when perhaps 60 percent of the San were full-time hunters and gatherers, this proportion has steadily dropped until the present (1976) when less than 5 percent of the San simply hunt and gather for a living. However, it is interesting

San language families

Bleek's division	Westphal's scheme (1963)	Main ethnographic representatives	Numbers of speakers and current status
Northern (!Kung zhun/twasi)	Bush A	Nyae Nyae !Kung[a] Dobe Area !Kung[b]	14,000, mostly on farms
Central (Nharo, /Gwi, //Gana)	Tshu-Khwe	Nharo (Naron)[c] /Gwi[d] Ghanzi Farm[e]	30,000, mostly on farms and cattle posts
Southern	Bush B	!Xo[f] !Xo[g]	3,000
	Bush C	n/uhki	1?
	Bush D	//egwi	100?
		Xam	extinct Cape Bushmen

[a]L. Marshall 1960; this volume, Chapter 15.
[b]R. Lee 1969; this volume, Chapters 1-3, 6, 8-14.
[c]D. Bleek 1928a.
[d]J. Tanaka, this volume, Chapter 4; G. B. Silberbauer 1965.
[e]M. Guenther, this volume, Chapter 5.
[f]H. J. Heinz 1966; Eibl-Eibesfeldt 1972.
[g]A. Traill 1973.

that in every San community, even the most acculturated ones, wild plant foods and game continue to play an important if not primary role in subsistence.

As modernization and industrialization of Botswana proceeds, the San are facing two further developments of crucial importance in their history. The first is the loss of their land base. On European and African farms where free-hold tenure is replacing tribal land tenure, the San are becoming, in effect, "squatters" on land they have traditionally occupied for centuries.

The second development is their incorporation by South Africa into the paramilitary units mobilized against the African liberation forces. In effect, the San are being caught in a pincer between the white settlers and the liberation movements.

A History of San Studies

For a people of such importance to science, surprisingly little has been known about the San. The Australian aborigines have a number of classic monographs done in the late nineteenth century such as the famous work of Spencer and Gillen on the Arunta and other peoples in central Australia (1899, 1904). No comparable body of work exists for the San. The early San literature was rarely based on field work. W.H.I. Bleek, the greatest of the nineteenth-century re-searchers, produced his language and folklore studies by interviewing San prisoners in the Cape Town jails (Bleek 1869; Bleek and Lloyd 1911). Even Schapera's classic, *The Khoisan Peoples of South Africa* (1930), was a compilation of library sources. Dorothea Bleek, the daughter of W.H.I. Bleek, carried out field work among the Naron (1928a), the Angola !Kung (Bleek 1928b), and the Hadza of East Africa as well as the editing of some of the Xam folklore materials collected by her father (see *Bantu Studies* for 1932 to 1936).

Although some medical research was carried out among the San in the 1930s (e.g., Dart 1937), serious ethnographic field work did not get underway until 1951. In that year, Laurence and Lorna Marshall began their work among the Nyae Nyae !Kung of South West Africa. The Marshall family expeditions have produced a dis-tinguished series of publications, films, and books through the fifties and sixties. An important paper by Lorna Marshall is reprinted in this volume.

Long-term research was opened up among the /Gwi and //Gana peoples of the Central Kalahari Desert by George Silberbauer in 1959 (Silberbauer 1965; Silberbauer and Kuper 1966). H.J. Heinz has made a detailed study of the !Xo peoples of southern Botswana (Heinz 1966) and of the "River Bushmen" of the Okavango Swamps.

Medical, ecological, and physiological research has been carried out by Phillip Tobias, C.H. Wyndham, and the other members of the Kalahari Research Committee of the University of the Witwatersand in Johannesburg (Tobias 1964). Mention has already been made of the linguistic work of Westphal (1963) and Traill (1973).

In 1967, a Japanese expedition did San field work in Botswana. The /Gwi and //Gana originally studied by Silberbauer were observed by Jiro Tanaka on three field trips, the second one under the auspices of the Harvard Kalahari Research group (Tanaka, 1969; this volume, Chapter 4). Mathias Guenther from Toronto studied a mission station on the Ghanzi farms in 1968–1970, and was among the first to work with San in highly acculturated situations (Guenther, this volume, Chapter 5).

The accompanying map shows the principal San field work sites up to 1976.

The Harvard Kalahari Research Group

Our interest in the San was sparked over a decade ago at the University of California at Berkeley by Sherwood Washburn and J. Desmond Clark. Washburn argued that the study of living hunting and gathering peoples might throw light on the evolution of human behavior and ecology. Clark believed that the study of campsite behavior would be an aid in the interpretation of prehistoric living sites. In the early 1960s, the anthropological world was excited by the new data pouring in from field studies of nonhuman primates and from the Leakeys' discoveries of ancient living floors associated with fossil man. The ethnographic study of a contemporary hunter-gatherer group seemed to be the next logical step.

Stage One: Lee and DeVore, 1963–1967. We chose to work in Africa rather than in Australia because we wanted to be close to the actual faunal and floral environment occupied by early man. After two months of survey in Bechuanaland in mid-1963, Lee and DeVore decided to concentrate on an isolated region in northwestern Ngamiland, named the Dobe Area after the waterhole where Lee first camped in October 1963. Lee spent fifteen months and DeVore two months in 1963–64 living in the Dobe Area. In line with our original research interests, we focused heavily on ecology—mainly hunting and gathering techniques, land use, and group structure. The results were summarized in Lee's doctoral dissertation (1965) and in several papers (Lee 1968a, b; 1969a).

This first field study yielded new data on hunters and gatherers that seemed to cast doubt on some of the then current views of the hunting and gathering way of life. At the suggestion of Sol Tax we organized the symposium on Man the Hunter, held in Chicago in April 1966. The conference brought together students of hunter-gatherers from all over the world and helped to stimulate new research directions on the hunters (Lee and DeVore, eds. 1968).

Two practical consequences emerged from the first field study and from the symposium. First, it became clear that before the hunter-gatherers could be of real use to students of human evolution,

11

Location of major San field work sites to 1976

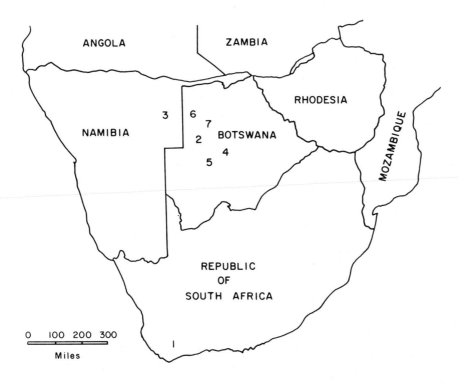

1. Cape Town — W. H. I. Bleek
2. Ghanzi — D. F. Bleek, M. Guenther
3. Nyae Nyae — L. Marshall, J. Marshall et al.
4. Central Kalahari Game Reserve — G. Silberbauer, J. Tanaka
5. Lone Tree — Takatchwane — H. J. Heinz, A. Traill
6. Dobe Area — Harvard Kalahari Research Group (R. Lee, I. DeVore et al.)
7. Kauri — M. Biesele

a great deal more had to be known of the ethnography, adaptations, and acculturation status of the contemporary cases. And second, it became clear that the range of specialized information required was so broad that it was more than any single investigator could hope to collect.

These considerations led to the planning of the second field study. The central ethnographic and ecological interests of Lee and DeVore were continued, but the research goals were expanded to include specialists in demography, child development, archaeology, population genetics, medicine, and nutrition.

Stage Two: Lee, DeVore, Howell, Draper, Harpending, Yellen, Physicians, Katz, 1967–1969. In 1967, DeVore and Lee returned to the Dobe Area to continue their work. In late 1967, Nancy Howell began research on San demography. Her study later grew to include reproductive histories of virtually all the adult women of the Dobe Area (see Howell, Chapter 6). Howell also studied the networks of kinship and acquaintance that held together the widely dispersed San population of Dobe and adjacent areas (Howell, in preparation).

In early 1968, Patricia Draper, Henry Harpending, and John Yellen arrived at Dobe. Draper did an 18-month study of child rearing and subsistence of both nomadic and settled !Kung. Harpending's work in genetic demography took him to camps all over northwestern Botswana where he interviewed and collected blood samples from close to two thousand San. John Yellen in collaboration with Irven DeVore did a two-part study of hunting behavior and settlement patterns. They followed hunters on actual hunts, and carefully traced the butchering and distribution of the meat and the final scattering of the bone remains. They also plotted the floor plans of recently occupied campsites (see Yellen, Chapter 2), and Yellen conducted excavations of Stone Age sites in the area.

In 1967–68, a medical team composed of Drs. Stewart Truswell and John Hansen made two trips to Dobe to examine !Kung adults and children. Truswell and Dr. B. Kennelly made a third trip in 1969 to work on heart disease. Medical research was also carried out by Drs. Trefor Jenkins and Jack Metz (see Truswell and Hansen, Chapter 8). In September 1968, Richard Katz, a psychologist, spent several months studying the !Kung healing dance in collaboration with Richard Lee.

Stage Three: Konner, Shostak, Tanaka, Biesele, 1969–1972. In mid-1969, Mel Konner and Marjorie Shostak joined the Harpendings and Yellen at Dobe. Konner worked on the ethology of early infant development (see Konner, Chapter 10). Later in the field study, he

was joined by Nicholas Blurton Jones from the Institute of Child
Study, University of London. Together they worked on several projects including the !Kungs' knowledge of animal behavior (Chapter
14). Shostak made studies of beadwork and musical instruments and
collected in-depth life-history materials from eight San women
(Chapter 11).

13

Jiro Tanaka of Kyoto University, who had worked with the /Gwi
in 1967–68, returned in 1971 to the Central Kalahari Reserve to
continue his ecological studies—paralleling Lee's ecological work in
the Dobe Area, 400 km to the north (Chapter 4).

In late 1970, Megan Biesele, a folklorist and anthropologist, arrived
in the Dobe area to study oral literature, myth, and ritual of the
!Kung. Most of her work was done at Kauri, about 150 km southeast
of Dobe (Chapter 13). Biesele, in addition to her ethnographic work,
focused on the problems of social and economic change among the
San. Biesele's findings showed that drastic changes were in the offing
for the remaining San groups.

Kalahari Hunter-Gatherers: The
Genesis of a Book

With the return of most of the field workers by 1971, the time
seemed ripe for a major presentation of our results. DeVore and Lee
organized the "Symposium on Bushman Studies" which was held in
New York in late November 1971. An audience of over four hundred people heard papers by Howell, Harpending, Yellen, and DeVore
in the morning and by Lee, Katz, Konner, Draper, and Guenther in
the afternoon. An important contribution was made by the discus-
sants who constructively criticized the papers and helped put our
data into perspective. These included Milton Freeman, Jean MacCluer,
Charles Nelson, and Sherwood Washburn on the demographic and
ecological papers; June Helm and Michael Harner on the sociological
papers; Margaret Bacon and Nicholas Blurton Jones on the papers on
child development.

Stimulated by the positive reception to the Symposium on Bushman Studies, DeVore and Lee were encouraged to go ahead with a
substantial publication of the San research. The book before you is
the result. Eight of the original nine papers have been included and
six new papers have been added: those by Tanaka, Shostak, and
Biesele, as well as the coauthored papers by Yellen and Lee, Truswell
and Hansen, and Blurton Jones and Konner. In addition we have
reprinted a revised version of Lorna Marshall's classic originally published in 1961: "Sharing, Talking and Giving: Relief of Social Ten-

sions among the !Kung." The book is divided into four parts corresponding to the research group's four main problem areas: Ecology and Social Change, Population and Health, Childhood, and Behavior and Belief.

14

Part I: Ecology and Social Change. These first five chapters introduce the basic adaptive strategies of the Kalahari San. In Chapter 1, John Yellen and Richard Lee describe the environment within which the Dobe !Kung operate, covering geology, climate, vegetation, and plant and animal resources, as well as the impact of the !Kung on their ecosystem. In Chapter 2 Yellen discusses !Kung settlement patterns from the perspective of ethnoarchaeology—the application of ethnographic data to the interpretation of prehistoric living sites. Yellen begins with the question "What can we reconstruct of !Kung behavior patterns strictly from the evidence of their abandoned campsites?" He goes on to suggest a number of possible answers, ending on a note of cautious optimism.

Whereas Yellen focuses on the spatial arrangements within a campsite a few hundred square meters in size, Lee (Chapter 3) enlarges the scope to encompass the spatial organization of several thousand square kilometers. He is concerned both with the way foraging groups move annually over the landscape and how land use changes over time—first as a result of climatic cycles and second as a product of secular historical changes. For this analysis Lee has chosen the dozen !Kung groups that have occupied the /Xai/xai and /Gam areas from 1890–1970. Lee demonstrates that the flexible land use patterns of today are part of the long-term ecological adaptation and not simply a response to recent acculturation and breakdown.

In Chapter 4, Jiro Tanaka reports on his ecological work with the /Gwi and //Gana San who occupy the Central Kalahari Game Reserve 300 km south of the Dobe Area. This region is more arid than Dobe, and its San inhabitants go for months each year without access to standing water; all their moisture requirements are drawn from water-storing roots and melons. Tanaka documents the success of this remarkable adaptation and draws a series of comparisons with the subsistence patterns of the Dobe area !Kung, placing the Dobe material in a broader perspective.

Mathias Guenther is one of the few anthropologists to work primarily among the acculturated San. Guenther lived with the Nharo and !Kung of the Ghanzi block, a district of freehold farms and ranches operated by Afrikaner and English white settlers from South Africa. Guenther portrays the complex ethnic mosaic of the Ghanzi District as a system of stratification with the whites (and now some wealthy blacks) at the top, the "African" Bantu-speakers in the

middle, and the "Bushmen" (San) at the bottom. The Nharo San
have become in effect squatters on their own land and the Ghanzi
District illustrates what could be the fate of all the San if they lose
free access to their hereditary lands.

15

Part II: Population and Health. Basic population and health parameters are presented in Part II. Nancy Howell reports on two
bodies of demographic data for the Dobe Area: a population register
maintained for the period 1963–1969 and the reproductive histories
of 165 Dobe Area women. Howell also discusses her newly-developed
techniques for estimating the ages of people, like the San, who do
not keep track of dates. An important finding is that fertility among
the !Kung is significantly lower than that of settled agricultural populations. This lower fertility may help explain why hunter-gatherer
populations tend to remain within the limited carrying capacities of
their land.

Henry Harpending (Chapter 7) draws on his observations of 2,000
San to provide a broad regional perspective on the Dobe !Kung. As
a geneticist, Harpending is particularly interested in inbreeding coefficients and in the distances traveled in order to find a spouse. On this
latter point the !Kung data are striking. Very long geographic distances separate the spouses before marriage, among the longest ever
recorded for a band or tribal population.

Stewart Truswell and John Hansen participated in three trips to
the Dobe Area and they have drawn together a comprehensive review
of !Kung medical research from their own and from others' investigations. The authors find the !Kung a basically healthy population
without evidence of malnutrition or degenerative heart disease. Their
studies of childhood growth indicate that !Kung children tend to be
small for their age, and they attribute this to undernutrition, an explanation that is at odds with the evidence for an abundant food
supply from other investigators. Further research will be needed to
resolve this question. In investigating heart disease, Truswell and
Dr. Brian Kennelly have made detailed studies collecting blood pressures, sera, and electrocardiographic data from over one hundred
!Kung. The results show not only that the !Kung have low blood
pressure and low cholesterol levels, but that these indicators do not
increase with age. The ECG studies indicated a striking absence of
degenerative heart disease in older subjects; explanations for this
enviable health status are sought in the nutritional, ecological, and
cultural background of !Kung life.

Part III: Childhood. Patricia Draper's study of !Kung childhood
(Chapter 9) is one of the first in which the dynamics of child development are closely related to ecological adaptation. The !Kung child

is pampered, weaned late, and has intense continuous contact with the mother, as he rides in the "back pack." Unlike children in most agricultural and pastoral societies, the young child is not assigned domestic tasks. Instead, the five-year-old enters a carefree phase of life with few responsibilities. Draper also uses her rich field data to show how childrearing practices change when San settle down and take up farming and herding.

Applying techniques developed largely for the observation of British and American infants and preschoolers, Melvin Konner's work on !Kung infants is among the first ethological studies of infancy in an African culture (Chapter 10). Konner made very detailed observations on children in the first year of life to determine the appearance of behavioral landmarks such as smiling, crawling, and walking. The !Kung infants' environment is rich in tactile and visual stimulation, and Konner seeks to show how this rich environment affects development—whether it retards or accelerates the appearance of new behaviors. Because these data on childrearing come from a hunter-gatherer population, they provide both a maximum contrast to the context of childrearing in industrial cultures, and some insight into the parent-offspring relations that characterized all humankind throughout most of its history.

Marjorie Shostak collected in-depth life history materials from eight !Kung women. From the rich corpus of hundreds of hours of taped interviews, Shostak has drawn a long excerpt in which N≠isa a 55-year-old woman, describes her own childhood with humor and feeling. In this unique document, the inner life and struggle of N≠isa, comes through; she expresses her early feelings about her parents and siblings, and her reaction to her husband when she was married to him at fifteen. In her careful translation from !Kung, Shostak has successfully captured some of the earthy flavor of !Kung dialogue.

Part IV: Behavior and Belief. In 1968 Richard Katz studied trance healing from the perspective of humanistic psychology. Beginning with the role of transcendent experience in human culture, he goes on in his chapter to describe the major features of the !Kung healing dance complex. A high percentage of !Kung adults are able to enter trance, and Katz considers how the society is able to absorb and utilize this high spiritual energy. He also considers the possibility for personal growth afforded by the trance experience, and goes on to compare transcendental experiences in the East and West with those among the !Kung.

Megan Biesele (Chapter 13) presents an introduction to her collection of over seventy-five !Kung myths and folktales. The !Kung of Botswana possess a series of myth cycles centered around a cast of characters that include a trickster god (Kauha) and his relatives. The beautiful Python of the dazzling costume is one of the most important of the central characters. She is the protagonist of a coherent cycle of adventures. !Kung folklore is unique among the San oral literatures in the prominence it gives to a female heroine. Otherwise the !Kung group of tale figures appears to correspond to the Mantis family members in the tales recorded by W.H.I. Bleek for the Cape Bushmen of the last century. The !Kung characters live together in a typical San camp and take part in a series of adventures filled with sex and violence. Trickster themes are prominent and are intimately connected with the origins of the necessities of life, of sharing, and of the social order.

In the field Nicholas Blurton Jones and Melvin Konner held "seminars" with the !Kung on their knowledge of animal behavior. The !Kung are keen observers of the habits of the animals on which they depend for a living. The depth and accuracy of their knowledge is set out in Chapter 14. The !Kung men became active participants in the research enterprise and clearly enjoyed the opportunity to share their knowledge with interested outsiders. What is most striking about this inquiry is what it reveals about the way !Kung think. The similarity of their thinking to our own suggests that the logico-deductive model of science may be very ancient, and may in fact have originated with the first fully human hunter-gatherers in the Pleistocene.

The final paper in this series is a reprinting of Lorna Marshall's classic, "Sharing, Talking and Giving: Relief of Social Tensions among the !Kung Bushmen." Originally published in 1961, this paper outlines the fundamental attitudes and behaviors that underlie the sharing way of life. Marshall points out how talking, much of it verging on argument, acts as a safety valve to keep people communicating effectively. For people to live at close quarters with little or no privacy, constant communication must be maintained. Gift giving serves a similar function in cementing relations between groups. In a strongly egalitarian society no person should gain a material advantage over another. Group norms strongly enforce the ethic of generosity and humility. With a wealth of case materials and details, Marshall documents how the !Kung successfully live up to the demands of a communal existence.

The Future of the San

From our twelve years of research on the San has emerged a sense of the accelerating pace of change. As concerned anthropologists we have begun to explore how our work could be of maximum benefit to the San. In order to deal with these issues we have to consider the trajectory of San development as it became clear to us through successive years of study.

In 1963, the San of the Dobe Area were the most isolated and traditional hunter-gatherers we could find in northern Botswana, Our choice of Dobe as a study site did not spring from archaism or romanticism. To follow out our stated purpose of preserving a record of the hunting and gathering way of life, it was necessary to find the most unacculturated group.

The Dobe Area is cut off from the rest of what was then the Bechuanaland Protectorate by a 100-kilometer stretch of waterless country that takes three days to cross on foot or two by donkey. When we first arrived at Dobe in October 1963, the area had no stores or schools and only intermittent contact with the outside world. A government truck would come out about once a month, but its main concern was the Bantu-speaking cattle people and not the San themselves. At that time, the San planted no crops and kept no domesticated animals except for the dog. The majority of the people lived mainly by hunting and gathering. The pastoralists lived at eight of the ten waterholes, but beyond these areas stretched a vast uncharted, unfenced hinterland of 10,000 km² used almost exclusively by hunting and gathering groups of San. For the foraging peoples, group structure was intact, traditional kinship patterns were very strong and the people moved freely back and forth across the unfenced boundary between Bechuanaland and South West Africa. In 1960–61, a government settlement station had been set up by the South Africans at Chum!kwe, 50 km west of the Dobe Area, but this had barely begun to affect the lives of the Bechuanaland !Kung. Dobe appeared to be an ideal area to study the hunting and gathering way of life.

As our field work continued, a more realistic picture of the "pristine" nature of the Dobe Area began to emerge. Most of the men of the Dobe Area had had some experience at some point in their lives herding the Bantu cattle, and about 20 percent of the young men were working on the cattle at any one time. Some had even owned cattle or goats in the past. Similarly, the !Kung were not total strangers to agriculture. Many had learned the techniques by assisting their Bantu neighbors in planting, and in years of good rainfall some had planted small plots themselves and had harvested crops. However, because of the extreme unreliability of the rainfall, none of the San had succeeded in establishing themselves on an agricultural basis. Hunting and gathering continued to be by far the most reliable and therefore dominant means of subsistence.

We sensed that the !Kung were on the threshold of great changes, but we could not have anticipated how rapidly these changes would come or what their consequences would be. In 1964, after the first census of the area, the !Kung were canvassed in a voter registration drive, in fact, one of their first direct contacts with the central government of the country. The Dobe Area San voted in the first election in 1965 and became, along with their fellow countrymen, citizens of the independent Republic of Botswana in 1966. In 1965, the unguarded international border that runs through the Dobe Area was fenced and began to be regularly patrolled by the South African occupation forces in Namibia (South West Africa). This fencing limited access to the western hunting areas of the Dobe Area, and in the mid-1960s, a number of Dobe Area families decided to emigrate permanently to Chum!kwe where the South Africans were providing jobs and rations. In 1967, a trading store was built at !Kangwa in the heart of the Dobe Area, and for the first time store-bought food and dry goods were available for cash. Immediately, the San women of !Kangwa set up a thriving business in home brew beer using brown sugar from the store as the main ingredient. The arrival of the store and the increase in government services after 1966 reduced the isolation of the Dobe Area, and in 1967–68, an average of one truck a week arrived at !Kangwa from the outside world. This improvement of transportation made it much easier for Dobe Area San to emigrate and in the years 1964–1968 about twenty young men went out to work in the gold mines of the Witwatersrand in South Africa.

The period from 1967 to 1970 was one of high rainfall, and the San took this opportunity to plant and harvest extensive crops of maize, sorghum, and melons. However, when the rainfall failed in 1972–73, they again fell back on hunting and gathering.

Perhaps the most important change in the mid-1960s was the increase in livestock holdings among the San. Whether purchased with cash from mine wages or obtained in payment for cowherding services, these goats, cattle, donkeys, and horses poured by the dozens into the San economy. By 1973, at least twenty families (particularly at !Goshe waterhole) were living as pastoralists and only part time as hunter-gatherers. Finally, in 1973, a primary school opened at !Kangwa with two teachers offering the first four grades.

A deeper change of potentially great importance is taking place in Botswana in a way that is only partially visible to the San themselves. In 1969, legislation was introduced to take land out of tribal tenure and put it into freehold tenure. Land Boards have been set up to hear applications from responsible individuals and groups, who, if their applications are successful, must survey and fence their land and limit herd size to ensure adequate grazing and prevent soil erosion. On first glance, these changes appear to be beneficial by promoting a more scientific, "rational" use of the land. However, on closer examination, the new land legislation could have potentially disastrous consequences for the San, since it makes them, in effect, "squatters" on the land they have traditionally occupied.

The experience of the Dobe Area over the last decade parallels that of many other San areas in Botswana. The problems of land loss, labor migration, shift to agriculture, and the cash economy are problems faced by the surviving San all over the Kalahari.

The Nature of the Problem

Of the 30,000 San people in the Republic of Botswana, fewer than 5 percent still pursue the hunting and gathering way of life. The majority have become incorporated as workers and clients into the tribal pastoral-agricultural life of their Tswana neighbors, while a large minority live and work as laborer-squatters on the freehold farming blocks particularly around Ghanzi. Smaller numbers of San have achieved semi-independent status in settled villages in the north and northeast (Lee 1965). Although part-time hunting and gathering continues to be important in many San communities, the major trend is clearly toward integration at the *economic* level with the national pastoral-agricultural economy of Botswana.

On the other hand, the extraordinary persistence of San culture, San language, and San identity (especially in the west of the country) in the face of several generations of contact with non-San peoples is eloquent testimony to the strength and vitality of the San people. Furthermore the people of Botswana are coming to recognize increasingly the rich contribution that San peoples have made to the national culture of the country. In fact culture historians of the future may argue that the cultural distinctiveness of Botswana derives from the unique blending of the aboriginal San cultures with those of the powerful medieval Tswana clans and other Bantu-speaking peoples. Tswana language, mythology, and folk culture reflect the interweaving of San themes through the fabric of the national life.

What then is the best way of assuring that the San will continue to be one of the elements in the ethnic and regional mosaic of Botswana culture?

Indigenous Peoples' Struggles

The experience of aboriginal minorities in many parts of the world

—Canada, United States, Sweden, Australia—has clearly shown that the most important single factor in their survival is the preservation of their land base. Without land on which to maintain their community-wide social and economic institutions, these peoples are rapidly and tragically absorbed into the poorest economic stratum in rural and urban slums. Even on the land, the picture for aboriginal peoples is far from ideal: poor housing, sanitation, and health facilities have been reported for many Indian, Eskimo, and Lapp reserves. Nevertheless these people still retain something that may ultimately prove to be far more valuable than physical amenities in this rapidly dividing world: a *continuing, functional community and family organization and a continuing sense of personal and social identity.* Land, Community, Family, Identity: these are the four cornerstones of cultural survival, not only for San people but also for any ethnic group which has traditionally lived off the land.

Maintaining these cornerstones is the goal in line with the aspirations of the San people themselves. As they have frequently stated to us in recent years, they want to grow food and have land to raise livestock, a place to water their stock, and an education for their children.

Unfortunately the San until recently have been politically silent. Under the tribal system they were discrimated against legally and economically. And despite recent government efforts to remove these legal disabilities, the San continue to exist in many parts of the country as second-class citizens. The long-standing Tswana policy of assimilating "subject" peoples into the clan and ward system of the various tribes, while admirable, is not an unmixed blessing. For when San people are incorporated, they may lose their language and culture and in return may gain entree to only the lowest economic stratum of Tswana society (Schapera 1952).

Our research has found that many San communities *want* to maintain their identity while at the same time move forward economically But they lack the means in terms of capital, education, and expert advice to take the necessary steps. Information on similar changes from other parts of the world is also lacking. Given their motivation, how can the San people close the gap between their aspirations and the means to fulfill them? At this point it is appropriate for us, as anthropologists, to specify our interest in the matter.

Toward a New Definition of
Anthropological Practice

For a number of years the Harvard Research Group, in keeping with then current anthropological research practice, stayed clear of involvement in social change. We gave freely of our time and effort when specifically asked by the government, and we have written down and transmitted to the authorities requests dictated by San groups; but for the most part our position followed the "paradigm" of "pure science" outlined in the following passage by the incoming president of the American Anthropological Association, Anthony F.C. Wallace:

> From the 1920s up to the mid-1960s, anthropology developed consistently along the lines of a clear-cut paradigm. As we all know, there were massive increases, especially after World War II, in numbers of anthropologists, in funding levels, in research and publication, but the pattern remained remarkably constant. It was a five-sided pattern which saw anthropology (1) as essentially a *graduate* academic discipline, (2) as a *basic science* with "application" following pure research, (3) as grounded in field work and excavation in *non-Western* cultures, (4) *as requiring no special ethical code* beyond what simple patriotism and common decency would suggest and (5) as entitled to call upon federal and foundation funds for unrestricted *support of the discipline as such* (via fellowships and research grants). (Wallace 1972, p. 10, emphasis in original)

Wallace goes on to discuss how in the mid-1960s this paradigm came under severe attack from several sources, including first "the increasing objection of foreign populations to ethnographic, physical anthropological and archaeological scrutiny under conditions of one-sided advantage to American anthropologists and their sponsors" (p. 11). A second source of pressure in Wallace's view, has come from "the movement of socially concerned students and others to reform the university and to influence anthropology (as well as other fields) to take up such moral and practical problems as war, poverty, social injustice and the misuse of the planet's natural resources" (p. 10).

The net effect of these and other pressures has been to radically challenge the old paradigm and to produce some fundamental shifts in the conditions of anthropological practice. The Harvard Research Group has participated in these ongoing debates, and we have reexamined our whole relationship to the San and other peoples of Botswana. In our view the implications of the shift in practice are four:

(1) We acknowledge that the responsibility of the scholar to the people studied goes beyond merely publishing the results of his or her studies in appropriate journals.

(2) This new definition of responsibility includes using our knowl-

edge in *working with the people* in their struggles to determine their own futures.

(3) Working with the people may take a number of concrete forms: (a) feeding back research results to the people studied and to their neighbors; (b) using knowledge acquired in scientific research to help communities achieve their development goals; (c) acting as advocates for inarticulate peoples, until their own political voice can be heard; (d) backing up our commitment financially with concrete aid to projects for the welfare of the people studied.

(4) Finally, we acknowledge that our responsibility extends beyond the San, with whom we did field work, to all the peoples of southern Africa in their struggles for freedom, dignity, and self-determination.

While actual proposals for action are being discussed, as a first step the Harvard Kalahari Group has agreed to turn over the royalties from this volume, as well as those from other works on the San, to a nonprofit body, the Kalahari Peoples' Fund, which would use its entire income annually for the working through of a new definition of anthropological practice. The Fund was founded by members of the Harvard Kalahari Research Group at a meeting in Hancock, New Hampshire, in January 1973. Its purposes are to promote understanding of the development problems facing the San and other small-scale societies and to assist them in their struggles for self-determination.

But what of the San themselves? Does this sort of "intervention" accord with their own definition of the situation? It is appropriate to conclude with the words of !Kun/obe, a !Kung woman who spoke with Megan Biesele shortly before the latter's departure from the field (see Chapter 13). After telling the story of the division of the social world due to the bumbling of Kara/'tuma (mythical forerunner of the San), !Kun/obe spoke of the current predicament of the San:

> Look what Kara/'tuma did to the San—that they hide their voices and hide their intelligence—they wouldn't do that if it hadn't been for Kara/'tuma. But I refuse this guy, I do. I'm telling you, I'm speaking out for myself and I'm not afraid of anyone! And even if all the white people came together and I stood in the midst of them I would still cry out for myself. People should cry out for themselves, Megan! People should protest. Black people cry for themselves, and they stay alive. The Afrikaaners cried for themselves, and they are alive. These people over there went about crying and crying, and they were

lifted up. We who are Zhū/twāsi (San), let us cry out, so we will be lifted up. Unless we do, we are just going to ruin.

Look, today San have goats, we have wretched donkeys. We ride them to travel around and carry home our things. Some of us have horses, some have cows. Where will they drink? What will these things drink? Where will they find enough water? I say to you, who in the course of your work have come here to live with us, "you should gather together the !Kung, let us all talk together," and then you write a letter to the government. Tell the government how we live, and ask them to drill bore-holes so that our stock may drink. Then if we have to pay taxes like everyone else that's just fine with us. That's what I say.

Ecology and Social Change

I

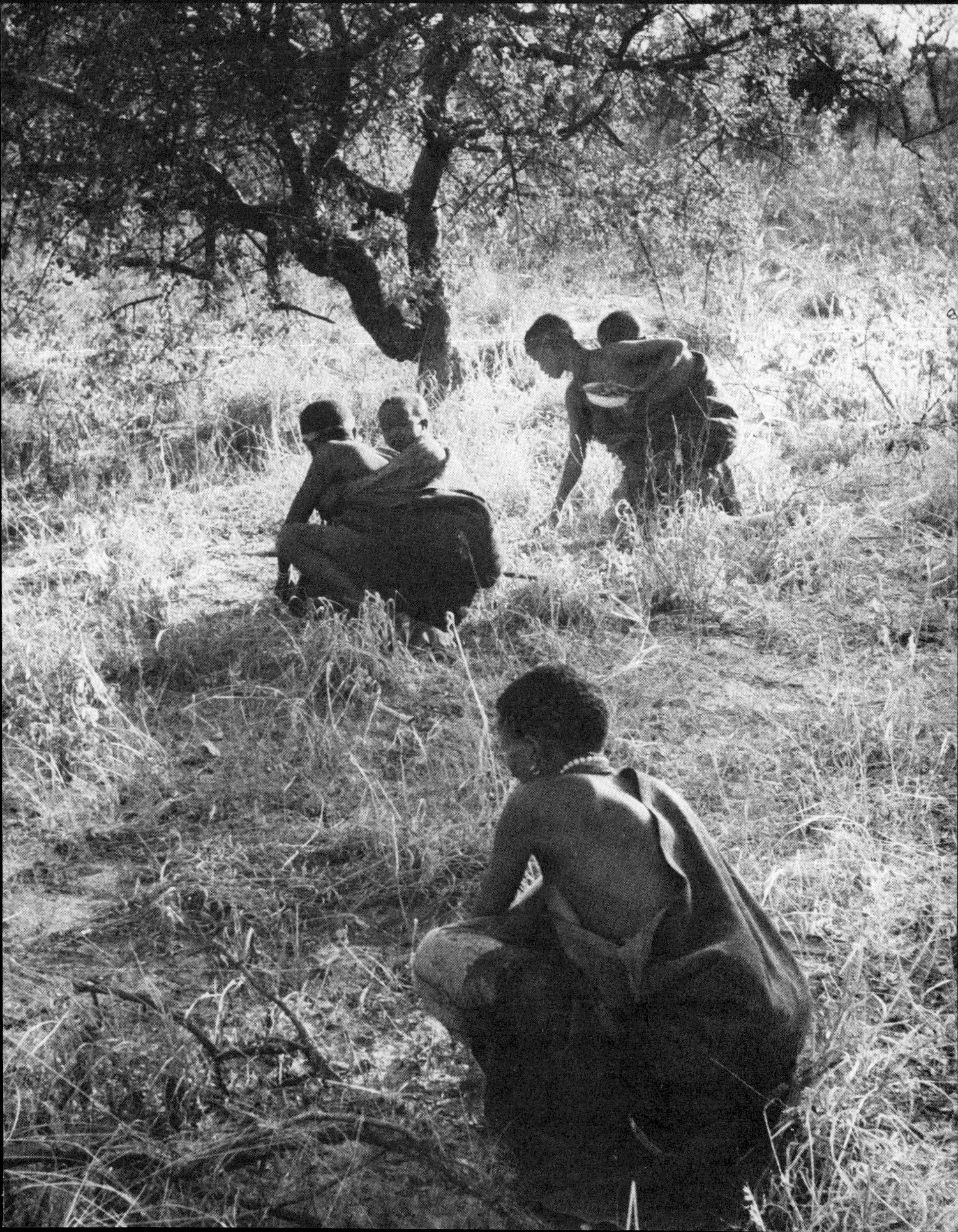

Women with infants digging roots

The Dobe-/Du/da Environment

Background to a Hunting and Gathering Way of Life

John E. Yellen and Richard B. Lee

The mongongo forests north of Dobe and the border road in 1964

The Dobe-/Du/da region[1] lies on the northern fringe of the Kalahari Desert, straddling the international border between Botswana and Namibia. Its limits lie between 20°30′ south latitude and 20°45′ to 21°20′ east longitude, encompassing an area of approximately 11,000 km². The Aha Hills, /Xai/xai (Kaikai), and !Kangwa (Kangwa or Levisfontein) are the regional features labeled on standard maps of southern Africa. "Dobe" and "/Du/da" are waterholes in the northern and southern reaches of this area respectively. This is part of a broader area approximately 290 km by 290 km or 84,100 km², bounded by the Okavongo River on the north and east, the Ghanzi Farms on the south, and the edge of the South West African Escarpment on the west. The topography, characterized by longitudinal or *alab* dunes and dry river beds (Grove 1969), is covered by Tree Savanna (Northern Kalahari Tree and Bush Savanna, and North West Tree Savanna) (Weare and Yalala 1971). Standing water is scarce during most of the year, and throughout the two areas there are only ten permanent water points.

The valleys of three dry rivers with tributaries run roughly from west to east, transecting the Dobe-/Du/da area: the !Kangwa, the /Xai/xai, and the Eiseb. Between the northernmost, the !Kangwa Valley (including the Dobe region), and the /Xai/xai Valley 35 km to the south, rise the Aha Hills, the only large formation of underlying rock exposed in the region. South of /Xai/xai, tributaries of the Eiseb Valley cut through the ≠To//gana, /Gəm, and /Du/da areas (Map 1.1).

A 90-kilometer waterless strip of land which separates the Dobe-/Du/da region from the Okavongo swamps to the east effectively limits east-west movement during most of the year. But north of Dobe and south of /Du/da other dry river valleys, conforming to the east-west pattern, contain permanent water points that support other !Kung populations. !Kung also live at the Nyae Nyae pans approximately 60 km southwest of Dobe.

The Dobe-/Du/da area lies on the northern fringe of the Kalahari. It forms part of a transitional zone between the drier shrub savanna (marked on most maps as the "Kalahari Desert"), which lies about 180 km to the south, and the lusher regions near the Okavongo river less than 180 km to the north. And as one moves from Dobe southwards to /Du/da changes may be noted on a smaller scale: the dunes become higher but are spaced further apart; the country assumes a more open character with fewer stands of large trees and more open grassland. Although exact figures are unavailable, the average mean annual rainfall may be slightly lower at /Du/da than at Dobe, and the ranges of the /Du/da ungulates are possibly slightly larger than those of their northern counterparts. Such small-scale variation, not considered in detail here, may lead to slightly different subsistence strategies for the Dobe as opposed to the /Du/da !Kung.

29

Temperature and Climatic Stress

The northern Kalahari Desert has a mean elevation of ca 1100 m above sea level; it lies within the summer rainfall area of southern Africa. These factors contribute to a climatic regime characterized by hot summers with a four- to six-month rainy season and by moderate to cool winters without rainfall. At 20° south latitude, the

Map 1.1. The Dobe-/Du/da Area

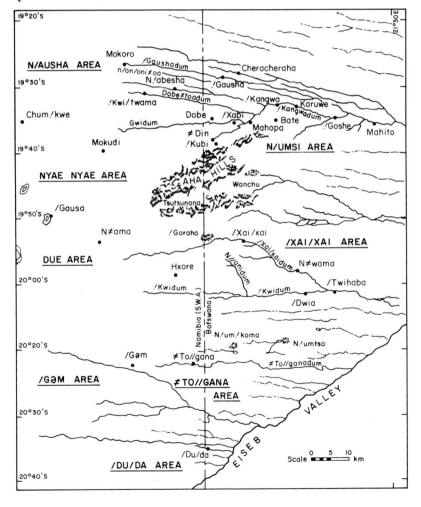

sun is directly overhead from early December to early January, but the highest mean temperatures are recorded in October, at the end of the dry season. In June and July, the coldest months of the year, night temperatures fall to freezing or near-freezing, with mean daytime highs of 25° Celsius (C).

The !Kung, in common with most high desert dwellers, experience both heat and cold stress (see Table 1.1). In terms of the work ecology, the critical temperature datum is the daily maximum since it indicates the heat conditions under which the people must hunt and gather. From October to March the people of the Dobe area can expect daily highs of 35°–45°C (95°–113°F), meaning that subsistence work must be carried out under conditions of extreme sweat loss. For example, a person walking in the sun at 38°C (100°F) will sweat at the rate of roughly 800 cc of water loss per hour, an equivalent of 3 liters (over 6 lbs of water!) in a typical working day. At the other extreme during the months of June, July, and August the !Kung can expect about 60 nights when the temperature falls below 5°C.

Rainfall

All the rainfall is concentrated in the hot summer months (October–May), while from June to September the Dobe area is completely dry. The relationships between two major air masses determine weather patterns in the Kalahari. The warming summer sun creates a region of low pressure which draws southward the heavier, rain-bearing equatorial system. The position of the southern and westernmost extension of this system, termed the "inter-tropical front" (ITF), depends on the relationship between this equatorial low and the cool dry air flowing northwards and eastwards from the Atlantic. The ITF, which may be up to 80 or more kilometers wide, is marked by widespread altostratus clouds and heavy rainfall and is followed by convectional rains. Its southward movement marks the start of the rains in the Kalahari, and its subsequent northward movement may account for later heavy rains (Wellington 1955, pp. 216–218). The extreme western edge of this front passes over the Dobe-/Du/da region; even slight year-to-year variations in its position can have a dramatic effect on the amount of rainfall the area receives. In such a climatic regime averages say little. The most striking fact is the enormous yearly variation in amount and distribution of rainfall. Figure 1.1 shows the rainfall at Dobe for two rainy seasons and most of a third. Rainfall varies from 239 mm in the drought of 1963–64 to

Table 1.1. Heat and cold stress in the Dobe Area: percentage of days each month with extreme temperatures

Conditions	1967			1968												1969			
	Oct	Nov	Dec	Jan	Feb	Mar[a]	Apr	May	June	July	Aug	Sept	Oct	Nov	Dec	Jan	Feb[a]	Mar	Apr
Heat stress																			
Percentage of days 33° C or over	56	38	42	40	5		7	4	0	0	39	100	100	50	76	70	0	0	58
Number of days of valid observations	$\frac{9}{31}$	$\frac{24}{30}$	$\frac{31}{31}$	$\frac{30}{31}$	$\frac{22}{29}$	$\frac{0}{31}$	$\frac{15}{30}$	$\frac{27}{31}$	$\frac{30}{30}$	$\frac{28}{31}$	$\frac{28}{31}$	$\frac{20}{30}$	$\frac{31}{31}$	$\frac{26}{30}$	$\frac{29}{31}$	$\frac{27}{31}$	$\frac{0}{28}$	$\frac{11}{31}$	$\frac{26}{30}$
Cold stress																			
Percentage of nights:																			
under 10°	0	0	0	0	0		10	44	93	96	96	75	26	0	0	0		0	0
under 5°	0	0	0	0	0		0	0	77	71	60	0	0	0	0	0		0	0
under 0°	0	0	0	0	0		0	0	37	0	0	0	0	0	0	0		0	0
Number of nights of valid observations	$\frac{3}{31}$	$\frac{28}{30}$	$\frac{30}{31}$	$\frac{30}{31}$	$\frac{21}{29}$	$\frac{0}{31}$	$\frac{16}{30}$	$\frac{27}{31}$	$\frac{30}{30}$	$\frac{28}{31}$	$\frac{25}{31}$	$\frac{20}{30}$	$\frac{31}{31}$	$\frac{26}{30}$	$\frac{30}{31}$	$\frac{29}{31}$	$\frac{0}{28}$	$\frac{11}{31}$	$\frac{26}{30}$

[a]No record.

597 mm in 1967–68, a swing of 250 percent. In addition month-to-month and place-to-place variations further increase the uncertainty of precipitation (see Lee, Chapter 3; Yellen and Harpending 1972).

Seasons

The !Kung divide the year into the following five seasons:

(1) *!huma*. The *Spring Rains* generally begin in October with the onset of the first rains consisting of light convectional thundershowers that often fall on one area and miss other areas entirely. The first rains trigger growth and reproduction in both flora and fauna and may transform overnight the landscape from a parched and dry state to one of lush greenery.

(2) *bara*. The *Main Summer Rains* generally fall from December

Figure 1.1. Rainfall at Dobe for three years

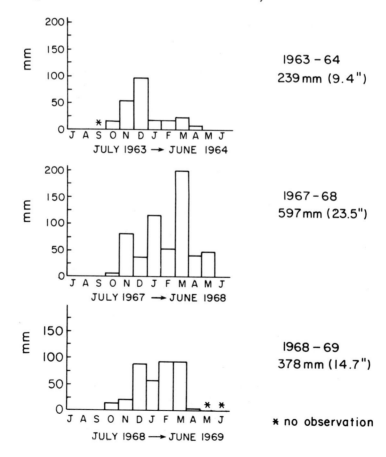

1963 – 64
239 mm (9.4")

1967 – 68
597 mm (23.5")

1968 – 69
378 mm (14.7")

* no observation

to March, but their time of onset and duration are highly variable. During the period of the main rains, the major summer foods appear.

(3) ≠tobe. The brief *Autumn* season lasts from the end of the rains until rapidly falling nightly temperatures mark the start of winter. The warm weather and lower humidity favor high rates of evaporation.

(4) !gum. The *Winter* dry season extends from May through August. It is heralded by a sharp drop in nightly temperatures to freezing or near-freezing. The days are clear and, by tropical standards, cool, often characterized by strong dessicating winds from the south and west with gusts estimated to 40 knots.

(5) !ga. The *Early Spring* season begins late in August with a rapid increase in daily temperatures and ends, usually in October or November, with the onset of the first rains. It is an extremely hot dry period during which the supply of water and food reach the lowest annual level.

Land and Water

Geological History

The Dobe area is situated on the western flank of an immense basin extending from the Namibian highlands to the highlands of Rhodesia. The Kalahari Basin was formed during the Tertiary era when surrounding areas were elevated by as much as a thousand meters. The lack of a corresponding rise in the central part of the subcontinent produced this gigantic basin which catches detritus from the surrounding highlands. The Aha Hills, formed of Otavi Dolomite, is one of the few places where these underlying rocks are exposed today. Dolomite, often riddled with sinkholes and caves, serves as an important underground reservoir; and most likely much, if not all, of the subsurface water now in the /Xai/xai and !Kangwa river beds is derived from this source.

Broad sheets of calcrete and silcrete, characteristic of arid and semi-arid environments, underlie much of the Kalahari and are widely exposed both in the dry river beds in the Dobe–/Du/da region and in the area between Dobe and the Aha Hills. Hardpan, composed of calcium carbonate, is derived from underlying bedrock. Slightly soluble, it is drawn upward in aqueous solution by osmotic pressure and deposited in sheets, some up to half a meter in thickness. The age of the oldest deposits is not known, but in some areas hardpan is still in the process of formation. These exposed hardpan areas have had important consequences for the past and present inhabitants of the Dobe area. Silcrete nodules, which form *in situ* in these layers, have provided a source of raw material for Late Stone Age tool-makers, probably ancestors of the modern day !Kung; and present-day inhabitants use small calcrete nodules as nut-cracking stones. Also, rock-hard layers of hardpan hold rainwater near the surface but, at the same time, they effectively prevent !Kung, using only wooden digging sticks, from excavating wells to tap the underground water supplies often not far below the surface.

Most of the Kalahari Basin is covered with a mantle of sand, generally between 3 m and 30 m in depth. The sands, varying in color from brownish-red to greyish-white, were probably originally derived and accumulated in pre-Quaternary times. However, it is likely that they have been redistributed more than once, with the most recent distribution definitely occurring in the last several thousand years. Conclusive evidence for this is found in the /Xai/xai region where Late Stone Age artifacts, no more than several thousand years old, have been found beneath 2 m of this sand.[2] The Dobe-/Du/da region is the only area of Botswana distinguished by well-established alab dune formations, which are discussed in detail below.

The Dune and Molapo System

Parallel longitudinal dunes, 8 km to 80 km in length and oriented 102°–282° roughly east–west, cover most of the Dobe-/Du/da region in a uniform pattern. The dune crests, situated from 1.5 km to 8 km apart, are designated "alab dunes" by Grove (1969), adopting a term first used by Monod (1958) to describe similar formations in areas bordering the southern Sahara. The term *molapo* is a Setswana word used here to describe depressions or small valleys between the dunes. It corresponds to *omaramba,* a Herero word used by J. Marshall (1957), Story (1958), and others. Formed by prevailing easterly winds at a time when annual precipitation was less than 250 mm, the dunes are presently stabilized by fixed vegetation. Similar formations in Senegal are believed to be younger than 20,000 BP (Michel 1967).

Drainage of rain water from the dune crests and flanks has largely removed the finer silty constitutents of the dune soils and concentrated them in adjacent molapo beds. On the lower flats and in the molapos, this water has reduced the ferric oxide component of the soil to soluble ferrous oxide which has been leached out. The result is a gradual and regular vertical shift in soil composition from loose, iron-rich sand on the dune crests down to a more compact soil, lacking in iron but richer in silt in the molapo bottoms. The consequences of this variation are extremely important since differences in soil closely correspond to differences in vegetation associations. The following zones have been defined: (I) Dune crest: loose reddish sand; (IIA) Upper flats: loose buff colored sands; (IIB) Lower flats: compacted white sands; (IIIA) Well defined molapos: compact grey silty sand with limestone sporadically exposed; (IIIB) Smaller molapos: light grey compacted sand with lower silt content; (IV) Hardpan (see Lee 1965, pp. 69–81).

Hydrology

Of the three types of standing water sources in the Dobe–/Du/da region—large pans in dry river channels, smaller molapo pans, and holes in large trees—the first is by far the most important, for only these river bed pans hold water throughout the year. The three large rivers probably have carried surface water during more than one period in their history, and the fact that the Eiseb and !Kangwa in places *transect* alab dunes indicates that these rivers were active at least once after the dunes were formed. All three carried water eastward toward the Okavongo swamps, and after exceptionally heavy rains water still flows down the !Kangwa for brief periods of

San herding Herero donkeys at /Xai/xai

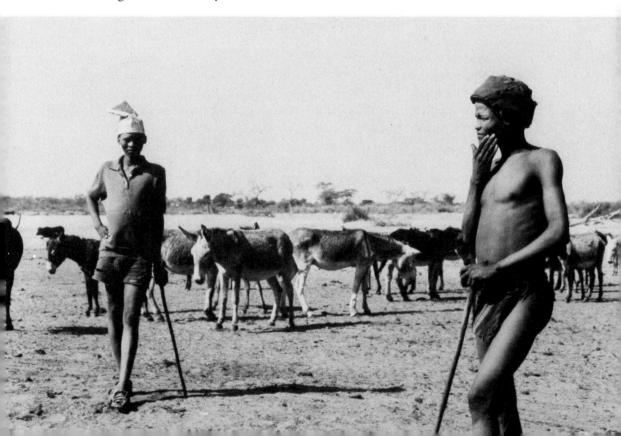

time. Some of the larger molapos such as !Gausha and /Du/da have served, during periods of higher rainfall, as small feeders representing tributaries channeled along the prevailing molapo pattern.

Presently the three main rivers carry underground water throughout the year. Transecting this flow at various points along their course are large, roughly circular pans, providing the only permanent water sources in the region. By far the largest concentration of these pans lies in the !kangwa valley, which has seven permanent (!Goshe, !Kangwa, Bate, Karuwe, Mahopa, !Xabi, and !Kubi) and one semi-permanent (Dobe) waterholes (see Map 1.1). The /Xai/xai valley has one permanent (/Xai/xai) and one semi-permanent (/Twihaba) source of water, while one permanent (/Gəm) and two semi-permanent (≠To//gana and /Du/da) sources are located in the sections of the Eisab valley tributaries that lie within our area.

The second source of water consists of small seasonal pans located in the bottoms of molapos and other low-lying areas. Ranging in size from a few meters to over a hundred meters in diameter, they serve as the focus for limited areas of internal drainage. Pans of this type, which fill during the rains, are numerous and widely scattered. Depending on their size and the areas they drain, they may hold water from only a day or two up to several months. In years of good rainfall, the largest may retain water until the winter or even to the start of the next rainy season.

The third source of water is from the hollows in the trunks and root systems of large trees which may hold tens of liters of water. While these supplies are continually replenished during the rainy season, they are quickly exhausted when the rains cease. Their main importance lies in their location on the food-rich dune crests for they provide the only water sources in these areas.

Fauna

Because of the broken nature of the vegetation, the area does not support the large herds of migratory plains game that are found on the open stretches of the southern Kalahari. Wildebeest, for example, which occur in herds of several thousand in the Central Kalahari Game Reserve, are seen in groups of ten to twenty in the Dobe area. There has been a diminution of game in the northwestern Kalahari over the past fifty years. Rhino, hippo, and springbok have disappeared completely, while zebra are rare. Buffalo and elephant were formerly numerous but now are only occasional summer visitors.

Of the 40 species of resident larger mammals, the most prominent are kudu, wildebeest, and gemsbok. Giraffe, eland, roan antelope,

and hartebeest are also present. Of particular importance to the San
as game are wart hog, porcupine, steenbok, duiker, and springhare.

The major African predators are all represented in the area and
include lion, leopard, cheetah, wild dog, and two species of hyena.
The smaller carnivores include caracul, wildcat, genet, jackal, and
several species of mongoose.

Unprovoked attacks by wild animals on San are extremely rare.
The people do not regard the bush as threatening or hostile. They
sleep in the open without fires when necessary and make no provision to protect or fortify their living sites. The most common
threat to the San homes, in fact, comes from the Herero cattle which
periodically blunder into camp to browse on the grass huts.

Bird life is abundant and varied. Some 80 species have been recorded. Ostrich are still common and continue to provide the !Kung
with a steady supply of ostrich eggshell water containers and materials for making beads. Only 8 species of birds are systematically
hunted by the San for food: guinea fowl, francolin (two species),
korhaan, kori bustard, sandgrouse, cape turtle dove, and the red-
billed teal.

At least 24 species of reptiles and amphibians, including five
poisonous snakes, are named and known by the San. Only two reptiles are of any importance as food: the rock python and the large
leopard tortoise.

Fish are not present in the Dobe area, but aquatic species such
as terrapins, leeches, clams, and snails found in isolated waterholes
indicate that at some time in the past the area was connected to a
river system by flowing water.

Of the invertebrates known to the San, there is an abundance
of scorpions, spiders, ticks, centipedes, and millipedes, as well as at
least 70 species of insects. The most important insects are the man-
tises (about whom there is a body of myths), bees (highly prized
for their honey), flying ants and click beetles (dietary delicacies),
and poison beetles (the sources of San arrow poison).

The Resource Base

Of the almost 500 species of local plants and animals known and
named by the San, some use is found for 150 species of plants and
100 species of animals. By virtue of their extremely extensive knowledge of the environment, the people are self-sufficient, with a single
exception: iron for knives, spear blades, arrowheads, and awls must
be obtained through trade and exchange.

The foundation of !Kung subsistence is the over 100 species of edible plants of the Dobe-/Du/da area. These include 30 species of roots and bulbs, 30 species of berries and fruits, and an assortment of melons, nuts, leafy greens, and edible gums.

To illustrate the richness and high nutritional quality of the !Kung diet, the composition of 5 of their major food species is set out in Table 1.2, along with 2 common Western foods for comparison. The most important of the food plants is //"xa, the mongongo or mangetti nut *(Ricinodendron rautanenii),* a superabundant staple which yields both an edible fruit and a kernel. The latter has a caloric content of 600 calories per 100 g and a protein content of 27 percent, a level of nutritional value that ranks it with the richest cultivated foods, such as peanuts and soybeans. Thousands of kilos of these nuts are consumed each year by the San, yet thousands more rot on the ground for want of eating.

The baobab fruit *(Adansonia digitata)* ≠m, is another staple. It yields a delectable and refreshing powdery fruit rich in vitamin C, calcium, and magnesium and a kernel which compares favorably in calories and proteins to domesticated nuts.

The tsin bean *(Bauhinia esculenta)* ts'hi, is comparable to the mongongo in calories and proteins and can be harvested for months after ripening because of its tough outer shell. In parts of our area, especially in the southern reaches where mongongo is scarce, tsin beans are the primary plant staple.

The vegetable ivory fruit *(Hyphaene ventricosa)* and the *!gwa* berry *(Grewia retinervis)* are very localized in distribution but yield hundreds of kilos of food during their four-month seasons.

These are only a few of the more abundant and attractive foods available to the !Kung. The nut and bean species (mongongo, baobab, and tsin) are particularly important since they contain high levels of high quality vegetable protein and fats that substitute for meat when game is scarce. Not all the foods are attractive, however. Some of the larger roots and melons have a decidedly bitter taste and a high proportion of roughage. These the people eat only when other more desirable foods are depleted.

The vegetable foods are so plentiful for most of the year that the !Kung can afford to exercise selectivity in their diet. They tend to eat only the most attractive foods available at a given season and to bypass those that are not as tasty or easy to collect. Over the course of a year only 23 species of plants make up about 90 percent of the vegetable diet by weight, and one species, the mongongo nut, accounts for at least half of the total (Lee 1968, p. 34; 1973b).

Game resources are less abundant and less predictable than plants. Meat provides 20–50 percent of the diet by weight, depending on the season and the number of men hunting in the camp. The general diminution of game in the northwestern Kalahari has not led to the collapse of the San way of life, however, because of excellent techniques for capturing smaller mammals; and the meat from these kills supplements a diet primarily based on vegetable sources.

At some camps for short periods the amount of game brought in may be much higher. In December 1964, for example, a camp with four hunters killed twenty-nine animals over a seventeen-day period.

The big antelopes, kudu, wildebeest, and gemsbok are regularly hunted with poisoned arrows, but a good hunter feels he has done well if he kills as many as six of these in a year. The general scarcity of game and their frequency of movement raises obvious difficulties for !Kung hunters. Except in a very rough way, it is rarely possible to predict on a day to day basis where the big antelopes will be located. This in part explains why considerable attention is given to the hunting with dogs of wart hogs, steenbok, and duiker—three species with very limited ranges. The owner of a well-trained pack of four or five dogs can count on twelve to fifteen of the 50–80 kg wart hogs a year. Duiker and steenbok, small antelopes weighing 10–20 kg, are next in importance. These are taken with dogs, trapped in rope snares, or, more rarely, shot with poisoned arrows. In the birth season (December to March) the young are often run down on foot or brought down with throwing clubs.

An unorthodox but highly effective hunting technique is the probing of underground burrows. Four important species are taken this way. The springhare is killed with a flexible 4-meter pole with a metal hook at the end. These nocturnal animals sleep in long narrow burrows by day. The hunter finds an occupied burrow, probes it with the pole until he has hooked his prey, and then excavates the soft sand until he can retrieve the animal. The large African porcupine is also an underground dweller which the !Kung hunt. They often light a fire at the burrow mouth in an attempt to half-suffocate the animal and drive it from the burrow. Sometimes they dig down on the den from above, or actually crawl down the narrow burrow to spear the occupant. The Antbear (up to 65 kg) also lives in burrows, and men dig down on the prey from above to spear it. Finally, warthogs, when run to ground, are flushed from their holes by lighting a fire at the entrance and then speared when trying to escape. The underground species are highly desired because they are very fat, and animal fat is one of the elements most scarce in the San diet.

The game birds, guinea fowl, francolin, and bustard, are captured in ingenious snares when the opportunity arises, as are the small mammals such as hare, bat-ear fox, mongoose, genet, and aardwolf. Occasionally the dogs flush these animals out of the bush and are allowed to eat them. When there is no other meat in the camp, however, the people eat these themselves.

Table 1.2. Composition of some major San wild foods, 100 grams as eaten[a]

Common name	Mongongo nut	Mongongo fruit	Baobab fruit and nut
San name	//"xa	//"xa	≠m
Botanical name	Ricinodendron rantanenii		Adansonia digitata
Season of use	year round	Apr–Nov	May–Sept
Composition in g/100 g eaten			
Moisture	4.2	13.4	5.2
Ash	4.0	5.7	7.3
Protein	28.3	6.6	14.3
Fat	58.4	0.6	13.9
Fiber	1.5	3.5	10.7
Carbohydrates	3.7	70.2	51.4
K calories	654	312	388
Composition in mg/100 g eaten			
Ca	249	89.6	272
Mg	500	195	630
Fe	2.07	0.74	9.51
Cu	1.90	0.45	2.47
Na	2.0	1.01	76.3
K	686.6	1760	4173
P	704	46.0	1166
Zn	4.09	1.39	6.96
B-Carotene	—	0	—
Thiamin	0.127	—	—
Riboflavin	0.139	0.113	—
Nicotinic Acid	—	0.121	—
Vitamin C	0.57	8.51	—

[a]Analyzed by A. S. Wehmeyer, National Nutrition Research Institute, CSIR, South Africa, based on samples submitted by Harvard Kalahari Research Group Oct.–Dec. 1967, June 1968.

[b]Watt, B. K., and A. L. Merrill (1963) Composition of Foods: Raw, Processed, Prepared. U.S. Department of Agriculture Handbook No. 8, Washington, D.C., p. 43 (Item no. 1495).

[c]Ibid., p. 52 (Item no. 1870).

The big leopard tortoise, weighing up to eight pounds, is a great favorite and is easily collected by men, women, and children. It is baked in the shell and can feed a family of four. The nonpoisonous rock python also makes a good meal. Few of the many other snakes, lizards, and amphibians are sought as food. Nor, for that matter, do insects play more than a negligible role in the diet. A species of

Tsin bean	Veg. ivory fruit	Grewia berry	Peanuts roasted w/skins[b]	Brown rice cooked[c]
ts'hi	!hani	!gwa	—	—
Bauhinia esculenta	*Hyphaene ventricosa*	*Grewia retinervis*	*Arachis hypogaea*	*Oryza Sativa*
Feb–July	June–Oct	Mar–June	—	—
5.2	6.6	10.6	1.8	70.3
2.9	9.0	3.7	2.7	1.1
31.6	4.9	5.4	26.2	2.5
31.6	0.4	0.2	48.7	0.6
1.0	9.6	12.6	2.7	0.3
23.2	69.6	67.5	20.6	25.5
544	302	293	582	119
136	103	157	72	12
258	196.5	172	—	—
3.3	2.04	4.7	2.2	0.5
1.0	0.47	0.4	—	—
89.0	544.9	31.0	5	282
849	2560	655	701	70
484	155.8	—	407	73
3.8	0.56	1.6	—	—
0.22	0.06	—	—	—
0.936	—	—	0.32	.09
0.815	0.096	—	0.13	.02
1.86	4.62	—	17.1	1.4
2.19	19.7	—	0	0

flying ant has an annual two-day outbreak around the beginning of December; thousands are collected and roasted, mainly by the young women and children.

By and large, the snakes, insects, and lizards that Service (1966: 101) says are the staples of the "Bushman" diet are despised by the San of the Dobe area.

The overwhelming bulk of the animal protein which !Kung consume is provided by mammals, and of these 14 are hunted systematically. These include antbear, duiker, eland, gemsbok, giraffe, hare, hartebeest, kudu, porcupine, roan, steenbok, springhare, wart hog, and wildebeest. The porcupine and springhare, both relatively abundant, easy to locate, and readily killed within their burrows, are the most frequently obtained. Less attention is paid to the hare which usually must be stalked and shot with bow and arrow, and to the relatively large antbear which must be dug from its burrow with a great expenditure of effort and a not very high likelihood of success.

Success in hunting ungulates appears inversely related to size. The steenbok, which may be either trapped, shot with poisoned arrow, or run down with dogs is most frequently killed, followed by the duiker, which is usually too large to trap. The wart hog, successfully run down and brought to bay by dogs as well as hunted by the bow and arrow, is the next most frequently killed. Of 151 hunters interviewed in the Dobe and /Xai/xai areas, 75 percent have killed at least one, and 39 percent have killed 10 or more.

The other larger ungulates, all of which are hunted with bow and poisoned arrow, are less common and more difficult to locate and stalk. After they are wounded, some may travel long distances and take several days to die. Consequently rates of hunting success are proportionally lower. About half of the animals wounded by !Kung hunters are allowed to escape, either to recover or to be eaten by carnivores. Among the !Kung, gemsbok is most frequently killed, followed by kudu, wildebeest, eland, roan, hartebeest, and giraffe. Of the same group of 151 hunters, only 28 percent would admit to killing a single giraffe, and only 6 percent claimed 10 or more kills.

People and the Environment

The Environment's Effect on People

In outlining briefly the most important environmental factors influencing the !Kung way of life and the resultant annual subsistence strategies, one finds the prime considerations include the relative scarcity of water during most seasons of the year, the occurrence of a number of discrete vegetation associations, an additional, uneven distribution of resources within vegetation zones, the relative abundance of plant and animal foods, and the effects of changing seasons. Each of these is discussed separately below.

43

This entire region of some 11,000 km² includes only nine permanent and four semipermanent water sources; the !Kung are forced to depend exclusively on them for four to five months each year and during this time must locate their camps near them. This means that even utilization of the entire range is not possible throughout the year, and in some areas abundant, readily available, and desirable foods are not collected since they lie too far from standing water. (While !Kung will sometimes make brief trips into this hinterland during the dry season, carrying water with them and relying on water roots, they do so only a few days or weeks at a time.) Thus, from May to October, utilization of the hinterland is extremely uneven, and intensity of utilization is related inversely to distance from permanent water. During a day's trip, an individual will rarely travel more than 15 km (on a straight line) from camp, and generally no more than 10 km. Thus scarcity of permanent water is the most crucial limiting factor with which the !Kung must contend.

The widespread system of alab dunes—the regular progression of dune crest, upper and lower dune flanks, and shallow and deeper molapos—each with its characteristic soil and floral associations, gives the region a varied character. All of these different associations may be reached in the course of an average day's collecting trip from most of the permanent waterholes. Added to these are the more limited areas of river valley and flatlands with exposed hardpan which also provide their unique food sources. Compared with flatter areas in the southern Kalahari which receive a similar amount of rainfall, the number of plant species is relatively large just because of this diverse character of the landscape, making the number of food plants available to the !Kung for exploitation unexpectedly large. The list now numbers some 110 species; and although many of these are only rarely utilized, they form a cushion in times of stress.

While all elements of the dune and molapo system can be exploited from most of the waterholes, a caveat must be added, for within the areas readily accessible to each of them, some resources are relatively abundant and others relatively scarce. The people of !Goshe, for example, have extensive mongongo groves located within 10 km of their waterhole, while, by contrast, Dobe lies about 7 km from the nearest dune, and the nut grove on it is small. Dobe is noted for its concentration of vegetable ivory palms, !Xabi for its morula trees, and !Kubi for its baobabs. The tsin bean is absent in the north but is superabundant south of the Aha Hills on the open flats west of /Xai/xai. Eland are relatively common south of the Aha Hills and rarer to the north, while kudu concentrate in the flatlands around !Kubi during the winter to utilize the winter browse there. The result is a movement of people throughout the year for either short or extended visits to other waterholes, and it is not unusual for some individuals to live alternately at two different waterholes. Ostensibly these visits are undertaken for social reasons, but in large part they reflect this fact of underlying resource variability.

It has been emphasized that, overall, plant foods are relatively abundant, varied, and easy to locate and collect while large game is scarce, difficult to find, and hard to kill. The result is that vegetable foods provide the mainstay of the diet while meat rarely constitutes more than 40 percent of it. (Incidentally, this is true of the great majority of hunters and gatherers in tropical and subtropical regions, see Lee 1968a.) The !Kung have a hierarchy of vegetable food preferences; they concentrate their attention on preferred species in times of plenty and broaden the variety of their diet during the less abundant times of the year. These plant foods are, of course, adapted to a semi-desert environment; and although they may be less plentiful in drier years, they never completely fail. They provide a secure, dependable subsistence base.

The subsistence strategy is, of course, closely related to the seasons. Briefly, under the precontact system, there was a movement of small groups away from the permanent waterholes during the rainy season and a gradual consolidation into much larger aggregations during the dry months of the year. Even today, with the onset of the rains, pairs or small groups of families move to the seasonal pans to eat roots and last year's crop of mongongo nuts. The main rains herald a time of plenty as the leafy greens, fruits, and berries ripen. Game is more plentiful at this time; and since water is available in most areas, the !Kung can move their camps to good hunting areas. It is at this time of year that people can afford to be most selective and concentrate on their favorite foods. In late summer, while pans still hold water, the new crop of mongongo nuts falls; and the !Kung can eat both the nut and sweet fruit surrounding it (see Table 1.2). This is also the honey season, when both men and women concentrate their attention on locating and opening hives.

In autumn the seasonal pools start to dry and population begins to concentrate, first at the larger seasonal pans and then back to the permanent water sources. From early winter until the start of the next rains food becomes increasingly scarce; people must work harder to obtain it and must utilize less-preferred species. Early winter is still a time of relative plenty, when the last of the summer berries and the mongongos near the water sources provide fairly easy pickings. In the later winter gums and roots provide major items in the diet. Men set out snares for the smaller buck and for birds. Late winter and early spring—before the first rains—is the most difficult time of the year. The areas within easy walking distance of the waterholes become depleted of choice foods, and diet consists largely of roots, edible gum, and whatever other less desirable foods may be found. People scan the skies and await anxiously the first rains.

People's Effect on the Environment

The !Kung hunt and set bush fires; both of these practices alter the environment to some extent, but how much and in what ways is uncertain. Our own guess is that the traditional hunting system has little, if any, adverse effect on the ungulate population. A possible explanation is merely that they have hunted with poisoned arrows for hundreds or perhaps thousands of years, and the equilibrium between predator and prey was reached long ago. The effect that burning has on vegetation patterns is quite substantial. The !Kung set fire to large areas in late winter and early spring in order to facilitate the growth of new grass which, in turn, attracts game. Tinley (1966) points out that the effects of burning can vary depending on where and when it is applied. He states that to maintain and favor the spread of grassland valuable for either wild or domestic grazing animals, burning should take place only after the first inch or two of rains have fallen, and that earlier burning, such as the !Kung practice, promotes the development of shrub at the expense of grassland. Thus, it is possible that San burning is working to decrease open grassland, a topic we plan to investigate in future research.

In contrast to the !Kung, the effect of Bantu inhabitants, who both plant crops and maintain herds of cows and goats, has been profound. Bantu hunters use rifles, horses, and donkeys; and the decrease in game since their advent in the early twentieth century has been significant. Not only do rifles provide a more effective means of killing than poisoned arrows which must be fired at close range, but also the use of horses and donkeys enormously extends a hunter's mobility. A mounted hunter can scout a significantly larger area than a man on foot; he can range farther afield and remain there for a longer period of time because he can carry water with him. He also can use his mounts as pack animals to bring fresh meat back to his village.

But more important is the effect of livestock which Bantu maintain at all the permanent waterholes in both the !Kangwa and /Xai-/xai valleys. Overgrazing is considerable, and both cattle and goats compete directly with the different species of wild grazers and browsers. Their effect on the vegetation is also considerable since they shift the balance away from the grasslands and in favor of extensive shrubland and thicket. As Tinley points out, in semi-arid environments this delicate balance is easily disrupted, so that it is essential for stock numbers to be kept low if equilibrium is to be maintained (1966, p. 79). Luckily domestic animals must drink regularly, and the effects of their overgrazing are limited primarily to the river valleys and the immediate surrounding areas. What is more, since they are excluded from Namibia by a patrolled wire fence, the western portion of the Dobe-/Du/da region remains off limits to domestic stock.

Left to their own devices the !Kung would continue indefinitely to carry out this skillful exploitation of their resources. Their present level of population makes only modest demands upon the environment, and the mechanisms that maintain this level of population appear to be functioning adequately (see Howell, Chapter 6). A mixed agricultural-pastoral way of life is rapidly replacing hunting and gathering in the Dobe-/Du/da area. Success, over the long run, depends on maintaining the natural vegetation cover. It remains to be seen whether such an adaptation can prove as viable as the traditional !Kung subsistence techniques.

Settlement Patterns of the !Kung:
An Archaeological Perspective

John E. Yellen

Plane-table survey of San rainy season camp

Archaeologists frequently lament the paucity of ethnographic data on settlement types and settlement patterns. Generally, it is easier to find out what an individual calls his cross-cousin than it is to obtain an accurate description of the house or the settlement in which he lives. It is worthwhile asking why ethnographers generally have paid scant attention to this aspect of material culture; an adequate explanation must take into account the fundamental nature of this class of data, and the inherent limitations placed on the interpretation of it.

It is explanation, rather than description itself, which is the anthropologist's goal; explanation involves demonstrating interrelationships and regularities between phenomena and attempting to discover the causative rules or laws reflected therein. Though types of camps and regularities in the form of patterns may be described, it is necessary to use other data to explain why a certain configuration is observed. The kind of settlements which an individual group may establish reflects decisions, either conscious or unconscious, by the members of a society about how they will relate both to their environment and to one another.

For example, the !Kung establish small, widely scattered, and short-lived camps during the rainy season and build larger, more permanent ones during the dry season. On the other hand, Gould (1969) notes that aborigines of the Australian Western Desert congregate in large camps when standing water is most plentiful and disperse into smaller groups during drier periods of the year. To understand why such different patterns exist it is necessary to examine the Kalahari and Western Australian Desert environments, the distribution of water, plant, and animal resources, and consequently the differing subsistence strategies employed by the !Kung and the aborigines. Similarly, the placement, spacing, and utilization of huts and work areas in a !Kung encampment can be described and striking regularities noted; but to explain them one is forced to speak in terms of group structure, social organization, and the division of activities among different units. In other words, to explain why an encampment assumes a certain form, one must use a different class of data for setting out the relevant variables and, from there, speak of "systems" and consider explanation and cause and effect. But one can not discuss the physical elements of settlements alone in this way, and it is easy to see why little anthropological attention has been focused on them per se. One may speak of religious systems, political, economic, or kinship systems, or ecological or social systems—and many of the classic anthropological works bear these terms in their titles—but for settlements, the term "pattern" or "type" is generally applied.

For the archaeologist, the study of modern settlement patterns and the reconstruction of prehistoric ones are most important. The obvious point should be made that at least limited information about the latter generally becomes available in the normal course of an archaeological excavation. It is possible to use even partial insight into a prehistoric settlement pattern as the basis for more general speculations, and to attempt to delineate at least some of the related cultural systems which are the underlying shaping factors. This is not a new argument and has been elaborated by Binford (1962) among others, although generally in a slightly different context.

49

It is useful to draw an operational distinction between ecologically oriented and sociologically oriented behaviors (Chang 1967b, p. 102) and to consider several studies which attempt to reconstruct one or the other of these systems in a specific prehistoric context, on the basis of inferred settlement pattern or settlement type. In the Epirus region of Greece, for example, Higgs and his colleagues (1967) have noted that Upper Paleolithic sites fall into three groupings: larger sites at the foot of the Pindhus mountain range and parallel to it, other large sites at a lower altitude near the coast, and finally smaller, open-air sites located between the coast and the mountains. Higgs postulates that a single group occupied all of these sites, moving to the higher ones in the summer when they are snow-free and to the lower, coastal sites in the winter. The smaller, intermediate sites he interprets as either transit stations or marginal hunting camps occupied for brief periods of time (Coles and Higgs 1969).

In a similar type of study, White (1971) has examined a series of sites in western Arnhemland, and after consideration of the location and contents of each site, she concludes that the prehistoric hunters spent the drier months of the year on the coastal plain where they depended largely on fresh water and estuarine resources. During the yearly rains, an inland movement to the highlands occurred, and hunting assumed a more important role. Both the Higgs and White studies, based on analysis of settlement pattern, are primarily ecological in their orientation. To cite another which deals with sociological variables one may turn to Movius's (1965, 1966) examination of Upper Paleolithic hearths at the Abri Pataud in southwestern France. Hearths in the earliest (Aurignacian) levels are consistently small, while their later (Perigordian) counterparts are greatly increased in size. To account for these differences, Movius postulates a shift from an earlier nuclear family type of organization to larger extended families in Periogordian times.

It is interesting to note that both Higgs and White in their arguments use ethnographic analogy. In western Arnhemland there is, most likely, historical continuity from their prehistoric counterparts to the historically known aborigines, who alternated their residence between the highlands and the coastal plains. Higgs notes the movement of present-day Greek pastoralists to and from the higher mountainous regions and points out that grazing for present-day domesticates is abundant and readily available in the highlands only during the snow-free summer months. Presumably the same held true for the wild prey of Upper Paleolithic man.

In western Ngamiland, it is possible to use ethnographic data in a similar way and to compare, for example, distributions of present-day dry season !Kung camps with their Late Stone Age counterparts. The conclusion drawn from striking similarities is that these prehistoric hunters and gathers patterned certain of their responses to the environment in the same way as their modern counterparts (Yellen and Harpending 1972). Given that environmental conditions during the late Stone Age prevail today, and that present !Kung are probably directly descended from these prehistoric ancestors, the analogies drawn are probably valid. But to what extent must analogies be limited to situations in which direct historical links may be established?[1]

In point of fact, the archaeologist, lacking practical alternatives, has little choice but to use general analogy, and both Ascher (1961) and Chang (1967a; 1967b) point out that no guidelines, other than the use of "common sense," exist to determine how analogy may properly be employed. Even when it is understood that recourse to analogy does not provide proof but only possible explanations for observed archaeological phenomena, scholars disagree violently on the acceptability of this approach. On the one hand, Chang (1967a, p. 230) argues:

> Indeed, in a broad sense, archaeological reconstruction *is* analogy, with or without explicit ethnological recourse. To claim any information at all, other than the stone or the potsherd that is actually discovered, is necessarily to presume knowledge of man and culture in general and to assume the existence of cultural regularities, however broadly conceived. Since each archaeological object and situation is unique, every archaeological reconstruction is analogy based upon a number

of such presumptions and assumptions. The ethnological recourse does not make analogy possible; it only renders its results
probable or even scientifically true.

One of the strongest critics of the analogical approach, on the other
hand, contends:

> The use of analogy has demanded that prehistorians adopt the
> frames of reference of anthropologists who study modern
> populations and attempt to force their data into those frames,
> a process which will eventually cause serious errors in prehis-
> toric analysis, if it has not done so already. (Freeman 1968,
> p. 262)

While the criticisms which Freeman raises are valid, and alternative
techniques for reconstruction should be encouraged, it must be noted
that different approaches are few; and without recourse to analogy—
either implicitly or explicitly—it would be difficult to make any

Two families leaving camp to hunt and gather, the men with springhare poles

statements about the lifeways of prehistoric hunters and gatherers.
One might add that to employ analogy does not preclude the use of
other approaches and techniques.

Perhaps the best case for the value of analogy based on ethnographic parallel can be made by offering specific examples. At some
Mousterian sites, for example, a curious and puzzling fact has been
noted: mandibles of larger animals are split along their entire length,
while mandibles of smaller species are left intact. The !Kung do the
same thing, and the reason is that inside the jawbones of larger
animals one finds a rich, fatty, edible marrow which is a highly
valued food. Dart (1957a; 1957b) argues that Australopithecines at
Makapansgat Cave used bone tools because an analysis of faunal remains shows that some kinds of bone fragments, such as the distal
ends of humeri in comparison to their proximal counterparts, are
proportionately more common than would be expected. He suggests
that distal humeri were used as clubs, and also interprets certain
alterations in some bone fragments' shapes as purposeful human
modifications. In an enlightening study of goat bone remains from
modern abandoned Hottentot campsites, Brain (1967; 1969) has
found similar nonrandom distributions and similar types of modifications, all clearly due to mechanical weathering and such natural
forces as differential strength and resultant preservation of different
bones. Another example of this type of ethnographic parallel can
be based on the interesting fact that !Kung camps are generally located at least one-half kilometer from their water source, even
though this entails a round trip usually twice a day for water. The
reason is that the !Kung do not want to frighten away from the area
game which also utilizes these water sources. If a similar pattern is
revealed in a prehistoric context, the modern case could be offered
as a possible explanation.

Analogies may serve to provide hypotheses, which are susceptible
to testing. Binford (1968, p. 270) has succinctly summarized this
approach in stating that "model building and testing can be related
to ethnographic facts, but verification of propositions (should) remain a problem to be solved by the formulation of hypotheses test-
able by archaeological data." The implication is that analogies, based
on the behavior of the !Kung, aborigines, or any other source are
believable to the extent they may be supported by testing with independent data. While Freeman (1968) may strongly argue to the contrary, I would reply that if one wishes to hypothesize about the
organization and methods of adaptation of prehistoric hunting and
gathering societies, one obvious and valuable place to turn for ideas

is to the modern counterparts with the most similar subsistence bases. The attempt to test the resulting hypotheses against archaeological data is the next step.

Thus far, I have argued that ethnographic fact may serve the process of archaeological interpretation in two ways: it may provide specific analogies or one of a number of bases for hypothesis formulation. Such data may be employed, as well, to test general deductive statements, underlying principles, which are supposed to apply to all hunting and gathering societies. The literature contains a number of such statements concerning the contexts in which specific activities take place (Longacre and Ayres 1968) or the kinds of camps which hunters and gatherers establish (Binford 1968; 1971). To take one specific example, Wilmsen (1972) has devised a model which describes the spatial and interactional conditions of band organization at any point in time and states:

> A band most effectively exploits stable food resources by dividing into smaller groups each of which is centered among a set of resource locations which it alone exploits. A single location centered in the band's region and from which members cooperatively hunt mobile animals is most effective for this type of resource. (p. 22)

Since deductive statements of this type are meant to apply to all hunting and gathering societies, a single counter-example will serve to disprove them, and one may look at an individual group to see if it conforms to the pattern. Thus, a first step in validating such propositions is to examine known, documented societies. Here !Kung data are of extreme value, as illustrated in the conclusion of this article.

There is one additional use which ethnographic studies may serve, and this concerns methodology. The archaeologist must continually draw inferences from the material which he recovers from the ground. Since he rarely has the assurance that his conclusions are correct, it is difficult for him to evaluate the techniques he used to draw them. What are the best ways, for example, for estimating the size of a site? How accurate are estimates of the number of animals eaten at a site, based on calculation of "minimum numbers" from faunal remains? Through study of a living group, it is possible to see what people do, then to observe the visible remains of activities, and finally, in this controlled situation, to determine what techniques are best suited for reconstructing the former on the basis of the latter. There is no

circular reasoning (often characteristic of archaeological recon-
structions) involved here, since only the techniques of reconstruction
are being tested.

The conclusion which may be drawn from this preceding discussion is that ethnographic data may be used validly in the reconstruction of the past. It can serve as the basis for hypothesis and
speculation. Observed analogies do not provide conclusions, but
they may suggest avenues for further research. General deductive
statements about the behavior of hunters and gatherers may also be
tested against single, present-day societies of this type. These societies may provide a controlled environment and, as such, serve as a
methodological testing ground. Not only is it permissible to use
ethnographic data in this way, but this approach is also a valuable
one which should be actively pursued. Several examples supporting
this view have been offered.

Dobe !Kung Settlement Pattern

Environmental Variables Influencing Settlement Pattern

While it is impossible to distinguish completely between ecological
and sociological factors, certain aspects of !Kung settlement patterns
may be understood best as responses to subsistence needs and considered as ecologically oriented behaviors.[2] A settlement's size, location, and length of occupation all reflect these variables, especially
the latter two which are directly dependent on conscious choices
about how the food resources in a given area are to be utilized.

The geographical units that form the basis for !Kung spatial organization consist of areas containing a sufficient amount and variety of
resources to support a group of individuals over the course of a year.
While it is convenient to describe such areas as "territories," this term
can be misleading. The boundaries of these regions are not clearly defined, and, in fact, !Kung have no single term in their own language
to describe them. To some extent areas overlap; they are not defended,
and in some instances more than one group will move within a single
area.[3] They may be described best as an informal and highly flexible
method for arranging the population in a workable relation to available resources.

One of these areas, which includes the Dobe waterhole, provides
the basis for the following analysis (Map 2.1). This region encompasses approximately 320 km[2], located mostly to the north and
west of Dobe, the only permanent water source in the area. The

waterhole itself is situated on the boundary between an extensive, flat, low-lying area of exposed hard pan which lies to the south of it and the rolling dune and molapo (valley) system which stretches away to the north. While the southern area is extensively exploited for several months during the dry season, no camps are established south of Dobe; and for most of the year, almost all movement is to the north and northwest where numerous camps are constructed and occupied. This northern area includes five pans which may hold water for several months during and immediately after the rains; one additional pan, !Gausha, is located in the eastern fringe of this region and is used primarily by groups based at !Kangwa. In this region are eight groves of mongongo trees which stretch roughly east–west along the dune crests. Aside from the nuts they yield, these trees may collect in their large hollows several gallons of water during the rains. In the far northern reach of this region used by the Dobe group, lie a series of *Hwanasi,* or salt pans, located in the bed of an old river; they are important because during the rainy season they attract herds of large game.

  !Kung subsistence strategy is based in large part on the desire to keep hunting and gathering trips as short as possible and to minimize the distance that must be traveled each day. Most, if not all, of a nuclear family's personal belongings can be carried by a single adult,

Map 2.1. Land-use division between Dobe and surrounding groups

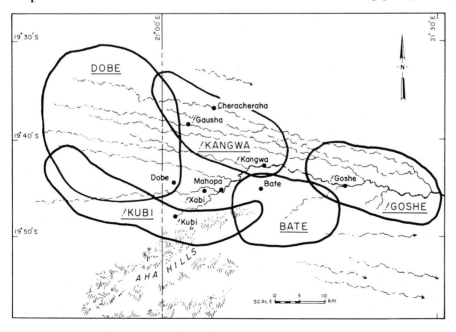

and a serviceable hut can be constructed in little more than an hour; these factors facilitate mobility and permit groups to shift residence to more desirable areas quickly and with a minimum of difficulty. The major constraining factor is water, which for most of the year is available at a single pan: Dobe (see Yellen and Lee, Chapter 1). The overall residence pattern is one of group concentration near the Dobe waterhole in relatively large, long-term camps during the dry months of the year, and an outward movement in smaller units to nut groves and seasonal waterholes during and immediately after the rains.

Table 2.1 shows the movements of the Dobe group over a six- and one-half-month period, from January 27, 1968 to July 11, 1968. This includes the season of heavy rains, autumn, and the first half of the winter, and encompasses most of the moves made by them during their yearly round. If the start of an annual cycle is marked by the first rains, it is likely that prior to January 27, 1968, the group made no more than one trip of perhaps eight to ten days to the north of Dobe. After July 11, 1968, the group remained in Dobe until the start of the next rains in late November 1968. During the study period, 37 moves from one camp to another were made. Excluding the large base camp at Dobe, 27 camps were occupied: 11 in nut groves, 14 near pans in molapos, and 2 in intervening areas. Twenty-three of these camps were occupied only once; 3 were reoccupied a single time, and one was reoccupied twice. The average length of a single occupation, excluding Dobe, is 3.1 days. Sites in nut groves were inhabited an average of 2.7 days while in molapos the average length of occupation is 3.6 days. Map 2.2 shows the placement of these camps.

Movements out of Dobe during and after the rains are basically cyclical in nature, as illustrated by Map 2.3. Typically, a group will move northwards, occupying a series of camps as it goes, and then head back toward Dobe again. Frequency of return to Dobe and length of time spent there are based largely on social factors: desire to visit other !Kung, to make brief trips to other waterholes, to collect or leave individuals or families, and also to visit Bantu cattle posts and anthropologists' camps. During rounds to the north, however, movement from one site to another and length of time spent in an area reflect decisions based primarily on subsistence factors. The general !Kung strategy is to camp in an area where a mix of resources—including water, plant, and animal foods—is readily available. Shifts in campsite reflect changes in food preference, the availability of new vegetable resources, or new knowledge about the location of wide-ranging and constantly moving large game. Thus, a

Table 2.1. Campsites occupied by Dobe Camp: January 27, 1968 to July 11, 1968[a]

Place	Location of site	Date of occupation	Number of days occupied	Site
1. Dobe	O[f]	?	?	Base Camp
2. N/on/oni ≠toa	G[c]	Jan. 27	7	_[b]
3. ≠Tum ≠toa	G	Feb. 3	8	New Site (n.s.)
4. N/on/oni ≠toa	G	Feb. 12	2	Reoccupy 2
5. /Tanagaba	M[d]	Feb. 14	2	n.s.
6. /Twi /twama	M	Feb. 16	3	n.s.
7. N!abesha	M	Feb. 19	2	n.s.
8. Dobe	O	Feb. 21	17	Reoccupy 1
9. N!abesha	M	March 9	5	n.s.
10. Shum!kau	M	March 14	2	n.s.
11. N/on/oni ≠toa	G	March 16	2	Reoccupy 2
12. ≠Tum ≠toa	G	March 18	2	Reoccupy 3
13. Hwanasi	SP[e]	March 20	3	n.s.
14. Chu!kon!a	O	March 23	2	n.s.
15. /Twi !ka hwanasi	SP	March 25	1	n.s.
16. /Twi !ka kwanasi	SP	March 26	1	n.s.
17. Chu!kon!a	O	March 27	2	Reoccupy 14
18. !Gum ≠toa	G	March 29	2	n.s.
19. Dobe	O	March 31	11	Reoccupy 1
20. Dobe ≠toa	G	April 11	1	n.s.
21. ≠Tum ≠toa	G	April 12	3	n.s.
22. //gakwe ≠dwa	M	April 15	12	n.s.
23. !Gausha ≠toa	G	April 27	1	n.s.
24. Dobe	O	April 28	26	Reoccupy 1
25. N!abesha	M	May 24	5	Reoccupy 9
26. Shum!kau	M	May 29	1	n.s.
27. N/on/oni ≠toa	G	May 30	5	n.s.
28. ≠Tum ≠toa	G	June 4	3	n.s.
29. ≠Tum ≠toa	G	June 7	1	n.s.
30. Dobe ≠toa	G	June 8	1	n.s.
31. Dobe	O	June 9	14	Reoccupy 1
32. North of Dobe	O	June 23	1	n.s.
33. N!abesha	M	June 24	1	n.s.
34. Shum!kau	M	June 25	6	n.s.
35. Mokoro	M	July 1	2	n.s.
36. N/on/oni ≠toa	G	July 3	1	n.s.
37. //Gakwe ≠dwa	M	July 4	8	n.s.
38. Dobe	O	July 11		Reoccupy 1

[a]In interpreting this table, bias caused by the presence of the author must be considered. At camp 5, a brief stopping point on the way back to Dobe, I persuaded the group to march north with me, retracing their route, after which I drove them back to Dobe. Camps 6 and 7, though never occupied, are included since the group was anxious to return to Dobe with planned stops of three days at /twi /twama and two days at N!abesha on their way back. At !gum ≠toa camp 18, the group walked to the border road in the hope I would pass by on my way to Dobe. When I did so, they asked for a ride there, and I obliged them. At //gakwe ≠dwa, I was present throughout the occupation and returned the group to Dobe again in my truck. If anthropologists had not been camped at Dobe during this period, the group would probably have spent less time there and more of it in the north, but our presence had negligible effect on !Kung choices of where to move their camps, camp composition, and the length of time a camp was occupied.

[b]This camp was built in May, 1967.

[c]G = Site in nut grove.

[d]M = Site in molapo.

[e]SP = Site near salt pans.

[f]O = Other.

group may spend several days beyond easy walking distance of a nut grove while the hunters scout likely areas for large game. If none is found, the next move may be to a nut grove, where nuts are plentiful, but where the men may have to walk further to hunt. If the hunters see a promising but distant area or perhaps kill a large buck, the entire group may move toward the kill, camp at the water source nearest to it, and remain there until the meat is consumed. Of course, in all such moves, water is the major, and most limiting, factor.

While the general destination of a move is a matter for careful consideration, there are no hard and fast rules about where within an area a camp will be located, save one: a former campsite will not be reoccupied unless the huts are standing and still in fair repair. The lifespan of such huts is short—usually under a year—so generally the reoccupation of a camp occurs within several months of the original construction, and families reoccupy their own huts. But most often a group will select a new site in the same general area. There are two

Map 2.2. Location of camp occupied by Dobe group

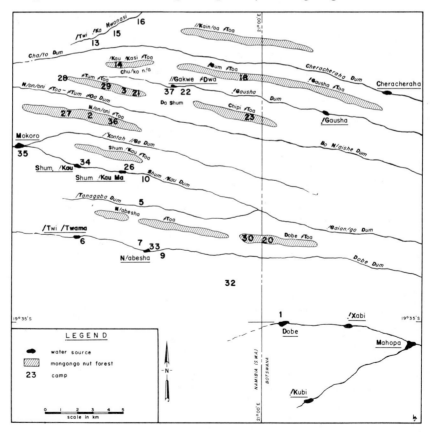

reasons for this: old sites tend to attract fleas, ticks, and other forms of insect life, so that it is more pleasant to start again at a fresh location. Secondly, if a group returns to an old site in the course of a single season, gathering will be slightly more difficult since the most easily collected resources, closest to the camp, will have been already exploited. At any rate, there is no overlapping of new and old but discernible sites. Either a group will reoccupy directly its old huts, or it will start completely afresh at a clean site. The archaeological implications of this fact are considerable.

Social Variables Influencing Settlement Pattern

The question of camp and group organization is considered in some detail by Lee in Chapter 3, and my basic purpose in this section is to apply, with slight modification, his observations to the Dobe group. Generally, a new dry-season camp is established at Dobe each

Map 2.3. Routes of Dobe group during two trips from Dobe

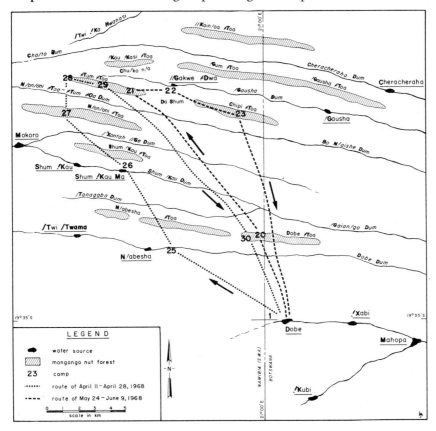

year, to be occupied until the next rains. By analyzing observations made of the 1964, 1968, and 1969 camps, one can not only look at camp organization, but also get some idea of change over time. As Table 2.2 shows, at one time or another during these three years, elements of four extended families were present. Three of these extended families (headed by /"Xashe n!a, ≠Gau n!a and Chu!ko n!a) are linked in the eldest generation by sib ties, while the fourth (headed by short Kan//ka) is linked by marriage in the next generation to both /"Xashe n!a and Chu!ko n!a's groups. This general pattern is typical in !Kung dry-season camps.

While two families are represented at Dobe during all three of the sample years, it is important to emphasize the changes that occur since they illustrate the fluidity characteristic of this settlement pattern. Of the 13 adults of ≠Gau n!a's family present in 1964, only two remain in 1969; no members of short Kan//ka's group occupy Dobe in 1964, but in the 1969 camp they have the greatest number of huts; and Chu!ko n!a's three married children appear for the first time in 1969. Five adults who had huts in the 1968 camp had none in 1969, and 11 adults in the 1969 camp were absent the previous year. A total of 33 different individuals lived in the Dobe camps in 1968 and 1969, and only 17 of them were present both years. During the overall six-year period, the core family of /"Xashe n!a and his adult sons remains fairly stable, but around it great changes take place. It might also be noted that while the turnover of individuals is significant, the total number of inhabitants of these Dobe camps

Table 2.2. Numbers of occupants of Dobe dry-season camps: 1964, 1968, 1969 (tabulated by extended family)

| Year | Extended families of— | | | | |
	/"Xashe n!a	≠Gau n!a	Kan//ka n!a (short Kan//ka)	Chu!ko n!a's children	Total
1964:					
adults	12	13	—	—	25 (+11? young)
huts	?	?	—	—	?
1968:					
adults	10	7	5	—	22 (+13 young)
huts	5	4	3	—	12
1969:					
adults	10	2	10	6	38 (+15 young)
huts	5	1	6	3	15

changes only slightly from year to year. In 1964 there were 12 adult males and 13 adult females; in 1968 the figures are 12 males and 10 females, and in 1969 15 males and 13 females. This suggests that while the constraints on individual movement are relatively weak, overall settlement size is tightly controlled.

There is also movement that takes place even during the occupation of a single, dry-season, camp; and very rarely are all of the same individuals present for more than several days running. Both extended and one- or two-day visits are made to other camps, and some huts may stand empty for a month or longer. Similarly, other people may "move in" as guests for varying period of time. Rarely, a family may maintain a hut at more than one dry-season camp, for the construction of a hut emphasizes the right of a person to live at a certain place, even though it is far from certain that he will actually be in residence there at any given time.

As might be expected, group composition is more variable in rainy-season camps which are both smaller and occupied for much shorter periods of time. Table 2.3 shows the composition of the Dobe group during their five trips from Dobe during the 1968 rainy season and immediately thereafter. This study is based on the movements of N!aishe and ≠Toma, two brothers, who along with their wives and children usually travel together and who were present during each of these trips. But for no two trips was the remaining party composition identical, although most often the brothers, both sons of /"Xashe n!a, were accompanied by other members of this extended family. During the main rains, when water was more plentiful, groups tended to be smaller; and as water sources decreased, group size increased as people congregated at the remaining water points. The average number of adult participants was 4.5 for the first two trips which took place during the main rains and 12.5 for the last two, after the rains had ceased.

!Kung Campsites: Organization
and Variation

!Kung camps are generally circular in shape, and the greater the number of huts a camp contains, the more nearly it conforms to this pattern. Huts are located along the circumference of the circle, generally about four meters apart, with their entrances facing toward the center. Huts are generally occupied by nuclear families: a husband, wife, and immature children share a single hut and hearth. Young married adults of the same sex usually have a separate hut, while widowers and co-wives have huts of their own. At the 1969

Table 2.3. Participants in trips from Dobe, 1968

Date	Extended families of—							Chu!ko n!a's children		Number of participants
	/"Xashe n!a				Tall Kan//ka	Short Kan//ka				
	N!aishe[a]	ǂToma	/"Xashe n!a	ǂGau ma		Short Kan//ka	Dəm	Debe	Kan//ka	
January 27– February 20	X	X								4 adults 7 young
March 9– March 30	X	X	X							5 adults 7 young
April 11– April 27	X	X	X			X	X			12 adults 11 young
May 24– June 8	X	X	X	X	X					10 adults 7 young
June 23– July 10	X	X	X	X[b]	X			X	X	15 adults 8 young

[a] These names refer to heads of nuclear families with two exceptions: ǂGau ma is an adult unmarried male and Dəm is accompanied by his very elderly father.

[b] During this trip, ǂGau ma is accompanied by his future wife, /Tasa.

Dobe camp, 12 of 14 huts were occupied by nuclear family groups; one by two young men, and one by an elderly widower. Placement of huts around the circle is generally by extended family, with huts of such a group contiguous to each other. Figures 2.1 and 2.2 serve to illustrate this point.[4]

Huts vary in type according to the season and to the length of time they will be occupied. At the one extreme are rainy-season structures, which are circular in shape, slightly under two meters in height, and about two meters in diameter. These domed houses are constructed from branches set around the circumference, bent inwards, and tied to form the high point of the roof. This frame is then covered with a thick layer of grass which is loosely tied in place; a small area is left open on one side as an entrance. The same type of hut is constructed at the dry season camp near the Dobe waterhole. On the other hand,

Figure 2.1. The 1968 Dobe Camp

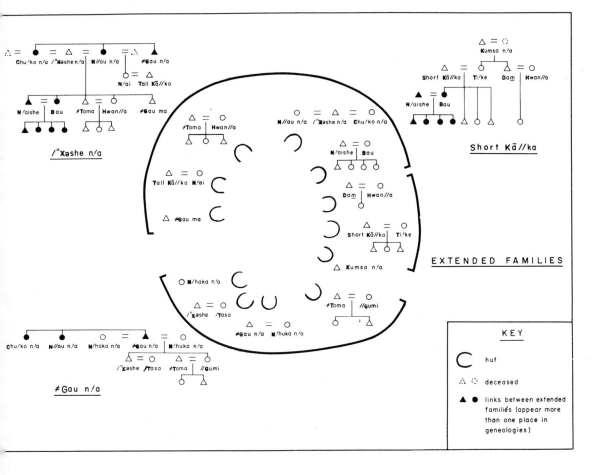

at temporary camps occupied just after the rains, a hut may consist
of no more than a few leafy branches stuck into the ground to provide shade. Huts provide shade and a place to store belongings; they
serve to mark out ground which belongs to a single family. Very
few activities take place inside a hut, and only during a rainstorm do
people sleep in them.

All camps have hearths which are used for cooking, warmth, and
as a focus of activities. Located in front of each hut, these hearths
are marked by charcoal as well as by small depressions resulting
from raking coals, ash, and hot sand during cooking. Very rarely,
cooking pits or scatters of surface charcoal mark special activity
areas. One other characteristic of all camps is debris scatter generally
confined to the area immediately surrounding each hearth. This
debris consists, for the most part, of vegetable remains (generally nut

Figure 2.2. The 1969 Dobe Camp

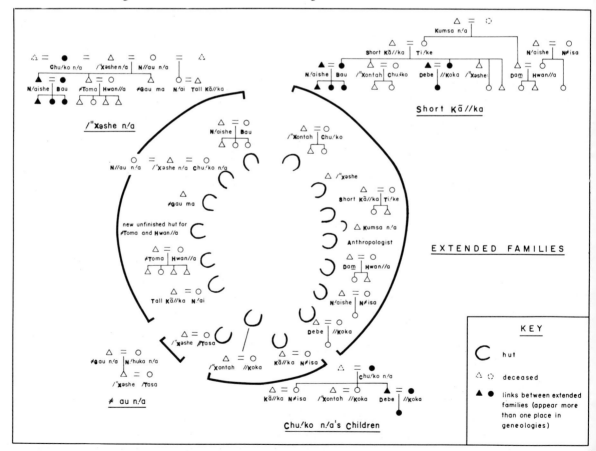

shells, fruit, and melon skins), bone fragments, and the waste products of manufacturing activities including bits of ostrich eggshell, bone and wood shavings, and fiber used for the manufacture of string. The fist-sized, or slightly larger, cracking stones are the only items of value left at a campsite when it is abandoned; and these are either used again when the camp is reoccupied, or are carried away when a new camp is established nearby. The iron knives, axes, and adzes forming the core of the !Kung tool kit are never left behind.[5]

In terms of type, a sharp distinction may be made between dry-season base camps and their smaller, rainy-season and post-rainy-season counterparts. The dry-season camps are larger: they contain more people and more huts, and are occupied for much longer periods of time; the huts in them are better constructed and more evenly arranged. A greater amount of debris piles up in them, and in winter when fires are fed through the entire night and part of the day, ash is carted away and dumped behind the huts. A single dry-season camp may be occupied for as long as six months. It would be abandoned for a site nearby, generally less than 100 m away, only if a death occurs in the camp, or if it becomes extremely rank and bug ridden. In contrast, the rainy-season camps are smaller, with fewer huts and occupants, are inhabited for shorter periods of time, and are consequently marked by less debris and no dumps. Since these huts are often rudimentary after the main rains are over, they are located to incorporate small trees and leafy bushes which provide natural shade since this lessens the amount of construction necessary. Also, they are placed to avoid thick clumps of bushes and to take advantage of small open spaces so that a minimal amount of clearing need be done. The result is that huts in these camps are more irregularly placed and rarely conform to an even circular pattern.

When the types—as opposed to amounts—of debris associated with camps are considered, differences may be noted between dry season camps and those more "temporary" ones occupied during and just after the rains. And within this latter group, between-camp variations may also be observed. There are two relevant variables which account for this: the food resources most readily available near a camp at the time of its occupation and the length of time which a camp is occupied. The effect of resource variability can best be seen by looking at the sample of "temporary" camps presented in Table 2.4. A series of camps from three slightly different environmental settings —the open southern molapos of N!abesha and /Tanagaba, the extensive N/on/oni ≠toa mongongo grove, and the Hwanasi area of salt pans are compared to show differences in subsistence activities that

65

are directly related to this variable.[6] The distances between these areas are short: 7 km—less than two hours walk—separates the Hwanasi area from N/on/oni ≠toa; /Tanagaba lies only 3 km further to the south. Distances of this magnitude are easily covered in a day's hunting or gathering trip. A comparison of the southern molapos to the nut-grove camps shows that while small game accounts for all the meat eaten in both areas, mongongo nuts were consumed only at two of the three molapo camps, and then only in small numbers. At N/on/oni ≠toa mongongo nuts were the prime food source at both camps. And at the Hwanasi camps, within easy walking distance of the nut groves, no mongongo nuts were eaten. Also, the Hwanasi camps are the only ones at which a large animal was killed, even though they were occupied less than half the total number of man-hours than their counterparts in each of the other two regions. These results are not statistically significant, but informal observation over a two- and a half-year period suggests that the pattern described above is the typical one.

The second variable affecting the types of debris that mark abandoned campsites is the length of time a camp was occupied. This is particularly true for by-products of manufacturing processes such as the production of wooden artifacts—bows, mortars and pestles, digging sticks—or of arrows, twine, ostrich eggshell beads, and so forth. These activities can take place in all types of camps because

Table 2.4. Game and major vegetable foods from camps in three areas

	N!abesha and /Tanagaba (molapos)	N/on/oni ≠Toa (nut grove)	Hwanasi (salt pans)
Number of camps in sample	3 (No. 5, 9,[a]33)	2 (No. 2,[b]36)	3 (No. 13, 15, 16)
Number of adult man-days spent in area	60	58	25
Game killed and eaten in area	Small game: 5 porcupine 7 springhare 1 hornbill	Small game: 5 porcupine 9 springhare 1 steenbok 1 duiker	Small game: 1 steenbok
	Large buck: none	Large buck: none	Large buck: 1 gemsbok
Notes on vegetable food	Mongongo nuts eaten at nos. 9 and 33 only in limited amounts	Mongongo nuts major veg. food at both camps	No mongongo nuts eaten

[a]This includes 1 reoccupation (No. 25).
[b]This includes 2 reoccupations (Nos. 4, 11).

the necessary tools are always carried from site to site; the needed raw materials, generally available in more than one area, are relatively easy to collect and carry. There is no close correlation between the location of raw materials and the camps at which they are processed. Furthermore, my general impression is that as much spare time from subsistence activities is available in transient camps as in more permanent ones. Thus, while it is possible to predict how subsistence activities will vary from area to area, the same does not hold true for manufacturing processes. The only general rule applicable is that, for any specific manufacturing process, the longer a camp is occupied, the greater the likelihood that an activity in question occurred there.

Activity Patterning within and about Campsites

A camp itself, the physical, observable entity, develops both through conscious acts such as the construction of huts and hearths and through incidental acts such as the discarding of debris from manufacturing or subsistence tasks. A relationship can be shown between any type of activity, the social context in which it occurs, and its spatial correlates.

Activities that take place outside of the campsite are limited almost entirely to gathering and hunting trips. The collection of raw materials for manufacture of goods generally takes place incidentally in the course of these food-collecting trips. With few exceptions, age and sex primarily determine the composition of hunting and of collecting groups, which are, of course, task specific. All members of a camp, for example, may go off together to collect honey. The size of such groups varies depending on the specific tasks at hand. Usually men hunt alone or with a single companion and only rarely in groups of more than two; but when following a large wounded animal, all men in camp will participate to help with the butchering and transportation of meat back to camp. Women generally set off in a large group to gather, and disperse slightly during the course of the trip, but usually individuals maintain voice contact. Both hunting and gathering activities leave few if any marks on the landscape, and the kill site of an animal such as an eland, which may weigh up to half a ton, is marked only by a few bones, the horns, stomach and intestine contents, and the scattered remains of a fire used to cook the liver and several other pieces of meat. From an archaeological point of view, it would probably be invisible.

Within a campsite itself, two types of space can be distinguished: (1) a communal area that includes the empty space in the center of the camp and belongs to no particular individual; and (2) family areas, each the domain of a single family, including the hearth, the hut, and the immediately surrounding area. From the point of view of an individual, there is a threefold subdivision of space: (1) the area belonging to him and his family, (2) the similar areas occupied by other families, and (3) the area shared by all inhabitants of the camp. Some activities, such as dancing or the first distribution of meat, are communal and involve either representatives of more than one family, or the majority, if not all, of the camp members. These activities generally occur in the center of the encampment and, incidentally, leave few if any material remains (Figure 2.3).

Conversely, individuals sleep and, generally, eat in family groups. Consequently these activities are spatially localized around individual family hearths. Thus, meat is cooked, divided into individual portions, and finally consumed around the individual hearths, where the observed bone scatters primarily reflect the last stage of this process. Manufacturing activities are also carried out within a familial con-

Figure 2.3. A camp in the ≠Tum≠toa Grove

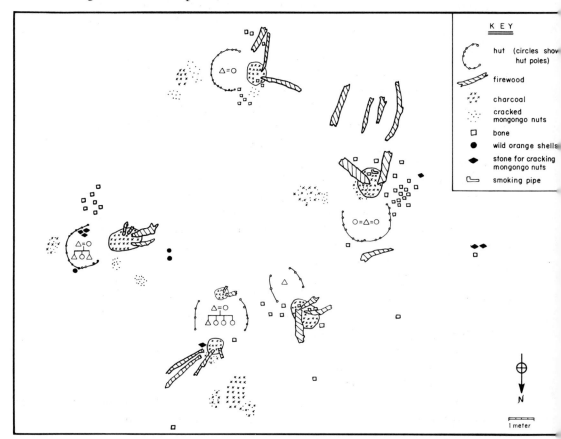

text, so that the incidental by-products of these activities are also found intermixed and clustered in the areas around the individual hearths. Often several men will work together to make and poison arrows, or several women and girls will cooperate to make ostrich eggshell beads. The important point is that cooperative manufacturing activities of this type do not take place in distinct separated areas. They are carried out around the hearth of one of the participants, and the other workers are, in effect, visitors at this hearth. One exception to this general rule is skin drying: fresh skins are pegged out horizontally on the ground to dry in an area outside the hut circle. The skins of larger buck take up a good deal of space; all skins attract not only vermin but carnivores as well, and, therefore, this one activity is spatially segregated. In addition, during the heat of the day, activity areas sometimes shift to utilize patches of heavy shade which lie outside the encampment; in almost all cases such areas are marked by thin scatters of charcoal and nut shells, which indicate the cooking and consumption of mongongo nuts, although other remains are, on rare occasions, also represented.

Conclusion

In conclusion, it would be profitable to examine several generalizations that have been used as starting points in the reconstruction of prehistoric hunter and gatherer societies and evaluate them in light of the !Kung evidence. One question which may be considered in this light concerns campsite typology. Binford, for example, has suggested that for hunters and gatherers two main kinds of camps may be postulated. One type, base camps, are "selected primarily in terms of adequate life-space, protection from the elements, and central location with respect to the distribution of resources." Maintenance activities, "related to the preparation and distribution of subsistence goods already on hand and to the processing of on-hand raw materials in the production of tools," Binford states, take place primarily at base camps (Binford and Binford 1966, p. 268), and on the basis of such activities this camp type is distinguished. The second kind of camp, work camps, are characterized primarily by extractive tasks—for example, "kill sites, collection stations, and quarries for usable flint" (p. 268). Binford goes on to suggest that maintenance and extractive tasks, and thus base and work camps, are

> not isomorphic in their distribution, extractive tasks more commonly being performed by work groups and minimal segments of the society at locations determined by the distributions of

resources within a territory. Maintenance activities, on the
other hand, would tend to occur at locations selected princi-
pally in terms of space and shelter requirements of the residence
group. (1966, pp. 291–292)

Applied to the !Kung, Binford's distinction is, in one way, correct,
since extractive activities are generally undertaken by special work
groups in specific locations where, of course, the desired resources
are available. But this has nothing to do with camps per se since
such activities occur away from any kind of camp at all. It is possible
to distinguish between !Kung dry-season camps occupied for long
periods of time and their more temporary wet and post-wet-season
counterparts, and to show for the latter that location influences
subsistence activities which occur. However, it is not possible to fit
this pattern into the base-camp—task-camp dichotomy. Given that
food is not stored, extractive activities of all types are carried out in
the vicinity of all camps regardless of type, and since raw materials
are not strictly localized and are easy to carry, maintenance activities
similarly are not confined to a specific type of camp. Thus, this
breakdown of base and work camps does not hold in this instance.

If one were to make a useful categorization for the !Kung, one
would first separate activities which occurred within a campsite from
those which took place away from it. (The latter category would include most of Binford's "extractive activities.") The next distinction
would be between food preparation and manufacturing activities
which took place within a camp (both considered maintenance
activities by Binford), and one would then observe that in smaller,
more temporary camps evidence of manufacturing activities would be
relatively rare or absent. The reason is that subsistence activities
occur daily, and proportionately less time is spent making goods;
thus, the shorter the period of occupation, the less likely that manufacturing activities took place. The problem is basically one of
sampling, and the relevant variable is the length of time a camp was
occupied. And in this instance, the dichotomy proposed by Binford
is neither correct nor useful.

A second problem to be considered deals with reconstruction at a
single site. Inference based on information recovered through excavation provides one technique of archaeological reconstruction,
which aims at learning something about the organization of people
responsible for the remains. This approach has been succinctly outlined by Chang (1967b, p. 108) who states:

To correlate objects or their dimensions into events, events into

categories of activities, and categories of activities—in relation
to categories of social groupings—into a micro-structure, are the
major steps of the micro-articulatory procedure.

One of the most difficult steps in this procedure, as Chang himself
realizes, is to determine the "category of social grouping" in which a
specific activity or set of activities takes place. Freeman (1968, p.
266) draws the distinction between "special-purpose groups made up
of members of one or more corporate groups, cooperating to perform specific tasks and, perhaps, immediately dissolving after a very
brief existence," and corporate groups themselves, which for the
!Kung consist either of individual nuclear families or the entire mem-
bership of a camp. Within a !Kung camp, most activities take place
in one or the other of these corporate contexts. But those activities
with the greatest "archaeological visibility" such as the preparation
of animal and vegetable foods and the production of goods are carried out within the nuclear family. Since the camp is composed of a
number of families, this means that one type of activity, making
arrows for example, occurs at a number of locations within a camp.
And since most family-related activities take place in the immediate area of the hearth, the making of arrows is not spatially segregated from the cracking of mongongo nuts or the cooking and
consumption of meat.

Given this example, it is easy to see the danger of assuming *a priori*
that most activities are performed by special-purpose, task-specific
groups, and that these tasks are spatially segregated from each other.
This is the underlying assumption of Watson, LeBlanc, and Redman
(1971, p. 119) when they state:

> Various members of a single culture may perform different
> activities in different parts of the same site at about the same
> time. The resulting horizontal distribution of cultural debris
> and features might indicate or delineate butchering, cooking,
> sleeping and tool-making activity areas.

This statement is misleading because it implies that the location at
which an activity is performed is determined primarily by the nature
of that activity and only secondarily by the social context in which
it occurs. A.E. Marks, in his analysis of Rosh Zin, an Epipaleolithic
site in the Negev, assumes at the outset of his study that just such a
correlation holds, and is surprised to note that "no specific area has
been located where primary workshop activities took precedence"
(1971, p. 1242). In light of the !Kung data, this observation is not

72

at all surprising.[7] Another correlate of the task-group assumption
is that in an archaeological context, objects found in association are,
in some way, related to a single task. Longacre and Ayres, for example, in their analysis of an abandoned Apache *ramada* (campsite)
accept this view from the outset and note (1968, p. 156):

> The cluster of tools near the ramada presented us with a prob-
> lem. Because they were found together, we inferred that they
> were used in a single task, but we were unable to suggest the
> exact nature of the task.

While their assumption was correct in that instance, it provides a
dangerous *a priori* base for archaeological interpretation.

In societies with relatively limited and simple technologies—and
this includes most hunters and gatherers—with lack of craft specialization, and in which an individual produces goods primarily for
himself and for his immediate family, I would hypothesize that a
large number of activities occur in a domestic context, and that the
correlations which hold for the !Kung are most likely to apply. This
I would argue, is an hypothesis that can be tested in an archaeological
context by first defining clusters of artifacts on the ground and then
by noting the distribution of different artifact types among these
clusters.

In both the above examples, I have tried to show how recourse to
ethnographic data can serve as a relevant yardstick for measuring an
archaeological hypothesis, for modifying it, and for proposing alternative formulations. It is especially encouraging that activity patterning within !Kung camps—presumably only the camps themselves
would have archaeological visibility—relates directly to corporate
groups, in this case nuclear families, for this suggests that it might
eventually be possible to trace the development, or evolution, of
such social structures through time. And this certainly is a question
worthy of consideration.

!Kung Spatial Organization:

An Ecological and Historical Perspective

Richard B. Lee

3

Winter camp at a permanent waterhole

ECOLOGY AND SOCIAL
CHANGE

This is a contribution to the study of how hunters and gatherers organize themselves in space and how this organization adapts to variations in population and resources. Using field data from the dozen !Kung groups that have occupied the /Xai/xai and /Gɔm areas from 1890 to 1970, I examine here the nature of the association between social groups and their space, in a search for the ecological and sociological determinants of this association.[1]

Since there has been extended controversy in anthropology on the question of sociospatial organization among hunter-gatherers, it is important at the outset to define the problem and pinpoint sources of confusion. All hunting and gathering peoples live in organized groups that move frequently through their ranges. Most modern hunter living groups are small—under 200 people—and these groups are observed to move their campsites from two to ten times annually. The existence of a group and a space necessarily implies the existence of two kinds of boundaries: social and spatial. A social boundary can be measured according to how open or closed the group is. At the open extreme, individuals moving at random within a space, encounter one another for brief periods and then move on. At the other extreme is a series of tightly organized groups whose members stay together throughout the year with minimal interchange with other groups. A spatial boundary can be measured along the dimension of overlap/nonoverlap. Imagine a large space containing five groups. At the "overlapping" extreme, all five groups have free access to the entire space; at the nonoverlapping extreme, the five groups divide the space into five exclusive sectors. In an intermediate condition, each of the five groups has a core area which is theirs alone, while they share the rest of the space with their neighbors. These two kinds of boundaries are illustrated in Table 3.1 (see Yellen and Harpending 1972).

The distinction between social and spatial boundaries is necessary, and much confusion has arisen from the fact that group boundaries and land boundaries have not been kept separate in analyses of

Table 3.1. Dimensions along which social and spatial boundaries may vary in hunter-gatherer groups

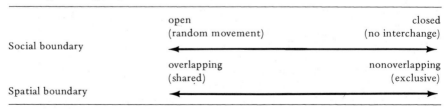

hunter-gatherer organization. Open groups may have nonoverlapping territories but still accommodate movement of personnel across the boundaries, and it is at least theoretically possible for a closed group to share overlapping ranges with their neighbors. As we shall see, both spatial and social boundaries are fluid for contemporary hunter-gatherers.

A second source of confusion has been the failure to distinguish between the *behavior* of groups in their space and the *conceptions* or *folk view* of the people about themselves and their land. The latter type of data, though important, is at best an imperfect reflection of the actual arrangements of persons on the ground. My prime concern here is with the behavior of groups and not with their ideology, although later some ideological aspects are introduced (for example, pp. 25–26).

Having defined the dimensions along which social and spatial organization may vary, we must now consider what formations are actually observed in the ethnographies of hunter-gatherer societies. Ethnographically, there is no case known of a society in which the members move randomly in a totally overlapping space. Toward the opposite extreme, however, there is apparent evidence in a number of societies for tightly organized groups maintaining exclusive territories. Such groups, reported in several parts of the world, have been lumped under the general rubric of the "patrilocal band model" of hunter-gatherer social organization.

In its essentials, the patrilocal band is based on three organizing principles: (1) band exogamy (everyone must marry someone from outside the group), (2) patrilocal post-marital residence (women move into *other* groups at marriage; men remain together and bring their wives in), and (3) band territoriality (each group controls a space, moves within it, and defends it against outsiders) (Radcliffe-Brown 1930; Steward 1936; 1955; Service 1962; 1966).

The operation of these principles results in a situation not unlike the "closed group/nonoverlapping space" extreme of our model. This is not to say that no interchange occurs: women move between groups at marriage, and all of these societies are acknowledged to have formalized visiting arrangements for the purpose of carrying out rituals and trade. Nevertheless, the dominant impression one gets from accounts of patrilocal bands is one of semi-isolated, male-centered groups, encapsulated within territories.

This patrilocal, territorial, exogamous band or "horde," as Radcliffe-Brown called it, has proven to be a remarkably persistent construct in the study of hunting and gathering peoples. For Radcliffe-

Brown in 1930 it was "the important local group throughout
Australia" (1930, p. 35); others have endorsed this view quite
recently and have presented some ethnographic data in support of
it (Stanner 1965; Birdsell 1970). Still others have sought to establish the patrilocal form as the basic grouping not only for Australians
but for all hunter-gatherers present and past (Service 1962; 1966;
Williams 1968).

Why do so many analysts continue to be attracted to the patrilocal
band model? At least part of its appeal is that it is an elegant and
parsimonious formulation. The society is seen as being structured by
the interaction of a small number of jural rules: territorial ownership
by males; band exogamy; and viripatrilocal, postmarital residence.
Similarly, the spatial arrangements are extremely neat: a mosaic of
territories arranged in a honeycomb pattern, each containing its land-
owning group. This apparent neatness and parsimony have proved
especially useful to model-builders seeking to characterize hunter-
gatherer group structure in an economic way for computer and
mathematical simulation.

However, the problem is that a society based on these rules would
find itself in severe adaptive difficulties. The patrilocal band makes
scant provision for a number of basic features of hunter-gatherer life,
such as the necessity to even out demographic variation in sex ratios
and family size, the continuing necessity to adjust group size to
resources, and the desirability of resolving conflict by fission.

In contrast to advocates of the patrilocal model, I argue that this
form of organization is empirically rare and that its rarity can be
proved by a careful ecological analysis. To the contrary, the model
of !Kung described in the chapter appears to account well for the
observed facts and, moreover, can be applied to the analysis of other
hunter-gatherer cases. A similar critique of the patrilocal model based
on !Kung materials is presented by Yellen and Harpending (1972).

We are, of course, not the first to question the universality of the
patrilocal band among hunter-gatherers. This was done as early as
1936 by Steward (1936; 1938; 1955), and criticisms of the patrilocal
model have become more frequent in recent years (e.g., Helm 1965;
Hiatt 1962; 1966; 1968; Leacock 1969; Meggitt 1962, pp. 70–71;
Woodburn 1968; and various authors in Damas 1969, and Lee and
DeVore 1968). According to these criticisms, a relatively open,
social group with overlapping shared territories seems to be the prevailing form among contemporary hunter-gatherers.

Yet the flexible group alternative to the patrilocal model is not
without its difficulties. Though different, it appears at first glance to

be equally unattractive. The recent observations of hunter-gatherer group structure present an apparently chaotic picture, in which a person may live wherever and with whomever he or she pleases. The situation is further complicated by the fact that all living hunter-gatherer groups have been strongly affected by contact with outside peoples. Service (1962) goes so far as to argue that the flexibility of modern hunter groupings is strictly an artifact of acculturation and breakdown.

Since so much of the recent controversy has focused on the Australian aboriginal materials, it may be refreshing to take a different but equally interesting case—that of the !Kung hunter-gatherers of southern Africa.

!Kung Local Groups and Their Space

We will consider the Dobe Area !Kung of Botswana (including the /Du/da !Kung) and the closely related Nyae Nyae !Kung across the border in Namibia (illegally occupied by South Africa). The following description is drawn from the Dobe material, although the main features apply as well to the Nyae Nyae !Kung, as documented by the Marshall family. Where specific points of disagreement exist, they are explicitly stated.

What are the major features of !Kung local groupings, land ownership, group affiliation, and boundary maintenance? The basic local grouping is a camp (Marshall's band), which is a noncorporate, bilaterally organized, group of people who live in a single settlement and who move together for at least part of the year. At the core of each of these camps are two, three, or more siblings and/or cousins, both male and female, who are generally acknowledged to be owners (K''xausi) of the waterhole. Around each waterhole is a block of land or n!ore. This contains food resources and other water points and is the basic subsistence area for the resident group. Lorna Marshall (1960, p. 344 ff.) has argued that the ownership of each waterhole resides in the person of a band headman who is always male and who inherits his position patrilineally, but my own research indicates that no headmen existed among either the Dobe or the Nyae Nyae !Kung. Instead the sibling-cousin group of K''xausi collectively held the waterhole. (Documentation on the problem of the headman will be presented elsewhere.)

Specific groups have histories of association with their waterholes that vary from a few years up to several decades in duration. Rarely does this association go back as far as the grandparent generation of the oldest people living. To put it another way, a first approximation of the "half-life" of a group's tenure at a waterhole can be estimated at thirty to fifty years.

An individual may inherit his or her n!ore from his father's or mother's family; or he or she may inherit it from both parents, or from neither. There is a discernible patrilineal tendency, at least among males. A survey of 151 men over the age of fifteen, representing 90 percent of the adult male residents of the Dobe area, gave the breakdown on inheritance of n!ore shown in Table 3.2. We see that while the majority take n!ores *not* in a strict patrilineal way, inheritance from father is the most frequent single alternative. Unfortunately, comparable data were not gathered for females.

The composition of groups at any one time shows little or no patrilocal emphasis. In fact, because of the frequency of bride service, there is even a slight tendency toward matrilocality (see Leacock 1955). Of 114 currently married couples, 22 were living with husband's parent(s); 24 were living with wife's parent(s); while 12 were living with *both* husband's and wife's parents. A further 15 couples were living neolocally, while in the case of 41 couples, neither husband's nor wife's parents were alive. Those couples in which both had living parents were observed to pay frequent visits to both sides. This and other processes of intergroup visiting created a fluid situation in which the composition of groups changed from week to week with the comings and goings of people (Lee 1972a).

Within a local group's area, subsistence resources are not exclusively reserved for the K"xausi and their families. By observing elementary good manners, anyone who has a relative in a camp may enjoy the resources of the area around the camp. Within the camp, food is shared in such a way that everyone—residents and visitors alike—receives an equitable share (see L. Marshall 1960; 1961).

In moving through the annual round, the !Kung groupings satisfy their subsistence requirements with surprisingly little friction with

Table 3.2. Patrilineal vs matrilineal inheritance of locality as reported by 151 !Kung men

Inherited n!ore from—	Number	Percentage
Father	60	39.7
Mother	40	26.5
Both father *and* mother	16	10.6
Neither parent	21	13.9
[Does not know, or no n!ore]	14	9.3
Total	151	100.0

neighboring groups. Subsistence space is bounded, but these boundaries are vague and not defended. In fact, a frequent pattern is for groups from two or more waterholes to join forces for the joint exploitation of a major resource, such as tsin beans or mongongo nuts. And during the winter dry season, it is common to find from two to six different groups camping together at a permanent waterhole.

79

Environmental Causes of Flexibility

How do we account for this flexibility of group structure? Before we conclude that it is due to the effects of recent contact and acculturation, we should consider what effect preexisting features of the environment would have on group structure. Two permanent features of the Kalahari environment appear to be salient: first, the high variability in rainfall; and second, the sparse distribution of standing water in the northern Kalahari. Let us consider each of these features in turn.

Summer camp near the mongongo forests north of Dobe

Rainfall Variability

Average annual rainfall has little meaning in an environment in which rainfall may vary by as much as 300 percent from year to year. During the 1963–64 rainy season, we recorded 239 mm (9.4 in), while during 1967–68, 597 mm (23.5 in) was recorded. Given this variability, it would be more useful to discuss rainfall in terms of extremes—for example, by tabulating the number of years out of every ten in which drought is experienced. Maun, 300 km by air southeast of Dobe, is the nearest weather station for which long-term rainfall records are available. Figure 3.1 illustrates the fluctuations in rainfall that Maun has experienced over the last half-century. Table 3.3 summarizes these data. In a run of 46 years, drought occurred in 17 years (37 percent), and of these, 12 years (26 percent) were

Figure 3.1. Variations in annual rainfall at Maun, Botswana, July 1922 to June 1968 (mean 462.3 mm based on 46 years of records)

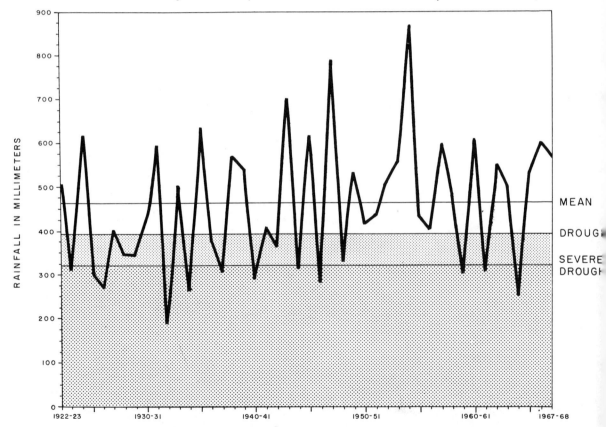

classified as severe drought when less than 70 percent of average rainfall occurred. In other words, the probability of drought occur- at Maun is about two years in five, and of severe drought, one year in four.

The situation for Dobe would be even more acute since rainfall is lower overall (about 350 mm at Dobe *vs* 462 mm for Maun) and therefore more erratic in annual fluctuation. Judging from our ex- perience over a 7-year period (1963 to 1969) and that of the Mar- shall's (1952 to 1959), drought conditions probably characterize about half the years. For reasons which are not clear, the northern Kalahari appears to experience alternating runs of good years and of bad years of varying length.

A second source of variability is the difference in rainfall from place to place in a single month or season. In a cluster of five stations within an area 200 km across, annual totals may be comparable, but the fall in a given month may vary from place to place by as much as a factor of ten. Table 3.4 shows the rainfall for 1966–67 rainy season at five stations in the Ghanzi district 300 km south of Dobe. In the early rains of October to December, this local variation is crucial, since it is these rains which largely determine the overall size of the wild food harvest later in the season. For example, in November, Kalkfontein received only 3.5 mm while Scarborough, 50 km away, received 34.0 mm. As a result, the desert may be blooming in one area while a few hours' walk away it will still be parched.

It is to such variable conditions that the spatial organization of the !Kung must adapt. Theirs is a *long-term solution* to the prob- lem, and it is unfortunate that an ethnographer will observe only a small segment of the pattern in any given year of fieldwork.

Table 3.3. Drought frequencies and intensities at Maun, Botswana over a 46-year period (Lat. S20°00′ Long. E23°26′)

		Number		Percentage
Years of normal rainfall[a]		29		63
Years of drought:[b]		17		37
1st degree (mild)	5		11	
2nd degree (severe)	11		24	
3rd degree (very severe)	1		2	
Total		46		100

[a]Normal rainfall is annual rainfall more than 85 percent of mean.

[b]Definitions of drought severity adopted from Wellington (1964, pp. 40–43): 1st degree, 70 to 84 percent of mean rainfall; 2nd degree, 55 to 69 percent of mean rainfall; 3rd degree, less than 55 percent of mean rainfall.

Water Source Scarcity

The sparse distribution of water on the ground is the spatial correlate of the temporal variability just discussed. Because of the porosity of the sandy soils, the high rates of evaporation, and the infrequency of exposures of water-bearing rock, standing water points are few and far between. Map 3.1 shows an area south of the Aha Hills and north of the Eiseb Valley. This includes the southern half of the Dobe area and parts of the Nyae Nyae and /Du/da areas on the west and south, respectively. The area straddles the international border and measures about 80 by 80 km for a total area of 6400 km^2 (2,500 mi^2). This entire region contains only five permanent water points, that is, waterholes that hold water throughout the year; and, of these, three have been known to fail within living memory.

In fact, the area contains a hierarchy of water sources arranged in order of their duration and reliability: (I) two have never given out in living memory (/Xai/xai, /Gəm); (II) three have not failed in the last five years (Twihaba, ≠To//gana, /Du/da); (III) five (at least) are strong summer waters which may last through the winter of good years (/Dwia, N≠wama, Hxore, !Kwidum, //Gum//geni); (IV) about 50 are seasonal water points holding water from a few days to several months; (V) about 100 are mongongo, baobab, and terminalia trees with small reservoirs in their hollow boles; (VI) about 150 are sites in which the water-bearing root !xwa (Fockea monroi) is found.

Table 3.4. Local variations in rainfall among five localities in the Ghanzi District, Botswana, 1966–67 rainy season

	Rainfall in mm at—				
	Kalkfontein	Scarborough	Ghanzi	Oakdene	Cume
1966					
July	—	—	—	—	—
August	—	—	6.3	—	0.5
September	—	12.0	41.2	14.5	25.7
October	16.0	10.5	24.1	—	24.5
November	3.5	34.0	35.2	43.2	29.0
December	73.5	116.0	111.6	90.5	75.4
1967					
January	127.0	167.6	242.0	183.0	223.2
February	81.0	136.0	139.2	161.5	131.3
March	38.0	35.5	14.5	6.3	50.0
April	25.0	89.5	6.2	55.4	86.3
May	18.5	13.5	9.1	21.0	6.5
June	—	—	—	—	—
Total	382.5	614.6	629.4	575.4	652.4

Map 3.1. Distribution of water sources in the /Xai/xai-/Gəm Area

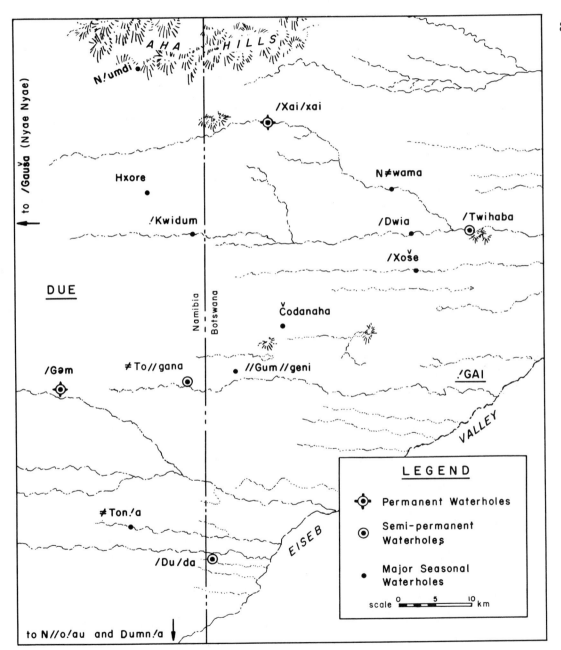

AHA HILLS

N/umdi

/Xai/xai

to /Gaušа (Nyae Nyae)

Hxore

N≠wama

/Kwidum

/Dwia

/Twihaba

/Xoše

DUE

Namibia

Botswana

Čodanaha

/Gəm

≠To//gana

//Gum//geni

/GAI

VALLEY

≠Ton/a

EISEB

/Du/da

to N//o/au and Dumn/a

LEGEND

◉ Permanent Waterholes

⊙ Semi-permanent Waterholes

● Major Seasonal Waterholes

scale 0   5   10 km

In general, the farther down the hierarchy of water sources they go, the harder it is for the !Kung to staisfy their moisture requirements. Access to tree water (class V) is usually difficult and often must be soaked up in a makeshift sponge or sucked out in a reed straw. (Sip-wells are known by the !Kung but rarely utilized.) Water root (Class VI) is even more difficult to reach since the root itself must be dug out from depths of up to 40 cm (15 in), and contents of as many as 20 roots must be consumed daily to provide the needs of one person (see Lee 1965, pp. 172 ff.). On the other hand, because root and tree waters are widely distributed in close proximity to valuable food sources, they are often utilized despite their difficulty of access.

The !Kung ability to operate successfully in this environment therefore involves them in sorting out a complex set of variables about the current locations of food and water, the ease or difficulty of getting it, and the whereabouts and current activities of adjacent groups. And their subsistence plans must be continually revised in light of the unfolding rainfall situation through the growing season and beyond.

Patterns of !Kung Spatial Organization

Given the ecological conditions, what land-use pattern has emerged? Today (1963–1969), international politics and pastoral occupation have restructured the land use in non--hunter-gatherer ways. The current situation and how it evolved are interesting questions in their own right and will be discussed below. In order to understand the hunting and gathering pattern, we must reconstruct the distribution of landholding groups as they were during the 1920s, before the Bantu settlement.

In Map 3.2 are plotted the landholding groups of the /Gɔm-/Xai/xai areas of forty years ago. The number is located on the map in the vicinity of the largest waterhole each group's area contains. An examination of Map 3.2 makes it apparent that there were many more groups holding land than there were permanent waterholes to support them. Eleven groups regularly wintered in the area, with occasional visits from at least four other groups; yet there were only five permanent waterholes and of these only two were really reliable. Eleven is the minimum number that operated in this area. There may have been more groups, especially in /Gɔm. The members of these groups have moved entirely out of the area to the larger "magnets" of the Ghanzi and Gobabis white farms, or to the Tswana and

Map 3.2. A reconstruction of the distribution of land-holding groups, 1920–1930

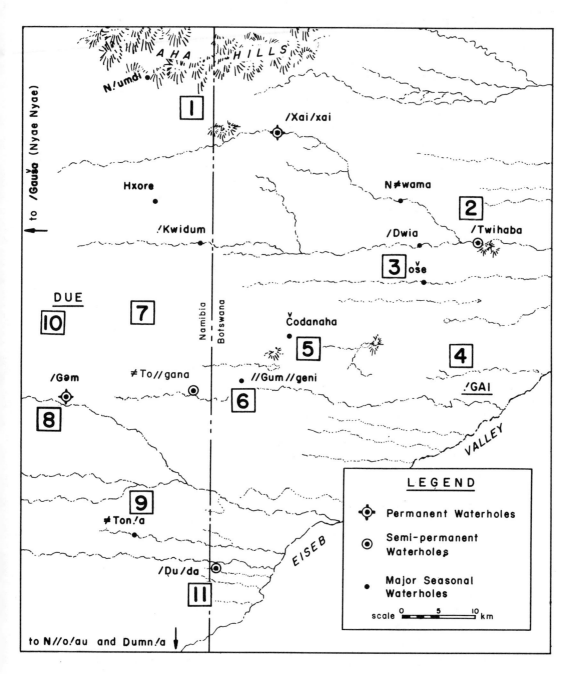

to /Gauš∙a (Nyae Nyae)

AHA HILLS

N/umdi

1

/Xai/xai

Hxore

N≠wama

2

/Kwidum

/Dwia

/Twihaba

3 oše

DUE

10

7

Namibia

Botswana

Čodanaha

5

4

/Gəm

≠To//gana

//Gum//geni

/GAI

8

6

VALLEY

9

≠Ton/a

LEGEND

⊕ Permanent Waterholes

◉ Semi-permanent Waterholes

• Major Seasonal Waterholes

/Du/da

EISEB

11

scale 0   5   10 km

to N//o/au and Dumn/a

Herero cattle posts around Lake Ngami. Further, this presentation does not take into account groups that have moved *into* the study area since 1930, such as the group from /Gausha (355) who moved to /Xai/xai in the 1940s, and groups from the Ghanzi farms who were moving into the /Du/da area in the late 1960s (625 and 729).

Such a large number of groups could be supported only if there were widespread agreement to maintain regular and free access to permanent water. The orderly, rather evenly spaced arrangement of groups in Map 3.2 is characteristic only of the height of the rainy season when water and food are available throughout the area. But as the summer waters evaporate with the coming of the winter, the eleven groups would converge to the pattern plotted in Map 3.3 and summarized in Table 3.5, Column 2.

Unless water was exceptionally strong, groups 2 and 4 would join group 3 at /Twihaba, and later in the season most or all of the people would pay a visit to group 1 at /Xai/xai. At the same time, groups 5, 6, and 7 would converge on ≠To//gana, while groups 8, and 9, and 10 would converge on /Gəm. Group 11 stayed around /Du/da, where it was joined by one or two groups from N//o!kau and Dumn!a (see Table 3.5 footnote). Later in the season, it was customary for groups at /Du/da and ≠To//gana to pay visits to relatives at /Gəm.

In good years, groups had the option of wintering in any one of several places: in the home area, at a permanent waterhole, or visiting relatives at waterholes outside the area. Also, the members of the groups that were primarily associated with one of the two very reliable waterholes—group 1 at /Xai/xai and group 8 at /Gəm—could spend most of their year enjoying the seasonal food resources of their neighbors. Reciprocal access to resources at all times ensured that key resources would be available at critical periods.

In moderate winter dry-season conditions, the eleven groups distributed themselves at five water points. Under very severe conditions, the groups underwent another phase of convergence (see Table 3.5, Column 3). Four groups fell back on /Xai/xai, four others on /Gəm, and three others alternated between /Gəm and /Xai/xai. Thus in the most difficult drought years there might be as many as seven groups at a single waterhole. Such a situation was observed by the Marshalls when seven groups converged on /Gəm in the severe drought winter of 1952 (J. Marshall 1957, p. 36).

Traditionally, waterholes such as /Xai/xai and /Gəm have played important roles as entrepots in the economic and social lives of the !Kung. Even before the Bantu built their cattle posts there, /Xai/xai

Map 3.3. Patterns of convergence of land-holding groups during the dry season and in drought years, 1920–1930

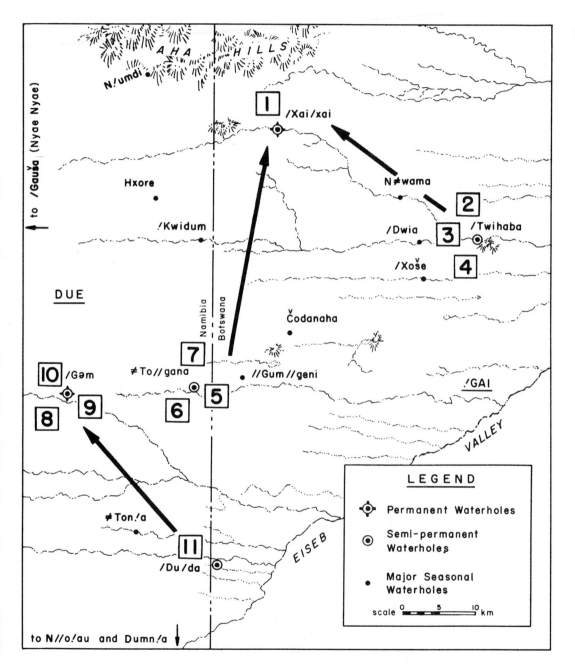

Table 3.5. Reconstructed groups of the /Xai/xai and /Gəm Areas, circa 1920 to 1930[a]

Group no.	Informant no.	Location Summer (1)	Winter (2)	Extreme dry recourse (3)	Current status
1	396	N!umdi	/Xai/xai	/Xai/xai	!Xumn!a's group at /Xai/xai
2	346	/Twihaba	/Twihaba and /Xai/xai	/Xai/xai	No longer functioning; descendants at /Xai/xai
3	414	/Dwia	/Twihaba and /Xai/xai	/Xai/xai	/Ti!kai's group at /Xai/xai
4	429	!Kai	/Twihaba and /Xai/xai	/Xai/xai	No longer functioning; descendants at /Xai/xai
5	335	Chodanaha	≠To//gana	/Gəm or /Xai/xai	Still utilize n!ore part of the year; winter at /Xai/xai
6	543	//Gum//geni	≠To//gana	/Gəm or /Xai/xai	A few families still utilize n!ore; winter at /Xai/xai or /Du/da
7	363	n. of ≠To//gana	≠To//gana	/Gəm or /Xai/xai	No longer functioning; descendants at /Xai/xai
8	336	Around /Gəm	/Gəm	/Gəm	No longer functioning; descendants at /Xai/xai
9	580	Due or ≠Ton!a	/Gəm	/Gəm	A functioning group now based at /Du/da
10	636?	Due	/Gəm	/Gəm	Moved to South African Government settlement scheme at Chum!kwe
11	684	/Du/da	/Du/da	/Gəm	A functioning group based at /Du/da

[a]There were several additional groups who moved into this area from the west and south during the summer and may have opted to winter at /Gəm and/or /Xai/xai during extremely dry years (e.g. Marshall's bands 1 and 2 from /Gausha, band 15 from Dum!na, and band 17 from N//o!kau) (L. Marshall, 1960).

was a trading center where people from all points of the compass
came to visit, dance, and do *hxaro*—a kind of traditional trading—
and sometimes to fight.

/Ti!kai 414 described the traditional role of /Xai/xai as follows:

> /Xai/xai has always been a meeting place for people even be-
> fore the blacks came. People came from the north, from
> !Kangwa and !Goshe, and from the south from /Gəm (and
> from the west from /Gausha), stayed here, did hxaro, drank
> *n!o* (a choice wild fruit), ate *//"xa* (mongongo nuts), and then
> went back.
>
> They asked Kan!o [one of the owners] for permission. They
> also asked ≠Toma!gain [Father of 396].
>
> /Xai/xai was favored because the water was so big. Choma
> [men's initiation ceremony] was danced here, but the main
> reason [to meet] was hxaro trade.
>
> People came in all seasons of the year—summer, winter, and
> spring. But they particularly came in spring [*!ga,* September-
> October] when the trees were in flower [before the onset of
> the rains]. When the summer pans dried out, they ate *!xwa*
> [the waterbearing root]. When the *!xwa* got thin, they came
> into /Xai/xai. This was because some of the n!ores did not have
> year-round water.

A closely comparable land-use pattern has been observed in the Nyae
Nyae area as recently as 1952–53 by the Marshall expedition. In a
little-read but extremely informative work ("Ecology of the !Kung
Bushmen of the Kalahari," Harvard senior honors thesis, 1957),
John Marshall discussed how the Nyae Nyae groups would arrange
themselves with reference to water first under "normal" and then
under drought conditions. Of the latter, he writes:

> In very dry years, more of the bands would be concentrated
> around /Gautscha [/Gausha], Deboragu, and perhaps Khumsa.
> I do not know for sure whether Khumsa is a permanent water-
> hole. I am sure that there is a permanent waterhole northeast
> of /Gautscha to which bands 8, 9, and 10 would shrink if a
> winter of desiccation was complete. The distribution of the
> interior bands in such a winter season that so utterly rejects all
> juicy things would probably be:
> Bands 1, 2, 3, at /Gautscha, the highest yielding waterhole
> in the area, therefore able to support the 85 people of these
> bands.
> Bands 4 and 5 might hold out at Deboragu and would be
> joined by band 6. Deboragu is a weak water. The 29 people of

bands 4, 5, and 6 would probably be able to survive, however. One man told us, speaking with affection for Deboragu, that, though it may look dry, scratch and you will find water.

Band 11 might flee to S'amangaigai [Tsamāgaigai] and so the people would endure. (J. Marshall 1957, pp. 32–33)

Hunter-Gatherer Spatial Organization

The spatial organization of many hunting and gathering peoples was similar to that of the two !Kung cases cited. For example, a division of the Eskimo year into a large-group phase and a small-group phase was first formally described by Mauss in a classic paper (1906), and documented by many observers (Boas 1888; Rasmussen 1931; Spencer 1959; Balikci 1964; Damas 1969; the last source is particularly useful). In the case of the central Eskimo, the time of maximum concentration was also in the winter, but the environmental determinant was the accessibility of good seal hunting rather than the availability of water. For other Eskimo groups, the maximal aggregation was associated with a variety of ecological strategies, as summarized by Damas (1969, pp. 135–138).

Among the Australian aborigines, the flexible land-use pattern was for a long time obscured in anthropological studies by a confusion of the patrilineal totemic ritual group with the on-the-ground *living* group. The totemic group indeed controlled real estate exclusively but only for occasional ritual purposes, and not for day-to-day living (Hiatt 1962; Berndt 1970). For the latter, the group that hunted, gathered, and lived together was made up of members of a number of patriclans and exhibited a genealogical composition and an annual pattern of concentration-dispersion similar to that of the !Kung. In Arnhemland and Cape York, the significant ecological determinant appeared to be the annual flooding of the plain which caused the people to congregate in larger groups on the seacoast (Thomson 1939, p. 209) or on higher interior ground (White and Peterson 1969; Schrire, 1972; see also Hiatt 1965, pp. 24–29). In desert Australia, the concentration-dispersion pattern has been known for many years. Particular attention has been paid to the maximal grouping in the form of the *corroboree* or ceremonial gathering (Spencer and Gillen 1899, p. 271 ff). The ecological significance of this gathering has been pointed out by Meggitt (1962, pp. 54–55) and Strehlow (1947, p. 65). Here, as among the San, the environment determinant was seasonal differences in water availability.

90

Examples could be multiplied: concentration-dispersion and reciprocal access to resources have been documented for subarctic Indians (Helm 1965; Leacock 1955; 1969), Great Basin Indians (Steward 1938; 1955), and Pygmies (Turnbull 1965; 1968); the case of the Northwest Coast is discussed below. However, central to all of these cases is a pattern of concentration and dispersion, usually seasonal, and a set of rules and practices for allowing reciprocal access to, or joint exploitation of, key resources.

The worldwide occurrence of this pattern of spatial organization in vastly different kinds of environments indicates the degree to which it was basic to the hunting and gathering adaptation. Several of the adaptive advantages can be spelled out. In the case of the !Kung, we see, first, that reciprocal access to resources allowed a much higher population density than could be supported if it were required that every n!ore contain a permanent water source (Map 3.1). Thus in the /Xai/xai-/Gəm areas, we find eleven groups in occupation instead of two. Second, the pattern contained a mechanism for responding to local imbalance in food resources. It had the capacity to adjust to conditions of scarcity and also to conditions of exceptional abundance. Third, the pattern offered many social advantages, not the least of which was the separating out of individuals and groups in conflict, thus keeping the threat of violence to a minimum. (Leacock 1969, p. 14 cites a very similar set of advantages for the flexibility of Montagnais groupings.)

By contrast, the patrilocal pattern of spatial organization that encapsulates a group of males with their spouses and offspring within a territory is far less adaptive. Indeed, it would be difficult to visualize how a patrilocal territorial organization could function in the San case. I would predict that such a society could survive only to the extent to which its members could slough off their patrilocality and territoriality and approximate the flexible model outlined above. (It is curious that Birdsell, one of the foremost exponents of the ecological approach in anthropology, should have chosen to espouse a model of hunter social organization that is as ecologically unviable as is the patrilineal band.)

In view of these adaptive advantages, it hardly seems likely—as Service has argued—that this flexible land-use pattern is strictly a product of acculturation brought about by the breakdown of aboriginal bands. Flexibility appears to be adaptive in both the precontact and the postcontact situation. In fact, we are now in a position to trace what actually has happened to change !Kung land use patterns over the last eighty years.

Contact and Spatial Organization:
1890 to 1969

Starting in the late 1880s and early 1890s, Tswana pastoralists began coming out to the /Xai/xai-/Gəm areas from their towns in the
east for annual hunting and grazing expeditions. At the end of each
rainy season, the various hunting parties, along with several groups of
San, would rendezvous for some weeks of hunting, dancing, and
trading. In the trade, the !Kung gave furs, hides, honey, and ostrich
eggshell beadwork, while in return they received tobacco, clay pots,
iron implements, and European goods. When the trading was done,
the oxen were inspanned, and the Tswana drove their wagons back
to the east for the winter. During this period of initial contact, an
annual concentration point occurred at this encampment known as
Koloi (ox-wagon, or ox-wagon camp in Setswana).

During the 1920s, permanent Bantu-speaking settlers began to
move into the area, bringing herds of livestock and enlarging and
deepening the waterholes at /Gəm´and /Xai/xai. A nucleus of semisedentary !Kung began to develop at these two points in a process
that has been observed worldwide among hunter-gatherers around
what L.R. Hiatt has aptly called "the magnets" of attractiveness.
Mission and Government Stations constituted the magnets in Australia, while, in the northern Kalahari, Bantu cattle posts were the
magnets (Lee 1972b).

Prior to Bantu settlement, the !Kung had spent most of the year
moving around the n!ores and a few months camped at the permanent water. Since the arrival of the Bantu, a reverse pattern has
evolved. Today, many !Kung remain most of the year camped at
/Xai/xai and spend only a few months of the year moving around the
n!ores. In fact, the point of major population concentration in recent
years has usually coincided with the Christmas feast offered the
!Kung by their Bantu neighbors (Lee 1969b).

The effects of contact on spatial organization are shown in Map
3.4 (and Table 3.5, last column). Acculturation has produced fragmentation and discontinuous utilization of n!ores. Four groups have
ceased to function as subsistence units, having become wholly attached to Bantu cattle posts (groups 2, 4, 7, and 8). One group, 10—
along with many others from the Nyae Nyae, outside our study area
—has joined the South African government settlement station in
Chum!kwe. Four other groups move in and out of /Xai/xai on hunting and gathering trips of varying length (groups 1, 3, 5, and 6).

Even though these semisettled groups spend most of the year at

Map 3.4. Current land-use patterns of active land-holding groups, 1963–1969

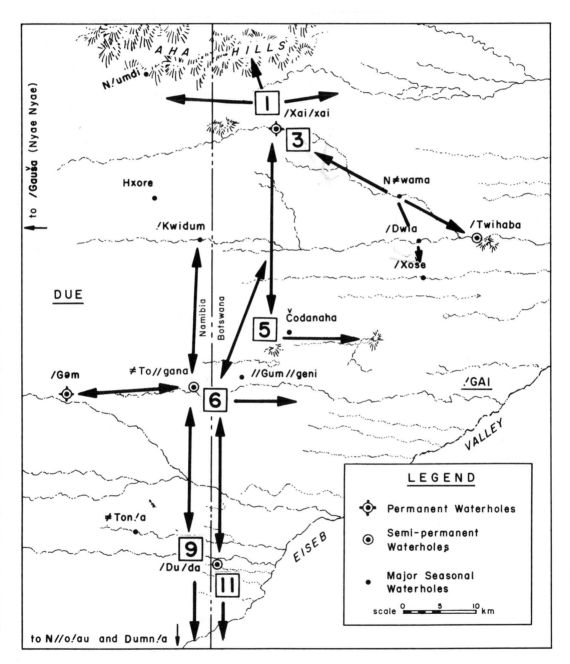

/Xai/xai (or Chum!kwe), each tries to spend at least a month or two in the home n!ore. Unlike the Australians, the !Kung do not maintain totemic sites within their home localities. Nevertheless, the ties to the n!ore are certainly based on sentiment as well as economic expediency; this emotional content is expressed in the following quotation from a young woman member of group 3 now living at /Xai/xai:

> [You see us here today but] you know we are not /Xai/xai people. Our true n!ore is east at /Dwia and every day at this time of year [November] we all scan the eastern horizon for any sign of cloud or rain. We say, to each other, "Has it hit the n!ore?" "Look, did that miss the n!ore?" And we think of the rich fields of berries spreading as far as the eye can see and the mongongo nuts densely littered on the ground. We think of the meat that will soon be hanging thick from every branch. No, we are not of /Xai/xai; /Dwia is our earth. We just came here to drink the milk.

In only two cases (groups 9 and 11), are the groups using their n!ores in anything like the traditional manner. And in the last three years, even these groups have been affected. South African police patrols have ordered these groups to confine their camps and activities to within a close radius of the border so that they can be easily checked up on. This has produced two rather bizarre effects on spatial and social organization: first, there is a highly unusual linear pattern of land use as the groups move up the border road from camp to camp and then down again, and, second, there are abnormally large groups of 90 to 120 people camping together at times of the year when one would expect them to be dispersed into much smaller groups. The !Kung say they are afraid to disperse for fear that the police patrols will go out after them (see Map 3.4).

In short, contact has produced in !Kung land use a spectrum of effects including fragmentation and sedentism in some groups and consolidation and mobility in others. The actual changes in land use can be accounted for by a combination of economic and political factors, although common to all situations is the introduction of an economic "magnet" and along with it an outside jural authority (Lee 1972a; 1972b). The highly flexible spatial arrangements of today appear to be a continuation of flexible spatial arrangements of the precontact era. And these flexible arrangements in turn are shown to be adaptations to the perennial problems of the arid environment: recurrent drought and scarcity of surface water.

Conclusion

It remains now to deal briefly with several methodological issues. First, I want to specify the operations of the method used in this paper so that it can be applied to other ethnographic cases. In the analysis of a given case, we consider first how the environment varies spatially in terms of the uneven distribution of resources, and, second, how the abundance and distributions of these resources vary through time. The resources that vary may be water supply, game populations, salmon runs, vegetable foods, or other factors. Each case will have its own constellation of factors. Then, invoking Elton's concept of Minimal or Economic Density (Elton 1927), we delineate the minimum area that a group of people must maintain access to in order to ensure its survival in the medium and long run. For example, a hunter-gatherer group may be able to satisfy subsistence requirements within 100 km² for four years out of five but it will still go out of the business unless it has access to a much larger area during the fifth year. And in order to ride out environmental fluctuation over the course of 50, 100, or 200 years, the area to which the group must maintain access must be even larger, probably on the order of ten times the area it covers in a single good year. Maintaining access to such a large area is really a question of maintaining cordial working relations with one's neighbors occupying the space. So the environmental problem has a social solution.

However, little of this long-term perspective is visible to an observer. When an observer arrives on the scene and finds a hunting and gathering population in a state of constant motion, he may be initially puzzled by this mobility, since the people appear to be moving even more frequently than necessary to exploit what appear to be rather stable resources. Faced with such a set of facts, the observer is liable to attribute this mobility—as Service does—to breakdown of aboriginal bands through contact (Service 1962, p. 108), or he may conclude with Turnbull that the mobility is *socially* determined and has nothing to do with environmental factors (Turnbull 1965, pp. 177–178).

Both these interpretations suffer from the short time perspective enforced by the limitations of anthropological fieldwork. An ethnographer in his stint in the field observes one or at best two repeats of the annual round, and on this basis tries to generalize about Pygmy life or Eskimo life. But we have seen that there is no such thing as a typical year for a hunter-gatherer population. Their adaptation is a long-term one, and the observer can catch only a very short segment of the whole in a year.

95

When we see hunters moving widely about their range, in the apparent absence of ecological necessity, we are watching intergroup, economic relations that take years and generations to unfold. Keeping up distant social ties against a possible future need and visiting neighbors who owe favors from previous years are only two of the factors that set hunter groups in motion. The ostensible purposes are social, but the underlying rationale is adaptive. This may also help to explain why hunter-gatherers trade beads with their neighbors in exchange for beads. The trade item in the perspective is a facilitating device for maintaining relations that may be ecologically crucial over the long run. Similarly, when an investigator reports an environment which is without significant regional or temporal variation (Turnbull 1965, 1968), we may suspect that he has not looked into the matter carefully enough or long enough.

Population density is also a key variable. An adequate analysis of environmental variability must also plot the minimal subsistence areas for varying levels of population density. A resource area that looks quite undifferentiated for 5 persons per 100 km² (13/100 mi²) may be highly differentiated when the population grows to 25 persons per 100 km² (65/100 mi²). For example, a population in the process of moving into a new area and occupying it at low densities would be immune initially to fluctuations in key resources, and its members thus might manage their affairs without elaborate arrangements for reciprocal access. But their population would grow after several generations to the level where environmental fluctuation *would* threaten their survival. Long before this point is reached, however, one would expect that the necessary mechanisms of reciprocal access would have evolved. At this point, other forces tending to limit population density become operative, and these prevent the population from threatening the overall level of resources (Lee 1972b).

Finally, it might be argued that the method presented here is applicable only in the most marginal environments with maximum unpredictability of resources. Again I invoke population density. Since all environments vary, for all environments there will be a certain threshold of population density at which point the resource base will become unpredictable. It is extremely interesting that concentration-dispersion land use and rules for reciprocal access to resources are found even in the "richest" environments among the most affluent of the world's recent hunter-gatherers. The Indians of the Northwest Coast (Drucker 1955) annually dispersed from their large winter villages into smaller summer settlements located nearer to prime fishing sites. And it was on the Northwest Coast that the pioneer research in the problem of environmental variation in relation to spatial organization was carried out by Wayne Suttles. Suttles (1960; 1962; 1968) has shown that even the rich environment of coastal British Columbia was subject to severe local and annual variation in salmon runs. Without the annual dispersion and the reciprocal access to resources offered by intervillage feasts and potlatches, many villages of coastal Indians would have gone out of business (see also Vayda 1961, Piddocke 1965).

If the method and the argument presented in this paper have merit, then it may be appropriate for us to discard models of prehistoric populations that encapsulate each group of males within a territory and to consider instead a more dynamic model in which interlocking aggregations of persons undergo continual reshuffling of groups in response to short- and long-term environmental fluctuations and to changes in population density.

4 Subsistence Ecology of Central Kalahari San

Jiro Tanaka

/Gwi San in the Central Kalahari eating *Bauhinia macrantha* beans

Some four hundred km southeast of the Dobe Area live a second group of isolated San who were full-time hunter-gatherers until very recent times (Map 4.1). These people, the /Gwi and //Gana San of the ≠Kade pan area, belong to a language group (Tshu-Khwe) that is unrelated to !Kung; but in spite of this, the central Kalahari mode of subsistence shows many similarities to that of the Dobe Area !Kung. Clearly different from Dobe, however, is the ecological setting. ≠Kade pan, approximately in the center of the Central Kalahari Game Reserve, is located in a much drier zone; plant foods are not nearly as abundant or of as high quality as they are in the Dobe Area, and standing water is extremely scarce.

These key differences in ecology have wrought a number of important shifts in adaptation and organization. This chapter examines central Kalahari subsistence in detail, and by drawing frequent comparisons with the Dobe material attempts to delineate the range of variation among the Kalahari hunting and gathering peoples. Field work on the ≠Kade San has previously been carried out by Silberbauer (1965, 1972). During my own field work (September 1967–March 1968; March 1971–June 1972) the ≠Kade San, consisting of the /Gwi and //Gana people who intermarry and have similar life

Map 4.1. Sketch map of ≠Kade Area

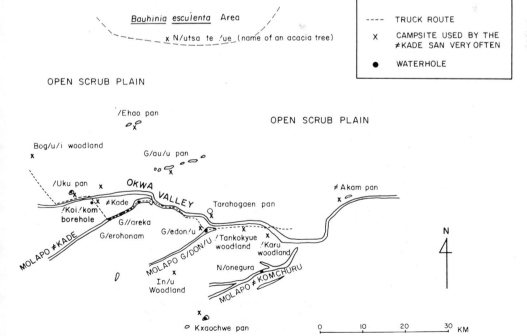

100

styles despite slight linguistic differences, led a self-sufficient life, depending almost entirely on hunting and gathering. Although they do keep herds of goats and donkeys, this chapter is primarily concerned with their actual hunting and gathering subsistence base.

In the middle of the Reserve, the long depression that is the Okwa Valley (the ≠Kade San call it "/a") runs from west to east. Within the entire ≠Kade area, there are three molapos[1] running parallel to each other to join the valley as well as many pans[2] of all sizes. Such variation in topography produces a rich variety of vegetation in the area. The acacia woodlands provide the people with plenty of firewood and building materials, while an assortment of food plants can be collected by comparatively short seasonal migrations. When rain comes, the shallow waterholes in pans and molapos become drinking water sources for the San, as well as convenient places for hunting herbivorous game animals attracted by the soft grass and water. For these reasons, the ≠Kade area is the most densely populated area in the Central Kalahari Game Reserve. Of the estimated 1000 San in the Reserve, about half use the ≠Kade area as at least a part of their nomadic range. During the period of my field work, I came across about 400 individuals there, including seasonal or temporary visitors. I would estimate that about 250 individuals are "permanent" residents of the ≠Kade area.

In a preliminary report,[3] I pointed out the following: (1) the ≠Kade people obtain more than 90 percent of their requisite water from plants; (2) vegetable food is more important than animal food and is the basis of their subsistence; (3) there is an abundance and rich variety of vegetable food; (4) food selectivity is high, that is, 13 species of plants comprise their staple diet. I also pointed out that (5) the ≠Kade are obliged to move their camps according to the seasonal change in food supply; (6) the amount of effort and time used in obtaining food is relatively small (about 5 hours per day); (7) their nomadic range is wide and population density low (0.03 person per sq km), but their travel route is almost always fixed and the area of intensive utilization restricted.

There are two remarkable differences between the subsistence economy of the !Kung of the Dobe Area and that of the ≠Kade people. First, the ≠Kade San have no standing water at all except for a few days after heavy rain, while the Dobe San almost always live in the vicinity of a waterhole. Second, the bulk of the ≠Kade San diet consists of 13 species of plants with no one dominant primary food as the mongongo nut is among the Dobe San.

It is important to describe how the ≠Kade San obtain water and the quantity obtained, since there are no other people in the world who lack standing water for such long periods of time. Then, as the mongongo tree (*Ricinodendron rautaneii*) is absent in the vegetation of the central and southern Kalahari, it is also important to describe the ≠Kade San subsistence method in order to understand the range of subsistence modes of the San.

101

Subsistence Activities

The ≠Kade San society is egalitarian with no differentiation in social status or occupation. Division of labor is based on age and sex only, with the adults providing food for dependent children under 15 years and for the aged. Hunting is done by men and gathering by women.

Gathering

Gathering vegetable food is divided into two types of activity: "picking" and "digging." The technique used in gathering depends on the location of the edible part of the plant—whether it is on or under the ground. Reaching tubers and bulbs requires a digging stick, except for a few species such as the truffle or the *Scilla* bulb. Although it has been observed that the chimpanzee occasionally exploits food resources with the aid of simple tools, no nonhuman primates are able to obtain tubers buried deep in the ground. The gathering technique of digging with a digging stick is specific to human beings.

Consequently, troops of chacma baboons live in other parts of the Kalahari but not in the ≠Kade area where they cannot survive the late dry season when necessary water has to be obtained from underground plants. Only humans are able to survive there by using the digging technique to obtain water resources. Even though this digging plays an important part in the San food life throughout the year, it inevitably becomes most crucial in the late dry season.

Although hunting requires skill and heavy labor the reward is small. On the other hand, gathering is a more stable basis for subsistence because food plants can predictably yield an adequate quantity of food for everyone with comparatively little effort. Gathering trips by women lasting from one to several hours are made almost every day. Food obtained on a gathering trip is partly consumed in the field, but most is carried back to the camp. Hence, "carrying" should be emphasized as being as important a part of the gathering subsistence activity as it is of hunting. Delay in the consumption of food by carrying back to the camp the gathered plants or hunted animals and their pooling and redistribution are important considerations when investigating the origin of the human family.

Hunting

Typical hunting tools used by the ≠Kade San are the bow-and-arrow to kill large antelopes and giraffe; the rope snare to trap small antelopes, small carnivores, and birds; and the long pole and hook for one man to hold springhare while another man digs down to the animal in its burrow. When dogs are available to help, antelopes, small carnivores, and warthog are hunted with a spear. Small animals are sometimes killed by clubbing.

The quarry of carnivores, such as the lion, leopard, cheetah, and hunting dog, is sometimes usurped by dashing to the spot where a large number of wheeling vultures have been observed.

Bow-and-arrow hunting is extremely difficult and requires hard work. Men carry weapons in their shoulder bags and are always prepared to shoot when they go out into the field, although more often than not they return to camp without finding any game. They usually stay in the field for several hours, covering 10–30 km in a hunting day which sometimes may last 10 hours. Men make such hunting trips about three days per week.

Food Sources

Drinking Water

As already mentioned, no permanent waterhole exists in the Central Kalahari Game Reserve, but small hollows in pans and molapos collect water during the rains and provide shallow waterholes for several days after heavy rain. The ≠Kade San move their camps to take advantage of these pans for about 30 to 60 days per year.

Table 4.1 shows how many days the ≠Kade people could use the waterholes in the area during the rainy season of 1967–68. "W" shows presence of water in a hole. "D" indicates utilization of water by the people. The table shows that the ≠Kade pan provided water for 39 days and the G//areka pan for 36 days (this group moved to the pan three days after rain) in one year. In this season, it did not rain for the 54 days from January 9 to March 2.

For the more than 300 days annually when the ≠Kade San cannot find any standing water, they are obliged to obtain water from plants and animals. Two species of melon, *Citrullus lanatus* and *Citrullus naudinianus*, two species of tubers, *Raphionacme burkei* and *Coccinia*

Table 4.1. Available dates of standing water

Date		Waterhole			
		G/erohonam	G//areka	≠Kade	G/edon!u
1967 Dec.	10				
	11				
	12				
	13			D	
	14				
	22				
	23				
	24	W	W	D	
	25	W	W	D	
	26	W	W	D	W
	27	W	D	D	W
	28	W	D	D	W
	29	W	D	D	W
	30	W	D	D	W
	31	W	D	D	W
1968 Jan.	1	W	D	D	W
	2	W	D	D	W
	3	W	D	D	W
	4	W	D		W
	5	W	D		W
	6	W	D		W
	7	W	D		W
	8	W	D	D	W
	9	W	D	D	W
	10	W	D	D	W
	11	D		D	W
	12	D		D	
	13	D		D	
	14			D	
	15			D	
	16			D	
1968 Mar.	1				
	2				
	3	W	D	D	D
	4	W	D	D	D
	5	W	D	D	D
	6	W	D	D	D
	7	W	D	D	D
	8	W	D	D	D
	9	W	D	D	D
	10	W	D	D	D
	11	W	D	D	D
	12	W	D	D	D
	13	W	D	D	W
	14	W	D	D	W
	15	W	D	D	W
	16	W	D	D	W

(continued)

Table 4.1. Available dates of standing water (continued)

		Waterhole			
Date		G/erohonam	G//areka	≠Kade	G/edon!u
	17	W	D	D	W
	18	W	D	D	W
	19	W	D	D	W
	20	W	D	D	W
	21	W	D	D	
	22	W	D		
	23	W	D		
	24				
	25				

rehmanii, and an aloe, *Aloe zebrina,* are the necessary water sources for them as well as important food resources. Although blood and moisture squeezed from the stomach contents of slain animals are good water sources, their use is not very significant since big game is so rarely caught.

Figure 4.1 shows the seasonal changes in water resources. *Tsama* melon, *Citrullus lanatus,* is an excellent source, as it consists of approximately 90 percent water and keeps for a surprisingly long time—throughout the year in some cases. At the end of December 1971, I observed a San group camping at Kxaochwe, about 30 km south of ≠Kade pan. They were still subsisting on tsama melon which they had collected with great effort, and they had also found the first fresh *Citrullus naudinianus* melons of the new season. The two species of plants that have juicy tubers are not really effective sources of water; both are fibrous, and *R. burkei* is particularly bitter. When tsama melon is available, it is always intensively collected, an illustration of the ≠Kade San's selectivity in choice of food plants.

It is very difficult to measure the quantity of water consumed by the people in a day when standing water is not available. Since it seems that tsama melon is the only water-bearing food consumed for many days during June, July, and August, I tried to determine the quantity of water obtained from the tsama melons during these periods. The mean weight of melon eaten by one person in a day is approximately 5 kg. Estimated water taken from it is approximately 70 percent because peel is discarded: $5000 \times 0.7 = 3500g$.

The estimated quantity of water obtained from melon consumed by the ≠Kade San is therefore 3500 ml per person per day, which includes hand and face washing water and about 100 ml to each person's dog. Melon flesh boiled with meat is drunk by both people and dogs. If the tsama melon becomes scarce or even disappears in the the late dry season, the ≠Kade San have to rely primarily on tubers for their water requirements. In that case, the quantity of water they can obtain is probably much less than when the tsama melon is available.

Vegetable Food

The bushveld and woodland of the Kalahari consists of more varieties of plants than presumed at first sight. Many of the species are used by the ≠Kade San as food, medicine, or material for various tools. The number of species of plants regarded as food by the ≠Kade San totals 79, of which 3 are major foods. These food plants are classified into 5 categories by their utility value:

I. Major food: Plants that occupy the major part of a diet in a certain season (13 species).
II. Minor food: Plants that come to be a staple when major food is not available (7 species). They are no less important than major food, but their period of utilization is rather short.
III. Supplementary food: Plants not eaten in any quantity but often added to the menu as a supplementary food that is important as a source of vitamins and other nutrients (15 species).
IV. Rare food: Plants sometimes collected as a supplementary food but less important (27 species).
V. Probable food: Plants regarded as food by some informants, but not observed by me as included in their diet; and plants whose food value is suspect (16 species).

Figure 4.1. Seasonal changes in water resources

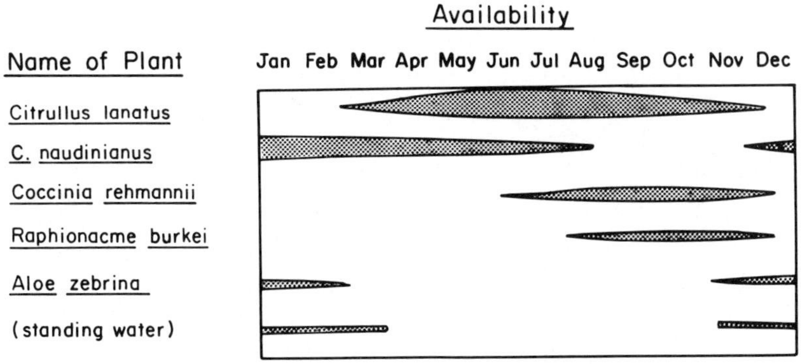

Availability

Name of Plant	Jan Feb Mar Apr May Jun Jul Aug Sep Oct Nov Dec
Citrullus lanatus	
C. naudinianus	
Coccinia rehmannii	
Raphionacme burkei	
Aloe zebrina	
(standing water)	

The entire list is found in Appendix Table 4.A.

In any season, some dozens of species of edible plants are available, but only a few species of favorite plants are included in the menu during each season. When the most desirable plants such as *Citrullus lanatus, Bauhinia esculenta, Bauhinia macrantha,* or *Terfezia sp.* are available together, only a single species is collected intensively on most days.

The tuberous plants, *Coccinia rehmanii, Rhaphionacme burkei,* and *Cucumis kalahariensis,* continue to be available well into the rainy season which usually starts in November. Green vegetables such as *Scilla spp.* and *Talinum spp.* that sprout soon after the start of the first rains are gradually added to the menu. Within a few weeks the *Ochna* berry ripens and the *Grewia* berry soon after. These two berries then become the staple food. When the *Citrullus naudinianus* melon ripens in December and is ready to be eaten, tubers are no longer dug.

By February, the *Bauhinia macrantha* bean is ready to be eaten and becomes an important constituent of San food for several months. This single species of bean constitutes the main element in the diet when standing water is available, while the other plants are almost never eaten despite the fact that this is the richest season for all food plants in the Kalahari bushveld. *Bauhinia macrantha* is rich in protein and fat and is abundant in the area. Since this bean is tasty, nutritious, and very abundant for a long period, it is among the most important foods for the ≠Kade San together with the two species of melons that serve as water resources for most of the year and the three species of tubers (*Cucumis kalahariensis, Coccinia rehmanii,* and *Rhaphionacme burkei*) that are precious food and water resources in the late dry season. The *Bauhinia macrantha* bean is collected and brought to camp in its pod even though the pod is not edible and accounts for 75 percent of the whole weight.

Tsama melon (*Citrullus lanatus*) ripens slightly later then the *C. naudinianus.* It serves both man and most animals of the central Kalahari as their main water source until the late dry season. Tsama melon looks like watermelon, though much smaller in size; none of the fruits are sweet and some are even bitter. It is eaten efficiently with only the peel, about 20 percent of its weight, discarded. With water available from two species of melon, ≠Kade San collect the *Bauhinia macrantha* bean intensively until May. Around April the bean dries up, turning dark brown in color, and soon drops to the ground from a burst pod after which it is no longer edible.

After the *Bauhinia macrantha* season, the ≠Kade San sometimes make trips lasting a few days to collect the *Bauhinia esculenta* bean. This plant grows only in an open scrub plain, over 40 km to the north of ≠Kade pan. The bean is round and about 1.5 cm in diameter; and since it is much bigger than *Bauhinia macrantha,* it may still be collected on the ground until the rains start in October. Many of them, nevertheless, are eaten by rodents. *Bauhinia esculenta* contains much more protein and fat than *Bauhinia macrantha.* It dries somewhat earlier than the other bean, so that the people say "/oi (*Bauhinia esculenta*) is a better food than n≠an≠te (*Bauhinia macrantha*). Frost makes n≠an≠te bitter, but /oi is already dry when the winter comes, so it remains palatable long after." Although the ≠Kade people prefer the *esculenta* bean to the *macrantha,* the former grows far from their usual campsites in a poorly vegetated area. Thus they cannot find suitable shade trees for rest during a collecting trip, and they must expend a great amount of effort in collecting and carrying melons for water and firewood to sustain such a trip. As both species of *Bauhinia* bean are hard and easy to preserve, the San collect larger quantities than they can consume in one day and store them for the coming difficult season.[4]

In April and May, another excellent food plant, the truffle *Terfezia sp.,* is introduced into the menu. It is uncertain whether this species is a root parasite or fungus. In size and shape it resembles the potato although the texture is like that of soft cheese. The truffle is located by the cracks in the ground it causes as it grows. But its growth depends on rainfall, and it is not seen in a drought year.

After June, the *Bauhinia macrantha* bean and the truffle disappear, and the *Citrullus naudinianus* melon decreases. Only the tsama melon remains continuously as a staple food, and tubers become significant food resources. However, because tsama melon is a guaranteed water supply in this early dry season, only the favorite tubers such as *Cucumis kalahariensis* and *Coccinia rehmanii* are selectively collected. Collecting these tubers is not easy, as reaching a single tuber necessitates digging in hard sand approximately 70 cm beneath the surface.

September and October are the most difficult months of the year for the ≠Kade people. All the trees and grasses wither away and every part of the Kalahari turns brown and barren. Apart from hunting for game meat which is unreliable, the people spend a great amount of time and effort digging up every kind of root and collecting the few melons which have not rotted or have not been eaten by grazing animals. The most important water resource in this season is the abundant and widespread tuber, *Rhapionacme burkei,* which is

108

utilized by ≠Kade San despite its bitter taste. *Strophanthus sp.* and *Brachystelma sp.* produce delicious tubers, but they are not widely distributed in the area and are consequently much less important. Even a bitter-tasting plant such as *Dipcadi viride* that would never be touched in other seasons is collected and its juice mixed with the other plants. The most important food plants in this season are therefore *Rhaphionacme burkei, Cucumis kalahariensis,* and *Coccinia rehmanii.* This hard life of digging roots continues until the next rains start and the new food plants become obtainable.

As shown in Figure 4.2, "desirable food plants" (that is, abundant, easy to collect and carry, tasty and nutritious) are intensively utilized whenever they are in an edible state. Those are *Citrullus lanatus, Bauhinia macrantha, Ochna pulchra, Grewia flava, Grewia retinervis,* and *Terfezia sp.* The plants that require great effort to collect—such as *Cucumis kalahariensis* and *Coccinia rehmanii;* the plant that has to be carried long distances back to the camp (*Bauhinia esculenta*); and the plants that are bitter, unpalatable, or fibrous, such as *Rhaphionacme burkei, Aloe zebrina,* and *Scilla sp.*—are rarely utilized when the other, more desirable foods are available. *Citrullus naudinianus* melon is very important, but tsama melon is preferred when both are available at the same time.

As mentioned above, there are only 13 species of food plants utilized intensively by the ≠Kade San, and they are introduced into

Figure 4.2. Seasonal changes in main food resources

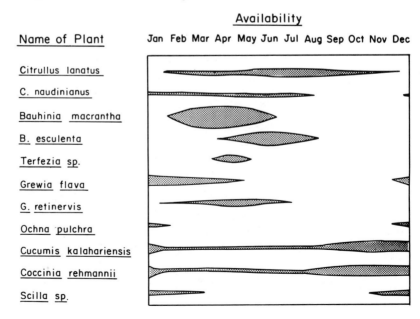

their diet in various combinations of a few species according to the season. Utilization of the other plants is quantitatively negligible. They are merely eaten as supplementary foods in order to supply water, calories, vitamins, and other nutrients.

Now let us consider which of the major species are the really important calorie sources in the ≠Kade San diet, excluding those species consisting of water or indigestible substances and those collected comparatively infrequently.

Rhaphionacme burkei and *Aloe zebrina* which are only used as water sources are excluded. The two species of melons consist mostly of water and fiber, though they are also eaten as food. Two species of *Grewia* berries mostly consist of indigestible seeds. *Scilla sp.* is a very fibrous bulk and is probably not digested to any significant degree. *Ochna* berry, rich in protein and fat, is not eaten much and is available for a short period only. The truffle is an excellent food probably containing carbohydrate; but growth of this species is heavily dependent upon rainfall, and its availability is unreliable.

Of the four remaining species of plants that are important ≠Kade San food, there are the two species of tubers (*Cucumis kalahariensis* and *Coccinia rehmanii*) and the two species of *Bauhinia* bean. The importance of the tubers is that, besides being eaten throughout the year, they also constitute the main food in the late dry season. Analysis of the nutrient composition of the two *Bauhinia* beans has been made by A.S. Wehmeyer and is shown in Table 4.2. The two *Bauhinia* beans are extremely nutritious and satisfying to the people, although they cease to be the main food in the mid-dry season. Thus it can be said that the basis of the ≠Kade San subsistence is primarily the tubers of *Cucumis kalahariensis* and *Coccinia rehmanii* and secondarily the seasonal concentration of the two species of *Bauhinia* beans.

To calculate how much food the ≠Kade people eat per day is difficult because the quantity differs from one day to another, and their eating times are not fixed. Table 4.3 shows the average weight in kilograms of food plants taken in a day, derived from a few observations made when more than 90 percent of the daily diet was provided by a single food plant such as tsama melon. One family represents a mean size of the ≠Kade San families: 1 man + 1 woman + 3 children. It is also difficult to estimate how much should be regarded strictly as food, because the requisite water is ingested together with the calorie intake. A fairly reasonable estimate is probably around 600–1000 gr per person per day for the weight of food ingested, excluding melons and truffle which contain 70–90 percent water.

Animal Food

The number of species of animals utilized as food by the ≠Kade
San is over 50: 33 mammals, 7 reptiles, 1 amphibian, several birds
and insects. The complete list is found in Appendix Table 4.B.

Because the big antelopes such as eland, kudu, gemsbok, hartebeest,
and wildebeest weigh 100–300 kg, the giraffe weigh up to 1300 kg, and
the springbok and ostrich weigh around 50 kg, one brought into the
camp is sufficient to satisfy the appetite of all camp members. But
since the small animals such as the duiker, steenbok, warthog, jackal,
fox, and the kori bustard weigh only 10–15 kg, they are distributed
only among a few families. The even smaller animals (hare, springhare, porcupine, genet, and guinea fowl) weigh 2 or 3 kg and are
usually consumed by a single family.

Table 4.4 shows the number of game animals hunted by the
≠Kade people in six months from September 1967 to March 1968.
Since the ≠Kade people migrate frequently and the number of camp

Table 4.2. Nutrient composition of the two *Bauhinia* beans

Component	Bauhinia esculenta	Bauhinia macrantha
Moisture	5.2	6.8
Ash	2.9	3.4
Fat	36.1	18.1
Protein	31.6	25.2
Calcium	136	144
Magnesium	258	188
Iron	3.3	3.82
Copper	1.0	0.93
Sodium	89	1.55
Potassium	849	961
Phosphorus	484	334
Zinc	3.8	1.9
Riboflavin	0.82	0.205
Nicotinic acid	1.86	1.245

(Moisture–Protein: g/100 g; Calcium–Nicotinic acid: mg/100 g)

members fluctuates from day to day, it is not strictly correct to express the number of animals per certain number of persons. The figures presented in the table show an approximate number of game per 50 persons, an average camp size, based on my continuous observations among several camps for the six-month period. The tortoise, small birds, snakes, and insects are negligible in weight. As Table 4.4 indicates, the total animal food taken by the 50 ≠Kade people in six months is 2048 kg, so that on an average only 220 g is taken by one person in a day.

Table 4.3. Estimated weights of food taken daily by the ≠Kade San

Name of plant	Per family	Per person
Citrullus lanatus (moisture)	20 kg	4 kg
Citrullus naudinianus (moisture)	25 kg	5 kg
Bauhinia macrantha (protein, fat)	5 kg	1 kg
Ochna pulchra (protein, fat)	4 kg	0.8 kg
Cucumus kalahariensis (carbohydrate)	3 kg	0.6 kg
Coccinia rehmanii (carbohydrate)	3 kg	0.6 kg
Terfezia sp. (probably carbohydrate)	15 kg	3 kg
Scilla sp. (carbohydrate with fiber)	3 kg	0.6 kg

Table 4.4. Number of game animals caught by the ≠Kade San from September 1967 to March 1968 (per 50 persons)

Name of animal	Number of animals recorded	Total weight of animals recorded (kg)	Estimated number of animals in a year
giraffe	0	0	1
gemsbok	7	1150	⎫
hartebeest	1	200	⎪
kudu	1	200	⎬ 20
wildebeest	0	0	⎪
eland	0	0	⎭
springbok	2	200	4
duiker	3	45	6
steenbok	17	170	30
warthog	0	0	2
jackal	3 (young)	3	6
fox	7	27	15
porcupine	0	0	2
springhare	22	53	50
genet	0	0	3
caracal	0	0	0 or 1
python	0	0	2
tortoise	many	negligible	many
ostrich	0	0	0 or 1
guinea fowl	0	0	2
		2048	

The ≠Kade San have many taboos about eating game meat. Generally those taboos depend on sex, age, or marital status. They believe that one becomes thin and dies upon eating a tabooed animal. The vulture and hunting dog as well as the domesticated dog are never eaten. The hyena is hated because of its scavenging habit, but its meat is sometimes eaten when hunger is beyond endurance. The lion is not generally eaten, except by the aged, because it eats man. The other carnivores (leopard, cheetah, jackal, fox, caracal, and genet) are not included in the taboo; they are regularly hunted by such methods as trapping. The most distinctive taboo determined by age and sex is the one concerning steenbok, springhare, kori bustard, and tortoise. Kori bustard and tortoise are not eaten except by infants and the elderly over about 40 years of age. Springhare and steenbok taboos are usually applied to a married couple who are nursing a newborn baby under about 6 months of age. These two animals are also taboo to a person who is able to fall into trance during the gemsbok dance.

The reason behind the ≠ Kade San's various taboos about animal food is not certain. However one possible ecological explanation may be given about the taboos determined by age. Animals (most strictly) tabooed (steenbok, springhare, kori bustard, and tortoise) are hunted most frequently, but all of them are small and cannot be distributed among many persons. The taboos probably function to give more opportunity of eating meat to helpless individuals, the infants and the aged.

Vegetable Food versus Animal Food

Let us consider the ratio of vegetable to animal food in the ≠Kade San diet. Previously, we estimated the weight of the vegetable food eaten by a person in a day as 600 g–1000 g, an average of 800 g for the weight of one day's consumption. On the other hand, ingested animal food has been estimated as 220 g per person per day. As bones, horns, hooves, and contents of stomach and intestine are thrown away, the edible portion is approximately two thirds of the figure: $220 \times 2/3 = 147$ g. The proportions by weight of vegetable food and animal food in the total diet are, respectively, 81.3 percent and 18.7 percent. If the plants taken as water sources (such as melons and tubers) are included in the vegetable food count, the ratio of animal food to vegetable food is even lower: vegetable food 96.4 percent; animal food 3.6 percent. Thus animal food is not very important in the ≠Kade San diet because vegetable food is more predictable and more easily collected. The ≠Kade area provides a necessary and sufficient amount of food plants to maintain the San subsistence. On the other hand, game animals are not so abundant, and they are scattered; the San's bow, arrow, and spear are primitive; and high skill and heavy labor are required to obtain the game. Even successful hunting does not bring enough food, and the mere process alone is risky. Therefore, it is not a suitable subsistence base (see Lee 1968a).

Although the proportion of animal food of the total (18.7 percent) diet is quite large, the ≠Kade San can survive in the Kalahari without it, whereas they could not survive without vegetable food. Animal food has great importance, however, in adding quality to the diet, and the ≠Kade people praise animal food, saying "meat is the real food."

Nomadism

Since the ≠Kade San food plants change according to the seasonal differences of plant growth; and since only a very small part of a wild plant is edible, people cannot live for a long time at one place. They must migrate at intervals of one to several weeks to the places where the food plants are ready to be eaten. Migration is one of the food-obtaining group activities, and it is a necessary activity for all hunting-gathering societies.

The time and place of the ≠Kade people's migrations are determined by the availability of food plants, and almost never by the convenience of hunting. This is easily understood in view of the ratio of importance of vegetable to animal food discussed above. Only when standing water is available in pans or molapos during the rainy season is a camp site prescribed by the accessibility of water.

Thus the ≠Kade San have a nomadic range of about 50 km radius centering on the Okwa Valley and three molapos, and they move an average of 300 km in a year, exclusive of daily hunting and gathering trips.

Discussion

The habitat of the San, the Kalahari Desert, is a marginal area with only 170 mm to 700 mm of rainfall per year. This conforms to the general rule that the contemporary hunter-gatherers in the world today do live in such marginal areas as tundra, tropical rain forests, and desert—all unsuitable for agriculture and pastoralism. These people have survived by very specialized adaptations to the harsh environment in these habitats. Since all hunter-gatherers share a common economic basis, they likewise have many similarities in social organization. But in other aspects, important differences are to be found between them resulting from differences in habitat and depending upon whether the subsistence base stresses hunting or stresses gathering.

Although the contemporary hunter-gatherers are, of course, *not the same people* and therefore do not have the same culture as the ancient hunter-gatherers who were distributed world wide in the Pleistocene, one may still ask why they have remained hunters to the present. Perhaps they could not incorporate different means of production developed by other people on account of their isolation, or perhaps such methods did not suit their particular habitat, or, again, they may not have needed other technologies at all because of the presence of abundant natural resources. Since the only surviving examples of hunter-gatherers are to be found in marginal areas, their societies might well have been different from the other ancient hunter-gatherers who lived in more fertile areas and whose societies adopted agriculture or pastoralism with the passage of time. And their societies may themselves have become altered during the lapse of ten thousand years, a period when the other hunter-gatherers achieved a revolutionary change as a result of the domestication of plants and animals.

The societies of some Arctic Eskimos and some San in the Kalahari are so specialized as a result of adaptation to harsh environments that it is sometimes difficult to change to another way of life. Or like the Siriono of South America who once started to follow the way to agriculture and then returned to the hunting-gathering life in the tropical forest, their societies might have experienced a "devolution phenomenon." When we attempt to reconstruct human history, however, the ethnographic facts of the contemporary hunter-gatherers undoubtedly provide important clues to these problems. Particularly when studying the evolution of human society, they are among the only data we have.

The first and most distinctive feature of the ≠Kade San subsistence is their dependence upon food plants for most of their water. There are few other peoples who have such meager water resources in their habitat. This is what makes ≠Kade San life so difficult. Most other San, including the !Kung of the Dobe Area, have at least one or more permanent waterholes in their habitats.

The next set of data concerns the staple food of the hunter-gatherer societies of the Kalahari. Part of the northern Kalahari contains a concentration of the *Ricinodendron rautanenii* trees that form woodlands on the ridges of dunes and produce the mongongo nut, the primary food for the Dobe San. This species, extending into Zambia and Rhodesia, is not common in the rest of the Kalahari, so that only the more northerly !Kung can utilize it as a primary food. The diet of the ≠Kade San shows a more varied pattern than the Dobe !Kung; that is, in most of the Kalahari there exists no plant that is so abundant and nutritious and, by lasting the whole year, provides a single key food. In the case of the ≠Kade San, thirteen species of plants form the main food group throughout the year. The presence of some stable plant food base is generally a necessary requirement for peoples whose subsistence depends on gathering, whether this plant base comprises only one species like the mongongo nut of the Dobe !Kung, the acorn of the California Indian, or two (and more) species observed among the ≠Kade San.

The ≠Kade San migrate over a much larger area than the Dobe !Kung. The difference in the range size between the two peoples is caused by the differences in their food life; the Dobe !Kung migrate around waterholes in a less dry area and depend on the widely distributed mongongo nut. The ≠Kade San inhabit a much drier area, have no waterholes, and have no single predominant article of diet.

Lee reported that "!Kung bushmen of Dobe devote from twelve to nineteen hours a week to getting food" per adult (Lee 1968b). On the other hand, the working period of the ≠Kade San is four hours and thirty minutes per adult per day: thirty-two hours and thirty-three minutes a week. The ≠Kade San have to spend approximately double the effort of the Dobe !Kung for obtaining their food. Here also, the difference of mode of life and effort required to obtain food between the two is obvious.

I have shown in the present study that the ≠Kade San subsistence is based primarily on gathering. Lee (1968b) has tabulated the pattern of subsistence of 58 hunter-gatherer populations and has pointed out that "half of the societies (29 cases) emphasize gathering, one-third (18 cases) fishing, and the remaining one-sixth (11 cases) hunting." He also pointed out the fact that "with a single exception (the Paraujano), all hunting-gathering societies derive at least twenty per cent of their diet from the hunting of mammals," and stressed the importance of hunting, though "hunting is rarely the primary source of food."

In Africa, where hominization is thought to have taken place, the hunter-gatherers (the Hadza and Dorobo in East Africa, the Pygmies in the Congo forest, and the San in the Kalahari) all have gathering as the basis of their subsistence (60–80 percent). Judging from the fact that the subsistence of the Hadza in the East African savanna, where game is more abundant than in the Kalahari, is based on gathering with approximately the same percentage (80 percent) as that of the San in the ≠Kade area, we can hardly imagine that the ancient inhabitants of Africa once derived their diet primarily from hunting even if we take into account the difference in environment between the Pleistocene and the present. Although the extremely perishable evidence of gathering is rarely found in archaeological sites, the Pleistocene peoples of Africa were probably "gatherer-hunters" whose subsistence base consisted primarily of the gathering of the *reliable* food plants rather than the hunting of animals. Among apes, the nearest kin of man, the gorilla and orangutan are strict vegetarians even though the chimpanzee occasionally eats meat. But since man habitually hunts and eats meat, it has been said that hunting has played an important part in a process of hominization. Meat was probably important in the sense that its attractiveness led to habitual hunting and caused qualitative changes in the mode of subsistence, rather than as a quantitatively dominant food input.

It is not unreasonable to postulate that there existed abundant and stable plant foods in the society of early man, as they exist in every modern gatherer society. The habitual food of the chimpanzee is usually leaf, flower, berry, and stalk; but those living in savanna-woodland largely depend upon the *Brachystegia* bean (which belongs to Caesalpiniaceae, the same family as *Bauhinia*) during the period of mid-late dry season (Itani 1966). The similarity in food habits of the ≠ Kade San to the savanna-woodland chimpanzee and the seasonal concentration on the Caesalpiniaceae bean may lead to the possible conclusion that these beans played an important part in the process of hominization, at a time when the ancestor of man could not utilize deep underground roots as a part of his diet, because of his lack of a digging stick. The importance of the beans ought to be noted, especially when one considers that the habitats of both the San and the chimpanzee are the bordering areas of forest and open-land.[5]

Appendix Table 4.A. Various species of plants eaten by the ≠Kade San[a]

Scientific name	G//ana name[b]	Edible part
I. Major food		
1. *Bauhinia esculenta*	/oi	bean (protein, fat)
	/am	tuber
2. *Bauhinia macrantha*	n≠an≠te	bean (protein, fat)
3. *Citrullus lanatus*	n//an	melon (moisture, sugar)
4. *Citrullus naudinianus*	kãn	melon (moisture, sugar)
5. *Coccinia rehmanii*	/a	tuber (moisture, starch)
6. *Cucumis kalahariensis*	om/e	tuber (moisture, starch)
7. *Grewia flava*	kxom	berry (sugar)
8. *Ochna pulchra*	≠kera	berry (protein and fat)
9. *Scilla sp.*	kyun	bulb, stalk
10. *Terfezia sp.*	kuche	truffle
11. *Aloe zebrina*	g//oru	stalk (moisture)
12. *Grewia retinervis*	//kane	berry (sugar)
13. *Rhaphionacme burkei*	bi	tuber (moisture)
II. Minor food		
14. *Brachystelma sp.*	//ore	tuber (moisture, starch)
15. *Oxygonum alatum*	n//au	stalk, leaf
16. *Cucumis angria*	n≠ann≠arugu	cucumber
17. *Scilla sp.*	kware	bulb, stalk
18. *Strychnos cocculoides*	/dua	fruit
19. *Talinum crispatulum*	//kape	stalk, leaf
20. *Ximenia caffra*	≠ori	plum
III. Supplementary food		
21. *Boscia albitrunca*	n/one	berry (sugar), leaf
22. *Brachystelma sp.*	//ao	tuber
23. *Brachystelma sp.*	//kaya	tuber
24. *Caralluma krobelii*	dadaba	stalk
25. *Corallocarpus bainesii*	/?orogu	stalk, leaf
26. *Grewia avellana*	n//o!ori	berry (sugar)
27. *Huerniopsis decidiens*	//kaya	stalk
28. *Kedrostis foetidissima*	chunane	leaf
29. *Scilla sp.*	g//wama	bulb
30. *Strophanthus sp.*	≠taba	tuber
31. *Talinum tenuissimum*	dam≠agugu	stalk, leaf
32. *Terminalia sericea*	g/a	leaf
33. *Vigna longiloba*	kareg/azuru	bean
34. *Vigna parviflora*	xane	tuber
35. *Ximenia americana*	g/ubi≠ori	plum
IV. Rare food		
36. *Acacia erubescens*	g//are	gum
37. *Acacia fleckii*	g≠are	gum
38. *Acacia giraffae*	//kara	gum
39. *Acacia hebeclada*	n//a	gum
40. *Acacia luederitzii*	go	gum
41. *Acacia mellifera*	//kowa	gum

(continued)

[a]Identification of the plants collected in the ≠Kade area was made by A. van Hoepen, Botanical Research Institute, Department of Agricultural Technical Services, Pretoria.

[b]The G/wi name is nearly always the same.

Appendix Table 4.A. Various species of plants eaten by the ≠Kade San (continued)

Scientific name	G//ana name[b]	Edible part
42. *Acacia nebrownii*	/ari	gum
43. *Albizia anthelminthica*	kxaru	gum
44. *Aloe littoralis*	≠oru	stalk
45. *Cephalocroton puschlii*	n≠enagu	bulb
46. *Casia biensis*	go/wa	tuber
47. *Commiphora angolensis*	!kana	tuber
48. *Commiphora africana*	za	tuber
49. *Commiphora pyrcanthoides*	/u	tuber
50. *Clerodendrum uncinatum*	gyuag//a	berry
51. *Dichrostrachys cieneria*	/oen	gum
52. *Dipcadi marlothii*	g!om	bulb
53. *Dipcadi viride*	n!au!kari	bulb
54. *Ehretia rigida*	g//a	berry
55. *Eriosema cordatum*	g≠ao	tuber
56. *Eriospermum sp.*	≠kon/uru	bulb
57. *Eulophia hereroensis*	!kauguna	tuber
58. *Grewia flavescens*	/ore	berry
59. *Ornithogalum amboense*	≠agubu	bulb
60. *Pergularia daemia*	murahari	stalk, leaf
61. *Solanum rautenanii*	manchu	stalk, leaf
62. *Tenaris schultzei*	?	tuber
63. *Ziziphus mucronata*	//karu	berry
V. Probable food		
64. *Strychnos pungens*	!koba	fruit
65. *Stapelia gettleffii*	?	stalk
66. *Vigna sp.*	/ide	tuber
67. *Walleria sp.*	n//u	tuber
68. Unidentified	g//ara	bulb, stalk
69. Unidentified	gera	tuber
70. Unidentified	!kon	bulb
71. Unidentified	kyomkyuchu	bulb
72. Unidentified	kuka	tuber
73. Unidentified	/uru	fruit
74. Unidentified	//a	tuber
75. Unidentified	//dokogam	tuber
76. Unidentified	iyazadam	stalk
77. Unidentified	/iki	tuber
78. Unidentified	xai	?
79. Unidentified	/in/u	bulb

Appendix Table 4.B. Various animal species utilized as food by the ≠Kade San

Scientific name	Common name	G//ana name[a]
Class Mammalia		
1. *Panthera leo*	lion	xam
2. *Acinonyx jubatus*	cheetah	!kao
3. *Panthera pardus*	leopard	//koe
4. *Canis mesomelas*	black backed jackal	g/ubi
5. *Octocyon megalotis*	bat eared fox	//a
6. *Vulpes chama*	Cape fox	shuri
7. *Hyaena brunnea*	brown hyaena	n/utsa
8. *Hyaena hyaena*	striped hyaena	/i
9. *Felis caracal*	caracal	!teme
10. *Genetta genetta*	genet	tsamba
11. *Felis libyca*	wild cat	!koru
12. *Felis serval*	serval	geerau
13. *Proteles cristatus*	aardwolf	/i
14. *Herpestes cauui kalahariensis*	slender mongoose	g≠ari
15. *Pedetes capensis*	springhare	g!yu
16. *Manis temmincki*	Cape pangolin	n≠ame
17. *Mellivora capensis*	honey badger or ratel	garu
18. *Orycteropus afer*	aardvark	gou
19. *Aonyx capensis*	clawless otter	≠koru
20. *Geosciurus inauris*	ground squirrel	n≠au
21. *Lepus capensis*	Cape hare	juba
22. *Lepus saxatilis*	scrub hare	juba
23. *Hystrix africae-australis*	porcupine	n//oe
24. *Phacochoerus aethiopicus*	warthog	//to
25. *Giraffa camelopardalis*	giraffe	n!gabe
26. *Connochaetes taurinus*	wildebeest	/e
27. *Alcelaphus buselaphus caama*	hartebeest	//kama
28. *Oryx gazella*	gemsbok	/o
29. *Taurotragus oryx*	eland	gyu
30. *Tragelaphus strepsiceros*	kudu	gyuwa
31. *Antidorcas marsupialis*	springbok	!kai
32. *Sylvicapra grimmia*	duiker	ng!owa
33. *Raphicerus campestris*	steenbok	g!aen
Class Reptilia		
34. *Python sebae*	common african python	lomma
35. *Typhlops sp.*	blind snake	kyuho!dom
36. *Dendroaspis polylepis polylepis*	black mamba	iyazam
37. *Bitis arietans arietans*	african puff-adder	g≠ae
38. Unidentified	giant lizard	?
39. Unidentified	leopard tortoise	g≠oe
40. Unidentified	tortoise	dam
Class Amphibia		
41. Unidentified	toad	gue
Class aves		
42. *Struthio camelus*	ostrich	g/ero
43. *Numida meleagris*	guinea fowl	//kane
44. *Afrotis afra*	black korhaan	di
45. *Lissotis melanogaster*	black bellied korhaan	?
46. *Ardeotis kori*	kori bustard	/deu
47. *Francolinus levaillantoides*	francolin	?
48. *Lophoceros flavirostris*	yellow billed hornbill	?

[a]The G/wi name is nearly always the same.

5   # From Hunters to Squatters:

Social and Cultural Change
among the Farm San of Ghanzi, Botswana

Mathias G. Guenther

Cattle post San near the Ghanzi District studying a Land Rover motor

There are practically no San in South Africa today; those that were not killed have become assimilated racially and culturally to the non-European population of that country. Some had moved northward and northeastward into the Kalahari wastelands; that is to Namibia and Botswana where most of today's San are still to be found. Subsequently Africans and Europeans have followed them into these areas, and for six or seven generations there has been close contact between San and other peoples. However, while the desert-living, hunting and gathering San have been objects of extensive study in recent years, and excellent research has been done, especially by the Marshalls and Lee,[1] very little research has been conducted among the more numerous San living on White-operated farms and ranches.[2] My own research has dealt with social and cultural change among the San of the Ghanzi district in western Botswana.[3] The district lies some 300 km south of the Dobe Area. Ghanzi is an area of San concentration: it contains almost a quarter of all the living San of southern Africa (which is estimated by Lee 1965, p. 19, at about 44,000). The 10,000 San constitute about 65 percent of the total Ghanzi population of 16,500 (official census 1964). The remainder are Africans (6,000), Europeans (300), Colored and Hottentot (200).

The Ghanzi San population is culturally heterogeneous with many different linguistic and cultural groups represented. Also, there is a wide range of variation of social and economic patterns because of differential degrees of acculturation experienced by the San. All three of D.F. Bleek's (1929) linguistic families are represented: the numerically strongest of these are the Nharo (Bleek 1928a) and the /Gwi (Silberbauer 1965), both Central San; followed by the ≠"Au//ei (or Auen) who are !Kung-speakers (and thus northern San); and then the !Xo who are southern San (Heinz 1966). The Ghanzi San have had close contact with Europeans for over seventy years; with Africans (primarily Tswana, Kgalagari, and Herero tribal groupings) the contact, though less intensive, has been going on for at least a century. A few Colored[4] and Hottentots[5] have also entered the area. The San of Ghanzi show a wide range of socioeconomic statuses, from independent full-time hunters and gatherers to third- and fourth-generation farm laborers fully incorporated into the cash economy of the non-San peoples.

Climatically and geographically the Ghanzi district is part of the Kalahari system. Thus, it has dry winters (from May to September) with warm days and cold nights. The rains fall in the hot summer (from October to April) and average 450 mm (18 in) per annum with extremely wide year-to-year fluctuations (see Yellen and Lee, Chapter 1 and Lee, Chapter 3).

Politically, the Ghanzi District is one of the administrative units of the independent republic of Botswana. It is nontribal State Land and is administered locally by a District Commissioner and his staff of civil servants and police. The district consists of three main areas: the Central Kalahari Game Reserve, the farming block, and the southern villages. The central Kalahari Game Reserve to the east, a huge area of 47,000 km^2 (18,000 mi^2), is set aside for wildlife and San. The farming block consists primarily of freehold farms owned by European cattle ranchers. The southern villages are inhabited by African and Colored ranchers and farmers.[6] The latter two areas are cattle country on which are grazed about 86,000 head of cattle representing about 6 percent of Botswana's national herd. Some crops are grown (maize, beans, pumpkin, vegetables, citrus fruit), but the yield is too low to meet the local needs because of the inadequacy and unreliability of the rainfall.

The contemporary situation of the San in Ghanzi may be categorized conveniently under three headings: the economic base, social and political conflict, and the level of consciousness attained by the San concerning their status and future. We will also consider the role of traditional San religion which, among the dispossessed laborers of Ghanzi, has almost reached the status of a revitalization movement. Finally an assessment is made of the degree of change with predictions about San future prospects. Since the latter may take the form of some kind of resettlement scheme, the peoples' attitudes towards such a scheme are brought to light.

Economics

The term "farm San" is appropriate because it reflects the basic way in which the incorporation of these people into White society has proceeded. A relationship between San and Europeans has developed almost exclusively in terms of their economic interaction, primarily because the European ranchers were dependent on San labor. In the Ghanzi case, the clearly defined ideology of racism and segregation of the South African settlers has prevented the economic relationship—of employer-employee—from ever expanding into a more pervasive social relationship.

While the farm San, on the whole, are dependent economically on the Europeans, this dependence is not complete. Not only do the less acculturated free-ranging San still live off the land, but even the most farm-oriented San leave their jobs at least once a year to hunt

and gather in the bush for a few weeks, usually during the late rainy
season. Most farm San thus utilize both the European and the traditional economic resources.

Regarding the European economic impact, the employment pattern and land tenure are the most conspicuous features. About one-
quarter of the San in the farming block are employed as seasonal
or intermittent farm laborers, the men as unskilled workers and the
women as domestic servants. The work of the farm laborer consists
of herding small stock, watering or milking cattle, and driving cattle
that have been bought or sold. Short-term employment is also found
in projects, such as erecting a fence or driving a large herd of cattle
through the Kalahari to the abattoir in Lobatsi, 600 km southeast
of Ghanzi.

Wages are low—between two and five Rands ($3.00–$7.50) per
month plus rations, which consist primarily of corn meal, tea, sugar,
and tobacco. The farmer also pays the tax and medical expenses for
his employed San. The cash wage a San is paid is about one-third to
one-half that of an African laborer and is insufficient to feed or
clothe the worker or any of the members of his household, which
usually includes the group of kin or non-kin hangers-on who live
with an employed San.

The land was alienated from the San in the 1890s when large
tracts were offered to prospective white settlers to "develop" the
area and to set as a barrier to white expansion from Namibia (German South West Africa) immediately to the west. The San bands
suddenly found themselves "squatters" on their own traditional
subsistence areas. The whites needed the San as labor to help run the
cattle and were prepared to give the San surplus milk and meat and
manufactured goods in return.

Today most of the land in the farming block is "owned" by Europeans, and a San, his family, and kinsmen may live on a farmer's
land only for as long as the San is employed on the farm. The number of kinsmen that may live with a farm San is usually prescribed
by the farmer in terms of his notion of a nuclear family. This is a
smaller social unit than the bilateral extended families which are the
basic social structure among the farm San as, indeed, among the
hunting and gathering bands. That is, while the number of San that
live on a farm (between 30 and 200) is usually larger than the residential unit of the veld San, these units usually consist of clusters of
kinsmen resembling in numbers and composition the band, the basic
sociopolitical unit of traditional San—or, heeding Lee's perceptive
criticism of this term (1965, pp. 50–51), the camp.

If the San laborer quits his work or is dismissed, he and his family group usually have to leave the farm. Thus, unless he is employed, a San's residence anywhere in the farming block is on the sufferance of the farmers, the "owners" of the land. Moreover, there are no areas in the farming block that are set aside for San. While the Central Kalahari Game Reserve east of the farming block is in theory open to any San, in fact it is habitable on a permanent basis only by full-time hunting and gathering San, the farm-associated San having lost some of the knowledge and skills necessary for veld life. The area is, however, visited periodically by farm San primarily in order to hunt and gather. The farm San often decry this lack of a home area and occasionally settle on abandoned farms in quite large numbers until forced to move on.

Regarding traditional economic activities, there is one basic pattern which has been retained, probably as much of necessity as of choice: the pattern of nomadism or mobility. Typically, a farm San will move from farm to farm in search of a sympathetic *baas* known not to enforce too rigorously the measures against San squatting. Squatting is a practice which, in the Ghanzi context, is defined as establishing residence on a farm, using the farm's borehole for water and its pasture for one's goats and donkeys, without being employed on the farm. Other favorite places for residence are the remote cattle posts which are situated up to 60 km distant from the farmer's home and which are visited infrequently by him. In moving about in search of work and of a place to live a farm San will be either alone, leaving his family with an employed kinsman, or he will move with his family and kinsmen, usually in a small group. However, sometimes the entire kingroup of ten to fifteen people may move with him, some of them riding on donkeys along with the family's possessions such as blankets and household goods. Also, the traditional transhumant pattern of seasonal concentration and dispersal still marks the yearly cycle of the farm San life to some degree; they alternate between living in large villages as farm laborers during the dry season, and hunting and gathering in small groups in the bush during the wet season. Thus, while changed in its content, the basic form, the pattern of mobility, is still a fundamental feature of the socioeconomic adaptation of the farm San (see Lee, Chapter 3).

In subsistence the farm San still utilize the traditional bush foods extensively. Throughout the year women go out on gathering trips that last from a few days to a few weeks. Along with this economic task there is the social one of visiting kinsmen and friends on other farms. Some plants are especially important—the marama bean (*Bauhinia esculenta*) known in the north as the tsin bean which grows abundantly in the district, and the raisin berry (*Grewia* sp.)

which is used for beer making. Ghanzi lies south of the distribution of the mongongo nut.

Hunting is restricted to the snaring of rodents and small antelopes such as duiker and steenbok; the large antelopes have become very scarce in the farming block. While not important economically, the hunt, nevertheless, is a male activity that enjoys high cultural esteem among the farm San. About once or twice a year, a San will leave the farm where he stays or works—with or without his employer's consent to hunt wildebeest or hartebeest in the bush. He either goes alone and meets with free-ranging San to hunt with them, or he will go with some friends or kinsmen from the farms. It is to be noted that by Botswana law, the San, unlike·the other ethnic groups in Botswana, may hunt freely throughout the year without any license, provided that they hunt on foot and use only bow and arrows and spears but not firearms.

Both of these activities, the women's gathering and the men's hunting, have been retained from precontact times. These periodic trips serve important economic and social purposes and are culturally valued practices that parents still teach their children.

Social and Political Conflict

Social interaction in Ghanzi society is marked by constant and intense conflict. It is especially marked in the relations between San and Europeans and between San and Africans. In fact, European–non-European relationships are generally conflict-ridden. Two important sources of conflict are the ethnic and racial pluralism and the pattern of economic exploitation.

A brief historic sketch on the settlement of Ghanzi will provide the background for these conflicts. The first European immigrants to settle permanently in Ghanzi were impoverished Boers from the northern Cape Province. They arrived in the area in 1899 with a few emaciated head of cattle—many of their herd had died during the 600-km trek through the Kalahari—and they eked out a precarious existence as cattle ranchers. The Boers came to be dependent on the San for labor, for at that time there were few Africans in the area. (Since 1950 the number of Africans has almost tripled.) The San worked for the settlers as unskilled, unreliable, intermittent workers in return for water, food (including a few head of small stock), and protection against raids from Africans (Tawana) from the north in Ngamiland. This unskilled labor pool was adequate since these early Boer farmers were impoverished, themselves victims of the economic system of Southern Africa. In fact, the early farmers were so poor that many came to depend to some degree on the San staple, the marama bean, collected each season by the wives of farmers' laborers and exchanged for meat, blankets, and tobacco. The economic relationship was basically a symbiotic one of mutual dependence. Socially the attitude of the early Boer settler to "his Bushmen" (San) was one of rough but benign paternalism—provided that the San "kept his place" in the set-down pattern of deference which also allowed some degree of prescribed joking and horse-play.

Thus, for the first fifty years of contact the relationship between San and Europeans was one of economic interdependence and social segregation; however, it was free of excessive conflict. The farm San maintained contact both with Europeans and with free-ranging San.

In the 1950s the district was resurveyed, and the number of farms in the farming block was more than quadrupled (from 36 to 166 farms). New settlers, British from South Africa, became attracted to Ghanzi. Their attitude toward farming was businesslike, and they were motivated by the aim of making a profit—and the ultimate goal of obtaining that swimming pool in the Kalahari (a goal which, to date, has been achieved by only one farmer). They came in with capital; they bred high-grade cattle; and instead of herding them, they kept them in fenced fields and paddocks. These changes in private cattle ranching concurred with the government's introduction of tight measures for cattle disease control, which included the erection of a sturdy, patrolled, cordon fence along the northern and eastern Ghanzi border, to control cattle movement in and out of the district. The road to the Lobatsi abattoir was improved, and cattle could now be taken in two days instead of the six-week trek of former times during which many cattle were lost to lions and thirst.

The new settler-businessmen could see little use in hiring San. They preferred Africans who were more educated and more "reliable," being more used to the European work attitudes learned in schools and on mission stations. In addition, having been pastoralists for centuries the Africans were more skilled with cattle. Finally, the new settlers had not "grown up" with the San; they did not know their language and culture and had not acquired the paternalistic concern about them which the old Boer settlers demonstrated.

Since the 1950s the number of Africans in the area has increased rapidly as more and more were hired as laborers. Many of them came from the settled and partially urbanized eastern half of Botswana where they had acquired education and work experience. San either got no jobs or were dismissed as ranching practices became progressively more sophisticated.

Tension between San and Africans in the farming block has risen accordingly. According to the San, during the latter half of the nineteenth century the Tawana of Ngamiland used Ghanzi as their game hunting ground. In the course of hunting expeditions they frequently raided San camps, killing the men and carrying the women and children off into serfdom. This practice ceased with the appearance of the European settlers who had secured the Ghanzi territory from the Tawana by treaties.[7] Consequently, the San in the northern half of Ghanzi have retained negatively stereotyped attitudes toward Africans. By contrast, early European-San relations were harmonious as the former were regarded as protectors against the tall, dark marauders from the north.[8]

Today, disgruntled farm San will sometimes say that the *n/ie/wa* ("clawed animals")[9] "have come again to kill us." The attainment of independence by Botswana in 1966 has heightened this fear on the part of many farm San who feel that now that the Africans are no longer restrained by the Europeans they will once again oppress the San. The fact that, upon independence, some of the Boer settlers left Ghanzi to return to South Africa or Namibia (because they were unwilling to live under Black government) has further contributed to the farm San's general feeling of apprehensiveness. Moreover, the San-African conflict is intensified by the Africans' power to transmit a certain type of disease fatal to San: witchcraft and sorcery. According to the San conceptualization, their system of medicine cannot deal with this "African disease." The heightened perception of witchcraft is stimulated by the increased incidence of organic diseases afflicting farm San, especially tuberculosis, upper respiratory infections, venereal disease, and smallpox (of which there was a devastating outbreak as recently as the mid 1960's).[10] Many of these diseases are a result of contact and did not afflict the San in the past.

In the last twenty years, San-European conflicts have also increased strikingly. San were dismissed from their work and driven from their "home" farms. Unemployment, squatting, and overpopulation of the farming district—exacerbated by the prolonged drought throughout the early 1960s which brought hundreds of free-ranging San to the permanent water supplies in the farms—have resulted in hunger and fighting.

Stock theft is the chief "Bushman (San) problem" in the district, as defined by the Europeans. For example, the Court Case Book of the Ghanzi District Commissioner showed that out of a total of 438 criminal cases tried in Ghanzi court in 1967, 140 cases involved San. Of these, 106 were cases of stock theft. Some farmers claim that

they lose up to one-tenth of their herd per annum through stock theft.
Thus, there is a great deal of ill feeling amongst the Europeans against
the San. The police force in the district has quadrupled in the last ten
years (to a current strength of about twenty men). However, in
many cases the San culprit is able to evade the policemen who have
difficulty tracking him into the practically uncharted Kalahari Desert.
Ranchers with unsympathetic attitudes toward the San suffer the
greatest losses.

Another basic source of conflict, an aspect of social organization,
is the system of stratification that has become established in Ghanzi
and is based on the racial and ethnic divisions of the society. The
system consists of two sets of categories of stratification: one is the
South African castelike dichotomy of European vs non-European;
this is a closed and rigid status system which contributes to much
tension in multiracial Botswana. The other is a ranking, in terms of
wealth and prestige based on the European mode, of the various
ethnic and racial groupings (San, Hottentot, African, Colored, European). This latter is less rigid, less discrete, and is defined with a
lesser degree of consensus except that all groups, including the San
themselves, are agreed that the San are at the bottom of the hierarchy.

It is of special interest that the farm San, in spite of the increasing
and pervasive conflict that defines his interaction with the Europeans,
nevertheless, like the African, admires the White man and demonstrates a marked desire to emulate his way of life. Also, there is an
underlying and vaguely affective bond which San feel toward Europeans (and which is reciprocal in the case of some of the old settlers)
partly, no doubt, based on the regard they have of the European as
protector against the African.

It is striking, indeed, to what extent the European ways are emu-
lated by the farm San. Possession of European objects—many of
them scavenged—accord prestige. Similarly, European foods are considered especially tasty; European medicine (symbolized by the
hypodermic needle) is considered all-powerful for many (but by no
means all) diseases; some European religious beliefs and deities set
standards for evaluating and redefining San religious beliefs and
deities. The old life and the old people in the bush are regarded with
contempt or embarrassment by a number of informants; old customs
and beliefs, as lies. Compared to a European, any San is a *k' 'amka-
kwe*[11], a "stupid," "weak," and "inconsequential" person while a
farm San is a *gaba kwe,* a "new" person, that is "advanced" in relation to a free-ranging San who is in the category of *kauka kwe*
"behind" person, that is, a "backward" person. Other San hold
quite different attitudes, as we shall see in the next section.

This then is the overall picture of the conditions and the way of life of the acculturated farm San in the Ghanzi district: farm San are economically exploited; they lack any reliable and nutritionally adequate subsistence base; they are unemployed, underfed, and overcrowded on land that does not belong to them; they are disease-ridden—partly through new organic diseases brought into the area, partly through diseases generated by social conflict. Social conflicts between San and Africans, between San and Europeans, and among San themselves are acute and constant; and the farm San is the focal figure and catalyst in these conflicts.

129

Level of Consciousness and Revitalization

The farm San are aware of their plight and talk about it a great deal: the hunger, the cruel *baas,* the fearsome Africans, the police, and jail. They summarize these conditions with the Tswana word *sheta* ("suffering"), and the term is in everyone's mouth. They also feel disillusioned, bitter, and resentful toward the Europeans for dismissing them from their work and chasing them off their farms and hiring Africans in their stead.

This situation of conflict and deprivation has led to the development of two psychological and cultural reactions. One of these is quite typical among deprived and marginal people in other parts of the world: revitalization of the past and the culture (see Worsley 1957; Sundkler 1948; Lanternari 1963). The other is the development of what might be called a sense of common "ethnic identity" as San.

The revitalistic orientation toward the old times and the traditional "pure" San culture is especially marked among those farm San in the most conflict-ridden and frustration-ridden settings. For example, residents on a South African Dutch Reformed Church mission to San where I was stationed during my research, are reassessing the "old ways" and regarding them with nostalgia and pride, while admiration for and emulation of the new is suspended. The past is held to have been a time of plentiful food and water and minimal disease (especially since there were no Africans and thus no sorcery and witchcraft); spouses were faithful; the young were respectful to the old; and there was an overall absence of intra- and intergroup conflict. In fact, these are not simply nostalgic fantasies; Lee and others have documented the relatively secure and easygoing life still enjoyed by the hunting and gathering San as recently as the 1960s.

The remarkable success of the religious specialist, the trance-dancer, who is accorded immense prestige, glamor, and wealth, can

130

be understood within this context. It is striking, by contrast, that in the religion of the Dobe San the trance-dancer is not a specialist and does not usually assume professional status.[12] Among Ghanzi farm San the dancer symbolizes more than just a healer; he dramatically and vicariously embodies the San cultural identity. His status and role are firmly based on the religious beliefs and "charter," and his frenzied ritual performance is an extremely intense social event, a Durkheimian *"corrobboree"* of *"dense moral interaction"* which generates feelings of solidarity, and allows for the cathartic venting of frustration and suppressed aggression (Durkheim 1961, pp. 245–251; Lee 1968b, p. 53; Silberbauer 1965, p. 98). At a night-long dance, sacred moods when the dancer is in trance, deities are present, and the sick are treated, alternate with secular moods of hilarity, drinking, and joking. The dance thus symbolizes and consolidates the farm San identity; it is dramatically objectified and celebrated at each of these charged occasions.

The development of an "ethnic identity" or a consciousness of "Sanness" that transcends the various cultural-linguistic groupings of the area is also emerging among the farm San. Among the free-ranging San, by contrast, this pan-Bushman identity is not found. All farm San regard themselves as *kwe* ("people") or *n/oa kwe* ("red people") or *masarwa* (the term applied to them by the Africans); however, they do distinguish the "wild" San from themselves both by the general category of *kauka kwe* ("behind people") and by their specific tribal names. The "wild" San are variously labelled "stupid," "ferocious," "skilled magicians," and other negative stereotypes. The sense of common ethnic identity is thus restricted only to the farm San.

One factor contributing to the development of this common identity is the social position of the San as part of an ethnically and racially heterogeneous setting in which the distinctions that obtain amongst the various San groups are not recognized by the other groups. To many Europeans in particular, all San look alike. A second unifying factor is the concept of *sheta*, a shared life of deprivation and suffering, which gives them a feeling of solidarity.

Furthermore, out of this suffering and emerging ethnic identity there is a widespread and growing political mobilization expressed in their demand that the government set aside land for the San, with their own fields and stock, and their own San headman. In fact, farm San often discuss suitable candidates for that office should it ever be instituted by the government, and there is wide-ranging consensus on two or three individuals whom the San regard as their potential leaders.[13]

Current Status and Future Prospects

Where do the farm San stand and where are they heading? To date, the most basic changes have been in the area of economics: farm labor, wages, pastoralism, and land tenure. Perhaps the most drastic and pervasive ideological shift has been away from the egalitarianism of the hunters and toward the pursuit of wealth and social status through the possession of cattle, small stock, and money. The neighboring Tswana and Herero have always valued wealth in cattle, but this is a sharp departure for the San whose traditional way of life was strongly opposed to the accumulation of property and wealth (e.g., Silberbauer 1965, p. 41; L. Marshall 1965, p. 158; Lee and DeVore 1968, p. 12).

Despite these changes in the economic practices, there are continuities in social organization: mobility, nomadism, and periodic dispersal and concentration. The bilateral, multifamily camp continues to be the basic living group. In other areas there have been a number of changes, such as introduction of new kin terms and new customs regarding child rearing and marriage, as well as changes in material culture (Guenther 1971). In addition to these numerous factors other cultural features have been introduced such as religious beliefs and practices, recreational activities, and healing practices. A number of traditional customs have almost disappeared such as boys' puberty rites, name relations, the concept of n!ow (L. Marshall 1957b), and other religious beliefs. These topics will be dealt with in detail in future papers.

Central to the present paper is the development of ethnic consciousness. The revitalistic reassertion and redefinition of San culture as a whole is an expression of important changes in San life that are of evolutionary proportions and significance. The farm San are moving, in effect, away from a band level of sociocultural integration. And, because of their situation of oppression, they are moving at the same time to some forms of proletarian consciousness.

These changes are being manifested in the development of a new pattern and scope of social organization. Instead of atomistic nomadic camps, each pursuing its own interests without any affiliation with other camps or without overall leadership, there is emerging a larger, sedentary tribal-like social unit consisting of many camps. The necessity for leadership is apparent, and the appearance of overall leadership seems imminent. Several candidates for this leadership are being considered, among them the charismatic and powerful trance-dancers. Instead of a fragmented, incoherent, religious charter differently interpreted by each individual, religious beliefs are showing signs of becoming standardized in a spirit of cultural revitalization. However, all of these changes are incipient in their development and have not yet pervaded the institutional forms and functions of San.

It is evident, then, that while many aspects of culture have changed considerably, and while some new values and practices have been introduced, in the final count, these changes do not yet amount to a basic transformation of the society. Important economic and social patterns and institutions still persist underneath the new forms. Along with farm labor and economic dependence there is also a continuing nomadic pattern of dispersal-concentration; and, while there are larger residential and social units, these are made up of smaller camps.

It would seem, nevertheless, that the farmer San of today, while in a state of transition, is still more a hunter and gatherer than he is a farm laborer. He has not yet undergone the degree of alienation and dispossession that is the prime feature of the proletariat class. If this view is correct, we are in a position to make informed guesses about the future of the San and to evaluate the feasibility of the plans that have been officially drafted for the future of these people.

Between 1958 and 1964 George B. Silberbauer was commissioned by the then Bechuanaland government to carry out an extensive investigation of the "present state of the Bushman population of the Bechuanaland Protectorate." He did so in various capacities: as anthropologist, Bushman Survey Officer, and District Commissioner of Ghanzi District. His *Bushman Survey Report,* published in 1965 contains a number of recommendations (pp. 132–138) with regard to San resettlement and establishment of San reserves. Silberbauer correctly pointed out that the farm San were at a serious disadvantage in all their dealings with Blacks and Whites, and that their oppression was likely to grow worse with time (pp. 117–126). A definite and carefully planned resettlement scheme had been drawn up upon Silberbauer's recommendations.

Although the original plan has now been set aside, it will be useful to review its specifics since it remains as a model for current, more extensive proposals being drafted by the Botswana government.

The plan was to resettle the Ghanzi San at Okwa, in the Central Kalahari Game Reserve 80 km south of Ghanzi, after a number of permanent boreholes has been drilled there. At Okwa, the San would have had the choice of three alternative economic adaptations: they could have followed the hunter-gatherer's way of life, participated in a supervised game-cropping scheme, or followed a supervised training program in animal husbandry and agriculture to be put into operation in the northern part of the reserve. Another part of the scheme was to train San in leather work, carpentry, tool-making, pump-maintenance, hygiene, domestic sciences, and handicraft marketing. The D'Kar San mission station in northwestern Ghanzi would have been expanded to include this training program which would have prepared San for their sedentary farm life at Okwa.

133

Most San with whom I discussed this scheme were in favor of it and emphasized what they regarded as its greatest asset, the chance to have their own area away from Europeans and Africans. Some said that they would return to hunting and gathering and the way of the old people; however, the majority made their participation conditional on there being stock available and on the demand that they have their own headman. Some doubts were also expressed as to how harmonious their relations would be with the free-ranging San of the Central Kalahari Game Reserve (the /Gwi, !Xo, and //Gana), some of whom are regarded by the farm San as dangerous and "wild."

This kind of scheme continues to have undeniable appeal for the Whites. It would remove the San "threat" from the farming area and park them somewhere out of the way on marginal land where the government can worry about them. The ranchers look forward to a decline in stock theft. Of course at the same time the scheme implicitly fails to acknowledge that the San have any legitimate claim to the land currently occupied by the ranchers. And, by moving an ethnic group to its own marginal land far away from its neighbors, the African government of Botswana seems to be emulating the South African policy of Apartheid. This consists of arresting the flow of social and economic change under the guise of "separate development." However, compared to the South African Bantu, acculturation of the farm San has been relatively slight over the seventy years of contact. Furthermore, the San are developing a sense of disillusionment with the European ways together with a new ethnic consciousness. Given that Botswana is committed to a policy of multiracialism and that the Tswana historically have offered abundant opportunities for upward mobility to subject peoples, the "Okwa" type of settlement scheme may yet succeed in stabilizing the San ethnic group and in strengthening their chances for long-term survival.

Further Studies to Part I

Ecology and social change have been among the central concerns of the San project since its beginning, and a considerable body of data has been published. Basic data on subsistence are found in Lee (1965, 1968a, 1969a, 1972a, and 1973b) for the !Kung and in Tanaka (1969) for the /Gwi. Group structure and social change are documented by Lee (1965, 1972a, 1972b, 1972c, and 1972e); and by Yellen and Harpending (1972). Additional work on ethnoarchaeology is reported by Yellen (1971, 1974, and in press). Important work on these topics is also found in Guenther (1971), L. Marshall (1960), and Silberbauer (1965, 1972).

A vigorous /Xai/xai man of seventy

The Population of the Dobe Area !Kung

Nancy Howell

A Dobe woman eight months pregnant with her husband, daughter, and a visiting uncle on left

138

Most of the peoples of the world today are going through a population explosion caused by sharp declines in mortality, followed at some later point by a slower decline in fertility. This striking phenomenon, called the "demographic transition," accompanied the change from agriculturally to industrially based economic systems. The present study may be relevant to a much earlier demographic transition, one starting approximately ten thousand years ago, when human societies made a change from hunting and gathering to agriculturally based economies.[1] Because of some of the rigors of life under hunting and gathering, for instance the absence of food surpluses on hand and the necessity of moving the whole group often, it is sometimes thought that the demographic transition that accompanies the economic change would be of the same kind as the current one, starting from very high levels of mortality and fertility that decline with the introduction of agriculture. Certainly it is undeniably true that the size of the human population increased enormously with agriculture.

The dynamics of that change, however, were probably quite different from the demographic transition that accompanies the shift from agriculture to industry. Detailed study of one contemporary hunting and gathering society, the !Kung, and consideration of the impact of various aspects of their way of life on demographic processes suggest that while we should expect some variation between different hunting and gathering populations, in general the hunters and gatherers are probably characterized by fertility and mortality levels that are relatively low by the standards of agricultural peoples, intermediate in level between agricultural and industrial peoples today.

Demographic Study of the !Kung

During the period 1963–1969, a total of 840 individuals who are linguistically and culturally !Kung (or Zhũ/twãsi, as they call themselves) were encountered and registered as members of the study population in the Botswana side of the northern Kalahari Desert (see map of study area, Chapter 1). These 840 people were not all alive at any one period of time; instead, people were added as they were encountered by the investigators, as they moved into the area, or as they were born; and their numbers were reserved to them even if they died or left the area.

Geographically, numbered persons are divided into two subgroups on the basis of their real separation in space. One subpopulation, composed of about 150 people who live in the /Du/da Area, has been completely omitted from this demographic analysis. Only the Dobe Area !Kung are included here.

The boundaries of the Dobe Area are, of course, easily crossed by !Kung, and visiting of relatives at distant points is an important feature of !Kung life. The composition of the population varies from day to day as people receive visitors from outside of the study area and as they make visits to the outside. We numbered all !Kung people as we encountered them and classified each person as a *Resident* or a *Marginal* person at the time of each census on the basis of whether the person claimed residence in the area or said he or she was going back where he came from. Persons who stayed in the area for about six months or who announced their intention of staying indefinitely were reclassified as resident; and, similarly, persons who left the area for six months or more were transferred to the marginal class. The number of persons who were both alive and resident in the Dobe area at some time during the year in the period 1963–1969 varies from 386 to 460 (Table 6.1). A figure of "person-years lived" during the year is calculated from the registration data for each year, and it serves as the denominator of many of the measures in the following pages.

Vital Statistics

One source of demographic data we have available is the vital processes in the population during the period of time we were observing it directly. These data tend to be highly accurate but of very limited usefulness, partly because the period of time is short and the population is very small. Like the wise men who investigated an elephant blindfolded, a demographer who depends upon such a small amount of information to learn about the "normal" or usual conditions of the !Kung population risks making very large mistakes.

The second problem in interpreting current vital rates is the unknown extent to which our expedition itself determined the level of those rates. This could happen, for instance, if we brought new causes of mortality to the population, if we saved lives with medical interference, and if we attracted (or repelled) people in the migration process. One must heed these warnings when reading Table 6.2. The Crude Birth Rate, which consists of live births per 1,000 persons living, varies between 18 in 1966 (similar to the CBR in the US in 1970) and 70 in 1967 (which is higher than any national rates; the Indian rate, for comparison, is about 42). The average CBR over

Table 6.1. Inventory of resident population only, 1963 to 1969

Year	No. who survived year (1)	No. born in year (2)	No. who died in year (3)	No. of immigrants in year (4)	No. of outmigrants in year (5)	Total residents (1) to (5)	Person-years lived by residents[a]
1963	367	16	1	0	2	386	377
1964	376	7	7	1	3	394	385
1965	367	11	10	0	7	395	381
1966	373	3[b]	4[b]	6	3	388	380
1967	373	25[c]	9[c]	20	3	426	397
1968	409	16	2	29	4	460	435
1969 (3 mos)	450	8	3	0	0	453	152
Total births		86					
Total deaths			36				
Total person-years lived							2507

[a]Person-years lived by residents is calculated by multiplying the numbers in columns (2) to (5), that is, the persons who either entered or left the resident population during the year, by 0.5 and adding that to the number who survived the whole year.

[b]One infant was counted both as born and died. The births refer only to numbered persons, and Crude Birth Rates cannot be calculated directly from these data.

[c]Four infants were counted both as born and died.

the six-year period is 41, which is also the rate for southern Africa
as a whole.

In the same period the average rate of immigration (that is, migration into the area) was 22 per 1,000. Additions to the population
per year, therefore, averaged 63 per 1,000.

The Crude Death Rates for the same period range from 6 per
1,000 in 1968 to 26 per 1,000 in 1965, with an overall rate of 16
per 1,000. For comparison, the CDR of the US in 1971 is approximately 9, and that of Botswana as a whole is 23. The highest national
CDR in 1970 are about 30 (in Angola, for instance) rather than a
possible 40 or 50, because almost all countries have some program
of provision of medical services to their populations. The !Kung
under study here, however, have no doctors or clinics to serve them
in the Dobe Area and must travel long distances to receive western-
type medicine. No doubt members of the expedition saved some
lives with antibiotics, and perhaps the physicians who worked with
us in the field for a few weeks at a time on several occasions during
the period had a substantial effect. More likely, the causes of death
in the area have been reduced in the recent decades, and the age-
composition of the population is such that the decline is very great
in this population. Whatever the reason, the mortality of the population was extremely low during the period of observation (Table
6.3). If this level of mortality persisted over a long period of time
(like 200 years), it would form a population very much like the US
or western Europe. We will see later that this has not been the case.

The second source of loss to the population is out-migration. The
average rate over the period is 8 per 1,000. Total reductions to the
population, then, in the period of observation, were 24 per 1,000.
The growth rate based simply on births and deaths for the period is
2.5 percent per year, which would cause the population to double in
28 years. With migration included, the population grew at 3.9 per-

Table 6.2. Annual variations in fertility, 1963 to 1968

Year	Crude birth rate[a]	General fertility ratio[b]
1963	55	169.4
1964	23	79.9
1965	39	114.5
1966	18	53.0
1967	70	212.1
1968	41	139.5

[a]Births per 1,000 person-years lived.
[b]Births per 1,000 women 15–49.

cent per year, which doubles a population every 18 years. These facts, while true, are not the important things to know about this population.

Retrospective Studies of Population Processes

In order to study the process by which the population has been formed over the lifetime of living people, and in order to gain as much information as possible about this small population, all the adult women living in the Dobe Area were interviewed in detail about their marital and reproductive histories. These interviews were collected individually in the !Kung language, and a small gift was given to each woman at the time of the interview to increase cooperation. May I say parenthetically that giving a gift in exchange for information was probably a mistake and is not something that I would do again or recommend to others. Most of the women were very cooperative in giving their histories in full. I know this because I maintained elaborate procedures to detect falsification or the more common oversimplification. In most cases I obtained a skeleton outline of the woman's marital and child-bearing career from some other !Kung person before starting the interview. Deviations from the outline were questioned at the time of the interview. Each interview was checked in detail later with Hakekgose Isak, an intelligent, partly literate observer of the !Kung population. Discrepancies between the interviews and other accounts were resolved in the field, and in almost all cases the woman was consulted and asked to help resolve the difficulties. I have considerable confidence, therefore, in the accuracy of the material.

All of the women past the age of menarche who were resident in 1968 were interviewed. In addition, a few who had not yet had

Table 6.3. Annual variations in mortality, 1963 to 1968

Year	Crude death rate[a]
1963	4
1964	15
1965	26
1966	13
1967	20
1968	6
1969	19

[a]Deaths per 1,000 person-years lived.

menarche but who were married were interviewed and are included in the final results. About twenty women who were visiting in the area were also interviewed, but their interviews are not being used here because it is not known what selective characteristics they might have to distinguish them from other women who did not travel during that time. The informants, then, consist of 165 resident women over the age of 15.

Before discussing some of the results of this study, we have to consider one other difficult subject, and that is age estimation. The !Kung, of course, have no notion of their own absolute age or year of birth, and knowledge of age is essential to demographic analysis. By 1968 we knew the exact age of that part of the population that had been born since 1963, and through interviewing we had a few reference points in the form of event calendars, referring to events which were known by the local population and which could be dated by reference to the outside world. Murders for which the accused was taken to court in Maun formed one of the main sources of information on dates.

Studies in other parts of the world, however, indicate that event calendars are not a satisfactory form of dating births; people are all too likely to remember both events clearly, but they do not remember them in relation to one another. The solution to the age estimation problem taken in this study uses another approach entirely, that of fitting a single curve to a rank order. Following the method developed by F.G.G. Rose (in *Kinship, Age Structure and Marriage of Groote Eylandt,* 1960), the population is first rank-ordered in age from youngest to oldest. This was done by the subjects themselves, who were asked whether they are older or younger than others who had already placed themselves in the age rank. Children were placed by their mothers; and adults placed themselves, or if they were not available, were placed by close relatives. In this way a sequence from youngest to oldest was established, and the event calendar dates were plotted on the time axis. Up to this point the method is the same as that of Rose. Rose speaks of the difficulty of curve fitting but does not describe how he solved it. Apparently, he either used a least-squares technique to minimize the deviations from his guessed ages, or he simply drew a curve by eye.

By contrast, the approach used in our study takes advantage of the known age distributions of stable populations, that is, the populations resulting from the long-term persistance of a given schedule of fertility and mortality. The model stable populations are the result of averaging the actual life tables of a large number of real populations to obtain the age distribution of deaths. These age distributions at death vary remarkably little between populations in their shape, although they vary widely in their levels of mortality.

The level of the mortality curve used to estimate age must be selected by the investigator; the level employed here corresponds to an expectation of life at birth of 30 years for women. To enter the tables, one must have one point in the age distribution at least; I used the proportion 6 years old and younger, which was known, and an estimated point for those 10 years old and younger. With this figure one can interpolate between columns representing different rates of growth for the level of mortality selected and simply read off the cumulative proportion to be expected at every other age.

Ages estimated in this way corresponded closely with most of the event calendar dates but completely contradicted a few points. This might be true of any single-curve method of age estimation. The estimates were checked for internal consistency and plausibility by measuring the difference in estimated age between mothers of various ages and their first child, if alive. On the basis of twenty pairs of mothers and first children in the age rank, mothers aged 60 and mothers aged 20 both tended to be about 19.5 years older than their oldest child.

It should be clear that this method automatically produces a completely smooth age distribution without any of the bumps and lumps one would find had fertility and mortality varied widely in the past. And yet, as argued above, it is almost certain that both fertility and mortality do vary widely from year to year in the small population. My conception of the relation between the wide variability in vital processes observed over the short run and the use of stable population parameters to estimate age is that the vital rates in the stable population model should be expected to characterize not a particular year but rather a much longer period, perhaps as long as a century. The stable population model, then, should describe the population on the average over many points of time, but not at every point. The stable population model estimates provide a picture of the population age structure which is very believable and internally consistent. The loss is that we cannot learn anything about the past history of the population by working backward from the age distribution.

Now let us look briefly at the results of the interviews with the women of the Dobe Area. The mean age at menarche in recent years (estimated upon 11 women who have had their first menstruation since 1963) is 16.5. About half of the 165 women married before their first menstruation and about half after. In recent years, at least, it tends to be the women who menstruate early who marry after menarche. The curve of first marriage frequencies starts as low as 9 but involves few women until about 15 and is essentially complete by 20. The maximum number who will ever marry is essentially the same as the number married by 20. The phenomenon of failure to marry is rare among these people. Only two women in the Dobe population had never married a !Kung, and both of these women had borne one child to a Bantu who did not settle down into marriage with her. The !Kung, when asked why no man married these women, say that it is because they both have no wits. One of these people is probably mentally retarded by western definitions, and the other is probably mentally ill.

First marriages often have little demographic or lasting social significance to the !Kung. If the young woman does not care for her husband, she may simply leave him and go home to her family. Women's wishes are generally respected concerning marriage, and women commonly form and dissolve several very brief marriages in the early, teen-age years. Both divorce and remarriage are simple and hold little handicaps for a woman at any age. Therefore while most of the women are married at any point of time during their reproductive years, the divorce rate throughout life is substantial.

The first live birth tends to occur around the age of 19.5. We will look at the chances of survival of infants a little later. At this point we might just indicate that the chance of death within the first year (and most of this occurs within the first few days) is about 20 percent for infants. If the baby dies, the mother may conceive again in as little as a few months, and probably within a year. For the 80 percent of live births who survive the mother breast-feeds the baby until either the baby dies, the baby outgrows the need or desire for breast milk (which does not seem to happen before the age of 4 or 5 or even 6), or the mother becomes pregnant again.

The timing to the next birth depends to some extent on age; younger women have their babies somewhat closer together than older women. Few of these intervals are less than 3 years long, and the modal length is about 4 years. Over the whole reproductive span, ages 15–49, women averaged 4.7 live births for the cohort born 45–49 years ago, and 5.2 for the cohorts born more than 50 years ago. The variance of the number of live births is small for the !Kung; the maximum number of live births is only 9. This level of fertility is considerably lower than any other population known that is practicing natural fertility (Table 6.4).

Table 6.4. Retrospective fertility: number of live births by current age of mother

Number of births	Age of mother											Total
	15-19	20-24	25-29	30-34	35-39	40-44	45-49	50-54	55-59	60-64	65+	
0	13	4	3	2	3	2	—	—	—	—	—	27
1	3	7	3	4	5	3	3	2	—	1	—	31
2	—	5	1	3	3	2	2	—	2	2	1	21
3	—	4	6	1	3	—	2	2	—	1	2	21
4	—	1	2	5	2	—	2	3	—	—	1	16
5	—	—	1	4	1	3	2	2	4	3	2	22
6	—	—	—	—	—	3	1	2	1	—	4	11
7	—	—	—	—	1	0	1	0	1	2	4	9
8	—	—	—	—	—	—	1	1	1	3	—	6
9	—	—	—	—	—	—	1	—	—	—	—	1
Women	16	21	16	19	18	13	15	12	9	12	14	165
Children	3	33	36	53	40	40	61	50	45	60	74	500
Mean	0.2	1.6	2.2	2.8	2.2	3.1	4.1	4.2	5.0	5.0	5.3	—
Total cohort fertility	—	—	—	—	—	—	4.1	4.2	5.0	5.0	5.3	—

Comparisons of the level of fertility in different populations require making a distinction between the levels of age-specific fertility to married women, on the one hand, and the proportion of the potentially fecund women who are not married on the other. Generally populations in which women do not marry until they are 25 or even older and populations in which some substantial proportion of the total never marry produce a relatively low level of fertility without necessarily affecting the rate of conceptions within marriage. In the !Kung population almost none of the difference between the maximum level of human fertility and the observed low level can be attributed to the marriage patterns. Women marry young and remarry relatively quickly when marriages end in divorce or widowhood.

Nor can the low observed fertility be attributed in any large part to high rates of fetal wastage or infanticide. The rates of miscarriage and spontaneous abortion reported are very low for remote periods in the past as women forget to report these events. During the past ten years the levels of fetal wastage reported are believable and comparable to schedules reported in other populations.

The !Kung women do not claim knowledge of any method of abortion that seems to be effective, but infanticide is practiced by !Kung women when in their opinion it is necessary: in all cases of birth defects; one of each pair of twins; and sometimes when one birth follows another too closely, and the baby would drink the milk of his older brother or sister; or when the woman feels she is too old to produce milk for another baby. All in all, only 6 of 500 live births reported to me died through infanticide, which is not a large contribution to infant mortality. Confidence in these figures is increased by the speed at which these same 6 cases were mentioned when other people were questioned about the incidence of infanticide; and, as mentioned before, the fetal mortality rate is not large enough to conceal vast numbers.

The age-specific fertility rates computed from the reproductive histories of these women are fairly consistent over time, given the small numbers which form the base of the analysis. The fact that age-specific fertility declines gradually with age supports the women's report that they do not control their fertility artificially. When asked, women report vague knowledge of several herbal teas which are said to cause sterility, but few people say they have used them. Instead, women claim that the cause of the low fertility is the stinginess of their god, who loves children and tries to keep them all to himself in heaven rather than let them come to earth and bring joy to their mothers and fathers. While in the field I received many requests for medicine to increase fertility and only one request from an overtired mother of four to help her stop having so many.

This raises the possibility that disease or malnutrition is the cause of the very low fertility. Many more women complained of the stinginess of god than felt that they had been troubled by venereal disease, but an increasing proportion with age do report that they have had venereal disease. The fertility of those 35 women who believe they have had gonorrhea is noticeably lower than those of the same age who say they have not had it (total fertility 2.4 for those who claim gonorrhea; 5.1 for those who have not). The fertility of the recent past, then, seems to point to a total completed number of live births of about 5 by the age of 45 for those women who have not had gonorrhea, and the proportion of women who have been affected by gonorrhea seems to have increased among all those who have not yet completed their child-bearing years. Whether this is due to a new introduction of gonorrhea from contact with Bantu and European men during the recent past, we cannot be sure, but the fact that the !Kung have a word for gonorrhea in their own language suggests that it is not completely a new phenomenon for them.

With this brief treatment of fertility, let us turn to look at some data on the levels of mortality that have formed this population over the lifetime of living people. To estimate the level of mortality on the largest number of observations, I computed what I call a "mini-life table" on the 500 children who were born to the 165 women interviewed (Table 6.5). Some are still alive within the intervals in which we are interested in estimating death rates, but it was possible to calculate the probability of death for each age on those who had already passed through the interval. The numbers are large enough up to the age of 15 to permit calculation of mortality rates among the children of these women. When these probabilities of death are translated into life-table terms, they form a life table which resembles model life tables for population in which the expectation of life at birth is 32.5 years for females, slightly less for males. This model life table also seems to fit the adult phase of mortality as far as we have data upon which to base it, checked in the following way. First we measure the differences in age between mothers and all of their surviving children, and fathers and their surviving offspring. We then calculate the proportions of persons of each age throughout adult life who have their mothers living and who have their fathers living. The model life table can be used to calculate the expected proportion of surviving parents, given the

Table 6.5. Retrospective estimates of mortality: deaths of the children born to interviewed women

Exact age	No. of persons–					q_x (6)	Life table functions	
	Entering interval (1)	Still in interval (2)	Subtotal (3)	Deaths (4)	Survived interval (5)		l_x (7)	d_x (8)
Birth to 1 yr.	500	25	475	96	379	.202	100,000	20,200
1 yr. to 5 yrs.	379	42	337	59	278	.175	79,800	13,965
5 yrs. to 10 yrs.	278	46	232	17	215	.073	65,835	4,806
10 yrs. to 15 yrs.	215	32	183	8	175	.043	61,029	2,624
							58,405	

q_x = probability of death from age x to x + 1. Calculated as col (4) divided by col (3).
l_x = number of survivors (of a birth cohort of 100,000) to the beginning of the age interval. Calculated as $l_x = l_{x-1}$ minus d_{x-1}.
d_x = number of deaths in age interval, out of the birth cohort of 100,000. Calculated as l_x times q_x.

mortality curve for adults and given, of course, that the parent was alive at the time of the birth of the child. These expected proportions surviving are then compared with the observed proportions to see if there is a match. For the 165 women who were interviewed, the match is very close indeed—within a few percentage points at most ages (Table 6.6). This comparison, and others, convince me that on the average the mortality forming this population conforms fairly closely with a model life table with an expectation of life of 32.5 years.

When that level of mortality is combined with the level of fertility of approximately 5 live births per mother over the reproductive span, we find long-term implications of a population with a steady growth rate of less than 0.5 percent per year. Given the fluctuations in mortality from one period to another, the rate is believable for this population which is growing slightly over the long run. The current fertility among younger women seems to be slightly lower than normal for the older women, probably due to gonorrhea, so that the rate of growth in the current phase should be less than expected in the long run, although still positive. On the other hand, we have seen a run of lowered mortality in the six years of observation, which may be partially due to real changes in the environment the people live in, perhaps partially due to the occasional contact they have with public health, as in the case of smallpox vaccination or in part to the increasing control of epidemic diseases that is being established in the surrounding populations of Botswana. In either

Table 6.6. Comparison of percentage of parents surviving to women by age, with expected proportion surviving under given conditions

Age of women	Survival of mothers		Survival of fathers	
	Expected[a]	Observed	Expected[a]	Observed
15–19	75	68	59	69
20–24	71	67	51	48
25–29	67	81	42	45
30–34	60	52	31	33
35–39	49	50	29	22
40–44	37	23	12	8
45–49	24	20	—	13

[a]Expected proportions are calculated by assuming that all mothers are thirty years old at birth of their daughters, and that they are from then on subject to the risk of mortality expressed in Model Life Table 6 "West," which has an expectation of life at birth of 32.5 years (Coale and Demeny, 1966). Expected proportion surviving is $L_x/_5 1_{30}$. The proportion of fathers expected to survive to various ages of their daughters is calculated in a similar manner, assuming that fathers are forty years old at the birth of their daughters and that they have the equivalent life table for males.

case the strictly demographic prospect for the population is good in that they are growing but not at a threatening level. Dangers to the existence of the population appear to come from the direction of assimilation and intermarriage with other groups, in other words, from the loss of their way of life and culture rather than from any predictable loss of the population itself.

7 Regional Variation in !Kung Populations

Henry Harpending

/Du/da people moving south along the fenced border road, 1969

The !Kung in Botswana are an ideal group in which to study the population processes of hunter-gatherers and the changes accompanying sedentism.[1] There are groups which subsist completely by hunting and gathering, groups which have entered into part- or full-time subsistence relations with neighboring Bantu-speaking peoples, and groups which have been sedentary for several decades. Among these it is possible to examine hypotheses about vital rates, breeding structure, and migration. However, it is important to recall the small total size of this group and the extreme difficulties in obtaining unbiased demographic information. The information presented here should be treated with caution in extrapolating to arid land hunter-gatherers in general, since this kind of ecosystem is especially subject to large temporal variations. Although the material in this paper is summarized and presented as statistics, the usual model in which these statistics are conceived to be estimates of underlying parameters does not seem appropriate; rather, they should best be taken as summaries of what did in fact happen in the population in the last several decades.

The demographic data were collected by fairly cursory interviews incidental to obtaining blood and saliva specimens for genetic and nutritional analysis (Jenkins et al. 1971; Metz et al. 1971; Harpending and Jenkins 1973a and b). The optimum methodology for obtaining demographic information from anthropological populations has not yet been worked out, and this paper and the paper by Howell in this volume represent two extreme approaches: intensive ethnographic investigation of a restricted sample versus extensive survey investigation of a very large sample. And though much of my material on reproduction and survivorship overlaps with that reported by Howell (Chapter 6), there are two vital differences. The sample of families reported here is from all !Kung groups in Botswana, while her sample is drawn primarily from the !Kangwa and /Xai/xai areas and is a larger sample of those areas than is mine. Second, she obtained information by very careful and meticulous interviews which were thoroughly cross-checked, while I did quick interviews, not necessarily with women and in much less detail than hers. Howell's methodological approach sacrifices sample size, while mine sacrifices the information obtained per subject. For example I could obtain no information on absolute or relative ages of people, but I surveyed many more families over a much larger region than could Nancy Howell.

Subjects

I attempted to sample every !Kung group in Botswana. There are about 2,500 !Kung in the country; of these the !Kangwa and /Xai/xai

153

groups which are the subjects of most of the papers in this volume
are about 20 percent. Map 7.1 shows the location of the nine groups
into which I have divided the sample. The census sizes are approximate since the continuous movements of individuals and families
would make more exact figures only arbitrary.

154

The /Du/da Area is named for a waterhole on the eastern margin
of the primary exploitation region of this group, which is almost

Map 7.1. Location of study areas

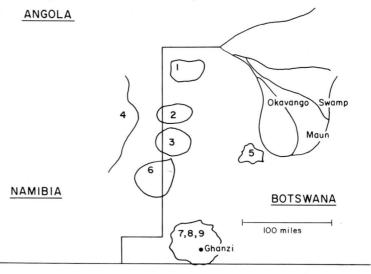

GROUP

	Approximate census	Genetic sample
!Kung		
1. North	200	102
2. !Kangwa	400	311
3. /Xai /xai	150	139
4. Namibia !Kung	?	50
5. Sehitwa	300	164
6. /Du/da	150	117
7. ≠"Au//ei (Kaukau)	1000	320
Other		
San		
8. Mixed	500	166
9. Nharo	2000	154

wholly in Namibia. There are no Bantu-speakers nor cattle in this area, and the group subsists entirely by hunting and gathering. It is interesting that hunting may assume somewhat greater importance in this area than in those where waterholes are shared with Bantu-speakers and cattle (Patricia Draper, personal communication). We do not know whether this is due to the lack of the occasional milk and meat available from cattle keepers in other areas or whether the invasion of cattle simply changes the vegetation enough to displace an appreciable fraction of the large animal population of an area.

The areas labeled /Xai/xai, !Kangwa, and North contain groups of !Kung representing the whole spectrum of adaptation from near complete dependence on foraging to complete dependence on employment by Bantu-speakers supplemented with a few goats and small gardens. The degree of dependence on cattle and on agriculture has been observed to vary from year to year depending on the rains and, hence, the productivity of gardens and the milk supply from the cattle. Generally in these areas an appreciable amount of anyone's diet will be the traditional bush foods such as mongongo nuts; and most men will own bows, arrows, and spears for hunting and will hunt regularly, although it does not seem to be the serious subsistence work that it is at /Du/da.

The !Kung who are labeled Sehitwa and who live just west of that town are families of employees of Tswana and Herero cattle herders. Very few of the older inhabitants of this region were born here; almost everyone immigrated from the west seeking wage labor. In this whole region I encountered only one man who claimed to hunt regularly, while most of the men denied knowledge of traditional !Kung hunting. This area then is slightly more advanced in the transition to sedentism and acculturation than the areas to its northwest, although it is possible to find specific villages in the !Kangwa or North regions which are comparable to those of the Sehitwa region.

Demography

The difficulties in obtaining good demographic data from "primitive" populations have been discussed by Neel and Chagnon (1968) and Howell (1973a) among others. People may not know their own ages and are often uncertain or unwilling to speak about past events, and so even the most careful ethnography can lead to contradictory and inconsistent results (Neel and Chagnon 1968). But even with perfect informants the numbers involved in anthropological studies

will almost always be so small that estimates of important demographic parameters will have no statistical stability. Howell concludes
that anthropologists interested in population phenomena would often
do better picking a reasonable life table from Coale and Demeny
(1966) than trying to obtain data from field studies. Further, even
rates estimated from a very large field study pertain only to the time
of the study; and in most populations year to year variances will be
large, and rates from one time period may be very atypical of long-
term rates.

Given these cautions, it may still be fruitful to spend resources on
studies of certain specific phenomena (e.g., infant mortality and
fertility interactions within families, Hinshaw et al. 1972), without
attempting to specify the global demographic configuration of the
population in any detail. This depends usually on the ease with
which the data are collected and on their prospective reliability. In a
population like the !Kung, where there is no reticence about discussing deceased kinsmen, mortality statistics may be useful indicators of adaptation. The Yanomamö of Amazonia, for example, is
a population where mortality statistics are probably not useful,
given the reluctance there to mention anyone's name, especially that
of a dead person (Chagnon 1968). Similarly, anthropologists usually
can ascertain the total fertility of women past reproductive age with
good reliability, and this is useful for comparative studies—even in
the absence of any information on mortality.

The material discussed in this section is extensively subdivided and
of varying reliability. This permits a very large number of comparisons and statistical tests and procedures, but it can be correspond-
ingly difficult to decide which to take seriously since many seemingly
significant effects will be spurious. These problems may be evaded
by simply presenting the tabulated statistics I have available and by
examining several prior hypotheses suggested by other studies or by
my own field impressions.

Table 7.1 shows the total number of live births for women in each
of the areas who had completed reproduction by reaching menopause and the fraction of their offspring who were still living at the
time of the interview. The definition of live birth which I used is not
the definition used by demographers. Therefore these figures should
be used with caution in comparisons with other studies, although
they ought to be perfectly acceptable for internal comparisons
among the areas. The !Kung define a birth as live if it received a
name, which means that it must have lived about three days. I chose
this definition because in my initial interviewing my language was

inadequate to explore the intricacies of whether or not a child was actually born alive. At the bottom of this Table is the same information, pooled for the groups north of Ghanzi, about all women who completed reproduction either through death or by reaching menopause. This tabulation is liable to be severely biased because the probability of inclusion of a dead woman increases with the number of offspring she had, but the statistic is of interest for population genetics in computing Crow's index of potential selection.

Table 7.2 shows frequency of infant and prereproductive mortality from data on sibships. Infant mortality is death before one year of age. Again, the infant mortality figures should only be used for internal comparison because of the peculiar definition of live birth. Each area was surveyed at least three times during the course of the study, so there is unlikely to be a systematic effect of observer experience. There is no correlation between sibship size and mortality in any area. The sex ratio in the births was 1.02 males per female. Sources of bias include faulty recall by older women, the poorer rapport I had with subjects in the Ghanzi area, and uncertainty about whether a child was more or less than one year of age

Table 7.1. Reproductive performance of !Kung women

	Number of women	Number of live births	Average	Number alive today	Proportion dead
Women past reproductive age					
North	17	68	4.00	35	0.49
Sehitwa	20	77	3.85	47	0.39
/Du/da	20	73	3.65	41	0.44
!Kangwa	37	157	4.24	103	0.34
/Xai /xai	15	76	5.06	47	0.38
1–5 pooled	109	451	4.14	273	0.40
≠"Au//ei (Kaukau)	65	288	4.43	230	0.20
Nharo	27	88	3.26	63	0.28
Xavante[a]	35	198	5.66	125	0.37
Yanomamö[a]	33	125	3.79	105	0.16
All women who reached reproductive age					
Groups (1–5 above pooled)	149	545	3.66 $(s^2 = 5.29)$	326 $(s^2 = 3.23)$	0.40
Xavante[a]	60	284	4.73 $(s^2 = 6.1)$	184	0.35
Yanomamö[a]	64	169	2.64 $(s^2 = 3.7)$	139	0.18

[a]Neel and Chagnon 1968.

158

at death. I suspect that I classified many infant deaths as postinfant deaths in comparing my figures with those of Nancy Howell, although the error could go either way. The ratio of postinfant to preinfant mortality which I observed is too low to be consistent with expectations from model life tables (Coale and Demeny 1966), but it is consistent with sporadic epidemics of infectious disease expected in this kind of environment (Dunn 1968).

I am more confident of the estimates of frequency of survivorship to reproductive age, although the numbers are smaller and there is wobble in the definition of reproductive age for males. To avoid biases in favor of high survivorship, the youngest sib to reach reproductive age was not included in the tabulation.

Variation in Reproduction

My most striking demographic impression was one of poor adaptation and high mortality in the North when compared with the central and southern !Kung groups. I first noticed this when collecting genetic samples there; I found only a few complete nuclear families in the whole area; either the children were dead or one or both parents were dead. There was no obvious cause of high mortality in this area; the people there seemed to have reached the same modus vivendi with the local Bantu-speaking cattle herders as had the !Kung of the areas further south. In contrast to the rest of !Kung land the North looked like paradise. It had thick forests with great large trees on the ridges and tall lush grass in the valleys. But to !Kung who accompanied me there from the south, and to me after a

Table 7.2. Sibship data

	Infant mortality			Prereproductive mortality		
	Live births	Deaths	Proportion dying	Live births	Deaths	Proportion dying
North	106	27	0.25	28	11	0.39
Sehitwa	164	18	0.11	50	20	0.40
/Du/da	121	17	0.14	41	10	0.24
!Kangwa	249	31	0.12	101	38	0.38
/Xai /xai	126	13	0.10	37	16	0.43
Pooled Ngamiland (1–5 above)	766	106	0.14	257	95	0.37
≠"Au//ei (Kaukau)	579	51	0.09	134	24	0.18
Nharo	129	8	0.06	52	15	0.29

year or so of field work, it was somehow unfamiliar and simply not terrain to which !Kung culture was adapted. Later, in confirmation, Kererwe Ledimo, a long-time resident of that part of the country, told me that before the intrusion of cattle there were very few !Kung there. He cited the absence of mongongo nuts and other traditional foods as a reason, and it is true that most of the place names there are not !Kung names.

Whatever the reason, the infant mortality there is much higher than in the other areas outside Ghanzi ($\chi^2_1 = 12.9$), though survivorship to reproductive age seems unaffected. The numbers on which the latter is based are small, and in this very mobile society a majority of the members of sibships on which survivorship to reproductive age was tabulated may have been born, twenty to thirty years ago, in areas far outside the North. The sibships yielding information on infant mortality are much more recent and reflect better the local conditions. There is an additional possible indication of higher mortality in the North: among parents there were 40 immigrants into the North from !Kangwa and /Xai/xai and only 27 from the North to these areas. While this difference is not significant in itself, it should be considered along with the other evidence, including the higher mortality among offspring of women past reproductive age in the North as shown in Table 7.1.

A possible mechanism for the higher mortality in the North is malaria. In their study in Namibia, Bronte-Stewart's group (1960) found the prevalence of splenomegaly to be a direct function of proximity to the Okavango River. Presumably the local ecology in the North is more similar to the riverine kind of environment of their study than to the desert. Another possible cause is a higher density of viruses. Kokernot and associates (1965) found that the variety of antibodies to arboviruses in Botswana was much higher near the Okavango Swamp and the Caprivi Strip than in the desert, where the inhabitants were remarkably free from evidence of past infection. If this difference in virus prevalence is due either to amount of ground water or to ecosystem richness and diversity, then the North should have a much higher load of minor virus infections than any other area. The North certainly merits further biomedical and sociological study. It is the extreme northeast extension of the !Kung range, and it is an intriguing notion that it represents an area of marginal adaptation maintaining itself by continuous immigration from core areas. It also gives a striking example of the fallibility of our impressions about "richness" and "suitability" of environments of hunter-gatherers.

A second hypothesis suggested by the anthropological and demo-

graphic literature (Binford 1968b; Polgar 1972; Lee 1972d) is that
acculturation and sedentarization will relax constraints on fertility,
so that in Ghanzi and, to a lesser extent, in Sehitwa, the number of
births should be higher than in the other areas. Table 7.1 shows that,
in fact, this is not happening for women who have reached menopause. An F-test for heterogeneity among the areas was not significant, and I conclude that the increase in fertility with sedentism
among !Kung does not exist to any great extent.

Children in the areas north of Ghanzi seemed uniformly healthy,
well-nourished, and active (Truswell and Hansen, Chapter 8). In
Ghanzi the children seem plagued with eye and respiratory diseases,
and they give the impression of being less vital and active than the
children in the bush. These impressions are either incorrect or irrele-
vant; both infant mortality and preadolescent mortality are lower in
Ghanzi by wide margins. This is a second example of the unreliability
of impressionistic assessments in fieldwork. This lower mortality
might be due in small part to the occasional availability of medical
attention and antibiotics in Ghanzi, but the regular availability of
milk is probably more important.

It is interesting that Cavalli-Sforza (1973) reports a four-year birth
interval for pygmies, who have been semisedentary for at least several
generations. These data, along with the data from the !Kung, imply
that the "first" demographic transition, from hunting and gathering
to settled agriculture, may have consisted primarily in a lowering of
mortality rates as in standard transition theory. For these two groups
at least there is scant evidence for the Binford hypothesis that
fertility will immediately rise when mobile people become sedentary
and constraints thus imposed on fertility are relaxed.

Migration

Figure 7.1 shows the distribution of distances between birthplaces of parents of children in the population. A difficulty with this
kind of tabulation is the large number of spouses who were born in
the "same place," which could be the same waterhole or the same
area of thousands of square miles. The shaded parts of the histogram
represent these cases, which were apportioned, simply by guess,
with knowledge of the place where the couple was born, the age of
the couple, and so forth. The mean and variance of the distances
should not be taken too seriously; the points of importance are the
very large distances over which mating takes place and the familiarity
with vast areas of terrain and large numbers of people implied by

such distances. Incidentally, when distances between birthplace and current residence are tabulated, there are no differences between the sexes; women are fully as mobile as men in this society. A consequence of this high mobility is very low genetic differentiation among areas compared with more sedentary preindustrial peoples (Harpending and Jenkins 1973a).

When the distances between birthplaces of parents and their offspring are plotted, they are almost as large as the marital distances. This is taken into account by considering the way in which these large distances are generated. !Kung families are continually moving around, seemingly at random, within large areas of land (Yellen and

Figure 7.1. Parental distance distribution

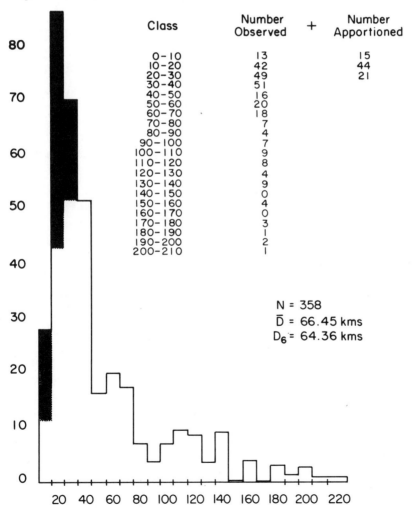

Class	Number Observed	+	Number Apportioned
0–10	13		15
10–20	42		44
20–30	49		21
30–40	51		
40–50	16		
50–60	20		
60–70	18		
70–80	7		
80–90	4		
90–100	7		
100–110	9		
110–120	8		
120–130	4		
130–140	9		
140–150	0		
150–160	4		
160–170	0		
170–180	3		
180–190	1		
190–200	2		
200–210	1		

$N = 358$
$\bar{D} = 66.45$ kms
$D_6 = 64.36$ kms

Harpending 1972). Hence the probability is appreciable that at marriageable age people will be far away from their birthplaces, and so the distance between birthplaces of mates will be large even if one marries the closest available partner.

Genetics

Much of the impetus for the study of the population genetics of primitive groups has been the goal of studying "microevolution," the processes of evolutionary change in these populations. That these studies would not, in fact, yield much information about human evolution was foreseen by Morton (1964) among others; and, indeed, they do not seem to have produced many new insights. Anthropologists traditionally have been interested in the history and status of biological relations among groups; and, although this sort of interest has been unfashionable, it has become more popular recently under the name of "population structure" (Morton 1969; Lalouel 1973; Harpending and Jenkins 1973b).

Harpending and Jenkins (1973a) presented genetic data on the various !Kung groups, and those same data are used here for a different purpose. They were interested in comparing the amount of genetic variation among areas with predictions made by considering rates of migration and gene exchange among the areas. In that study the agreement between prediction and observation was very close. In this paper the pattern of genetic variation is used to make inference about internal migration and recent population history, using indirectly the notion of genetic distance. Blood samples were taken from about 1,800 people and typed for various hereditary chemical differences, and the proportions of the various types were tabulated for each area and converted into gene frequencies. Genetic distance is simply a measure of how similar the gene frequencies of two areas are. For genetic and algebraic details see Harpending and Jenkins (1973a and b).

It is expected that areas which are close together will have similar gene frequencies because they exchange mates more often than areas further apart. Consequently genetic distance should be small in proportion to geographic distance. Further, genetic distances among several areas can determine a map just as mileage among cities can be converted back into a map of the relative locations of the cities. An important difference between genetic distance and geographic distance is that the latter defines always a two-dimensional space, while genetic distances can define a higher-dimensional space. The tech-

nique of principal components analysis then is used to find the best
two-dimensional representation of the genetic distances (nonmetric,
multidimensional scaling yields almost exactly the same configuration). It should be emphasized that this is simply a graphical aid to
allow rapid visual comprehension of the genetic distances. The technique permits inference about population history because the genetic
consequences of large-scale migration may take several generations to
come about. Thus two areas widely separated on the ground but
genetically very close together probably separated and moved apart
in the last several generations.

Figure 7.2 shows the two-dimensional principal components map
for genetic distance calculated from gene frequency variation, and
Figure 7.3 shows such a map for genetic distance predicted from the
pattern of mate exchange obtained from interviews with the older
generation. Because there has been a great deal of movement in the
last twenty to thirty years, the mating patterns of younger adults
were not included in the tabulation. The actual geographic positions
of the areas are on the map as the area names, and the arrows indicate where they are moved or displaced by the "map" given by the
first two principal components of observed (Figure 7.2) or predicted
(Figure 7.3) genetic distance.

As was mentioned previously, the Sehitwa area is a colony of
employees of Bantu cattle-keepers who were drawn from areas to
the west in recent decades. The genetic distance map places them
right back in the !Kangwa-/Xai/xai areas from which they came.
There is an indication that the /Du/da and Namibia populations are
separated from the populations immediately to their east more than

Figure 7.2. Genetic distance map (arrows) as displacement from
geographic location (place names)

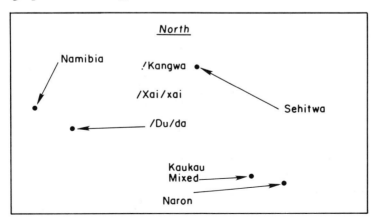

geography would predict. This may be an accident of small sample
size, or it may be a genetic consequence of the international border
between Botswana and Namibia. It makes good sense for /Du/da
since most of that population is in Namibia most of the time, and
the border camps we knew were on the eastern periphery of the
area.

The Nharo and mixed villages of Ghanzi are no further from the
!Kung as a whole than single !Kung areas are. This implies a high
degree of genetic homogeneity for the Khoisan peoples of southern
Africa since the Nharo speak a language mutually intelligible with
Nama and are, hence, linguistic Khoi ("Hottentot"). This is in
accord with other evidence in Harpending and Jenkins (1973b) that
Khoi and San (or "Hottentot" and "Bushman") in southern Africa
are genetically very much the same people, and that differences between them are much the result of diet and differential admixture
with other groups.

The genetic distances predicted by historical mating patterns
(Figure 7.3) are in excellent accord with geographic distances. This
means that mating patterns among the !Kung areas are very regularly determined by simple geographical proximity uncomplicated
by major irregularities of the Kalahari landscape.

The most striking result ·of the distance analyses in Figures 7.2
and 7.3 is the extent to which geography is reflected in the data, and
that the deviations from geography make good sense. This indicates
that this sort of approach may be very useful in many kinds of
anthropological studies of the recent population history of areas.

Figure 7.3. Genetic distances predicted from migration. Arrows displacement from geographic position (place names)

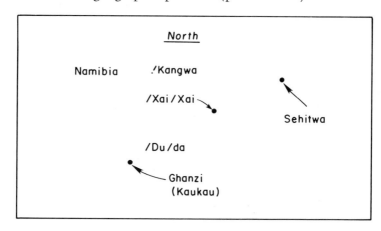

Conclusion

These demographic tabulations confirm in general the analysis given by Howell (Chapter 6), except that I detected a considerably lower infant mortality. She found an infant mortality rate of 20 percent in a series of 475 births compared to an average rate of 14 percent in my figures. If my peculiar definition of live birth accounts for this discrepancy, then her figures for completed fertility should be slightly higher than mine, as in fact they are. She obtains an average of 5 births for 47 women estimated to be older than 50 while I obtained an average of 4.65 in 80 women in !Kangwa and /Xai/xai who claimed to have reached menopause. When one considers that our interview techniques were so different and were done up to a year apart, that our figures should agree so well for these areas is remarkable and adds confidence to both sets of data.

Comparison with the results of Neel and Chagnon (1968) on the Xavante and Yanomamö is difficult because of the clear underreporting of fertility in their subjects, especially in the Yanomamö; but extrapolation suggests that fertility among these hunter-gatherers is slightly lower than among slash and burn agriculturalists while mortality may be comparable. This is in good accord with the hypothesis (Binford 1968b; Cavalli-Sforza 1973) that the advent of agriculture in human evolution led to a rise in fertility levels and a consequent increase in the rate of population growth. On the other hand, direct examination failed to detect any fertility increase after sedentarization within Ghanzi, where there were clear indications of a drastic drop in mortality.

Evidence from migration and population genetics presented shows that this population is very mobile and wide-ranging compared to most tribal and preindustrial groups, and that this mobility is a very regular function of simple geographic distance, because historical mating patterns predict a genetic distance map nearly identical to actual geography. It has been suggested (Yellen and Harpending 1972, and others) that this mobility is characteristic of hunter-gatherers, who have no ties to fixed resources as do agriculturalists.

The genetic distances also reconstructed geography very well, and the discrepancies were clearly interpretable in terms of known recent migrations of groups. It is suggested that this sort of "genetic topology" will be a valuable technique in studying the history of population movement in various areas of the world.

8 Medical Research among the !Kung

A. Stewart Truswell and John D.L. Hansen

San mother on the move with her baby and her possessions

This paper reports the results of three research trips to the Dobe !Kung. The purpose of our study was to provide a medical profile of a hunting and gathering population. Particular attention was paid to three sorts of questions. First, which kinds of medical conditions were present and which were absent in the population and what effect did these have on the population's fitness? Second we were interested specifically in the problem of heart disease. We wanted to follow up the lead of previous investigators that indicated a lower incidence of degenerative heart disease among the San than has been found in other populations. And if this turned out to be the case, we wished to explore the possible causes in terms of nutritional, social (life-style), and other factors.

A third area of investigation concerned the nutritional status of the !Kung population. What clinical signs of nutritional deficiencies, if any, were present? And what was the overall adequacy of the diet in terms of the maintenance of adult health and provision for the special needs of pregnant and lactating women and growing children?

Each of the three medical research trips to the Dobe Area of northwest Botswana consisted of ten days of field work. Our first visit, in October 1967, was at the end of the dry season—the weather was dry and hot, and water and food were scarce. We worked at Dobe in a specially equipped medical tent where we examined 45 adults and 30 children (under 15 years of age).

In late April to early May 1968 we returned to the area. We first worked at /Xai/xai, where we examined 51 additional adults and 28 children. Then we moved our equipment to Dobe to reexamine 34 of the San adults and 24 of the children whom we had seen the year before. The purpose of this second visit was to see whether there were any changes in the San's medical or nutritional state after the advent of the rainy season, when food and water were more abundant.

During our first visit we spent a great deal of time taking medical histories from the San with the help of interpreters. Each person was examined individually and thoroughly, and any unusual sign was checked by the other investigator. On the last day of both visits we collected 24-hour urines from a few of the San at Dobe. Preliminary findings from these first two visits have been published in abstract (Truswell and Hansen 1968a, p. 1338; Truswell et al. 1969, p. 1157; Hansen et al. 1969, p. 1158).

The third visit was made in July 1969. On this occasion Stewart Truswell was accompanied by a cardiologist, B.M. Kennelly. The special object of this visit was to record the San's electrocardiograms

(ECGs). We took with us a Cambridge "Transrite 4" portable ECG machine, powered by fourteen torch batteries. Dr. Kennelly made clinical cardiac examinations, and we measured the ventilatory function of some of the San with Wright's peak flow meter. We also went south of the Aha hills to examine San whom we had not seen before at ≠To//gana and /Du/da.

During each visit, blood samples were taken from 29, 39, and 31 adults (mostly male) respectively. Sera were allowed to separate by clot retraction in a cool place: they were decanted into tubes containing dried merthiolate and stored in a portable gas-driven refrigerator. Serum samples in a coolbox packed with ice were brought back with us when we returned to Cape Town by jeep and airplane. The samples were analyzed in the Clinical Nutrition Unit of Cape Town University Medical School.

Since our third visit, two other medical teams have made short visits to the Dobe area (Metz, Hart, and Harpending 1971, p. 229; Joffe et al. 1971, p. 206). We will summarize their findings in this chapter. However, we are not covering the highly specialized, biochemical genetic studies that have been made by H.C. Harpending and collaborators (see Chapter 7), and will deal only with biomedical studies that have been made on the !Kung in northwestern Botswana. Reports on San in other areas—the Central Kalahari, Namibia, and Angola—will be referred to only when they shed light on our own findings.

In general we found the San to be small and delicate and graceful, with light movements. Their skin is reddish-colored, often covered with a certain amount of earth. Their hair is short, peppercorn type; noses broad; cheekbones high; eyes somewhat Mongoloid; and external ears without lobes to the pinna. The San are nearly all thin. Most have lumbar lordosis, which was often striking. Many have potbellies, and a few of the women have mild-to-moderate steatopygia. The skin becomes very wrinkled and thickened, with loss of elasticity, from about the age of 45 to 50 years (but certainly not at 25 years as was once represented in the *Reader's Digest,* Ratcliffe 1967, p. 129). This is presumably from excessive exposure to the sunlight and perhaps additionally from squatting round the fire for hours when it is cold.

Medical Conditions Present

Lumbar lordosis and potbellies, often with divarication of the rectus abdominis muscles, are very common. These seem to go together and to be less common in the few young San living with Bantu pastoralists in the area. Likewise, the most striking steatopygia we noticed was in a woman married to a Herero. We think the potbellies may result from the large amount of indigestible residue and fiber in the bush diet, whereas San living with Herero have regular supplies of milk, meat, and cereals to eat instead of bush food. Chronic bronchitis and emphysema are common and perhaps result from the San's addiction to tobacco. It is, in fact, the tradition that all visitors, whether scientists or administrators, enlist the San's cooperation by giving them handfuls of *shoro,* a strong Rhodesian tobacco that men and women smoke almost universally from about ten years of age.

169

Tuberculosis appeared to be fairly common. We saw a few San with actual symptoms and signs of pulmonary TB, as well as a number of positive tuberculin Tine tests. Lupus vulgaris was evident, active and healed. Tonsillitis, rheumatic fever, and mitral valve

Three generations roasting, cracking, and eating nuts

disease appeared to be relatively common. Venereal diseases are fairly common in young adults. There was gonorrhea, which responded to penicillin, and there were some positive blood tests for syphillis. Gonococcal infection, clearly a cause of infertility, may have been introduced from the Herero, in whom it is rife.

Although there are no open pools of water at Dobe for most of the year, it became clear to us at our second visit that, in the wet season, malaria is an important infection, producing fevers in children and a few adults and an increase in the percentage of spleens palpable at Dobe from 40 to 53 percent. The pan at Dobe was swarming with mosquitoes at our second visit, and *Plasmodium falciparum* and *P. vivax* have both been found there (H.C. Harpending, personal communication). There appeared to be less malaria at /Xai/xai, where intensive cattle rearing by the resident Bantu has caused the original pan to dry up.

In addition to the inevitable atrophic skin in parts of the body exposed to the sun or fire, some skin infections were seen: occasional impetigo and *witkop*. The latter scalp-fungus infection is much less common than in the southern Kalahari (Murray et al. 1957, p. 657). We also saw a variety of eye problems: purulent conjunctivitis and pingueculae are common, and we suspect that trachoma is present. Joan Hickley, an ophthalmologist, found trachoma among !Kung in the northeast corner of Namibia (Bronte-Stewart et al. 1960, p. 188). Some degree of lens opacity (cataract) is the rule in the older San.

The teeth are very interesting in that they do not show caries or fluorosis but with age become worn down to the gums; the crowns of the teeth are lost and the dentine exposed. Periodontal disease is common, but scurvy was not seen. Our findings are similar to the results of more detailed dental examinations among Central Kalahari San (Van Reenan 1966, p. 703).

In elderly San, Heberden's nodes are evident in the fingers and sometimes mild osteoarthritis elsewhere, for example, in the knees. During heart examinations we sometimes encountered extrasystoles and heard a mild aortic sclerotic murmur (see below).

Bizarre results of old injuries were noted, such as one man whose foot had been pierced by a poisoned arrow and had gone septic. He later amputated his own foot at the ankle and now walks long distances on the light crutches he made for himself. Another man had survived an unarmed fight with a leopard. He is left with a facial paralysis, weakness of the extensor tendon of his bowstring finger, and chronic osteitis of his humerus. But he *had* killed the leopard with his bare hands.

Medical Conditions Absent or Rare

Perhaps of more interest and importance are some of the diseases which were *not* encountered in this isolated group of hunter-gatherers. Obesity was not seen; as a rule there is no middle-aged spread. The one or two women who are plump have moderate steatopygia There is no high blood pressure (see below) or evidence of coronary heart disease (see below).

171

Of the infections, we could elicit no history or signs of trypanosomiasis. It does occur 100 miles to the east, near the Okavango. Only one man gave a history of hematuria, which suggests bilharzia, but schistosomal infestation is reported to be uncommon throughout the Ovambo and Okavango systems (Geldenhuys et al. 1967, p. 767).

Silberbauer, among others, has pointed out that the San have an unusual system of sanitation. They live about a mile from their water and defecate into the sand some distance from their camp (Silberbauer 1965). The feces, rapidly dried by the sun, are disposed of by dung bettles. Furthermore the San are not crowded and move camp several times a year.

The hunting and gathering San had no alcohol. We found no evidence of cirrhosis though soft palpable livers were common. Gynecomastia (breast development in males) is uncommon, in contrast to its high prevalence in South African Bantu men. We did not see varicose veins, hemorrhoids or hernias, other than traumatic.

Jarvis and van Heerden (1967, p. 63) were struck by the well-preserved hearing of old San. They made audiometric measurements on 10 old Hei//kom San in Namibia and found no loss of hearing. One possible explanation for this is that the San are not exposed to noise in their environment. We also noticed that signs of previous otitis media were very rare. The drums could nearly always be seen; it was surprising how little wax there was in the external auditory meati. We saw only one old perforation.

There was some mild undernutrition, but malnutrition is not evident. This aspect is discussed more fully below.

Injury from interpersonal violence is rare, and suicide does not occur, as far as we could tell. We saw no neurological disease.

Anthropometry

The mean height of 79 men (15–83 years) examined was 160.92 cm (5 ft 3.4 in) with a range from 141 to 175 cms.

The mean height of 74 women (15–75 years) was 150.14 cm

(4 ft 11 in) with a range from 139.5 to 159 cms. To take into account that people aged 15–20 may not have reached their final height and to see if younger or older adults were taller, the population analyzed in Table 8.1 is subdivided into three age groups.

Tobias (1962a, p. 801) reviewed the measurements of San stature that have been recorded from the late 19th century to the 1950s. The average height of northern San males in the early studies was 156.97 cm, and in the 1950s it had reached 159.65 cm. These values are less than the average in our survey of 160.92 cm (for ages 15 years and older).

For northern San females the corresponding values are 148.5 cm in early studies, 149.93 in the 1950s, and 150.14 cm in the present study. Tobias suggested that these secular changes were not the result of examiners' selection but could be attributed to better nutrition and generally improved environmental circumstances.

Tobias has also suggested (1970, p. 101) that adverse nutritional and other environmental circumstances have less effect on the height of females than of males: the harder the environment, the closer the female to the male height. From the early studies to the present, the difference between female and male heights expressed as a percentage of male height has moved up from 5.4 percent in the earlier studies to 6.7 percent in our present study. The modal percent sex dimorphism is 7 to 8 percent in European populations.

In the present study the younger generation of adult San are 2.3 cm (nearly one inch) taller than men over forty. Part of this difference may result from loss of vertebral and intervertebral thickness and kyphosis (spinal curvature) with increasing age (Khosla and Lowe 1968, p. 742), but the difference between the generations in the men is greater than in the women. It therefore seems likely that our data show a continuation of the secular increase in San heights.

The average weight of the 79 San males was 47.91 kg (105.6 lbs). The women's weights averaged 40.08 kg (88.38 lbs). These are unclothed weights. Most women were weighed in a light kaross or underskirt, but an average figure for the same size and weight of garment was subtracted.

Table 8.1. Mean heights in cm (and number of subjects)

	15–20 years	21–40 years	41 years and older
Men (79)	151.38 (4)	162.75 (33)	160.43 (42)
Women (74)	150.06 (8)	150.93 (30)	149.50 (36)

At the height of the average San, the "desirable" weight in the US for small-framed men is 53.5–57.2 kg (118–126 lbs) (Diem 1962, pp. 623–624). The corresponding desirable weights for small-framed women 150 cm tall (without shoes) are 44.9–48.5 kg (99–107 lbs). Unfortunately the desirable weights are quoted for people wearing indoor clothes, which might weigh up to 4.0 kg for men or 2.5 kg for women. But even if these are subtracted, the desirable weights remain larger than the San weights.

In Table 8.2, the weight/height ratios (metric) of the San are shown for the different decades together with ratios calculated from "average" US weights (Diem 1962). All San values were relatively low, and there was little change with age except below 20 and over 69 years. For additional comparison, the weight/height index of young US men in the Minnesota experiment (Keys et al. 1950, p. 146) was 38.8, and it fell to 29.5 in the same men after 6 months' semi-starvation with loss of 25 percent of their body weight. The average weight/height ratio of Olympic long-distance runners (5,000 and 10,000 m; Tanner 1964), despite their very thin skinfolds, works out to 34.8.

The skinfold thicknesses measured with Harpenden calipers in San over age 20 are shown in Table 8.3. All these measurements were made in 1968 after the rainy season. (Measurements were lower in October 1967). These are low values, for example, compared with the oldest age (16½ years) in the only percentile charts we have seen for skinfolds (Tanner and Whitehouse 1962, p. 446). San male triceps skinfolds are on the 10th percentile and subscapular on the 25th percentile, while the San women's measurements are on the 10th and 3rd percentiles respectively. The FAO Committee on Calorie Requirements (FAO 1957) considered that average triceps

Table 8.2. Mean weight/height ratios: 100 × weight (kg) ÷ height (cm): San compared with ratios calculated from average US weights

	Age (years)						
	15–19	20–29	30–39	40–49	50–59	60–69	70–83
SAN							
Men	24.2	30.0	30.4	31.1	28.8	30.2	24.2
Women	24.0	27.5	26.4	27.0	27.1	26.1	24.7
AVERAGE US[a]							
Men[b]	34.0	38.7	40.4	41.3	41.6	40.7	—
Women[b]	31.6	33.4	36.0	38.1	38.9	39.3	—

[a]From Diem 1962, pp. 623–624.

[b]Calculated for men in shoes (1-in heel) 5 ft 4 in and women in shoes (2-in heel) 5 ft 1 in.

skinfolds in men of less than 5.0 mm would indicate definite under-nutrition.

In an attempt to obtain some simple index of the degree of steatopygia, we made three circumferential measurements in a sample of Dobe women: bust, waist, and hips. We had difficulties doing this for the reasons that most women's breasts are very de-pendent, their waists are not well-defined because of potbellies, and they are very modest about having their hips measured. The results (Table 8.4) show that most San women have smaller hip circumference than the British average (Thomson, personal communi-cation, 1969), but proportionately they have more of their subcu-taneous fat on their hips than on the upper parts of their bodies. The very low subscapular skinfold thicknesses in San women (Table 8.3) are another reflection of the distribution of fat.

The mean mid-arm circumference was 22.9 cm in 39 men aged 20–69 and 20.8 cm in 29 women of the same age range. Arm cir-cumference measurements were smaller in the pretwenty and post-seventy age groups. Between these two limits, arm circumference did not change with age. Standard arm circumferences (age 17) given by Jelliffe are 26.8 cm for males and 24.9 cm for females (Jelliffe 1966).

Pediatric Analyses

The children are born well spaced. Families had 0 to 4 children and larger numbers were uncommon. Childbearing is said to be easy as a rule. All children are breast-fed for a long time. The baby is carried on the mother's back in her kaross all day as she walks, works, or squats. Babies are completely covered from the sun for the first few months, and in three such infants we detected craniotabes, the first sign of rickets. Once the babies are exposed to the sun, the rickets disappears.

As they grow up the lives of the children are strikingly different from those of children who have to go to school. The San parents do not give their children formal training or lay down rules. For

Table 8.3. Skinfold thickness (mm) in adults (over 20 years); mean (and range)

	Midtriceps	Subscapular
Men (n = 37)	5.01 (3.1 to 9.0)	6.64 (4.5 to 10.1)
Women (n = 34)	9.42 (3.2 to 17.3)	6.61 (4.1 to 15.4)

example, young children are not told when they should go to sleep; they wander round between the adults at night until they are tired. Boys do not accompany their fathers on hunting expeditions until they are grown up. Children of even 10–15 years have no duties which they have to perform for the community.

Young children frequently have mild respiratory, skin and eye infections. Gastroenteritis is uncommon. We think this is because all the infants are breast-fed. We saw only one case of mild protein-calorie malnutrition. This was a baby about twelve months old who appeared to have been suffering from malaria. In seven blood samples from children taken at Dobe in 1967 the mean serum albumin was a 3.73 g per 100 ml, γ-globulin 1.52 g per 100 ml and vitamin A 90 μg per 100 ml.

Nevertheless H.C. Harpending and N. Howell have found from taking detailed family histories that there is considerable childhood mortality which is not apparent at first when one spends a short time with one or two bands of San. Pneumonia and malaria would appear to be more important causes in this community than gastro-enteritis and malnutrition, and from time to time in the past there seem to have been epidemics of smallpox and measles.

Growth

The Harvard growth curves have been used for comparative pur-poses. The word "standard" represents the 50th percentile of weight or height. The weight and height data of children of various age groupings are shown in Figure 8.1 and Table 8.5. Of twelve infants from birth to one year the majority (50–60 percent) are within the normal range for weight and height; the boys in this small sample appear to be somewhat bigger than the girls.

From 1 to 5 years it can be seen that most children drop below the 3rd percentile in weight and height. From 6 to 12 years this

Table 8.4. San women's dressmaker measurements (in)

	Bust (b)	Waist	Hips (h)	Ratio $\frac{h}{b}$
SAN WOMEN				
Average (of 17)	30.4	27.7	34.7	1.15
3 fattest (mean)	31.7	29.4	39.0	1.24
3 aged 15 or 16 years (mean)	29.4	26.6	31.8	1.08
BRITISH WOMEN (mean)[a]	35.2	25.2	37.5	1.06

[a]From A.M. Thomson, personal communication (1969).

tendency is aggravated, the average weight being only 63 percent of standard.

During the adolescent years, ages 13–19, weight and height remain at a low level compatible with the adult weight and height. Mean weight for height drops from 98 percent in the first year to 87 percent in the age group 6–12 years. After this there is a slight improvement.

In summary, the growth data show that San infants, while on the

Figure 8.1. Weights and heights of San boys and girls plotted in the 97th, 50th, and 3rd percentile lines for Boston children

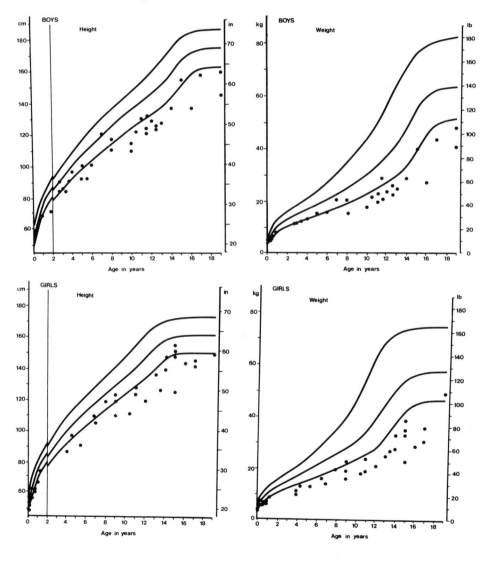

Table 8.5. Children's weights, heights, and head circumferences

Age and sex	No.	WEIGHT below 3rd percentile	Average % of standard weight	HEIGHT below 3rd percentile	Average % of standard height	Mean weight for height, % of standard[a]	Head circumference below 3rd percentile
0–1 year							
Boys	4	0	95.3 ± 6.0	1	93.8 ± 4.0	99	1/4
Girls	8	5	80.1 ± 14.0	6	90.5 ± 4.9	98	0/5
Total: 12		5 (40%)		7 (50%)		98.6	
1–5 years							
Boys	9	3	81.6 ± 6.8	7	90.7 ± 4.5	95	0/9
Girls	6	6	66.8 ± 6.9	5	89.2 ± 9.4	85	0/6
Total: 15		9 (60%)		12 (80%)		91	
6–12 years							
Boys	14	10	62.8 ± 9.9	13	86.1 ± 5.0	88	1/4
Girls	10	8	63.9 ± 11.4	6	86.9 ± 5.8	85	4/10
Total: 24		18 (75%)		19 (79%)		87	
13–19 years							
Boys	7	6	63.6 ± 10.0	6	86.4 ± 5.1	95	2/7
Girls	12	11	62.0 ± 11.6	9	89.0 ± 5.4	88	3/10
Total: 19		17 (89%)		15 (79%)		91	

[a]See Jelliffe (1966).

breast, compare favorably with western infants. However, after weaning, this growth is not maintained; and there is moderate growth retardation persisting to adult life. The low weight for height and thin skinfolds (Figure 8.2) with normal serum albumins suggest an energy (calorie) deficit throughout the growing period which could reasonably account for eventual short stature in adults. During the wet season the skinfolds increased somewhat (Figure 8.2), and growth increment over a six-month period was comparable to the Harvard average.

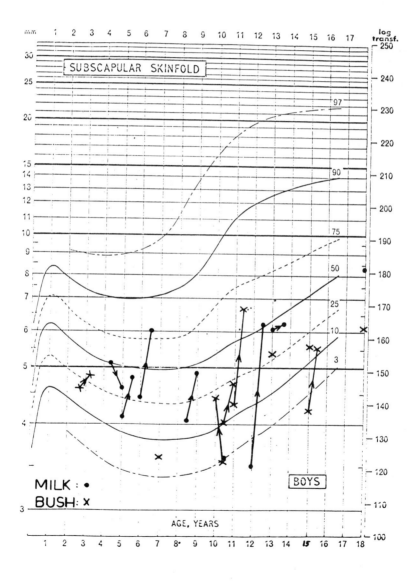

Figure 8.2. Subscapular skinfolds of San boys and girls in October 1967 (dry season) and April–May 1968 (wet season). For each child the two measurements (6 months apart) are joined by a line; the arrow indicates the direction of change from dry to wet season. The percentile lines on the charts are Tanner's for healthy British children. Note that most of the children's skinfolds are below the British 50th percentile and that skinfold thickness usually increased after the rains.

179

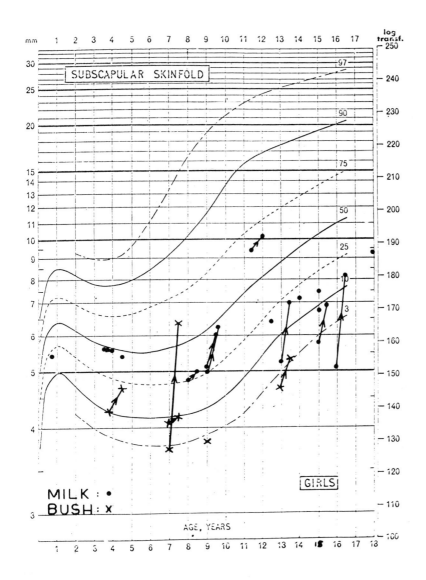

Head circumference is within the normal western range for most children but 17 percent (mostly older girls) are just below the 3rd percentile.

Puberty

Breast development starts in girls at about thirteen years; the menarche occurs late, at about fifteen years. At this stage the girls show the areolar hypertrophy of their breasts, illustrated in E.M. Thomas's book (1959).

Biochemical Measurements in Sera and 24-Hour Urines

The San's sera (Table 8.6) show slightly low albumins and increased γ-globulins; serum lipids are all very low, particularly the cholesterol. While vitamin A concentrations are above the average, carotenoids are rather low (ICNND 1963). Urates and electrolytes appear to be normal.

The 24-hour urines (Table 8.7) needed much care and explanation to obtain, and the question will naturally arise whether the collections were complete. For example, one of the subjects in 1967 took his foldable, plastic, urine-collecting containers with him when he went out hunting for the day! It will be noticed that creatinine

Table 8.6. Mean biochemical concentrations in adult sera

SERUM	SAN 1967	1968	1969	CONTROLS
Total proteins, g/100 ml	7.37			
Albumin (chemical), g/100 ml	3.48	3.88	3.84	4.97[a]
Albumin (electrophoresis), g/100 ml	3.73			
γ-globulin (electrophoresis), g/100 ml	2.10			
Cholesterol, mg/100 ml	119	110	128	202[a]
Triglycerides, mg/100 ml		111	91	
Phospholipids, mg/100 ml		130	159	193[a]
Carotenoids, μg/100 ml	15	26		87[a]
Vitamin A, μg/100 ml	101	53		71[a]
Urate, mg/100 ml	3.78 (males)			6.30 (males)
Sodium, mEq/L		139		152[a]
Chloride, mEq/L		100		99[a]
Potassium, mEq/L	4.26			

[a]Controls: one or two sera from the authors collected in the field. They do not therefore show the range but rather serve as a check that there was little or no loss of the substance in the San samples.

excretions (an indication of muscle mass) are lower in the San than in the controls. However, the San are smaller and weigh less than the controls. When creatinines are expressed per kg body weight, the San's come to 83 percent of the controls in 1967 and 86 percent in 1968, indicating that collection was almost complete for the group. While urinary nitrogens and potassium are the same or even higher in the San's urine than in the controls, the San excrete far less sodium, chloride, and phosphate.

Because we could not carry strong mineral acid with us in the airplane, we added iodine in 1967 and oxalic acid in 1968 to help preserve aliquots of urine while we carried them in a coolbox back to our laboratory. On both occasions the control urines were treated in exactly the same way.

Special Topics

Blood Pressures

The mean blood pressures of 152 San, measured under standard conditions with a mercury sphygmomanometer, are shown in Table 8.8. The methods are described in detail by Truswell and colleagues, 1972, page 5. The San mean blood pressures by decade are compared

Table 8.7. 24-hour urines from San adults at Dobe compared with controls collected at the same time (amounts excreted per day)

	SAN		CONTROLS[b]	
	1967	1968	1967	1968
Number of subjects	6	4[a]	2	3
Volume (ml)	873	1342	890	1367
Specific gravity	1.017	1.013	1.022	1.017
Creatinine (g)	0.84	0.98	1.36	1.42
Nitrogen (g)	10.4	10.6	8.7	11.4
Sodium (mEq)	31	29	212	147
Chloride (mEq)	30	36	173	121
Potassium (mEq)	70	103	68	61
Magnesium (mEq)	7.4		3.2	
Calcium (mg)	104		99	
Phosphate (mg)	157		737	
Osmolality (mOsm)	968		963	
N'methylnicotinamide (mg)	2.2		3.2	
Copper (μg)		99		98
Zinc (μg)		654		619
17-ketosteroids (mg)	4.8		9.6	
17-ketogenic steroids (mg)	3.8		7.8	

[a]The 4 subjects who provided samples in 1968 had been among the 6 subjects who gave urine samples in 1967.

[b]Collected at Dobe under the same conditions as San samples.

with London pressures (Hamilton et al. 1954, p. 11), which are typical of any developed community. Mean blood pressures do not rise with age in the San, and we did not find anyone with hypertension. This is very unusual: in most societies one would expect to find diastolic blood pressures over 110 mm Hg in about 5 percent of men 50–60 years, 8 percent over 60 years, and in 8 percent and 11 percent of women at corresponding ages (Ask-Upmark 1967). None of the San had mean diastolic pressures over 110 mm Hg. Kaminer and Lutz (1960, p. 289) found a similar absence of high blood pressure in Central Kalahari San in 1958, even though they did not have the good age estimates which we had in the present study. We have been able to find reports of only about a dozen communities whose mean blood pressures do not increase as they get older (Truswell et al. 1972, p.5). They are nearly all very isolated groups of people with simple technology.

In our full report on the San's blood pressures (Truswell et al. 1972, p. 5), we considered why they should be free of hypertension. First, they are living on a low salt regime. Their urinary sodiums and chlorides (Table 8.7) are very low and correspond to NaCl intakes around 2.0 grams per day. There is no salt available to the San at Dobe; the nearest source is 35 miles away at the South West Africa Administration's Bushman Settlement at Chum!kwe. A very low salt diet will cure high blood pressure: it would seem likely that a low salt diet will prevent it. Secondly, the San are thin—not only their arm circumferences, where blood pressures are measured by the indirect sphygmomanometric method, but their bodies as a whole. It is known that increased adiposity is correlated with increased blood pressure (Kannel et al. 1967, p. 48). The San do not have the increased adiposity seen in middle age in developed countries. Yet thinness cannot be the sole explanation because hypertension is sometimes seen in thin people. The third possible explanation for the San's freedom from high blood pressure is freedom from mental stress. We are not enthusiastic about this explanation. Living on a Hebridean island or on the edge of the primeval forest in the Congo

Table 8.8. Mean blood pressure of San in different age groups compared with London measurements by Hamilton et al. (1954). Men and women combined: systolic/diastolic

	15–19	20–29	30–39	40–49	50–59	60–69	70–83
San	117/74	119/74	117/74	116/75	121/75	122/70	120/67
London	117/70	122/74	124/77	132/80	145/87	160/90	168/90

does not protect against hypertension (Hawthorne et al. 1969, p. 651; Miller et al. 1962, p. 432). Furthermore it is notoriously difficult to quantify mental stress.

Heart Disease   183

Clearly the San are not troubled by hypertensive heart disease, the second most common type (Wood 1956). Nor did we find clinical evidence of coronary heart disease, the commonest type in industrial countries. In taking histories we did not find anyone who was subject to angina pectoris or who had heard of sudden death. Any chest pains we encountered were unilateral, probably related to pneumonia or originating in the chest wall. We saw no one with arterial disease of the legs.

In our examinations in 1967 and 1968 we found three cases of mitral valve disease, doubtless of rheumatic and streptococcal origin. Extrasystoles were encountered in three people over the age of 50 years. Six old people (58–72) had mild to moderate aortic ejection murmurs. We noted some degree of emphysema associated with chronic bronchitis in six San, all but one over the age of 60 years. Only one showed heart failure, a child of four who appeared to have active rheumatic fever. The other people with mitral murmurs, all those with aortic murmurs, and those with extrasystoles were asymptomatic. A minority with emphysema complained of shortness of breath on exertion; more of them complained of cough or unilateral chest pains.

Rheumatic heart disease and emphysema are certainly present among the San and appear to be relatively frequent. The aortic ejection murmurs heard in elderly people are not associated with signs of valve narrowing and we think they are caused by either aortic valve roughening or dilation of the aorta with age. This appeared to be a fairly benign condition. Systolic murmurs like this are common in the aged (Editorial 1968b, p. 530).

On the third medical visit, Dr. Kennelly confirmed the foregoing observations and found more subtle, innocent cardiac murmurs in some young adults. One man appeared to have had cardiomyopathy or myocarditis.

The main purpose of the third visit was to record electrocardiograms (ECGs) of the San. Nothing has been published before on this aspect. We were interested first to see if we could detect ECG evidence of silent coronary disease and secondly to see whether their ECGs showed any unusual features. Ninety-seven resting ECGs were recorded in clinically normal adults; some of the adults were retested after sprinting in the soft sand. We found no indication of coronary disease; no case of T wave inversion or flattening over the left ventricle was seen, and Q waves were absent (Kennelly, Truswell, and Schrire 1972, pp. 1093–1097).

However, the ECGs show a number of differences from the usual Caucasian patterns. The patterns resemble those which have been previously found in a percentage of apparently normal African and black U.S. subjects (Walker and Walker 1969, p. 441).

(1) 21 subjects (16 men) had high voltage in precordial leads. This might perhaps be explicable by thin chest walls.

(2) ST-segment elevation in precordial leads is seen in more of the San than in any other reported study of normals (Kennelly, Truswell, and Schrire, 1972). It is twice as common in males, occurring in mild degree in 89 percent. Elevated ST-segments usually become isoelectric after exercise.

(3) In a smaller proportion, more often women, T wave inversion is seen over the right ventricle. The cause of these two patterns is not clear, but they do not seem to have adverse prognostic significance (Walker and Walker 1969, p. 441).

Serum Lipids

Serum cholesterols were found to be very low. Many international surveys have shown that there is a negative correlation of serum cholesterol with the frequency of coronary heart disease both between populations (Keys 1970) and within populations (Kannel et al. 1971, p. 1). The Japanese and the Bantu, well known to have little coronary disease, have serum cholesterols averaging around 170 mg per 100 ml (Bronte-Stewart et al. 1955, p. 1103; Keys et al. 1958, p. 83). The San's serum cholesterols (Table 8.6) are about 50 mg per 100 ml lower again, which makes them one of the populations with the lowest serum cholesterols in the world. This alone might be a sufficient explanation for their apparent freedom from coronary disease.

The serum phospholipids are low, though not as far below western values as the cholesterols. The San were not always necessarily fasting when their blood samples were taken. If they had had a little to eat, it would not have affected their cholesterol or phospholipid concentrations but could have increased triglycerides. Despite this, their triglycerides were low as well. Our cholesterol values agree closely with the mean of 121 mg per 100 ml reported by Bersohn and Tobias in Central Kalahari San (Tobias 1966, p. 190). Miller and his associates have reported even lower serum lipids in a small number of

Central Kalahari San (Miller, Rubenstein, and Astrand 1968, p. 414; Editorial 1968a, p. 315); however their methodology was somewhat unorthodox.

We found that serum cholesterols show no significant variation with age or sex. They were a little higher in those who were getting some milk from Hereros in the district (Truswell and Hansen 1968b, p. 684) and in three pregnant women examined in 1969.

The very low cholesterols in the San can be explained largely by their diet which is very low in saturated fat and rich in polyunsaturated fat. Their major source is mongongo nuts (*Ricinodendron rautanenii*), which contain 57 percent fat. (Wehmeyer, Lee, and Whiting 1969, p. 1529). On gas chromatography (Engelter and Wehmeyer 1970, p. 25) this contains only a trace of myristic (14:0) and 10 percent of palmitic acid (16:0), but there is 43 percent linoleic acid (18:2) and 22 percent of a very late peak on gas chromatography which is probably α-eleostearic acid (Chisholm and Hopkins 1966, p. 390), a conjugated 18:3 fatty acid. The high ratio of 18:2 to 14:0 + 16:0 fatty acids should produce low serum cholesterols (Hegsted et al. 1965, p. 281). There is apparently no information on the nutritional effect of α-eleostearic acid; but since it is polyunsaturated, a cholesterol-lowering effect would be expected.

The other major source of dietary fat for the San is the meat of wild animals obtained by hunting. Although the meat and fat of farm animals in developed countries is very saturated, wild game in Africa have much less fat on and between the meat fibers, and the fat is less saturated and contains appreciable amounts of polyunsaturated fatty acids (Crawford 1968, p. 1329; 1969 p. 1419).

Our measurements of serum triglyceride fatty acids (Table 8.9) reflect the San's dietary intake of fatty acids. They show low proportions of the saturated fatty acids myristic (14:0) and palmitic (16:0), but high lionleic (18:2) and arachidonic (20:4) acids together with an acid, "x" which we were not able to identify completely. It is an 18:3 isomer and might therefore be derived from

Table 8.9. Mean percentage of fatty acids in fasting serum triglycerides

	Fatty acid									
	12:0	14:0	16:0	16:1	18:0	18:1	18:2	"x"[b]	20:1	20:4
San	2.0	1.0	25.1	2.6	6.1	34.2	25.9	1.8	0.7	0.5
Controls[a]	0.7	3.6	34.5	6.7	4.8	40.4	9.3	—	—	tr

[a]Controls were white office workers (35–55 years old) in Cape Town.
[b]"x" is an unsaturated 18 carbon fatty acid, probably an isomer of linolenic (18:3).

186

α-eleostearic acid, the unusual fatty acid in mongongo nuts. It is not present in the serum triglycerides of other population groups in southern Africa (Truswell and Mann 1972, p. 15), except for the Ovambos of northern Namibia (Watermeyer et al. 1972, p. 1390) in smaller concentration. They eat moderate amounts of mongongo nuts.

An additional factor probably helps to determine the San's low serum cholesterols. Although large amounts of exercise have little effect, repeated *prolonged* exercise *does* lower serum cholesterol (Gsell and Mayer 1962, p. 471). There is no reason to postulate that the unusual feedback mechanism which may keep Masai serum cholesterols low (Bliss et al. 1971, p. 694) is important in San. Unlike the Masai the San eat very little saturated fat. The low triglyceride concentrations seen in the San can be attributed to their low carbohydrate diets (Mann et al. 1970, p. 870) and lack of adiposity (Albrink, Meigs, and Granoff 1962, p. 484).

Hematology

During the clinical examinations we checked hemoglobin concentrations in anyone who appeared to have pale mucous membranes. We found no one with anemia except a baby with malaria. We assessed that the San's iron and vitamin B_{12} intake was adequate because of their regular consumption of meat and that they should be receiving adequate folate from liver and green leaves.

A more detailed examination of the San hematological status was carried out by Metz and Hart in collaboration with H.C. Harpending (1971) during a visit in late September 1969 to Dobe, Mahopa, and as far south as ≠To//gana. The first point of importance is that hookworm *Necator americanus* ova were found in 3 out of 18 fecal samples. If hookworm infestation is heavy, it can cause chronic occult blood loss from the bowel and lead to iron deficiency. Forty percent of the San showed mild eosinophilia, suggesting infestation with this or other helminth parasites.

However, the San are very rarely anemic. Only one out of 38 males had a hemoglobin under 13 g per 100 ml and only one out of 113 nonpregnant females had a hemoglobin below 11.5 per 100 ml. Serum iron concentrations averaged 117 μg in men and 97 μg per 100 ml in nonpregnant women. They ranged from 20 to 224 μg per 100 ml. Only 16 in all had serum irons below 70 μg per 100 ml and only 6 (5 women) had subnormal transferrin saturation. Metz and his colleagues pointed out that the Bantu iron cooking pots, which many San have adopted, are an important source of dietary iron.

There is a low incidence of folate deficiency. Only 8 percent of men and 3 percent of women neither pregnant nor lactating had serum folate concentrations below 3 ng/ml. Of 9 pregnant women 2 had low serum folates; another one had low transferrin saturation, but all the pregnant women had hemoglobins of at least 11 g per 100 ml.

The San's vitamin B_{12} concentrations averaged 650 pg/ml. They were all above the lower limit of normal for other populations, and in some subjects they were elevated, ranging to over 1,500 pg per ml. Vitamin B_{12} binding serum proteins were increased, however. It is therefore difficult to be sure whether the serum vitamin B_{12} levels result from this or from good dietary intakes or both. Vitamin B_{12} binding proteins increase in liver disease; but when they do, only the α-binding proteins are increased. In the San both α- and β-vitamin B_{12} binding proteins are elevated. Increased vitamin B_{12} binding proteins have been reported in other non-Caucasian people in Africa, such as Bantu and Cape Coloreds.

Glucose Tolerance Tests

In October 1970 Joffe's party visited Dobe and carried out oral glucose tolerance tests on 15 San (8 men, 7 women). They reported that plasma glucose concentrations were a little higher than in white controls in Cape Town (Joffe et al. 1971). Plasma growth hormone concentrations were not significantly different from controls and were promptly suppressed by glucose. Plasma insulins were low. Serum albumins were normal (averaging 3.7 g per 100 ml).

These results certainly do not indicate that the San have diabetes. The deviations are well within the normal, nondiabetic range (Jackson 1964). Joffe and associates compared their results to similar findings in central African pygmies. However, we find it difficult to draw any conclusions from this work, which fell into a number of methodological pitfalls. Their controls, unlike ours, did not have their tests done and samples collected in the field and carried back to the laboratory under the same conditions. The investigators measured the San's glucose tolerance tests in the afternoon, an unconventional time. Although their 10 control subjects also had afternoon tests, the latter did not have morning tests. Jarrett's group has now clearly shown that plasma glucose is higher and insulin lower in afternoon glucose tolerance tests, compared with the standard morning test (Jarrett et al. 1972, p. 199).

Joffe's group does not appear to have matched the ages of its subjects to those of the controls; plasma glucose levels increase with age. In addition the San were given relatively large doses of glucose because they were not adjusted for body weight. Lastly the study assumed that the San had been eating a high carbohydrate diet for the week before the tests, which seems rather improbable.

Lactose Tolerance Tests

Jenkins and colleagues (1974) did oral lactose tolerance tests on 40 adult bushmen at Tsum!kwe in Namibia. Only one subject absorbed well; in other words 97 percent were lactose intolerant. With a sample this size, this figure is not distinguishable from around 90 percent of Bantu who have adult lactase deficiency (Jersky and Kinsley, 1967; Cook 1973). Indeed adults of most populations in the world have lactase deficiency. Adult lactase *persistence* is the exception, occurring only in northern Europeans and Hamitic Africans.

The San do not drink milk but intestinal lactase is not an inducible enzyme. Jenkins and colleagues thought that special caution would be needed if the San were to be offered milk or milk powder. In fact none of the San tested by the Jenkins group had any adverse symptoms following 50g of lactose used for the test meal, which corresponds to the lactose in over a liter of milk, consumed rapidly. In adult lactase deficiency milk tolerance is unusual with ordinary intakes of milk (Pettifor and Hansen, 1974) presumably because there are still low activities of brush border lactase, unlike congenital lactase deficiency in which this enzyme is virtually absent.

Seasonal Changes in Nutritional Status

Thirty-three adults (over 20 years), 17 girls and 13 boys were examined at Dobe first at the end of the dry season when food and water were scarce in October 1967. The same individuals were re-examined in the same way and by the same examiners after the wet season in April–May 1968. Some of the changes in the *adults* are summarized in Table 8.10. Skinfold thickness and serum albumin increased despite evidence that malaria had been prevalent. In April 1968 spleens were palpable in 16 as aginst 12 people in the previous dry season and where a spleen had been palpable in 1967, it tended to be larger after the rains.

In the *children* mean weights and heights increased during the 6 months in almost all, no doubt because of growth. We have nothing to compare the growth rate against in these individuals. It is not very helpful to group children of different ages but the mean gain of height was substantial, 2.7 cms in girls under 15 years and 3.0 cms in the boys. In 5 San who had finished growing there was no change in height which indicates that the change was not methodological. Skinfold thickness (the sum of measurements at 3 sites, mid-triceps, subscapular and abdominal) increased in 16 and decreased in 9 of the boys and girls combined (see Figure 8.2).

In summary the Bushmen had more varied food to eat in April 1968. Our measurements indicate that the adults were fatter. The children had been growing satisfactorily and most were fatter.

Nutrition—Energy or Calories

We have paid particular attention to the question, Are the San adequately nourished? They *are* thin. Are they too thin? Is there evidence that they suffer in any way because they do not get or do not eat enough food? In the section on Anthropometry we have described the San as very thin by all the standards of developed countries. Hammel (1964, p. 413) states that they have one of the lowest adiposity coefficients in the world. Tobias considers them undernourished: "The Bushmen have probably improved but slightly from an extremely poor nutritional state to a still poor one" (Tobias 1971, p. 27). "It has long been known that, under conditions of better nourishment, Bushmen grow taller than otherwise" (Tobias 1962). De Almeida wrote about the San in nearby southern Angola that they "are a clear case of semi-starvation" (de Almeida 1965, p. 5). Birch and Gussow have concluded that there is a growing body

Table 8.10. Changes in adult San (over 20 years) October 1967 to April/May 1968[a]

Measurement	n	October 1967	April/May 1968	Change	P (Wilcoxon)
Weight (kg)	28	43.74	43.99	+0.26	NS
Subscapular[b] skinfold (mm)	33	6.41	7.51	+1.10	0.001
Spleen (mean number of fingers enlarged)	33	0.42	0.76	+0.34	NS
Serum albumin (G/100 ml)	8	3.51	4.03	+0.52	< 0.01
Serum cholesterol (mg/100 ml)	13	120.8	119.6	–1.2	NS

[a]Only people older than 20 years are included because those between 15 and 20 may have grown in the interval.

[b]Triceps skinfolds not shown because the measurement site was changed for some of the subjects between the 2 visits.

of evidence "that among groups who are endemically short, increase in stature follows an improvement in economic status, and that the shortness of such groups under their original environmental conditions arises not from 'short genes' but from social and environmental inadequacies" (1970, p. 113).

Richard Lee has disagreed (Lee 1969c, p. 47) with our provisional view that "chronic or seasonal calorie insufficiency may be a major reason why San do not reach the same adult stature as most other people" (Truswell and Hansen 1968a). One of Lee's points was that in July 1964 he estimated the nutrients available to one group at 2140 calories and 93 grams of protein for each man, woman, and child. But that was in July when, though food is not abundant, the minimum has not been reached. Between August and October, water is most limited and food most scarce. Elsewhere, Lee has written that "the San must resort to increasingly arduous tactics in order to maintain a good diet, or, alternatively they must content themselves with foods of less desirability in terms of abundance, ease of collecting, or nutritive value. It is during the three lean months of the year that the San life approaches the precarious conditions that have come to be associated with the hunting and gathering way of life" (Lee 1965). In these lean months, the foods eaten are mostly roots and bulbs, which would be expected generally to contain much water but to have low caloric density.

L. Marshall (1968, p. 94) has commented:

> It has been suggested that because they [the !Kung] do not have to work every day they can be said to have an "affluent society." This is a *bon mot* but does not add to the understanding of the reasons. . . . The !Kung we worked with are all very thin and . . . constantly expressed concern and anxiety about food. There must be reasons why they do not gather and eat more. I think energy for digging and the daylight hours come to an end for one thing. It has been suggested that they cannot eat more roots, berries, and seeds than they do, because the roughage is too much. Also, I believe we might look more into a possible social reason. If a woman gathered very much more than her family needed at a given time would it turn out that she was working for others?

As Lee himself showed, San who had obtained extra food from Hereros while they were growing were taller than average (1969c, p. 47).

After much analysis and discussion, our own view is that the San eat considerably less for their energy output than western, industrialized people, particularly during the three dry months, August to October. They have, in consequence, thin layers of subcutaneous fat, which are an advantage when walking long distances in the sand in the prevailing hot weather. On the other hand thinness is a disadvantage in the cold winter nights (Wyndham et al. 1964, p. 868). Another consequence of the relatively small energy intakes during childhood in those living entirely on bush foods is that final stature is less than their maximum genetic potential. We do not know the maximum height of which the San are capable, but the tallest man we examined was 175 cm (5 ft 9 in) tall. Insufficient energy (calorie) intake is not, we believe, the only influence which prevents the San from reaching their maximal potential height. Malaria and other infections could also have some growth-retarding effect (McGregor, Billewicz, and Thomson 1961, p. 1). Even the early age when they start tobacco smoking might have an effect. The relatively short stature of the San is not a bad thing in itself, and by keeping the Kalahari San light it has considerable advantages in their environment. However, we do not consider that the available evidence entitles us to say that their small size is mainly determined genetically.

Qualitative Nutrition

Having considered overall energy intake, we are left with the question whether the San are qualitatively malnourished: is their diet lacking in any essential nutrient, and/or do they show clinical or biochemical signs of specific nutritional deficiency? We will discuss the important specific nutrients one by one.

Protein. Meat from animals, mongongo nuts, and *Bauhinia esculenta* are rich in protein (Wehmeyer, Lee, and Whiting 1969). Babies and young children receive breast milk for their first three years of life or more. We saw no child with kwashiorkor, and the San did not seem to know of such a disease. Edema was not seen in adults either. Serum albumins were within normal limits except in people who had an illness or a problem with obtaining food at the time we took blood. In a small sample (Table 8.10) mean serum albumins were lower in the dry season. Urine nitrogens (Table 8.7) were as high as in controls. Plasma aminoacid patterns were within normal limits (Table 8.11) except in a girl of eight years who was thin and said her father had not been able to hunt recently because he had been ill. However, a plasma aminoacid pattern reflects fairly recent protein intake (Saunders et al. 1967, p. 795), and this girl did have a normal serum albumin of 3.95 grams per 100 ml. Upon comparison of our plasma aminoacids in San with findings reported in Babinga adult pygmies (Paolucci et al. 1969, p. 1652, and 1973, p. 429), both showed no signs of protein deficiency, though there were some interesting differences from controls, such as relatively high phenylalanine, serine, and glycine.

Vitamin A. High intakes would be expected from animals' livers. The serum vitamin A concentrations (Table 8.6) showed that the San were all very well nourished with Vitamin A[1]. They ranged from 51 to 194 μg per 100 ml in 1967 and from 26 to 126 μg per 100 ml in 1968. The low serum carotenoids indicate that their vitamin A must be eaten direct and not formed by splitting β-carotene.

Thiamin and Riboflavin. Thiamin and riboflavin should be adequately provided in the mixed diet the San eat. No clinical signs of deficiency were seen.

Niacin/Tryptophan. Niacin/tryptophan should be provided by the meat and some of the other foods of the San's mixed diet such as *Strychnos pungens* (Wehmeyer 1966, p. 1102). We saw no pellagrous

Table 8.11. Serum-free amino acids (mg per 100 ml)

	San adults 1967 men & women (n = 10), mean (& range)	Fasting controls[a] our laboratory 12 men & 12 women, mean (& range)	San girl of 8½ years (no. 147)
Taurine	1.92 (1.45 – 2.68)	1.42 (0.85 – 2.55)	2.44
Threonine	1.65 (1.43 – 2.24)	2.03 (0.69 – 3.45)	1.16
Serine	3.27 (2.80 – 3.99)	1.30 (0.63 – 2.84)	2.44
Glutamine	7.01 (5.67 – 8.19)	7.12 (4.21 – 11.08)	7.52
Proline	3.34 (2.37 – 5.78)	3.49 (1.15 – 7.23)	—
Citrulline	0.67 (0.56 – 0.81)	0.71 (0.46 – 0.96)	0.33
Glycine	3.56 (2.71 – 5.06)	2.11 (0.75 – 3.92)	2.95
Alanine	4.31 (3.12 – 6.34)	4.02 (2.11 – 6.20)	4.21
Valine	3.56 (1.66 – 6.11)	3.31 (2.20 – 4.59)	1.38
Methionine	0.39 (0.31 – 0.51)	0.47 (0.27 – 0.60)	0.21
Isoleucine	1.01 (0.81 – 1.26)	1.17 (0.79 – 1.83)	0.38
Leucine	2.56 (2.19 – 3.20)	2.05 (1.12 – 3.22)	1.43
Tyrosine	1.07 (0.80 – 1.67)	1.22 (0.83 – 1.63)	0.73
Phenylalanine	2.13 (1.75 – 3.04)	1.24 (0.73 – 2.25)	1.47
Ornithine	1.90 (1.03 – 3.73)	1.24 (0.53 – 1.93)	1.14
Lysine	2.87 (2.25 – 3.51)	2.91 (1.32 – 3.95)	1.58
Histidine	2.04 (1.30 – 2.70)	1.74 (0.87 – 2.32)	1.46
Arginine	2.71 (1.57 – 3.48)	1.49 (0.77 – 3.48)	1.69
Tryptophan	0.44 (0.25 – 0.52)		0.39

[a]Collected in Cape Town, not in the field.

skin changes. Urine N'methylnicotinamides (Table 8.7) were comparable to controls (both were somewhat lower than expected because of high blank readings). Plasma tryptophans seemed to be below normal values, but we did not have enough control serum left to compare with serum taken in the field.

193

Folic Acid and Vitamin B_{12}. Intakes and blood levels have been shown by Metz's team (Metz, Hart, and Harpending 1971) to be very satisfactory.

Vitamin C. Some of the bush foods are exceptionally rich in ascorbic acid, such as baobab flesh, *Adansonia digitata* (Wehmeyer 1966), and morula fruit, *Sclerocarya caffra* (Wehmeyer 1966; Fox 1966). Though there was periodontal disease, it did not have the features of scurvy.

Vitamin D. Despite the abundant sunlight, we saw craniotabes, the earliest sign of rickets, in three young infants who had been completely protected from sunlight since birth. In older infants and all other San there was nothing to suggest cholecalciferol deficiency.

Iron. Iron intake was adequate (Metz, Hart, and Harpending 1971; see this Chapter under Hematology).

Calcium. Calcium is present in the San's drinking water in the Dobe region since it comes from limestone wells. Urinary calciums were the same as in the controls (Table 8.7).

Sodium and Chloride. Lacking salt, the San's intakes were very low, and, consequently, so were urinary excretions. As discussed above, this may protect the San from hypertension. As expected, their kidneys had adjusted to the low intakes so that serum sodiums were normal.

Phosphorus. The San's urinary phosphates were very low. We wonder if this may not be because their diet lacks the cereals from which nearly all other population groups obtain large amounts of phosphate.

Iodine. Goiters were uncommon. Apart from mild physiological thyroid enlargements we only saw goiters in San who had been brought up on Gobabis or Ghanzi farms further south. We therefore conclude that dietary iodine is adequate in the Dobe region, and that the San do not obtain antithyroid substances in their bush food.

Other Trace Elements. With one or two exceptions we saw no fluorotic mottling of teeth. Urinary zinc and copper were normal.

To conclude, we do not know the significance, if any, of the low urinary phosphates. The low sodium chloride intakes are probably beneficial, rather than harmful. With these exceptions we found no evidence of any qualitative nutritional deficiency in the San. This was not unexpected since mixed diets should protect against malnutrition. As a rule, barring accidents and illness, it would seem that the only nutritional weakness of the San's diet is a shortage of energy (calories) usually in the dry spring season.

Further Studies to Part II

Aspects of !Kung demography are also discussed by Howell (1973, 1974), Harpending (1971), and Harpending and Jenkins (1973a, 1973b). See also Lee (1972d), and Yellen and Harpending (1972). Medical and nutritional studies have appeared on various special topics: on the problem of heart disease see Truswell and Hansen (1968); Truswell, Kennelly, Hansen, and Lee (1972); Kennelly, Truswell, and Schrire (1972); and Truswell and Mann (1972). Nutritional studies are reported in Truswell et al. (1969); Hansen et al. (1969); Metz et al. (1971); Wehmeyer et al. (1969); Engelter and Wehmeyer (1970); Truswell (1972a, 1972b); and Lee (1973b).

Mother nursing older child

Social and Economic Constraints on Child Life among the !Kung

Patricia Draper

Two children sharing water from a hollow tree

200

The usual approach in studies of socialization is to look at the interaction among cultural values, social structure, and child-training practices. The approach used here evolved during my two years in the field living with the !Kung, when it became clear to me that the major constraints on child life derived from the nature of adult work and from the organization of people in space. By the "nature of adult work" I refer to the hunting and gathering subsistence economy, to the rhythm of work routines, and to the accommodation to scarce and unevenly distributed water sources. By "organization of people in space" I refer to the actual settlement pattern of !Kung living groups and to the overlying network of social use to which the living space is put.

In approaching child life through a focus on these more concrete features of social life, I hope not to skimp on the rich ethnographic detail that can be conveyed in writings about child-training practices in other cultures. Instead, by specifying more fully the stage settings and the traffic rhythms of the social actors in camp life, I hope to open to the reader a view of the niche of children in this society.

The /Du/da people were the most isolated and traditional of all the !Kung on the border area. During 1969 about 120 people frequented the /Du/da area with usually 60–80 people (separated into two or more camps) at any one time. Camp size averaged 30–40 people, and the bands were separated by 5.0–50.0 km. The people lived by traditional hunting and gathering techniques and occupied lands not used by Herero and Tswana pastoralists, who lived at /Xai/xai, 66 km north of the /Du/da well.

Children living in these groups have lives which are markedly different from the lives of western children and different even from the lives of Bantu children in the same geographic area. The most striking contrasts stem from the settlement pattern, the small size of the local group, and the paucity of material goods.

It is difficult to convey a sense of the closeness, intimacy, and isolation of these bush camps. We Westerners combine intensely private domestic life (shared with five or fewer individuals) with daily exposure to hundreds or thousands of total strangers. The !Kung conduct their daily domestic life in the full view of 30–40 relatives and friends and rarely see a stranger. Even when a person visits a camp where some few individuals or families are unknown, he can always establish a connection with them via mutual relatives and in-laws at other locations.

Some /Du/da camps were sufficiently isolated that casual visiting between bands was not a daily event. During the rainy season camps were separated by 16–48 km though, as the dry season wore on, people retreated to lands near permanent water holes. As an example, in August 1969, 82 people lived in two separate camps near the ≠To//gana well. These people were all well known to each other. The nearest other !Kung at that time were at /Xai/xai (45 km to the north) and at /Gəm (15 km to the west).

For someone unaccustomed to the !Kung ways of building huts and laying out a village, it would be possible to walk within six meters of a village and never know it was there. Standing on the outskirts of a !Kung camp for the first time one thinks of birds' nests clinging with frail strength in the branches of bushes. The low, inconspicuous huts are built of branches and grass and so are entirely camoflaged. During most months of the year the people make no effort to clear away grass and bushes from the periphery of the village to mark the disjunction of the open bush with the settled village. People prefer to build their huts backed into the bush and facing into the center of the common village space.

The children living in these camps are limited in their range of movements. It is hardly an exaggeration to say they have almost no place aside from the village and its near periphery where they can go to be by themselves to play games or whatever. There is simply the cleared village space; and in back of each hut stretches the Kalahari bush which from a child's vantage point is vast, undifferentiated, and unsocialized. It was a surprise to me to see what little use children made of the bush hinterland. Older children use the bush beyond eyesight of the village to some extent, but children under about 10 years stayed close to home and most often were inside the village circle in close association with adults.

Inside, the /Du/da camps are small, compact, and densely settled places. The women build the traditional huts at the outer edges of a circular village space. The inner area is usually bare; grass, bushes, small trees are removed so that nothing remains which might have provided shade or privacy. The huts themselves are small (around 1.5 m tall by 1.8 m in diameter); and since they are located at the edge of the village space, they do not break up the inner space or create microneighborhoods for certain families. !Kung do not actually live in their houses or use them for privacy. Instead they use their huts primarily for keeping food, skins, and tools dry and as a kind of marker signifying the residence of one nuclear family.

Not only are there no physical barriers to communication within and across the village, there are also no social barriers which restrict the access of people to each other. Women and men, for example, have equal access to all points inside the village, as do children. The only restriction of access is to the inside of another person's hut. Most adults do not go inside the hut of another family, though children may do so. In practice, one rarely finds anyone inside a hut except during a heavy rain or when a person naps there during the heat of an afternoon.

Space within the village is not only small and well-populated, it is also undifferentiated as to function. There is, for example, no children's play area set apart from an "adults only" place. In the village are clusters of interacting people which include people of both sexes and of different ages. In an average village a person can hear the murmur of any conversation anywhere in the village. He might not understand the content of a conversation, but he would hear the voices. In this context everyone is visible at a glance; people are continuously aware of each other's presence, doings, and emotional states. Family huts are often so close together that the people sitting at the different hut fires can converse without raising their voices.

The custom of living in small groups gives a unique stamp to a child's life. Perhaps the single most striking feature is the close association children have with a variety of adults in the band. A child spends most of his days living with a variable assortment of 30–40 people who share the intimate village space. The group includes his own nuclear family and other families and individuals who are usually related to him by blood or marriage. At /Du/da the average band size was 34 people with a range of from 16 to 61 people. The average number of children per band was 5 girls and 7 boys ranging in age from infancy to 14 years. (Table 9.1 shows the age and sex composition of the /Du/da camps during 1969.)

As a consequence of such small total numbers, a child spends little time in the company of age-mates. A typical gang of children joined temporarily in some play in the village might include a 5-year-old boy, an 11-year-old girl, a 14-year-old boy, and a 2-year-old toddler hanging on the fringe of the action.

The limited and heterogeneous assortment of playmates available to a child poses interesting constraints on the kind of games which children can play. Competitiveness in games is almost entirely lacking, and it is interesting to see that in this respect !Kung cultural values against competitiveness and environmental constraint have such a fortunate congruence. To compete in a game or skill one needs one or preferably more children close in age and perhaps sex with whom to compete, but the smallness of group size among !Kung usually ensures that several age-mates are not available. Team sports are similarly unrealistic. Not only can the children not fill out a team; but the players are at such different levels of motor skill, motivation, and cognitive development that it is difficult and unrewarding to play a game involving intense competition, rules, and fairly complex strategy.[1]

An example of a game played by the children may illustrate these remarks. The game, called zeni, is played by both girls and boys; each player takes his turn alone. A feather is joined to a weight (a pebble or an uncracked mongongo nut) with a leather thong about 15 cm long. The player hurls the weighted feather (zeni) into the air by means of a stick. When the zeni descends, the weight falls first. The feather flutters behind, in a downward spiral, acting as a kind of sail or parachute. The object is for the player to reach the zeni before it lands and to send it back into the air by hooking the stick around the leather thong and hurling it.

The game requires skill, both in timing the catch and in rethrowing the zeni so that it can be hooked and thrown still another time. Each player is clearly striving to perfect his own technique but is not interested in doing better than the previous player. I never observed the children counting the number of times one child threw the zeni without missing; it appeared to me that each new player came into the game for the joy of it and for practicing his own skill.

The setting for zeni play and the typically unequally matched players did not promote a competitive spirit. The children who played usually ranged in age from about 6 to 15 years of age. Their

Table 9.1./Du/da Area: Band size, age and sex composition, places and months of observation

Period	Date	Place	Census	Adult males	Adult females	Young males	Young females
1	Jan. '69	/Du/da	—	—	—	—	—
2	Feb.–Mar. '69	/Du/da	16	5	6	3	2
3	Mar.–Apr. '69	≠Ticha	36	12	12	7	5
4	May '69	≠Tebi !guasi	45	13	16	11	5
5	May–June '69	≠Tebi !guasi	56	17	19	12	8
6	July '69	≠To//gana	17	4	6	6	1
7a	Aug. '69	≠To//gana (1)	21	6	7	7	1
7b	Aug. '69	≠To//gana (2)	61	19	22	9	11
8a	Sept. '69	≠To//gana (1)	24	7	10	3	4
8b	Sept. '69	≠To//gana (2)	32	10	12	4	6
9a	Oct. '69	≠To//gana (1)	24	9	8	3	4
9b	Oct. '69	≠To//gana (2)	40	14	13	6	7
		Averages	33.8	10.6	11.9	6.5	4.9

skills were so unequal that any rivalry would have been pointless.

In their choice of setting for the game the children reveal a lack of interest in manipulating the environment in order to facilitate the goal of the game. Far from setting the game in a cleared area where the player could have an optimum chance of reaching the zeni as it comes down, the game goes on in the middle of the village or on the periphery just behind the huts. When they play inside the village, the children stumble into huts, narrowly avoid stepping into smoldering hearths, and so forth. When they play on the periphery, they are in the open, unimproved bush and have to dodge around holes in the ground, thorn bushes, ant hills, and fallen logs. As one used to the orderly progress of games played according to rules on a green, graded field, I wondered that the children derived as much satisfaction from throwing the zeni as they did.

More often a youngster is not found in the exclusive company of children but is interacting in a cluster of people which includes at least one and often several adults.

Mother with her four children cracking nuts

As part of my study of children I collected a series of randomized spot observations at various times during the day on 36 children who lived at /Du/da. The spot observation was designed as a quick way of collecting certain data on a child: his location in space; the numbers, ages, sex, and identification numbers of the people who were interacting with him or, who were on the nearby premises. In 173 observations of this type, I recorded *no* instance in which a child was beyond eye or ear communication with at least one adult. In the same 173 spot observations there were only 5 instances in which a child was "alone" in the sense that he was not in the immediate presence of at least one other person. In these cases the child was either sleeping or walking by himself from one conversational group to another. In about 70 percent of the recorded spot observations children were in face-to-face interactive clusters which included one or more adults.

As described above, the area of village settlement is so small that continuous close physical proximity to adults is unavoidable. Aside from constraints of space, children have great freedom of social access to the adults of the band. During an average day one can expect to find at home half or more of the adults and all the children who are not being carried by their mothers. Adults work 3 to 4 days a week and often less than 8 hours per day. When men and women are not working, they usually stay in the village, sitting in conversational clusters in front of the huts, talking, resting, mending tools and leather garments. Children make virtually no economic contribution to subsistence for reasons which will be discussed more fully later.

Children over 3 years of age are in the village more hours in a 24-hour period than any one else with the exception of very old people who rarely leave camp. If it should happen that a child has neither his mother nor his father within reach, he is nevertheless under the informal but continuous surveillance of the remaining adults and adolescents who are taking the day off from work.

The relationship between children and adults is easygoing and unselfconscious. Adults do not believe that children should keep to themselves: be seen but not heard. The organization of work, leisure, and living space is such that there is no reason for confining children or excluding them from certain activities. Everyone lives on the flat surface of the ground; hence there is no need to protect children from falls or from becoming entrapped behind doors. With the exception of spears and poisoned arrows, adult tools do not constitute a hazard to children. Those weapons are simply kept hanging in trees or wedged on top of a hut, safely out of reach. When the men

206

are making spear and arrow points, they do not attempt to exclude children (or women) from the area. Usually a man sits at his own hearth while he hammers and files the metal.

One afternoon I watched for 2 hours while a father hammered and shaped the metal for several arrow points. During the period his son and his grandson (both under 4 years old) jostled him, sat on his legs, and attempted to pull the arrow heads from under the hammer. When the boys' fingers came close to the point of impact, he merely waited until the small hands were a little farther away before he resumed hammering. Although the man remonstrated with the boys (about once every 3 minutes), he did not become cross or chase the boys off; and they did not heed his warnings to quit interfering. Eventually, perhaps 50 minutes later, the boys moved off a few steps to join some teenagers lying in the shade.

Though the !Kung children are closely supervised, they have considerable leeway despite their continuous physical proximity to adults. Adults are ubiquitous, but they have a nondirective attitude toward the nearby children. In another type of behavior observation I recorded the activity of a child for a 60-minute period. I varied the time of the observation period over the day and randomized the order for observing each child. During the hour I recorded the child's actions, the actions of others to which he reacted (so far as this could be determined), his commands and commands received, as well as the shifting setting and the shifting set of interactants with whom he was engaged.

Analyzing these data allowed quantification of various aspects of child life. Given the intimate contact between adults and children I wanted to know the extent to which adults (in an overt way) were shaping a child's behavior. I counted the number of times an adult interrupted and changed the behavior of the subject child and as I expected, incidents of this type were infrequent. Girls between the ages of 4 and 14 years received about 1½ adult interruptions per hour; boys of the same age range received about 2 adult interruptions per hour.

If adult supervision of children is informal and unobtrusive, it is by no means lax; adults are habitually cognizant of the emotional states and whereabouts of children. Parents are quick to stop aggressive interactions especially when they involve children of unequal ages. They could inform me with great accuracy how to find a child who was beyond eye- and earshot of the village although frequently I was not sensitive enough to the subtleties of the directions to find my subject without guidance from another child. To me, !Kung directions were as unhelpful as verbal instructions in how to ride a bicycle would be to a novice cyclist.

The women are especially mindful of the 5- and 6-year-olds who are old enough to wander but too immature to keep oriented in the bush. One hot afternoon at ≠To//gana I was sitting with five women and a few infants. We were all huddled in the shade thrown by a single hut. It was almost too hot to talk; we all sat listlessly, waiting for the sudden lifting of the heat which came everyday at about 5:30 PM. Suddenly one woman jerked herself to a sitting position, neck arched, eyes darting to all directions. "Listen . . . listen!" she whispered. "Where are the children?" All the women leapt to their feet, looking about and calling to other people sitting farther off in the village. About that time we hard a child's voice calling in the distance and looking in that direction we saw the missing children: N//au, a 5-year-old girl, Hwan//ka, a 4-year-old girl, and N!ai, a 9-year-old girl, who were walking through the bush toward the camp. The wave of alarm which had galvanized the women, raised them from torpor, and scattered them twelve or more meters in a few seconds, subsided immediately. Three of the women drifted back to their original positions in the shade of the hut; the other two went to their own hearths and busied themselves at some task. I waited around to see what else might happen. The three girls entered the camp clearing and were apparently oblivious of the concern they had raised for they did not approach any of the women. In the next hour none of the women spoke to the children about their alarm. Probably they felt that there had been no real danger since the 9-year-old girl was present, and since they had apparently not wandered beyond earshot of the camp.

Also quantifiable from the hour observations was the amount of exposure of varying closeness which children had to adults. In developing meaningful parameters for describing the spatial proximity of children to adults I could not rely on the more obvious measures such as being in the same room or village with an adult or being separated by some unit of distance. These measures do not have much meaning in the context of the small, open space of a !Kung village. There are no true rooms in a village, as has been described previously. The village itself is a kind of big room which is the setting for its communal life. A measure of being in the same village with one or more adults contributes no information since children were usually in the village; and when they were, there was at least one (usually several) adult present with him. In fact, in the spot observations *and* hour observations, when the subject child was in the village, there were no instances in which he was not near at least one adult.

In the course of recording hour observations there were times when the subject child wandered away from the circle of huts and beyond eye and/or ear communication with the adults of the village. A game or an impromptu gathering expedition was usually the occasion for such an excursion. Such intervals away from adult monitoring were quite brief as is attested by Table 9.2 which shows the average number of minutes per hour observation in which a child was beyond eye and/or ear contact with any adult. My interest in the data of Table 9.2 and those following is in the order of magnitude of the behaviors of various types for !Kung children and not in the heterogeneity among the age-sex categories, for which the numbers are too small to make statistical manipulations useful or meaningful. The distribution of subjects by age and sex category by the hour observations appears in Table 9.3.

The number of subjects is small, and the absence of female subjects in two age categories makes any discussion of the effects of sex and/or increasing age of the variable extremely tenuous. Still, in absolute terms the numbers speak for themselves: /Du/da children are well-supervised; they are seldom left to shift for themselves. These figures also give indirect support for my generalizations earlier to the effect that children make little use of the village hinterland. Similarly, adults do not often go into this hinterland except on their way to work.

Table 9.2. Average number of minutes per hour in which the subject child was completely unsupervised (subjects distinguished by age and sex)

	2–3 years	4–6 years	7–9 years	10–12 years	13+ years
Girls	—[a]	0 min.	3 min.	—[a]	0 min.
Boys	0 min.	18 min.	0 min.	5 min.	22 min.

[a]No subjects available in the given age-sex category.

Table 9.3. Ages and numbers of hours observed of /Du/da children[a]

	2–3 years	4–6 years	7–9 years	10–12 years	13+ years
Girls	—	2 subj. 4 obs.	3 subj. 4 obs.	—	1 subj. 1 obs.
Boys	1 subj. 1 obs.	4 subj. 5 obs.	2 subj. 3 obs.	3 subj. 5 obs.	2 subj. 3 obs.

[a]Total number girls, 6; total number boys, 12: total number of hours observed, 26.

I settled on two different measures to assess the closeness of child-adult relations. One measure was of spatial proximity. It recorded whether or not there were one or more adults nearby such that the child could see them merely by turning his head. The names and identification numbers of all people in the visual vicinity of the child were recorded. Another measure was of the composition of the child's immediate group of interactants—the people who were in the immediate presence of the child. By "immediate presence of a child" I included only those people who were orienting toward each other and toward the child to the exclusion of other people.

The distinction is meaningful in the context of !Kung culture though it no doubt seems elaborate and unwieldy to people unfamiliar with their customs, particularly as they relate to the maintenance of personal distance. To gain a better understanding of the latter I recommend viewing the excellent ethnographic films by John Marshall which were taken of the !Kung of the nearby Nyae Nyae region. These films convey better than words how physically close they like to be and now much physical contact there is among members of the common living group.

The people live in a rather thick human press; but they screen out (from some levels of consciousness) faces, bodies, and sounds which are not relevant to the immediate activity. For example I occasionally saw five or six individuals squatting around a fire engaging in raucous, bawdy hilarity while another cluster of people not a meter away remained sober-faced and preoccupied with another conversation. We are all familiar with this technique which people employ (or try to) when they are among strangers in a crowded restaurant. What is remarkable to a western observer is that !Kung are able to do this among life-long friends and relatives.

I felt the sociability factor in adult-child dealings was at least important as the proximity factor for the data quantification to be culturally sensitive. Table 9.4 shows the average number of minutes per hour observation in which a child had one or more adults in his immediate presence.

Previously I mentioned that children make virtually no economic

Table 9.4. Average number of minutes per hour in which children have one or more adults in their immediate presence (subjects distinguished by age and sex)

	2–3 years·	4–6 years	7–9 years	10–12 years	13+ years
Girls	—	37 min.	35 min.	—	10 min.
Boys	47 min.	28 min.	42 min.	47 min.	5 min.

contribution to subsistence. In comparison with those in more settled societies, !Kung children are late in being held responsible for subsistence tasks. The girls are around 14-years old before they begin regular food gathering and water and wood collecting. (This is in spite of the fact that they may be married before this age.) Boys are 16 years old or over before they begin serious hunting. The fact that the !Kung can ignore their children for help in subsistence stems chiefly from the nature of adult work and the particular ecological adaptation these people have made which allows a wholesome diet in an apparently inhospitable and intractable environment. The !Kung are able to feed themselves with relative ease and predictability, and there is little reason to train children for economic self-sufficiency.

Richard Lee has documented for the northern Dobe Area !Kung the amount of work required to support members of the group and the inventory of animal and vegetable species which are used over the years (Lee 1965; 1969a). Although Lee's data refer to another population, the !Kung of the /Du/da area follow weekly work routines essentially similar to those in the north. Some regional dietary variations exist; for example, the /Du/da people ate less mongongo nuts and more game meat than did the Dobe inhabitants. In 1969 some /Du/da groups lived away from standing water for two or more weeks and at these times collected and consumed more water root (*!xwa*) and prickly melon (*ja*) than was common in the north where !Kung are more reluctant to dry camp.

At /Du/da, as at Dobe, that part of adult work which is concerned with actual food-getting goes on at a distance from camp. Women are the chief gatherers, and they prepare to make gathering trips about every other day. The trips last anywhere from four to ten hours depending on the location of the food and the length of time the group has been collecting from the same base camp. Men also gather, but not routinely. They collect mongongo nuts; and when the group is dry camped (as at ≠Ticha in April, 1969) or camped about 4.8 km from the waterhole (as at ≠To//gana in August, September, and October 1969), men and women may spend an hour or two per day collecting water root to supplement the standing water which had to be carried from the well to the village.

If children's work is not actually required, it is also true that children can be a hindrance to the work groups of men and women. I found that children do not often accompany adults on their food-getting rounds. Though it is true that children *could* follow their parents on their rounds (girls and boys with the women, older boys with men on long hunts), typically they did not. Children prefer to stay in the village, to gossip, to play among themselves, and to hang around with the adults who were not working. The children know that the women may wander far on their foraging expeditions, and that the days are extremely hot eight months of the year. The women cannot carry an older child when he becomes tired, for generally they are already carrying an infant or toddler in addition to the day's harvest of bush food. In the dry season when there were no water pans along the way, women actively discouraged children from following them because they didn't want to carry the additional drinking water which the children require.

There are, of course, times when children accompany gathering groups and, to a lesser extent, the hunting parties of the men. These episodes are surprisingly infrequent—just how infrequent I was slow to appreciate. In the first month or two after contacting the /Du/da people I did not carry out formal observations on children, but concentrated on learning the new names and faces, collecting genealogies, making camp diagrams, and trying to overcome the initial unfamiliarity of the /Du/da dialect. In the early weeks I joined the women on gathering trips, primarily intending to build rapport but also to learn how far the women walked, what foods they collected, and how the children behaved on the trips. I was glad to see that several children came along but was puzzled by what I detected as an "air of outing" among them. They were not helping fill their mothers' karosses with the foodstuffs which could be easily collected, and the 8- and 9-year-olds rarely carried even child-size pouches in which to carry food. Off and on they ate handfulls of berries and plugs of sweet edible resin, both of which they gathered themselves. More of the time they scampered through the bush racing each other for first grab at some delicious item, and they hung around me, scrutinizing my dress, my gait, my every move, sometimes with open stare, sometimes surreptitiously.

As the weeks passed and my presence became less of a novelty, I observed that older children seldom accompanied the gatherers even when I did. Several more passing months convinced me that the usual pattern is for children to stay at the village, that in the early weeks they "went gathering" to keep tabs on the strange woman who had inexplicably moved in with their people.

Analysis of the spot observations gives a good indication of the infrequency with which children accompany adult work groups. From a total of 77 spot observations on /Du/da girls there were 8 out of 76 observations (in one case the associates of the girl were not ascertained) in which the subject was absent, and it could be deter-

212

mined for each of these cases whom the girl was with and what she was doing. In 7 instances the girl was absent and reported to be gathering with the women. All but one of these 7 cases represented a girl 3 years or younger. These girls were so young that they were not weaned from the breast and were still carried by their mothers during a day's work. Needless to say, they were not making any contribution to subsistence.

From a total of 96 spot observations on /Du/da boys, there were 18 out of 93 observations (in 3 cases the associates of the boy were not ascertained) in which the subject was absent. Again, it could be determined whom he was with and what he was doing. In only 7 instances were the boys with the men hunting. Six of the 7 observations represented boys 11 years or older. Bush boys accompany women on gathering trips with the same infrequency: 7 in ·93 observations. Most of these boys were youngsters, still being carried by their mothers. In no case did a girl go hunting with the men.

Children do not do tasks in the village though they are in the village or close to it most of the day and in close interaction with adults who might easily parcel out the routine work done by adults. For example, cloth garments are scarce in the bush, and the work associated with preparing leather is common, absorbing a fair portion of the days which adults spend in camp. In the /Du/da camps there was usually at least one antelope hide staked out to the rear of the huts. When a hide is completely dry, a man scrapes it with a steel adze. It is monotonous work; the man hunches uncomfortably over the skin and scrapes carefully to avoid gouging a hole in the hide. Children sometimes stand watching this work; they pick up the curly shavings and eat small amounts. I never observed a man who was working at this job attempt to get help from his own or another child. Nor did the man volunteer information or advice about how the job was done. He simply worked with the children squatting at the edge of the hide watching and nibbling with apparent abosrption, then moving on to some other pastime.

When the scraping is finished, women take over the hides and treat them with a softening agent. In the last stage of preparation women spend hours rubbing the hides with a reddish aromatic powder made from a tree bark. They prefer to work the hides with the help of one or two friends; each woman sits with a portion of the skin in her lap, facing her helpers, chatting and smoking. Again, I never observed children helping in any of these tasks, nor in the sewing and tending necessary to make various leather devices. As with the hide scraping by men, I never saw a woman who was working a hide attempt to get help from a nearby child.

There is one area of daily routine where children give help; this is water collecting. Usually ten or more people (men and women) walk to the waterhole once each day. An adult hands a child a container which he then carries filled to the village. Children do not go every day to the well; they go when they want to, but they help out if they go.

In the course of recording hour observations on the /Du/da children I noted the child's activities and the duration of various activity-episodes. It was possible to derive from the hour observations an estimate of the average number of minutes in an hour in which a child was doing a task. I defined a task as work carried out by a child either because he was told to do so (in my hearing) or because he understood it to be his regular chore. (The latter I determined by interviewing the child's parent when the observation was finished.) I considered that a task was something useful to adults or to the group as a whole. (Child care was not included in the category of children' s tasks, but was scored separately and will be discussed later.)

By this measure, children do amazingly little work. The adolescents, theoretically the most capable of their group of doing useful work, were observed doing the least of any age class. Table 9.5 shows the average number of minutes of work per hour done by /Du/da children. Note that an empty cell indicates there were no subjects available in the population of a certain age-sex category.

The short intervals of child work represented in this chart are chiefly cases in which a child executes an informal command by an adult. Typical examples are: fetching a glowing coal for an adult who wants to light his pipe, fetching some utensil as a mortar and pestle for a woman who wants to pound meat or food. Note that the analysis of the hour observations reveals no clear finding of sex difference in task behavior for the /Du/da children. Boys and girls do equally little work. Surprisingly this applies equally to child-tending work by boys and girls.

Since their parents are away from home for three to four days per week, one might expect that !Kung children are assigned responsibility for younger children. In most preindustrial societies, particular-

Table 9.5. Average number of minutes per hour in which /Du/da children were observed doing a task (subjects distinguished by age, sex, and subsistence group)

	2–3 years	4–6 years	7–9 years	10–12 years	13+ years
Girls	—	1 min.	2 min.	—	0 min.
Boys	0 min.	.25 min.	3 min.	2 min.	0 min.

ly where there is no schooling, older children are expected to take care of younger children. The institution of child nurse is widespread in sub-Saharan Africa in societies where women have a heavy workload (usually agricultural) and must walk some distance to work. These women leave children at the homestead under the tutelage of an older child, usually female. The child nurses are making a substantial contribution to subsistence because they free adult women from continuous child tending.

In actual fact !Kung children devote almost no time to child care as Table 9.6 shows. The data are derived from analysis of the hour observations. Child care is defined to include the following kinds of behavior: the subject wipes face, feeds, amuses, protects from harm, helps dress, or comforts a younger child. Merely talking to a younger child was not counted unless it was accompanied by one of these described acts. Each episode of holding or carrying a younger child was counted once. Originally I tried to score the hour observations for the number of minutes in which the subject was doing something for a child. This proved unsatisfactory; such acts were so fleeting that I had to estimate their duration in seconds, not minutes. A better strategy seemed to make a tally of the discrete acts of child caring.

Various factors are at work to produce the very low scores on child caring. Children do not act as caretakers, because in almost any setting which includes a child there will be several adults present who themselves monitor young children. As I have indicated before in describing adult work routines, children who stay in the village rather than follow the women on gathering trips do not have the village to themselves. They are still in the company of other adults who are taking the day off. Those child-caring acts which were recorded in the hour observations occur chiefly when the subject child and other younger children are outside the village and out of easy communication with adults.[2]

Still other factors are related to the low scores of /Du/da children on child caring. These are long birth spacing, late weaning from the breast, and late weaning from the back. Children under 3 who need

Table 9.6. Average number of child-caring acts by a subject child per hour of observation (subjects distinguished by age and sex)

	2–3 years	4–6 years	7–9 years	10–12 years	13+ years
Girls	—	0	1	—	1
Boys	0	1	.5	1.6	3.8

the most caretaking stay close to their mothers. When the mother gathers, she normally carries a child under age 2 and is quite likely to carry a child over that age. (Richard Lee 1972d, makes interesting use of the same facts in calculating the work load for mothers of infants of varying ages.) Should a toddler's mother be away temporarily, the child will stay around some other familiar adult, typically the father or a grandparent. The long birth spacing (average 3.8 years) means that most mothers of 2- to 3-year-olds are not occupied with another infant and can still devote much of their attention to the knee child (Howell n.d.).

Most children are nursed for at least 3 years and sometimes longer if the mother does not become pregnant. The nursing promotes close ties between mother and child and makes him less independent of her. When a woman miscarries late in pregnancy or produces a stillborn, and she has an older child who is partly or recently weaned; she will put this child back on the breast to drink a renewed supply of milk for several additional months. Normally, in the absence of such a development one would expect that a nursing 3-year-old derives little nutritional benefit from his mother's milk for by then he is eating regularly a standard adult diet. Still, it was obvious to me observing nursing children of this age that the suckling was pleasurable and important to the child's sense of well-being.

At /Du/da I knew a mother, N!oshe, and her son, Kan//ka, who was then about 4 years old. The child was still nursing, though infrequently. I wondered how much if any milk Kan//ka was getting. When I asked N!oshe if her breasts still had milk, she answered, "No, when he nurses he just swallows his own saliva."

This paper has dealt with two dimensions of child life: the high degree of adult supervision and the almost negligible task assignment. The position of children with respect to these dimensions seems in large part determined by the ecological adjustment of !Kung living groups. The high adult supervision of children derives from the interaction of many factors. For example, the semi-nomadism, foraging, and hunting subsistence require minimal investment in housing and communal facilities since each encampment is abandoned after one to several weeks of occupation. Minimal camp furnishings, together with small group size (in turn adapted to efficient extraction of limited and unevenly distributed resources), result in an unusually close, densely occupied, and visually open settlement pattern. The mobility and small size of the groups and the sparse distribution of the entire population over the bush enable the !Kung to exploit a variety of variable food resources and to avoid overharvesting in one area.

216

Adults have considerable time which is not taken up by primary subsistence work such as killing game and collecting vegetable food. They stay at home several days per week and are in close physical proximity to children. The availability of many adults makes possible a loose rein on children in a primarily harmless environment.

The absence of child work seems related both to the predictability of the food supply and to the low level of technological development and the consequent simple, limited material inventory. Living in a relatively rich environment, a normal couple can feed their children and dependent relatives with ease. The nature of adult work (taking place far from camp and away from standing water) means that children cannot be inducted conveniently into adult work.

A simple material technology is both necessary for a people who carry all their possessions on their backs and sufficient if they live wholly off the bounty of the environment. Yet, the very technological simplicity of adult work and the lack of specialization of work conspires to exclude children from early learning of subsistence skills. !Kung subsistence is deceptively simple. It is so uncomplicated that it is easy to overlook the fact that the food-getter must be a mature adult. In more complex societies with more complex economies, food getting is highly rationalized and broken down into smaller packages of work that can be carried out simultaneously by different persons differing in strength, skill, and maturity. In more sophisticated systems there is not food getting but food production, maintenance chores (weeding of crops, husbanding of animals, mending of the tools needed to render food usable), and storage and protection of food surplus.

!Kung economy looks simple in comparison with other more diversified economies with greater division of labor, but from the point of view of the individual actor, subsistence is quite complex. For example, though it is simple enough to pick up nuts or melons once one is standing where they are found, it requires strength to walk 16 km or more per day carrying a full day's harvest and perhaps a child. A woman needs to know where various foodstuffs are to be found, in what season they are edible, and how to keep oriented in the bush. !Kung women, like their men, pay close attention to animal tracks as they pass through the bush; and they tell the men about recent game movements when they return home in the evening.

The tracks of dangerous animals, particularly snakes, but also big cats and elephants, are immediately noted; and women will sometimes change their course to avoid an unwelcome encounter. When I began accompanying the gathering trips, I learned quickly to follow someone's exact footsteps rather than to walk alongside the women who themselves sometimes walked abreast. This was after several occasions when a woman had showed me a snake lying only a few steps away—a snake which my untrained eye never could have spotted. On each occasion my informant knew the name of the snake, whether or not it was dangerous, and enough of its habits to know whether it would be aroused by our nearness. All such bush skills must take years to consolidate before an individual can subsist effectively in the bush.

Other contributors to this volume have mentioned that one justification for studying the !Kung is that they are relatively pure hunter-gatherers living in an ancient territory, and they in many ways may be typical of South African hunter-gatherers in Paleolithic times. It is interesting to consider the factors I have described and to speculate how typical they may be of hunter-gatherers in general—how factors of small group size, mobility, simple technology can affect the interaction of children with adults and the nature of their training in childhood.

10 Maternal Care, Infant Behavior and Development among the !Kung

Melvin J. Konner

A man laughing with an infant

At the time this study was conceived, infancy had become a major focus of interest for psychologists (Kessen et al. 1970), ethologists (Hinde and Spencer-Booth 1968), and students of the evolution of behavior (Bowlby 1969). Draper's excellent work on !Kung childhood (Chapter 9) was beginning to produce some interesting results pertaining to infancy, but was to focus ultimately on the effects of subsistence ecology on later childhood. So it seemed wise to plan a specific study of infancy as part of the long-range Harvard project.[1] Like other aspects of the expedition, this study suggested itself with a certain amount of urgency. Hunter-gatherer life did not seem destined for a lengthy future, and with it would pass an important chapter in our knowledge of human infancy, especially of the evolution of human infancy. That is, its importance lay not mainly in its uniqueness as an ethnological variety, but in its position as representative of a group of societies resembling, in their basic subsistence ecology, the original human sociocultural form.

The study of infancy was carried out over twenty months between 1969 and 1971 in the !Kangwa, Dobe, and /Du/da areas of northwestern Botswana. It was made technically possible only by the context of the larger expedition, since an infant study cannot be carried out without a secure rapport with the community, or without exact ages for the infants. The ages were available from the basic demographic work of Howell, Lee, and Draper; and the rapport, thanks to all the previous expedition participants, was excellent.

A preliminary descriptive account of !Kung infancy (Konner 1972b) has appeared; as well as a theoretical treatment of its meaning for an overview of the evolution of attachment, especially Bowlby's theory of attachment (DeVore and Konner 1974); and a study of sex differences in the behavior of two- to five-year olds (Blurton Jones and Konner 1973). The present chapter attempts a more quantitative presentation of some test data, and extends the earlier theoretical perspective in terms of quantified new data.

There are several reasons for taking an interest in !Kung infancy, in terms of behavioral science strategy. One is that, like any cross-cultural research, it broadens the variability available to us for study. It has the effect of giving us more variance with which to address any theoretical issue; and occasionally, it may disabuse us of false notions, explicit or tacit, of the universality of some western infant behavior or caretaking procedures. Unlike, however, most cross-cultural research, it adds a temporal or evolutionary and (potentially) causal dimension to the extent that we can guess, by extrapolation from modern hunter-gatherers, what adaptations in infant care and development must have characterized *ancestral* populations of

220

hunter-gatherers. That is, we reason from what we know of hunter-gatherer sociobiology and subsistence ecology and how it appears to affect infancy. Finally, it gives us leads, to be checked in an appropriately broad cross-cultural context, on possible universal features of human infant care, infant behavior, and development. This, in turn, gives us a basis for cross-species comparisons.

By way of introduction to the material to follow, three general features of the social context of !Kung infancy should be emphasized. First, the !Kung mother-infant bond is close, of long duration, and characterized by general indulgence of infant demands while remaining low in restriction of infant operations. Second, this relation rests in a very dense social context. The mother-infant pair is typically in constant contact with other adults (relatives and friends). This is in marked contrast to the relative isolation of American mothers, and probably goes a long way toward making the very indulgent !Kung pattern emotionally *possible* for mothers. Third, the infant graduates from his strong attachment to his mother to an attachment to a multiaged child group. This transition begins at the end of the first year and is largely complete several months after the birth of the next sibling, usually at age three or four. It is important to note that this child group is *not* a peer group (see also Draper 1972a). Indeed, given the demographic limitations of foraging subsistence, the likelihood that there would ordinarily be enough children of the same age at the same place at the same time to *form* a peer group is very slender. Multiaged groups have the following implications: 1) older children in the group will discharge many caretaking functions of the mother and father, thus largely obviating the need for parental vigilance after age three or four; 2) the infant's transition from interaction with parents to interaction with children is facilitated by the fact that much of the behavioral equipment he already has for social relations, exercised in relation to adults, is also appropriate in relation to older children, whereas the behavior would not work so well with peers; 3) cultural transmission in general can be carried out more on child-to-child basis, as opposed to adult-to-child only; 4) the acquisition of caretaking behaviors themselves is greatly facilitated by older children's experience with infants in these groups.

Typical Infant Positions and the Infant Sling

From the earliest days of life and throughout the first year, three positions characterize infant posture: 1) awake, held sitting or held

Newborn, older sister and mother

222

standing in the lap of the mother or other caretaker (since there are no chairs, adults are typically sitting on the ground); 2) awake or asleep, in the infant sling at the mother's side; 3) asleep, lying on a cloth on the ground beside the mother. Later, sitting on the ground beside the mother is added to these three. Infants are rarely permitted to lie down while awake. Mothers consider that this is bad for infants and that it retards motor development. (This is the opposite of the folk belief in the northeastern United States where grandparents, at any rate, say that vertical posture is bad, at least for very young infants. Hence, presumably, the American parental practice of laying babies down most of the time.)

The sling merits specific description because it differs in important ways from carrying devices in many other nontechnological societies, and from all the carrying devices now acquiring some commercial success in the northeastern United States. It is maximally nonrestrictive, leaving the arms and legs moving freely. It allows constant skin-to-skin contact between mother and infant. And it keeps the infant on the mother's side (hip) rather than on her back or front. The side position has the following noteworthy features: 1) the infant sees what the mother sees, thus sharing her view of the social world and the world of objects, especially a close view of work in the mother's hands and eye-level contact with children, who take considerable interest in babies; 2) the infant has constant access to the mother's breasts, which are uncovered, and after the development of visually directed reaching feeds himself whenever he likes (more or less continually); 3) the infant has constant access to cosmetic and decorative objects hanging around the mother's neck, and often occupies himself in playing with them. These objects appear to function for the infant as do objects hung in American cribs. This is important because the latter have been shown to significantly accelerate sensorimotor development during the first six months (White and Held 1967). (See Figure 10.1 for nursing data.)

Infant's Physical Contact with Mother and Other Caretakers

The extent of physical contact between the infant and mother during the first two years is shown in Figure 10.2. The graph shows passive physical contact only, excluding active touching of the mother by the infant (unless passive touching is going on at the same time) in order to reflect a more stable aspect of mother-infant contact without the infant's actual initiative playing the dominant role.

The sample in this graph consists of 31 babies ranging in age from one to 94 weeks, each observed at from one to four age-points for a total of 54 age-points. The data are drawn from three spot observations per infant per age-point. Each spot observation was done as the observer approached the mother-infant pair for the purpose of doing longer timed observations. The spot observation, a brief note of the juxtaposition and activity of mother and infant, was made immediately upon entering the village-camp and before the mother or infant noted the observer's presence. The observations were not formally randomized either with respect to time of day or order of mother-infant pairs. The latter is unlikely to have affected the data since there was typically only one mother-infant pair per village-camp. All daylight hours are represented though the earliest are under-represented. The data should therefore offer a fairly pure index of mother-infant contact under natural conditions.

The proportions of observations per age-point per child for which there was passive physical contact were averaged over arbitrary age groupings to give the dots on the solid-line portion of the graph (males and females separately). Each dot represents from two to eight infants at from four to nine age-points.

Figure 10.1. Percentage of infants and children nursing at time of contact, by age and sex groups. Cross-sectional data. Sex difference not significant.

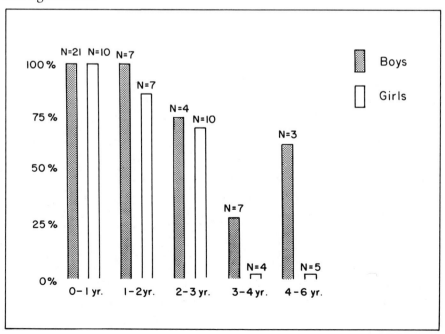

The data indicate a gradual decline in passive physical contact from a high of about 70 percent in the first months to about 30 percent in the middle of the second year. There is also a nonsignificant divergence of the sexes after about twenty weeks, with the females having more passive physical contact than the males.

Other data (Blurton Jones and Konner 1973) from observations of two- to five-year-old !Kung children in the same study area show that girls are more likely than boys to be passively touching, or within two feet of the mother, and suggests that the sex difference in infancy persists (as measured by the Mann-Whitney U test, p < 0.05). Draper's (1972a) study of the behavior of !Kung children of all ages shows tendencies for girls to be more in the presence of adults, more in the immediate village-camp vicinity, and less in contexts where there were only children than was the case for boys.

The dotted line graph in the lower left of Figure 10.2 is an effort to present some sort of comparison from already published data on English and American infants. The first star on the graph represents one eight-day-old infant studied by Richards and Bernal (1972) in Cambridge, England. They published a twenty-four-hour diary kept

Figure 10.2. Amount of passive physical contact with the mother. Straight lines, !Kung infants. Dotted line, American and English data from other studies. R-H and R-I, home and institution reared infants in North Carolina, Rheingold study (1960). T, Tulkin (1970). R&B, Richards and Bernal (1972).

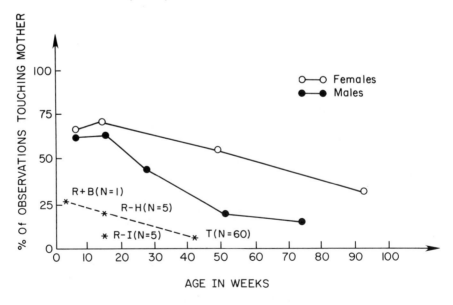

for this infant by its mother as typical of their much larger sample. The percentage noted includes all time spent out of the cot, either being fed or being bathed, as a proportion of total waking time. The next group of infants is drawn from Rheingold's study, done in North Carolina (Rheingold 1960), comparing home-reared and institution-reared infants (three and one-half months old). These data are from observations rather than diaries (one instantaneous observation every fifteen seconds for several hours). Again, the percentages include all time the infant was held, plus basinette time, on the theory that infant bathing may be a parental effort to establish contact in a culture where "purposeless" physical contact is largely unacceptable. The ten-month data are from Tulkin's study of social class differences in infant girls in Boston (Tulkin 1970; Tulkin and Kagan 1972). The data, from timed-sequence observations, show no class differences in physical contact, so the sixty subjects were pooled to form the proportion.

Both the !Kung and the admittedly makeshift "western" curve show declining physical-contact with age, the total amount of physical contact being very much greater for the !Kung infants. Note especially that the order of magnitude of the difference, in the Rheingold study, between the home-reared infants is small compared with the difference between normally reared American and !Kung infants. If orphanage infants in North Carolina are "deprived" of physical contact as compared with infants living at home in the same area, then normally reared infants would appear to be similarly "deprived" as compared with !Kung infants.

Whether this sort of statement makes any sense will depend upon studies of the consequences of different degrees of early physical contact which have yet to be done. Several facts, however, point to the importance of this issue. 1) American child-training practice (middle-class, as of 1940) is found to be low in the indulgence of dependency (which would include physical contact in infancy) as compared with a worldwide ethnographic range (Whiting and Child 1953). 2) Whiting (1971) in a recent cross-cultural study of mother-infant physical contact found it to be directly correlated with mean annual temperature. Since man evolved in a context of tropical hunting and gathering, the likelihood is that the !Kung pattern of high mother-infant physical contact characterizes human populations during the Pleistocene. 3) Laboratory studies of macaques (*Macaca mulatta:* Hinde and Spencer-Booth 1968; *Macaca nemestrina:* Jensen et al. 1968) show a curve of mother-infant physical contact starting at close to 100 percent, declining to 50 percent during the first fifteen weeks, and thereafter declining much more gradually until the end of the first year. Apart from the greater amount of contact for the first few weeks, the curve is similar to the !Kung curve. Even though these are laboratory curves, Hinde and Spencer-Booth show that the presence or absence of social context does not alter the pattern drastically. DeVore (1963) and Jay (1963) describe mother-infant relations in free-ranging baboons and langurs, and their data indicate high physical contact as well. The research in general indicates that high mother-infant physical contact is a basic higher primate pattern. The !Kung infant data together with the Whiting (1971) study suggest that man did not evolve away from this pattern, at least not to the extent of the major departure exhibited by Western infant care, until the tropical hunting and gathering mode of subsistence was left behind.

Contact with Other Persons

Figure 10.3, based on the same spot observations collected as described above, shows passive physical contact with anyone, including the mother. This makes the earlier part of the contact curve even more similar to the laboratory monkey curve, although the latter is for mothers only. Wild monkey species are known to vary

Figure 10.3. Amount of passive physical contact with anyone, including mother.

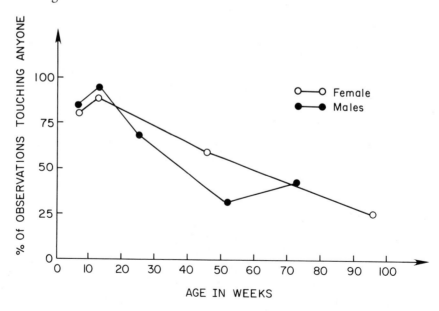

in the extent to which contact between infants and other individuals is permitted by mothers (Lancaster 1971), but descriptions of some, Lancaster's own vervets (*Cercopithecus aethiops*), for example, suggest that two graphs corresponding to Figure 10.1 and Figure 10.2 would make vervets and humans seem very similar.

Figure 10.4 shows an analysis by age of infants of any sort of participation by older children in the course of an infant observation. These are not spot observations but 15-minute timed-sequence observations, 6 per age-point per infant. In these, the observer's presence was known to those being observed. Other sampling characteristics are as described for Figure 10.2 above.

Girls play more with infants of both sexes than do boys. There also appears to be a same-sex preference operating so that girls play more with girl infants, and boys play more with boy infants. These two factors together would explain the graph. It should be noted that the Y-axis does not necessarily reflect the amount of time the infant spent with the child or the number of interactions but only the number of children involved with the infant per 15-minute observations.

Figure 10.4. Mean number of children of either sex appearing in 15-minute observations of infants, female and male.

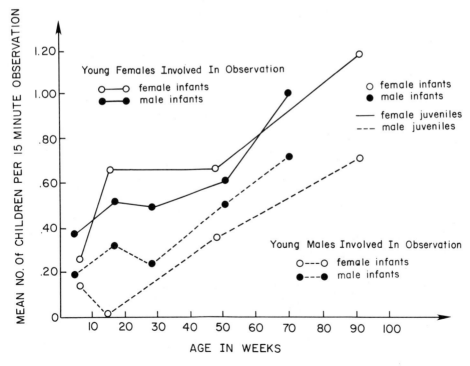

Data from observations of two-to-five-year-olds in London and among the !Kung, conducted by Blurton Jones and myself, show that English children in this age group are more likely to be face-to-face with the mother than are !Kung children (Mann-Whitney U test; girls p < 0.02; boys, p < 0.002) and less likely to be face-to-face with other children (girls, p < 0.02; boys, p < 0.10). This finding suggests that despite early intensive contact between !Kung mothers and infants, these infants do not become excessively attached toddlers or children. The maximum number of feet from the mother during the hour of observation is greater for !Kung than for English children (girls p < 0.10; boys p < 0.02), and there is no difference between the cultures in the amount of time touching or within two feet of the mother. If anything there is a suggestion that English children in this age group are more concerned with their mothers than are !Kung children, and independently recorded facial expression data (Blurton Jones, personal communication) support this tendency.

To summarize: while !Kung infants have very much more physical contact with their mothers than do English and American children, they also have a good deal of social contact with others. Although they face a difficult and often depressed separation experience at the time of weaning and the birth of a sibling (around age three or four, see Shostak, Chapter 11), they eventually adjust to this separation, and become closely involved with the multiaged child group which becomes the focus of their social interest.

Neuromotor Maturation and Neuromotor Learning

As part of an effort to assess as many different aspects of infant development as feasible, neuromotor development tests were administered. A neurological assessment schedule for infants up to ten days of age (Prechtl and Beintema 1964) was administered to ten infants. For older infants, a neuromotor development schedule based on the work of McGraw (1963) was used (Richards and Bernal MS). That this test has the advantage of more elaborate and detailed descriptions of motor behavior and stages than is usual in other infant tests should improve one's confidence in comparisons of samples assessed by different investigators.

Figures 10.5–10.9 show the results of such a comparison between the sample of !Kung infants and the original McGraw (1963) sample on the age of attainment of one phase of sitting, one phase of the assumption of erect posture, and three phases of erect locomotion, respectively. In each case the Y-axis shows the proportion of infants tested who give phase-appropriate behavior; the X-axis shows age in days.

The !Kung sample consists of twenty-one infants tested mainly cross-sectionally at various ages, though with some semilongitudinal data mixed in. The McGraw sample is a larger and completely longitudinal one tested weekly and thus monitored much more closely than the !Kung sample, some of whom were tested only once, while others were tested two to four times a month or two months apart. This would mean that the entry of one of McGraw's infants into a phase would have been noted within one week of its occurrence, whereas a !Kung infant's entry into a phase might be noted only a month or more later. This would tend to bias the data so as to make the McGraw American sample appear to attain phases earlier, relative to the !Kung sample, than they actually do.

In spite of this bias, in three of the five graphs, the !Kung infants are performing in phase earlier than the American infants. The dots on the !Kung solid line graphs are percentages of groups of infants whose ages fall within 100-day blocks. The stars on the McGraw graph are percentages of infants all actually at the specific age indicated.

Figure 10.5 shows the attainment of the phase of sitting characterized by the ability to maintain an erect sitting posture without

Figure 10.5. Attainment of independent sitting in !Kung infants, compared with McGraw (1963) data. For description of phase (F) see text.

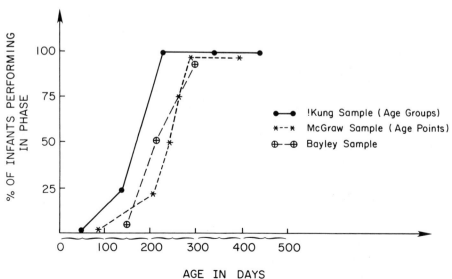

230

support from the arms. Figure 10.6 shows the attainment of the rising phase characterized by the ability, in the testing situation, to rise from the supine position on the ground, without assistance and without holding on to anything, to the erect standing position. Figure 10.7 shows the highest phase of walking, characterized by "synchronous arm-swinging with associated opposite leg movement." Compared with the behaviors shown in the other four graphs, this behavior is less dramatic and probably less reliable from one observer to another. In consequence, one might want to be more skeptical about the comparison between the two studies in this instance than in the other four. Figures 10.8 and 10.9 show the phases of walking with both hands held, and initial walking without assistance but without heel-toe progression or synchronous arm movements, respectively. These latter two graphs show descending as well as ascending segments because they do not represent the highest stage of a given locomotor development sequence, and so show infants passing out of the phase as well as into it.

While Figures 10.5–10.7 indicate a clear motor advancement of !Kung infants compared with American infants, Figure 10.8 shows no difference and Figure 10.9 shows a slight reversal of this effect. The Bayley age norm (including both black and white American

Figure 10.6. Attainment of independent rising from lying to standing in !Kung infants, compared with McGraw (1963) data. For description of phase (F) and sampling see text.

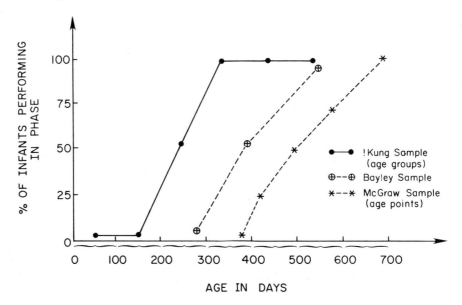

infants, Bayley 1969) for independent walking is shown on Figure 10.9 to indicate that the McGraw sample may be walking a bit earlier than the American norm, assuming that McGraw and Bayley were looking at the same thing. On the whole, considering that the procedures biased the data in favor of the McGraw longitudinal sample, it seems reasonable to conclude that !Kung infants are advanced in motor development in general as compared with their American counterparts.

The question of why this is so is a very complicated one. The precocity of African infants in motor performance as they develop (though not at birth) is a well-accepted phenomenon (LeVine 1970); and Warren's (1972) cogent critique of the research, although it points to the need for more careful work in this area, does not convincingly dispel one's belief in the phenomenon.

The first explanation that comes to mind, of course, is that the genetic basis of the developmental rates exhibit some sort of racial polymorphism. One would expect, if this were so, to find differences at birth. While one well-known study has found such differences (Geber and Dean 1967), its methodology has been heavily criticized (Warren 1972). Warren's restudy of the same Ugandan population failed to find evidence of precocity at birth, and Geber's own study of African newborns in Zambia (T.B. Brazelton, personal communi-

Figure 10.7. Attainment of highest phase of independent walking in !Kung infants, compared with McGraw data (1963). For description of phase (G) and sampling see text.

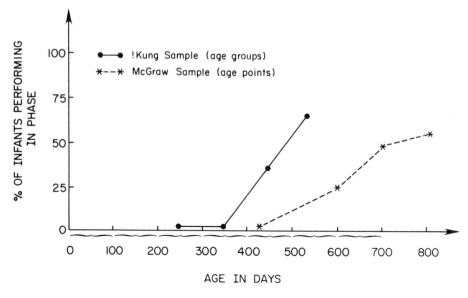

cation) also failed to find evidence of precocity. Infants of the
!Kung, who are considered racially distinct from these other African
populations, likewise do not give evidence of perinatal precocity.
(These findings are described in somewhat greater detail in Konner
1972b.)

232

While the absence of differences at birth makes the existence of
genetic differences less likely, it is still possible for postnatally
emerging differences in developmental rate to be genetically based.
Before reaching this conclusion, however, one would want to rule
out the possibility of environmental influence. It was the opinion of
Ainsworth (1967) that the precocity of her and (Geber's) Ugandan
infants in the first two years resulted from the exercise and stimulation of unrestricted freedom of movement and from being held all
the time.

Though the question of how much these neuromotor developmental rates are subject to environmental influence and learning has
been a controversial one, Zelazo and his associates (1972) have
demonstrated indisputably that exercise of the placing and walking
reflexes of the newborn for only twelve minutes a day during the
first eight weeks not only greatly increases the response rate for these
reflexes, but also accelerates the attainment of walking alone by
from six weeks to two months as compared with different groups of

Figure 10.8. Attainment of walking with hands held in !Kung infants, compared with McGraw data (1963). For description of phase
(D) and sampling see text.

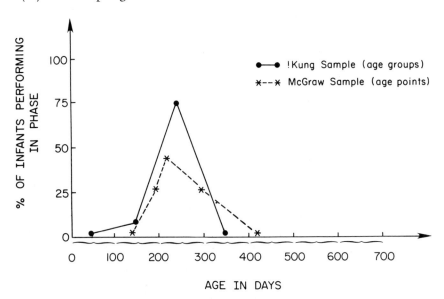

controls. Passive exercise of the legs also has an accelerating effect, but one significantly smaller than that of active exercise.

The Zelazo finding strongly suggests that neuromotor maturation of the !Kung infants may be accelerated by their exceptional amount of experience in the vertical position, since they are held sitting and held standing from the earliest weeks throughout infancy. While the age of independent walking itself is not accelerated, neither is the walking reflex at birth specifically exercised. Perhaps, as Zelazo (personal communication) has suggested, the marked acceleration of the age of walking alone depends on exercise of the centrally organized mechanism of walking, rather than just muscle exercise. This would help explain why !Kung infants walking alone at the same age as their American counterparts reach the mature phase of walking (synchronous arm-swinging) earlier. Once the central mechanism emerges, the months of previous muscle exercise then greatly shorten the clumsy-walking phase and accelerate the attainment of mature walking.

Another factor which demands attention is the !Kung parental attitude toward motor development. This attitude was among many aspects of parental belief studied in child behavior seminars[2] held with various groups of !Kung men and women. Although their be-

Figure 10.9. Attainment of first phase of independent walking in !Kung infants, compared with McGraw (1963) data and Bayley (1969) norm. For description of phase (E) and sampling see text.

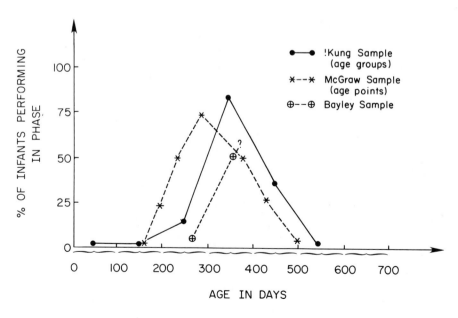

234

lief about most aspects of development involves a sort of cognitive-alimentation-adaptation view (the child plays and tries to do it and teaches himself) with some basis in maturation for the behavior, they do not believe in the maturation of motor milestones. They insist that a child not taught to sit, crawl, stand, and walk will never perform these behaviors (even as late as age three) because the bones of his back will be "soft" and "not tightened together." So they go through a training routine for each of these behaviors. Infants too young to sit are propped in front of their mothers in the sand with a wall of sand around their buttocks to support them. When they fall, they are propped up again. Incipient walkers are lured with bits of food to push the limits of their ability. And so on.

In general, it seems reasonable to accept the explanation of environmental influence for the partial precocity of !Kung infants. In view of recent evidence for the lability of these developmental systems, it would be wise to investigate this possibility in all cases of population differences in motor development rates. The burden of proof seems to have shifted to those who believe these differences are genetically based. They will have to either 1) show conclusively that there are population differences in motor capacity at birth, and that these are not the result of differences in prenatal care, maternal nutrition, or perinatal insult or 2) show that there are population differences in postnatal development rates where there are no differences in aspects of parental care and experience which are likely to affect these rates.

Cognitive Development in Early Infancy

In an effort to assess some dimensions of mental or cognitive development, data were collected by means of the Einstein Scales of Sensori-motor Development (Corman and Escalona 1970; Escalona et al. 1969), based on the infant studies and sensorimotor development theory of Piaget (1954; 1962). Only the results from the Prehension Scale, for infants in the first six months, have been analyzed so far. These results are presented in Figure 10.10.

The scale is ordered into stages, each consisting of several items all believed to reflect the same level of cognitive maturity. The scalability of the items, that is, the consistency of clustering within the stages, has been demonstrated for a sample of American infants (Corman and Escalona 1970). It was our impression that the clustering is very similar for !Kung infants, but our sample (18 infants in all, from 5 to 8 per stage) is not sufficiently large or sufficiently longitudinal for a numerical demonstration of clustering. Strictly speaking, this is a flaw in the comparison.

The graph in Figure 10.10 shows the four-stage levels of prehension discontinuously along the Y-axis, and age on the X-axis. Each !Kung infant performing at a stage level is represented by a dot. The rest of the data represented are from Corman and Escalona's (1970) fully presented results on their longitudinal American pilot sample (14 infants). For the American infants the median and mean age of entry into the stage is shown, as is the mean and range of ages of all infants in the stage, whether having just entered or on the verge of "graduating." It is the latter measure which is most appropriate for the comparison with !Kung infants because, again, the American infants are closely monitored while the !Kung infants are "catch as catch can," and therefore most likely to be in mid-stage.

Important items in the various stages are shown in Table 10.1. According to the instructions in the manual (Escalona et al 1970), infants are scored as performing in stage if they make two or more separate responses appropriate to the stage, or if they make one response on two or more separate trials. There were two observers,

Figure 10.10. Prehension scale, Einstein scales of sensorimotor development. Y-axis, discontinuous graph of four stages of sensorimotor development in the first six months. Points are !Kung infants. Other data are from Corman and Escalona (MS) sample. For description of scale see Table 10.1. For sample description see text.

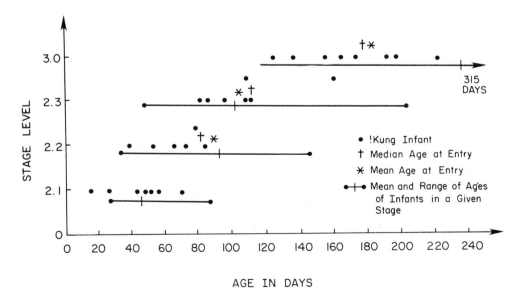

and both had to agree that a response had been made before it could be scored. The ages of the !Kung infants in a stage on the graph are compared with the midpoints, for individual American infants, between age at entry and age at leaving the stage, using the Mann-Whitney U test (two tailed). The !Kung infants are younger than the American midpoint ages for Stage 3 ($p = 0.002$) and Stage 2.3 ($p < 0.002$) and younger than the American age at entry for Stage 2.2 ($p < 0.02$).

Thus the general trend is for !Kung infants to be ahead of American infants in the Corman Escalona sample on these indicators of very early cognitive or sensorimotor development. Clearly these items are not free from the influence of motor maturation. No available test of infant intelligence is (although Tulkin's [1971] study has made made important progress in this direction). Still, behavior such as

Table 10.1. Prehension scale items administered (brief summary)

(1) Infant touches, rubs, scratches or grasps objects or surfaces. Stage 2.1.
(2) Infant touches, grasps, releases, re-grasps, releases and re-grasps in continuous sequence. Stage 2.1.
(3) Infant brings any portion of his hand to his mouth. Stage 2.1.
(4) Infant touches hands together in any way. Stage 2.1.
(5) Object placed in infant's hand, out of visual field:
    Response 1: After three seconds or more, object is brought to the mouth, without visual regard. Stage 2.1.
    Response 2: As above, but with no delay. Stage 2.2.
    Response 3: Visual regard, three seconds or more, before bringing to mouth. Stage 3.
(6) Object presented visually, infant's hand out of visual field:
    Response 1: Sucking movements or mouthing of hand (3X). while looking at object. Response must begin only after presentation. Stage 2.2.
    Response 2: Energetic arm waving or groping following presentation. Stage 2.3.
    Response 3: Reaching following light touch of infant's hand with object. Stage 2.3.
    Response 4: Hand to mouth followed by reaching and touching object. Stage 2.3.
    Response 5: Coordinated reach and grasp. Stage 2.4.
(7) Object presented visually, infant's hand in visual field:
    Response 1: Infant looks alternately at object and at hand. At least four shifts in focus. Stage 2.3.
    Response 2: Infant reaches for and contacts object. Stage 2.3.
(8) Hand regard:
    Response 1: Transient but repeated hand regard. Stage 2.1.
    Response 2: Longer continuous regard, at least four seconds. Stage 2.2.
(9) Infant's hand grasped and restrained by examiner, out of infant's visual field (twice with each hand):
    Response 1: Infant tries to free hand, without visual regard. Stage 2.2.
    Response 2: Infant turns to look at hand and/or face of examiner. Stage 2.3.
(10) An object is placed in infant's mouth. Infant brings one or both hands to object as if holding at his mouth. Stage 2.2
(11) Infant transfers object from one hand to the other with visual regard. Stage 3.
(12) Sustained shaking of rattle while facial expression and movement indicate attentiveness to sound. Three separate occasions. Stage 3.

the Stage 3 items "shakes rattle with regard to sound" and "transfers object from hand to hand with visual regard" have as their crucial features not motor adeptness but the mutual articulation of two separate sensorimotor systems (or schemata) reflecting, presumably, the maturation of some central organizing mechanism. It seems reasonable to suggest that !Kung infants are advanced with respect to a cognitive development factor (in the first six months) which is separate and distinct from their advanced neuromotor maturation.

In attempting to explain this difference, one thinks first of environmental enrichment, since many studies (e.g., Robinson and Robinson 1971; Fowler 1972) have now shown that social and environmental enrichment significantly enhances the cognitive development of infants. Figures 10.2 and 10.3 above indicate that infants are getting very considerable social stimulation in the first months, both from the mother and from other individuals. White and Held (1967) have shown that one aspect of sensorimotor development, the growth of visually directed reaching, can be accelerated significantly by the presence of hanging objects in the infant's crib. Observations suggest that cosmetic and decorative objects hanging around the !Kung mother's neck within reach of the infant on her lap or in the sling serve much the same function as the White and Held crib mobiles.

One final factor deserves mention in relation to this cognitive advancement: the fact that !Kung infants have much more experience in the vertical position than do their American counterparts. Vertical and horizontal positions have very different effects on levels of alertness, particularly in early infancy. A number of investigators of infant cognition (Bruner 1968; Bower et al. 1970) have found that positioning young infants (who cannot as yet sit) in a vertical or semivertical posture in an infant seat improves their performance on cognitive tasks. Vertical posture is also linked to a phenomenon known as the "orthostatic pressor reflex." This homeostatic reflex, present in most mammals, is a response to vertical positioning which activates the sympathetic nervous system. The adrenal medulla, part of the sympathetic nervous system, produces epinephrine which causes arousal and which may facilitate the cognitive process.

Vertical posture is well known as a soothing device for crying infants (Oken and Heath 1963), including newborns (Korner and Grobstein 1966). Korner and Grobstein demonstrated that eye-opening and visual scanning occurred more frequently ($p < 0.01$) in newborns held upright against the shoulder than in controls. The combined stimuli of this experimental treatment would be quite similar to those present for the !Kung infant in the sling. One would predict, on this basis, more visual scanning in !Kung infants than in American and other Western infants. Korner and Thoman (1970; Korner 1972) extended these experiments, finding that of six interventions in crying newborn infants "vestibular stimulation had a far more powerful effect in evoking visual alertness than did contact" (Korner 1972, p. 90) and that raising the infant in an infant seat to the vertical position, without contact, was effective, although it was not as effective as the same intervention with contact. In sleeping newborns "the only two interventions which elicited any visual activity were interventions entailing vestibular stimulation and the upright position" (Korner 1972, p. 91). Referring to Humphrey (1965) and Langworthy (1933), Korner reasons that the vestibular system is a likely principal mediator of early stimulation effects because it is one of the earliest myelinated (beginning at four months gestational age) and is fully mature at birth.

In another study, unrelated to infant posture, White and Castle (1964) showed that twenty minutes of additional physical handling per day increased the amount of visual exploration in infants observed after thirty days of such handling (beginning at one week of age). While this treatment did not significantly affect sensorimotor test performance, the authors hypothesized that "increased visual attentiveness together with increased mobility in an enriched environment should constitute the optimal circumstances for visual-motor development." These are essentially the conditions experienced by !Kung infants. Korner would probably argue that the key independent variable in the handling here was vestibular stimulation rather than contact. The important point here would seem to be that all the candidates for "key variable" in these studies—vestibular stimulation, upright posture, and physical contact—have some effect on attentiveness, at least in crying infants. All are almost continuously present in the !Kung infant's stimulus envelope, whether in the sling or on the lap of the mother or other caretakers.

Comparative Data: Density of Social Context and the Course of Mother-Infant Interactions

The notion that density of social context may regulate the degree of maternal indulgence of infant dependent demands (and/or the extent of dependent demands) is supported by laboratory studies of three primate species (Hinde and Spencer-Booth 1967; Kaplan 1972; Kaplan and Schusterman 1972; Wolfheim, Jensen, and Bobbitt

1970). Hinde and Spencer-Booth observed mother-infant pairs of rhesus monkeys (*Macaca mulatta*) longitudinally with or without the long-term presence of other animals. In isolate pairs, they found that mothers avoided and left infants more, although infants approached and followed more, than in group-living pairs. Isolate pairs were more frequently physically separated than group-living pairs. The amount of time spent more than two feet from the mother, expressed as a proportion of total time off the mother, showed the following developmental course: for the first ten weeks, isolates more; from eleven weeks on, group-living more. This may suggest that when infants are still motorically immature, and have little control over this distance, isolate mothers will maximize it. When locomotor facility emerges (eight to seventeen weeks), isolate infants can minimize the distance, subverting their mothers' attempts to escape them. Finally, isolate mothers tended to carry infants on their backs rather than in the ventral position during transport, after the infants climbed on them from behind, instead of from in front, as was more common in group-living infants.

In Kaplan's (1972) similar study of squirrel monkeys (*Saimiri sciureus*), mothers in isolated pairs avoided and punished their infants more and retrieved them less than mothers in group-living pairs; and isolate-pair infants made more attempts to play with mothers and stayed closer to them, although (at least at some ages) group-living infants nursed more. Grooming and looking at infants, likely indicators of maternal concern, were done more by group-living mothers. Thus the pattern, for isolate pairs, of greater infant dependent demands with lower maternal indulgence of them, resembles that found for rhesus monkeys. One anomalous finding was that group-living mothers make more attempts to shake off their infants. This could conceivably arise from their greater frequency of nursing, at least at some ages.

Wolfheim, Jensen, and Bobbitt (1970) found a similar pattern in pigtailed monkeys (*Macaca nemestrina*). Mothers in group-living pairs (infants age fourteen to fifteen weeks) were more retentive, spent more time in ventral contact with their infants, and nursed more than mothers in isolate pairs. Data from later ages were not presented. The authors interpret this in terms of protectiveness of infants who may come to harm from other group members. Hinde and Spencer-Booth interpret their data similarly, and this seems a plausible explanation. However, Kaplan's explanation that isolate mothers are under so much steady pressure from the infant that they are not inclined to indulge them ("familiarity breeds contempt") seems equally plausible. Hinde and Spencer-Booth (1971) summarize the effect as follows:

> . . . the infant's relations with its mother are affected by the other females present, for infants living alone with their mothers were off them more and went to a distance from them more, than did infants with group companions present. Since the infants living alone with their mothers were rejected more and played a larger role in maintaining proximity with their mothers, the difference was primarily due to the mothers. (p. 113)

This is the view most pertinent to the human data.

Two cross-cultural studies of human groups take a similar view. Whiting (1971), in a study of fifty-five societies, found that "the degree of infant indulgence is roughly proportional to the number of adults living in the household" (p. 358). The percentage of societies with high infant indulgence, according to family type, is: extended, 87; polygynous, 83; nuclear, 42; mother-child, 25. Minturn and colleagues (B. Whiting 1964), in a more detailed and thorough study of six cultures, found the operationally derived clusters "maternal warmth" and "maternal emotional stability" in relation to children to be correlated with the number of adults in the household (see especially chapters 2, 3, and 17). This relation holds both within and among the six cultures.

A comparison between !Kung and American or English early childhood would seem to be analogous in some respects to the laboratory and cross-cultural comparisons above. Roughly speaking, the situation of the !Kung mother-infant pair in the band context resembles that of the group-living monkey pairs, while the Western middle-class mother and infant, alone together much of the time, resemble the isolated monkey pairs. Exhibiting high physical contact and frequent nursing in the first two years, !Kung mother-infant relations seem to produce, nonetheless, two- to five-year-olds who, in familiar group contexts, interact less with their mothers and more with other children as compared with English two- to five-year-olds (see above), and also tend to go a greater maximum distance from their mothers (boys, $p < 0.01$; girls, n.s., $p < 0.10$). This cultural difference in developmental course parallels the greater initial indulgence of the group-living mothers and the developmental course of proximity to the mother in rhesus monkeys.

Two other parallels are of interest. A subsequent experiment with the same squirrel monkeys (Kaplan and Schusterman 1972), placing the infants in a choice situation so that they could either be near their mothers, a strange adult female, a strange infant, or an empty cage, revealed that the group-reared infants showed a greater preference for their own mothers than did the isolate-pair infants. The authors interpret this as indicating "preference" and the "closeness" of the relationship. To view it another way, the "choice" situation in the experiment is extremely frightening to the infants, given the authors' description of their behavior. It may simply be more frightening to the more indulged group-reared infants, just as fearfulness in !Kung infants is greater than that in American infants (Konner 1972b).

Finally, Hinde and Spencer-Booth (1967) found that locomotor milestones and certain aspects of sensorimotor development (corresponding to several behaviors in Items 5 and 6 of Table 10.1) appear earlier in infants from group-living as opposed to isolate pairs, just as !Kung sensorimotor development is advanced relative to American.

To summarize, the theory proposed to account for the developmental course of attachment found in these data is as follows. The dense social context by providing ample alternative stimulation for both mother and infant improves the likelihood that mothers will accept the dependent demands of infants. Paradoxically, this results in decreased proximity seeking and other dependent demands at later ages, except in intensely fear-provoking situations. This proposed relationship between early indulgence of dependency and later reduced dependency runs so contrary to classical notions of reinforcement and even common sense that even with convincing evidence it is difficult to accept.

But a major recent review of the attachment literature (Maccoby and Masters 1970) found this relationship to be confirmed by almost all the studies of human children which raised this question (p. 140).

Some theoretical adjustment to these data seems in order. An ordinary reinforcement model would predict that indulgence of dependency, that is, reward of dependent behaviors with satisfaction of the infant's needs, would increase the incidence of the behaviors. Actually the reverse is the case.

In Ainsworth, Bell, and Stayton's (1972) longitudinal study of infant attachment, infant crying and maternal response to crying were unrelated in the first three months, but lack of maternal response in the first quarter was related to infant crying duration and frequency in the second quarter (episodes ignored by mother vs crying frequency: $r = 0.56$, $p < 0.01$; mother's unresponsiveness vs crying duration: $r = 0.45$, $p < 0.01$). The same relationships obtained between quarters two and three and quarters three and four. This is the opposite of the effect predicted by the "spoiling" theory (e.g., Spock 1968, Section 300).

242

If we assume, as Bowlby (1969) has tried to show, that attachment behaviors are part of the normal biological functioning of the infant—instinctual, if you will—and thus difficult to extinguish without drastically disrupting the basic homeostasis of the organism, the data begin to make more sense. Attachment behaviors are not randomly occurring operants. Some, at least, such as crying and contact seeking, are behavioral manifestations of organismic distress. They cannot be extinguished by ignoring them any more than shivering in response to cold can be extinguished by ignoring it. Ignoring them simply increases the distress and so increases the manifestations of the distress.

Ainsworth, Bell, and Stayton (1972) suggest that mothers who respond promptly are reinforcing manifestations of distress which occur at progressively lower arousal levels. In other words, infants who come to feel confident of their mothers' basic responsiveness will come to signal their needs less dramatically, while infants with less responsive mothers will habitually proceed directly to higher arousal level manifestations. This is not only because they have learned that higher levels are necessary (an operant strengthening), but because their mothers' unresponsiveness gives them added cause for distress (a positive feedback cycle).

"Spoiling" theorists might argue that what Ainsworth and her colleagues are comparing are not responsive and unresponsive mothers, but responsive and inconsistent mothers. That is, the unresponsive mothers are ultimately responding, but erratically, thus applying the most effective reinforcement schedule (intermittent reinforcement) to the strengthening of the high arousal-level distress manifestations. The biologically based view would argue that this "inconsistency" is almost inevitable, stemming from the fact that mothers are organisms not well suited to ignoring their offsprings' distress. Some background variables, such as isolation of the mother-infant pair, make them better able to do this. It may be that such conditions in the long perspective of human evolution are in some sense abnormal.

Recommendations such as those of Spock (1968), encouraging maternal unresponsiveness, enhance the impact of these background variables on a mother-infant relationship which has evolved away from maternal indulgence of early dependency since the hunter-gatherer era. Whether proposed as practical solutions to parental annoyance and exhaustion or as "ultimate goods" for the child, these recommendations must be viewed with skepticism by developmental scientists in view of the current available evidence. (Ainsworth, Bell and Stayton's "cry-babies," who had had less responsive

mothers, reached the point where they fussed in greeting the mother
as well [crying when mother leaves vs negative greetings, r = 0.54,
p < .001]. That is, the unresponsive mothers were faced with infants
who began to fret at their mothers' mere appearance. This is not
what mothers are hoping for when they follow Spock's "unspoiling"
advice.)

It is ultimately possible to stop crying by ignoring it. This is what
happens in infants completely separated for long periods from their
mothers after the development of attachment (Ainsworth 1962;
Bowlby 1952). It is described as protest, followed by depression,
followed by a kind of affectless adaptation. There is evidence (works
cited) that such separations are not conducive to optimal mental
health. There is also evidence on the long-term effects of short
separations. In rhesus monkeys (Hinde and Spencer-Booth 1971)
infants who had their mothers separated from them for one or two
six-day periods between twenty and thirty weeks proved, at twelve
months of age, to be significantly more reluctant to enter and stay
in a strange environment than were controls and, at thirty months,
were less active and engaged less in social play and more in nonsocial
manipulative play. Thus even short separations at certain ages can
have significant long-term effects. As for less drastic varieties of
unresponsiveness, such as letting a child cry himself to sleep, or the
relative physical separation characteristic of Western mother-infant
pairs, long-term effects are still unknown.

Evolutionary Considerations: Mother-Infant Contact

Blurton Jones (1972) has analyzed comparative data from a number of mammals on patterns of infant care and concluded that those
in continuous proximity to their young differ from those which
cache or nest their young in certain predictable ways (see also Ben
Shaul 1962). Most important are that the "cachers" feed their young
at widely spaced intervals, have high protein and fat content in their
milk, and have high sucking rates, whereas "carriers" (including
followers) feed more or less continuously, have milk with low protein and fat content, and have low sucking rates. Humans, along
with all other higher primates studied, have the milk composition
and sucking characteristics of continuous proximity or "carrier"
species.

Considering the comparative data on these features in relation to
the hunter-gatherer data on mother-infant contact, it makes sense to

suggest that such contact was close in man during most of human evolution. (!Kung infants are fed more or less continuously.) The data would seem to warrant some investigation of the relationship of spacing of feeds to digestive difficulties in Western infants. However Harlow's (1958) now classic research on deprivation in infant rhesus monkeys clearly demonstrated that in the development of attachment "contact comfort" alone is more important than feeding alone. This suggests that mother-infant physical contact has an importance of its own completely distinct from its relation to the spacing of feeds.

This entire complex of adaptations—milk composition, sucking rate, the need for "contact comfort"—evolved in response to strong selection pressure favoring close mother-infant contact. This pattern is characteristic not only of foraging people, but of higher primates generally, and so must have considerable antiquity. As Bowlby (1969) cogently argues, the danger of infant loss through predation is a part of this selection pressure, especially in an altricial species. Close contact, however, has other selective advantages. It results in an attachment which prevents the newly mobile toddler from getting lost, and produces long-term proximity to adult models of subsistence-related behaviors. It may also reduce the likelihood of contracting illnesses which constitute the major threat to life in infancy. One adaptive risk of strong attachment, the later failure to separate, is probably much reduced in the dense social context characteristic of human foragers, where the mother has the constant company of adults and the infant has the constant attraction of a multiaged child group.

Summary and Conclusion

A number of findings from a study of !Kung infant care, behavior, and development have been presented. Some of these are as follows:

(1) Infants are in physical contact with their mothers or other individuals a very large portion of the time, in keeping with the pattern common to hunter-gatherers and higher primates in general.

(2) Infants are not restricted and have ample social and environmental stimulation and opportunity for self-stimulation.

(3) Infants are held vertical during most of their waking time and receive extensive vestibular stimulation.

(4) The transition away from close mother-infant contact is facilitated by the presence of a multiaged child group which becomes the focus of the child's attachments after a sibling is born.

(5) Infants are advanced compared with American infants in neuromotor development. This is probably attributable to their extensive experience in vertical postures and to conscious training efforts undertaken by their parents.

245

(6) Infants in the first six months are advanced compared with American infants in certain measures of cognitive (sensorimotor) development. This is probably attributable to the unusually high density of social and cognitive stimulation, both generally and in specific relation to behavior tested, in their developmental milieu. Their cognitive development may also be influenced by vertical posture, insofar as the latter appears to facilitate alertness and sensorimotor exercise.

!Kung infant life is far from ideal. Infant mortality is very high (Howell, Chapter 6). In spite of mitigating factors, many infants respond to weaning and the birth of a displacing sibling with a long period of depression, and they may remember this disappointment throughout their lives (Shostak, Chapter 11). However, the general rules are indulgence, stimulation, and nonrestriction.

The data on accelerated neuromotor and cognitive performance must be viewed with caution. Early acceleration of development in African infants has sometimes been found to disappear or even reverse itself after infancy (LeVine 1970). The best explanation for this is the change to a protein-poor diet at weaning, which does not happen for !Kung infants. Still one cannot assume that these early advances are lasting, or that sensorimotor intelligence is related to later intelligence. It has even been argued (Warren MS) that accelerated development may be harmful, since man is an altricial animal needing his long immaturity for learning. This argument, which by a logical extension would constitute a defense of retardation, must be taken with a grain of salt. But much more needs to be known about the long-term effects of specific early experiences and the long-term fate of specific early advances.

The data do show, however, that intensive mother-infant contact and extreme indulgence of infant dependency are not incompatible with adequate neuromotor and cognitive development. They may even encourage it, as Ainsworth (1967) has argued. The data also confirm the lability of developmental systems in relation to early stimulation and learning. Finally, they emphasize two independent variables, vertical posture and vestibular stimulation, which are receiving increasing attention from developmental scientists, and which may prove to have marked effects on infant development.

11   A !Kung Woman's Memories of Childhood

Marjorie Shostak

Girls dancing the springhare dance

The !Kung have engendered a great deal of interest during the past twenty-five years. Research, such as that set forth in this volume, has been done on their social structure, cultural institutions, subsistence ecology, physique, health, and growth, providing a broad base from which to understand the !Kung way of life. The most striking features of the adult society include hunting and gathering, frequent mobility and fluid band structure, lack of privacy, sharing of food and possessions, ample leisure time, the birth of children every three or four years, and a 50 percent mortality before adulthood; childhood is marked by late weaning, multiple caretaking, multiaged play groups, sex play, lack of responsibility throughout adolescence, and occasional early marriage for girls.

All these aspects have been noted and discussed by Western scholars, but how is this way of life experienced by !Kung women and men? How do they perceive their childhoods, their families and friends, death, birth, hunting and gathering as a way of life? How do they feel about themselves? As essential as these questions are, almost no attention had been given them. I wanted to try and find some answers before the acculturation process that has been gradually changing the traditional !Kung way of life, and that of all other known hunting and gathering societies, had progressed so far as to make a search of this kind impossible. Therefore, while in the field from 1969 to 1971, I undertook an exploration of the inner experience of being a !Kung. What follows is a description of how I used the interview technique to approach this problem and a presentation of edited sections from interviews with one woman. Her memories of early childhood and adolescence have been selected for this chapter.

When I first started to live among the !Kung, I hoped to be able to establish informal relationships with several people in which we would exchange feelings about experiences we shared in common and those that were different. As I became fluent in the language, however, I realized this was not possible. Apart from being a foreigner, I was seen as someone with unlimited wealth, who did not freely share her possessions as they did (for the most part) among themselves. If I wanted something from them, they in turn wanted something back from me. After considering carefully how payment might affect both the type of information I wanted and the delicate economic balance of a seminomadic people, I finally decided that some form of payment would be appropriate. People felt this was fair and became more responsive to my probing. After a period of experimenting with different interview techniques, I settled on one which

247

I used for all subsequent, long-term interviews: I would ask someone to "enter talks" with me, and for an hour or more at a time over a period of about two weeks, we would sit talking while I taped the conversation. By the end of a full set of interviews, I would have spent, on the average, twenty hours with each person.

Because of the intimacy required by this technique, I could not select my subjects completely objectively. After interviewing one man, I quickly learned that I could not achieve the same degree of intimacy with men. This was probably due to !Kung men's reticence in talking about masculine concerns with women, and to our mutual embarrassment in dealing with intimate matters. The women I chose were ones with whom I felt I could establish a good rapport, and ones who would reflect the widest range in !Kung conditions of life. Therefore, my sample included both fertile and barren women; married and, as yet, unmarried; happy and, as it seemed to me , unhappy; and women of a wide range of ages.

All the women I approached were eager to participate, partly for the payment and partly for the chance to talk about themselves. At the onset, I told each woman that I wanted to spend many days with her about her experiences. I mentioned some of the topics I hoped to discuss: memories of early childhood; feelings about parents, siblings, relatives, and friends; adolescence and experiences with other children; dreams; marriage; the birth of children; sex; rela- tionships with husband and/or lovers; feelings about the death of close family members; and thoughts about the future. I made it clear that anything she told me would not be repeated while I was living there and that the purpose of our talks was so women in my country could learn about !Kung women's lives.

Although the interviews began with my mentioning the kinds of things I wanted to discuss, I encouraged the women to initiate the conversations themselves. I felt that the way one memory led to another was of potential importance, and I tried to interrupt as little as possible. Aside from asking questions of clarification, I asked women to expand on topics which seemed interesting or important, but which might have been spoken about only briefly. When a wom- an found it difficult to sustain a topic or start a new one, I suggested other directions. With some women, I had to direct each interview, while others, once they understood the procedure, were able to go ahead with little assistance.

I interviewed eight women, and a unique relationship developed with each. This was not only because we spent close to twenty hours talking together, but also because of the marked personality differences among the women. Generally, as I learned to see the subtleties in the way each woman expressed herself, I was able to understand her better and, presumably, ask better questions. In turn, as each woman came to realize that I kept her confidences, she learned to trust me more. The women often openly expressed their pleasure in talking with me. They were proud they had been chosen to teach me about their customs and experiences. They told me that the things we discussed would never be spoken about with a man, because men had "their talk" and women, theirs. They became silent whenever a man walked by the hut we were in. It would be in a low and excited voice that a woman told me her lover's name, or discussed an early sexual experience, or talked of the time she went from the village, by herself, to give birth to her child.

Talking about experiences and telling stories is one of the main sources of entertainment for the !Kung. They have no written forms in which to express themselves; people sit around for hours talking to one another. It is common when a man describes a hunt or a woman describes something that happened while she was out gathering food, to see the speaker gesture broadly, suddenly raise or lower his voice and imitate sounds of animals, birds, and physical movements. Elements of the stories are repeated over and over again, and there is much use of exaggeration and hyperbole. Stories are usually accompanied by drama and excitement.

As with any skill, some people are more proficient at it than others. Among the eight women I interviewed, one woman was exceptional in her ability to tell a story vibrantly, expressively, and dramatically. I will refer to her as N≠isa. Her life has been difficult: in her fifty years she has experienced the death of all three of her children, her much loved husband, and both her parents. Her only living relatives are two brothers, one older and one younger. Although she derives pleasure from being a "substitute mother" for her brother's two small daughters, she feels her life is somewhat empty, that few people care if she lives or dies. She envies a woman of her age in another village who not only has seven children living nearby and many grandchildren, but whose father, husband, and older brother are alive as well. N≠isa feels that God has abandoned her; she does not understand why he has refused to help.

Like most !Kung women, N≠isa loves and has always wanted to have children. Although she was married five times, her only children came from her third marriage. She had been married twice before she reached menarche. These marriages were unstable and brief (see note 17). After her third husband (the father of her children) died,

250

she married for the fourth time. During this fourth marriage she did not conceive again, and, because of other difficulties, they separated. By the time she married her present (fifth) husband, all three of her children had died. She became pregnant for the last time in this marriage but miscarried. Though she wanted to have another baby, she was not able to conceive again. At the time of our interviews she was going through menopause, causing her much emotional, and some physical, pain. Now she knew she would never have another child.

In addition, N≠isa seemed to be questioning her sexual role. Along with the difficulties brought on by the onset of menopause, her husband, within the previous months, had not shown much interest in having sexual relations with her, or, she believed, with other women. He complained about being tired and old, while she often felt full of sexual energy. She wavered between thinking of herself as an old woman, and as one attractive (and attracted) to men. She still had a few lovers, as she had had for years, but none seemed steadily interested in her, as others had been when she was younger. On occasion, she said she did not feel healthy and that she was too thin to continue the relationships she already had. At other times, she talked positively about the prospects of new men in her life and said she would start "looking again" when our interviews were finished.

N≠isa's life has been a full though difficult one, marked throughout by death and sorrow. Yet, despite the pain and despite her present loneliness, she has been able to find humor and value in her experiences. Even had she not been so gifted in her ability to express herself, her interviews would be a valuable document. But the combination of this attitude, her expressive gift, and her confidence, intelligence, and sensitivity make her narrative an exceptionally moving account of the life of a courageous woman.

This is what I wanted. I hoped getting behind objective facts, getting "into" who the people are would provide a deeper insight into !Kung life. But, more important, I hoped it would touch us _humanly,_ in terms of the felt experience, in a way a body of strange facts cannot. Such facts often emphasize differences rather than similarities.

N≠isa's twenty hours of tape produced 350 single-spaced pages of typewritten transcript, written mostly in English, with some !Kung expressions retained so that the final version would reflect nuances unique to the !Kung language. Achieving a fluid English reading in the final version involved modifying or deleting awkward elements in the first transcription, particularly my interruptions for clarifications and the excessive repetition of words and phrases. Although repetition is a natural way to emphasize ideas in the !Kung language, it is unnatural in ours. Wherever possible, I have incorporated literal translations of !Kung idioms.

251

The texts presented here are edited excerpts of close to half of all N≠isa's memories of her childhood. (The entire collection of these early memories comprises about one-third of the total narrative.) They do not reflect the order in which they appeared in the interviews; here, they are organized chronologically. In a few cases, a memory presented as a continuous narrative is, in fact, taken from two different accounts of the same incident. Apart from these changes, the excerpts are faithful to N≠isa's narrative.

The memories are organized into four sections as follows: (I) weaning and her relationship with her younger brother; (II) relations with other family members; (III) experiences with other children; (IV) marriage. Both N≠isa's style of narration and the content of her stories raise a number of important questions about the factual validity of her narrative. It is not necessary to take literally everything she says for reasons which will become clear in the discussion found at the end of each group of memories.

Part I: Weaning and Her Relationship with Her Younger Brother[1]

(1) Long ago my mother gave birth to my younger brother Kumsa. I wanted the milk she had in her breasts and when she nursed him, my eyes watched as the milk spilled out. I cried all night, cried and cried, and then dawn broke.

Some mornings I just stayed around and my tears fell and I cried and refused food. That was because I saw him nursing, I saw with my eyes the milk spilling out. I thought it was mine.

Once, when my mother was with him and they were lying down asleep, I took him away from her and put him down on the other side of the hut. Then I lay down beside her. While she slept, I squeezed some milk and started to nurse and nursed and nursed and nursed. Maybe she thought it was him. When she woke and saw me, she said, "Where . . . tell me . . . tell me where did you put Kumsa? Where is he?"

I told her he was lying down inside the hut. She grabbed me and shoved me. I landed far away from her; I lay there and cried. She took Kumsa, put him down beside her, and insulted me by cursing my genitals.

"Are you crazy? By your large genitals,[2] what's the matter with you? Are you crazy that you took a baby and dropped him somewhere else and then lay down beside me and nursed? I thought it was Kumsa."

I stayed there crying and crying, and then I was quiet. I got up and just sat, and when my father came home, she told him:

"Do you see what kind of mind your daughter has? Hit her! Hit her, don't just look at her. She almost killed Kumsa. This little baby, this little thing here, she took from my side and dropped him somewhere else. I was lying here holding him and was sleeping. She came and took him away, then left him, and lay down where he had been and nursed me. Now, hit her!"

I said, "You're lying! Me . . . daddy, I didn't nurse. I refuse her milk and didn't take him away from her."

He said, "If I hear of this again, I'll hit you. Now, don't ever do that again!"

I said: "Yes, he's my little brother, is he not? My brother, my little brother, and I love him. I won't do that again. He can nurse all by himself. Daddy, even if you're not here, I won't try to steal mother's breasts. That's my brother's milk. But when you go to the bush, I'm going to follow along with you. The two of us will go and kill springhare, and you will trap a guinea fowl and then give it to me."

We slept. When dawn broke my father and my older brother went and I ran behind. I knew that if I stayed in the village, mother would stinge[3] her milk and wouldn't let me nurse. But when my older brother saw me, he pushed me away and told me to go back to the village, because the sun was too hot, and he said it would kill me.

(2) It was like that even before he was born, when mother tried to wean me. One night, my father took me and left me in the bush.[4] Mother was pregnant, and I cried because I wanted to nurse. When night sat, my father took me and said,

"I'm taking you and leaving you in the bush so a hyena will kill you. Hyena! There's meat over here! Come and take it!

"Are you a little baby? If you nurse the milk that belongs to your little sibling, you will die."

He set me down in the bush and began to leave. I started to run and ran past him. Crying, I ran back to mother and lay down beside her. I was afraid of the night. I ran back and lay beside her. When my father came back, he said, "I'm going to hit you! You can see that your mother's stomach is big, yet you still want to nurse. Your sibling's milk will kill you."

I cried and cried and finally was quiet. Then father said,

"Now, stay quiet and lie down. Tomorrow I will kill a guinea fowl and give it to you to eat. Today your mother's breasts are bad for you."

I heard what he said and was quiet. The next morning he killed a guinea fowl, and when he had cooked it, he gave it to me to eat. But when I finished, I still wanted to take mother's nipple. He took a piece of leather and hit me.

"N≠isa, are you without brains? Why don't you understand? Why do you want your mother's breasts again and again. Leave her breasts be."

I cried and cried. She was pregnant with Kumsa, wasn't she? I cried, and soon I was quiet. I ate many other things because it was the rainy season, but I still asked to nurse. Mother said, "Daughter! these things are things of shit! Shit, and you don't eat it. It kills you. Yes, it is shit, and it smells terrible. If you nurse, you'll go, 'whgaaah, whgaaah' and will throw up."

I said, "No, no. I won't throw up. I'll just nurse and drink the milk."

She refused, "You don't know what you're talking about. I'll explain to you. If you nurse the milk you'll die! Tomorrow your father will kill another springhare, and he will give it to you."

When I heard that, my heart was happy.

(3) One day my older brother ≠Dau went out, and while he was digging some //xaru bulbs, he saw a duiker and struck and killed it with an arrow. I was playing when he came back. He skinned it and gave me the feet, and I went and roasted them. He took some meat off the leg and gave that to me, too. I roasted it with the other, and then I ate and ate and ate. Mother asked me for some, but I refused.

"Didn't you stinge your breasts? Didn't I say I wanted to nurse and you stinged the milk? Are your breasts a good thing? No, your breasts are a bad thing, and I alone will eat this meat. I won't give you any. Just ≠Dau and I will eat it, and you won't."

(4) My younger brother Kumsa grew up and when he was just walking, my mother was pregnant with my younger sister, the one who died when she was still a little girl. When mother was pregnant this time, I was older and hated Kumsa. I always did bad things to him. We hated one another. When Kumsa said he wanted to go to mother and nurse, I picked him up and dropped him down somewhere in the bush. I hit him and pushed

him down and told him that mother was pregnant and that he shouldn't nurse.

(5) Some people just live, and others live and set animal and bird traps. If it is your father who is carrying the animals back home, you say to yourself, "My father is bringing home meat, and when he comes back I can eat it, and I can also stinge it."

Because when you are a child, you play, and you also do bad things to one another. You do bad things to someone, and he does bad things back to you. You tell him, "My father brought back meat and I won't let you have any of it."

You are mean to one another and hit and fight all the time. My younger brother Kumsa and I were like that. We hit one another. Sometimes I bit him and said, "Ooooh . . . what is this thing that has a horrible face and no brains and is mean? Why is he so mean to me when I'm trying to rest?"

He'd say he would hit me. I'd say I would hit him. We stayed together and played like that.

(6) Once when our father brought back meat, we both said, "Daddy . . . daddy . . . !" When I heard my brother say "Daddy . . . daddy . . . !", I said, "Why are you greeting my father? He is *my* father, isn't he? You can only say, 'Oh, hello father'."

He said, "Daddy . . . daddy! Hello, daddy!"

I said, "Be quiet! I alone will say hello to him. Why are you greeting him? When I say, 'Daddy . . . daddy . . . !', you be quiet. Only *I* will talk to him. Is he your father? I'm going to hit you!"

We argued and argued and argued. Later mother began cooking the meat father had brought back. She put a few pieces in the coals, and the rest she put in a pot. When the meat in the coals was done, she brushed the ashes off and gave me some. I sat and ate it, but while I was eating, Kumsa grabbed it and ran away. I ran after him, got it back, and bit him. He started to cry and I left him. I came back and cooked the piece again, then finished it.

When the meat in the pot was done, they took the pot out of the fire and gave me a plate of meat that I was supposed to share with Kumsa. I refused:

"I refuse Kumsa, his fingers are dirty. Kumsa has dirty fingers and I won't eat out of this plate with him. I'm going to eat out of this plate myself. Take some of it and give it to your son. Why should Kumsa and I eat together?"

Then we both ate. Kumsa and I were without brains, we were always fighting with one another. I hated him, and Kumsa, he hated me.

Discussion

The memories in Part I raise a number of questions that are difficult to answer. First, can we assume that N≠isa remembers in such detail, not only the event of being weaned, but verbatim accounts of conversations between her parents, her brother, and herself? It seems unlikely. Late weaning (age three or four) makes it possible that at least some of the feelings could have been remembered. But the exact detail in which N≠isa describes these events is best regarded as her own stylistic invention. N≠isa enjoyed the interview situation with the machine that "grabs your voice," and this, as well as her desire to tell her stories dramatically, may account for her seemingly unusual memory. However, other women I spoke with said, quite directly, that people do not remember anything from when they are such little children. It seems fair to assume then, that her earliest memories are a combination of facts, generalized experiences, and fantasy. (Verbatim accounts of conversations characterize her entire narrative. Even from later sections, much of this is probably reconstruction rather than actual memory.)

The second memory in which she said her father took her out to the hyenas because she was bad, raises the question of exaggeration. This is almost certainly the remembered fantasy of a little girl who was deeply frightened by her father's verbal threats. He might have gone as far as to pick her up, perhaps he even took her out of the hut, but it is very doubtful that the event took place as she described it. As indicated in Draper's and Konner's accounts (Chapters 9 and 10) of child-training practices, the !Kung are very lenient and indulgent with their children and rarely are observed using any form of physical punishment. This second memory can best be seen as the product of the fanciful imagination of N≠isa the little girl who eventually believed her own fantasy, or N≠isa the woman exaggerating a feeling that she still remembers from her childhood. This kind of exaggeration, especially when it involves parental physical punishment, will be encountered repeatedly throughout the sections that follow.

N≠isa's parents seem severe in the first weaning memory but they were very concerned that she stop nursing. The !Kung believe that a child should be weaned as soon as the mother realizes she is pregnant again. The milk that remains in her breast is thought to belong to the fetus and not to the child. If the child continues to nurse, they believe that the life or health of either the child or the fetus may be endangered or that the infant will be born wanting to injure his older sibling. Observations of the weaning period confirm the feelings of misery N≠isa expressed. Konner (1972) describes this stage as one in which children usually are depressed and resentful of the birth of the new sibling. N≠isa still carries some of these feelings with her. She believes that her relatively slight build and short stature came from having been weaned too early and from not having been given enough to eat.

!Kung children are encouraged to share things from infancy, because exchanging food and possessions is so basic to adult social interactions. Among the first words a child learns is *"na"* ("give it to me") and *"i"* ("here, take this"). This type of socialization is hard for children, especially when they are expected to share with someone they resent or dislike. Then, giving or holding back becomes a way of exercising power and expressing anger. Evidently, this is what is occurring with her brother, in memories 3, 5, and 6.

Part II: Relations with Other Family Members[5]

(7) During the time I cried because I wanted to nurse and couldn't, I sometimes took food from our hut when mother was away gathering. My parents hit me when I took things; they left me alone when I didn't. Some days I remained in the village and I didn't take and ruin[6] their things. Other days, when they were not there, I did. That's when they hit me and said I was without brains.

Once my mother took a digging stick and hit me. She hit me so hard my back hurt. I cried and cried and cried. Then I was sick.[7] My father said to her: "What did you do? You took your digging stick rather than a soft branch and hit the child? You hit that small child with a stick? You might have broken her back!"

I said, "I won't eat any of your //xaru bulbs. I'm going to go and eat grandma's //xaru."

I went to the village where mother's mother lived and told myself I would eat with her. When I arrived at her hut, grandma roasted //xaru, and I ate and ate and ate. I slept beside her and lived there for a while.

Once, when it was getting dark, I got up and walked back to mother's hut and lay with her and father. Another day, when they were away, I climbed the tree where the little pouch hung and took the //xaru again. I took the big bulbs and put them in a little pouch my father had sewn for me. I sat there and ate them, and when my parents returned they accused me of eating the //xaru. I said I didn't. They said I did. Then I started to cry;

my father hit me and my mother yelled at me: "Don't take things! You don't understand? I tell you and you don't understand. Your ears don't hear me when I talk to you."

I thought: "Uh-uhn, mother's making me feel terrible. I'm going to go stay with grandma again. Mother says I take things and hits me until my skin hurts. I'm going to go to grandma's and sleep beside her. She will prepare //xaru for me to eat."

I went to my grandmother's, but she said: "No, I can't take care of you. If I try, you will be hungry because I am old and just go gathering one day at a time. In the morning I just rest. While we sit together, hunger will kill you. Now, go and be good. Sit nicely beside your mother and father."

I said, "No, they will hit me. Today my skin hurts and I want to stay with you."

I stayed with my grandmother for a while that time. Then, one day, she said she was taking me back to my parents' village. She carried me there and gave me to my mother. Then she said: "Daughter, today I refuse N≠isa because I can't take care of her well. She's just a child, and you shouldn't hit her and hit her. If she is someone who likes food—then she *likes* it—and has a good appetite. Some of you are lazy and left her without enough to eat and she didn't grow well. Maybe that's what happened. When I used to take care of her, there was a lot of food, and I fed her well. She grew up with me for a while and when she went back with you, you killed her with hunger. With your own hands you hit her as though she weren't a !Kung. She cried and cried and was just a little thing. Yet, you yelled at her."

When my grandmother said that, I was happy. I held happiness in my heart because grandmother scolded mother. That made me so happy and I laughed and laughed. Then grandmother went back to her village. When she left, I cried. My father scolded me. "When you left us, we missed you. We wanted you to come back. Yes, your mother even came and looked for you. But today you refuse to be with her. Your mother was the one who gave birth to you. Now you'll start to do things with her and go gathering with her."

But I cried and cried and refused to be with her. I said, "Mother, let me just stay with grandmother. I want to follow her to her village."

My father said, "Be quiet, quiet. There is nothing here that will hit you. Now, be quiet."

Then I was quiet, and my father dug //xaru and *chō* bulbs and I ate them. I ate the roots and bulbs and nuts they gathered, and they didn't scold me.

When I was growing up, I sometimes stayed with my mother's

sister for days at a time and then went back to my mother. I stayed with her for a while and then passed on to my grandmother. I would go there for many days. Everybody helped bring me up—my mother's sister, my father, my mother, my grandmother. Look at how I am today, I'm very small. That's because people brought me up badly. I was too difficult for them.

(8) Let me tell you about my mother, my father, and myself. My father sometimes hit me. I remember the day I broke the ostrich eggshell water container. The shell was on the ground, and I picked it up and carried it in my kaross to get water. But it fell and broke! When I came back, my father took a thin branch and told me he was going to beat me. So, pffht! I ran away.

Another day, when I went again to get water, I took another eggshell and BAMM! But I said, "Today I won't run. Even though father may beat me, I won't run."

He did hit me, and I said I didn't care. But I cried and cried, and he hit me, and I cried. Then it was over. Whenever they asked me to take an ostrich eggshell and bring back water, I refused. When I did go to the well, I just took my thumb piano[8] with me, drank some water, then left and went home. I wouldn't collect water for them. I thought, "If they want me to get water in the ostrich eggshell, I refuse."

I stayed behind with the other people, and only mother went to fill the containers. Because if I went, I might break another eggshell, and they'd hit me.

I told them I wouldn't help them, that I wouldn't touch their ostrich eggshells because I was afraid they'd beat me. Instead, I took a small can, if I had one, and drank water from that. I was afraid.

We continued to live there, but I didn't touch any more ostrich eggshell containers.

(9) One day we were walking, gathering food, and the sun was burning. It was the hot, dry season, and there was no water anywhere. The sun hurt! As we walked along, my older brother saw some honey. He and my father took it from the tree, and we ate it. I was so thirsty I practically drank it! I carried some with me, and we continued to walk. Thirst was killing mother, and I was crying for water. I cried and cried. We rested somewhere in the shade and there was still no water. My father said to my older brother: "≠Dau, your mother and I will remain in the shade of this baobab tree. Take the water containers, go and

fill them with water. There is a big well way over at the Homa⁹ village."

≠Dau got up, took the ostrich eggshell containers, took a clay pot, and went. I was lying down, thirst killing me. As I lay there, I thought, "If I just stay here with mother and father, I will die of thirst. Why don't I go with ≠Dau, go and drink some water?"

As soon as I thought that, I got up and ran. I cried after him and ran and cried and ran and followed his tracks. He still didn't hear me. I kept on running and cried after him. When he finally heard me, he turned around and saw me behind him and said, "N≠isa's here? What am I going to do with her now?"

When I finally caught up with him, he picked me up and carried me on his shoulder. My older brother liked me. The two of us went together and walked and walked and walked until we finally reached the water well. When we got there, we drank. I drank the water and my heart was happy. Then we filled the containers. ≠Dau got them together, picked them up, picked me up, and carried me on his shoulders.

We started walking back and walked and walked, and then he put me down. I ran along with him and soon I started to cry. He told me: "N≠isa, I'm going to hit you. I am carrying these containers and they're very heavy. Now, keep running along, and let's get back to mother and father and give them some water. Thirst will kill them. What are you crying about? Are you without any sense?"

I said, "No! Pick me up. ≠Dau, pick me up and carry me on your shoulders."

He refused, and I cried. I ran along with him and cried and ran and cried. After a while he said he would carry me again. He picked me up and put me on his shoulders and carried me a long way. It was far! Then he set me down again, and I ran until I was tired, and he picked me up and carried me. We finally brought the water back to our parents. Then we drank it and they said, "Yes our children brought water back and did well— we are alive once again."

After we rested, we left, and all of us went to live in Homa village, where the well was. We walked and rested and walked and rested until we got there. I didn't cry along the way and carried my honey with me. When we arrived, we drank plenty of water and settled there for a while. There was a lot of water and we had all that honey and my heart was happy.

(10) The rainy season came. The sun rose and set, and then the rain spilled itself, and it fell and kept falling. It fell tire-

somely, without ceasing, and it seemed to tease people like a naughty child. The water pans were full and my heart was happy, and we lived and ate mongongo nuts. We ate more and more mongongos, and they were delicious. I was like a dog wagging my tail, and I ran around and wagged my tail. Really!! I went like that with my tail, just like a dog.

My heart was so happy because water had come that day. Yes! I was also thankful. We ate caterpillars,[10] ate many of them, and people collected food; people just kept collecting food. And there was meat, because people had killed meat, and it was hung up. My heart was so happy. I ate meat and wagged my tail. I laughed with my little tail and laughed a little donkey's laugh, a little thing that is. I wagged my tail and said, "Today I'm going to eat caterpillars. CA-TER-PIL-LLLEEERRRS!"

I ate them, and people kept roasting them in the coals and cooking them, and I kept eating them and ate and ate and ate them and then went to sleep.

Discussion

Again, in this section, N≠isa makes some puzzling statements. The first is about being beaten for having broken the ostrich eggshell water container. It is likely that she was severely scolded for breaking it since emptied eggshells are relatively scarce and are used for carrying and storing water. That she was actually physically beaten, however, is conceivable but doubtful. As in the hyena memory in Part I, memory 2, this is probably an exaggerated account of threats that were internalized and carried out only in the imagination of a little girl.

N≠isa makes still another statement that is surprising—that she was punished for taking food. It is difficult to believe that she was either beaten or scolded because parents are concerned that their children have enough to eat and food is given freely. When parents go away for the day, they either leave food for their children or arrange for someone else to feed them. If there is a scarcity of food, it is the children who get preferential treatment. Draper (1972) did observe withholding of food as punishment for wasting or destroying food, but this was short-lived, and there are no observations of beating for taking food. This is why N≠isa's account of her parents' reaction to her taking the //xaru when they were away is difficult to understand. One explanation could be that //xaru has some significance we do not yet know about and that parents do not want their children eating large quantities of it. This seems plausible because it is the only food N≠isa described being scolded for taking.

Another possible explanation involves N≠isa's relationship to her mother. Her memories suggest that this was a time of great tension between them. She portrayed her mother as someone who was always hitting, scolding, and criticizing her. She portrayed herself as someone who kept doing things her mother did not like, especially involving food: she took food which, for some reason, her mother did not want her to have; and, as indicated in other memories, she took food from other people's huts as well. These tensions may have distorted her view of this period and resulted in her remembering only the hostile feelings that existed between them. Whether it was her feelings of being unloved, or some resentment held over from the time of weaning, or simply the general !Kung anxiety about food availability that may have caused her to exaggerate, it is impossible to determine. It is also conceivable that her accounts are accurate; it is possible that her family was unusual in this regard. Also, physical punishment could be so rare that it is almost never observed, and yet be very important in the memories of a child. It is difficult to separate fact from fantasy.

Playing the Antbear game. "It" burrows under the legs

In Part I, memory 3, N≠isa refused to give her mother meat. In this last section, she refused to get water after having been scolded. She also left her mother's home for her grandmother's because she did not like the way she was being treated. Leaving was made somewhat easier by the !Kung tradition of multiple caretaking. Children often spend extended period with close relatives, and at least some do this when there are tensions resulting from the birth of a sibling. These actions, though, are indications of N≠isa's emerging independence as she learns to assert herself against the authority of her parents. !Kung children are encouraged to respect their own needs and may refuse to do things they feel strongly enough against, even when the requests come from their parents. Unlike western children, !Kung children are not strongly pressured to obey authority (see Draper, Chapter 9). This is reflected in the adult band structure in which there is no real chief.

At the time a child is weaned from the breast (usually when the mother realizes she is pregnant), he is still carried in her kaross while she engages in daily activities. This continues throughout her pregnancy and often even after the next child is born. Children love to be carried; they love the contact with their mothers, and they love not having to walk under the pressure of keeping up. But as a child grows older and gets heavier, and the demands of the younger child become greater, mothers begin to expect the older child to walk beside them.

This being "weaned from the back" (Draper 1972) elicits, in a slightly lessened form, similar kinds of behavior that weaning from the breast did: the child throws temper tantrums, refuses to walk by himself, demands to be carried, and refuses to be left in the village while his mother goes gathering. The adjustment, a difficult one for the child, is made easier by other people carrying him. This is why memory 9, in which N≠isa's brother carries her to the water well, is recalled with such tenderness.

Part III: Experiences with Other Children[11]

(11) When a child sleeps beside his mother, in front, and his father sleeps behind and makes love to her, the child watches. Perhaps this is the way the child learns. Because as his father lies with his mother, the child watches. The child is still senseless, is without intelligence, and he just watches.

Then, when he and the other children are playing, if he is a little boy, he takes his younger sister and has sex[12] with her. Because he saw his mother and father do that. So he takes her.

And as he grows, he lives in the bush and continues to play, now with other children, and they have sex with each other and play and play and play. They take food from the village and go back to the bush and continue their games. That's the way they grow up. When the sun is low in the sky they return to the village and sit down. They return when evening is just beginning to set and play in the middle of the village. That's what they do.

263

(12) I remember my parents when they lay together. Night . . . at night my father lay with my mother. I still wouldn't have fallen asleep; I'd just be lying still. My father slept with her, and I watched. Why wasn't my father concerned about me, that I might be up? I was fairly old by then. Why wasn't he respectful of me? Why wasn't he respectful? Adults should be concerned that a child may be awake. I couldn't sleep, and why were they making love? That's what I thought. I thought that my mother and father didn't care if I were dead asleep or not. If they had, then they could lie together, and no one would hear; then I'd be asleep and wouldn't wake up. That's what I thought.

Then, long ago, I refused to sleep in their hut. I said, "No. Today I won't lie down with mother and father. Today I will sleep alone in another hut."

I refused to stay with them because they weren't respectful of me.

(13) A child that is nursing doesn't know anything because he still has no intelligence. When he is nursing, he has no thoughts. The milk is the only thing he knows. Then he learns to sit. Even when he sits, he still doesn't think about things because his intelligence hasn't yet come to him. Where could he take his thoughts from? The only thought is nursing. But when he grows and is bigger, and he is walking, he has many thoughts. His thoughts now exist, and as he sits, he thinks about the work[13] of sexual intercourse. He sits and thinks about it, and if he is a little boy, he plays with the other children and teaches it to himself. The little girls also learn it by themselves.

They play and play and have sex with one another, and when they see a little girl by herself, they take her. She cries and cries. That's how boys teach themselves, and that's how girls teach themselves. They play and play and teach themselves. Little boys are the first ones to know its sweetness. That's why they do that when they play. Yes. A young girl, while she is still a child, her thoughts don't know it. A little boy has a penis, and perhaps, while he is still inside his mother's belly, he already knows about having sex. Because boys know how to do things with their genitals. They take little girls and push them down and have sex with them. Even if you are just playing, they do that.

Sometimes the boys ask if you want to play a game with your genitals, and the girls say no. They say they don't want to play that game, but they'd like to play other games. The boys tell you that having sex is what playing is all about.

I didn't know about it, and they taught it to me. After they taught me and taught me, I didn't cry. Some of the others knew about it long before I did, they had taught themselves and knew it. The little boys used to ask me why I always cried when they played. I said, "You all . . . you all are playing and say we should have sex together. That's why I'm crying. I'm going to tell mother you said we should do that."

Some days I refused and remained in the village and just stayed with mother. Some days I went with them. Sometimes I refused to play, other times I agreed. The little boys entered the play huts where we were playing, and then they lay down with us. My boyfriend came to see me and we lived like that and played. We would lie down and they would have sex with us.

(14) /Ti!kay taught it to me and because of that I liked him. I really liked him! When we played, the other children said I should play with someone else, but I refused. I wanted /Ti!kay only. I said, "Me, I won't take a horrible man."

They teased /Ti!kay. "Hey . . . /Ti!kay . . . you are the only one N≠isa likes. She refuses everyone else."

He taught me about men. We played and played, and he grabbed me, and we played and played. Some days we built little huts, and he took me. We played every day. I used to think, "What is this thing that is so good? How come it is so good and I used to refuse it? The other children knew about it and I had no sense. Now I know when you are a child, this is something you do. You teach it to yourself."

(15) We left the area where I played with /Ti!kay and the other children and went to live somewhere else, far away. When we got there, I thought about my friends and said, "I miss the children I used to play with. Mother, say we can go. Mother, father, let's go back east."

When they asked me why, I said, "So I can find the children I used to play with. I've come here and don't see any children."

They told me, "Yes, we'll go. We'll go where you want—we'll go to your cousins Dem and /Tasa. You can play with them."

I said, "No, I refuse! Let's go to the east so I can find the children I used to play with. I don't want to play with my cousins in their village."

I cried and cried, but they wouldn't go as far away as I wanted. They said I was being silly and that we would go to where my cousins lived.

When we got there, I just watched my cousins and their friends. I watched and watched and said to myself that I wouldn't play with them. Then /Tasa came and took me from my hut and asked me to play with her. I refused. Then she asked me to go and play with her in the water, but I refused that too.

At first I refused everything, then later I went with her to where her friends were playing and I joined them. They didn't have sex with one another. Maybe they didn't know it. We went to the water pan and played and then returned. We stayed in the village and rested. Then we went again to the water pan. We just stayed around and played and played and played.

(16) When you are a child you play at nothing things. You build little huts and play. Then you come back to the village and continue to play. If people bother you, you get up and play somewhere else.

Once we left a pool of rain water where we had been playing and went to the little huts we had made. We stayed there and played at being hunters. We went out tracking animals and when we saw one, we struck it with our make-believe arrows. We took some leaves and hung them over a stick and pretended it was meat. Then we carried it back to our village. When we got back, we stayed there and ate the meat and then the meat was gone. We went out again, found another animal and killed it. We threw more leaves over a stick, put other leaves in our karosses,[14] and brought it back. We played at living in the bush like that. We pretended to get water and we ate the meat. That's how we played.

We made believe about everything. We made believe we cooked food, and then we took it out of the fire. We had a trance dance,[15] and we sang and danced and danced and sang, and the boys made believe they were curing us. They went—"Xai--------i! Kow-a-di!"[16]

They cured us, and we sang and danced and danced, danced all day. Sometimes the sun set while we were visiting in our friends' village, but even though night sat, we stayed in the center of the village and played. We stayed into the night, dancing and singing and finally left one another and went to sleep. We were up again in the morning and started playing again. Sometimes we played with the children from another village, sometimes we just played by ourselves in the bush. That's what we did, and that's how we lived.

We took food from the village, went to our little village, and shared it with one another, ate it and gave it and took it. We stayed together and danced and sang and played. Most of the time we played the play of children, that of having sex with one another. We all did that. That was our work. Did we have any sense? No, we didn't have any sense and just did our work.

(17) One day, when I was fairly big, I went with some of my friends and with my younger brother and my younger sister away from the village and into the bush. We walked a long way. As we were walking, I saw the tracks of a baby kudu in the sand. I called to everyone and showed them. "Everybody come here! Here are tracks of a baby kudu. Let's see if we can find it."

We walked along, following the tracks, and walked and walked and walked. As we followed the tracks around, we saw, in the shade of a tree, the little kudu dead asleep. I jumped and tried to grab it. It cried, "Ehnnn . . . Ehnnn. . . ."

I cried out as it freed itself and ran away. I hadn't really caught it well. We started following the new tracks. I ran on ahead of everyone, ran so hard and so fast that I was alone. I came on it, jumped on it and then killed it. I grabbed its legs and carried it back. I was breathing very hard. "Whew . . . whew . . . whew . . . whew . . . whew . . . !"

When I came to where the rest of them were, my older cousin said to me: "My cousin, my little cousin killed a kudu! The rest of you here, what are you doing? How come we men didn't kill the kudu? This young girl has so much 'run' in her that she killed the kudu!"

I gave the animal to my cousin, and he carried it. On the way back to the village, we saw another small animal, a steenbok. One of my girlfriends and her older brother ran after it, and then he killed it. That day we brought a lot of meat back with us to the village. We cooked it and had plenty to eat.

Discussion

The !Kung have little privacy, either in the village or within the family. Parents and children sleep together in huts that have no dividers or private sections. This arrangement is inconvenient for parents when they want to engage in sexual activities. Occasionally they go to the bush to make love; most of the time they wait until they think their children are asleep and try to be discreet. But !Kung children are curious and have many opportunities to observe their parents' lovemaking. Several of the other women interviewed expressed feelings similar to the ones N≠isa described. One woman remembered telling her mother, the morning after observing her parents' lovemaking, that she refused to help any more because her mother had engaged in sexual activity the night before. Her mother scolded her and told her not to mention that kind of thing again. N≠isa's behavior in memory 12 is typical of older children, who often move out of their parents' huts and build small huts of their own, or share them with other adolescents.

267

!Kung children are sexually aware at a very early age because of the relative openness and acceptance of adult sexuality. They also have many opportunities to experiment with what they have observed. All the women I interviewed said that their childhood sex play included sexual intercourse. Parents say they do not approve of this among young and adolescent children; they say it is a good thing to do only when you are older. But the parents played this way when they were children and, although they usually deny it, they know their children are playing the same way. As long as it is done away from adults, children are not prevented from participating in experimental sexual play. If they are seen by an adult, they are scolded and told to play "nicely" (that is, nonsexually).

!Kung children have few responsibilities. They spend their time watching and participating in some adult activities and playing in small groups of children of different ages. For the most part, their games do not reflect a separate children's culture. They are usually imitations of adult activities: hunting, gathering, singing adult songs, trancing, playing house, and playing marriage. Many times, as in the case of gathering food or as described in memory 17 (when N≠isa killed the kudu), the children actually perform subsistence activity, rather than merely playing at it.

The memory in which N≠isa kills the kudu (17) also sheds light on the process through which !Kung boys and girls come to think of themselves as men and women. While it was made clear to the boys that they should have been the ones to kill it, N≠isa herself was highly praised for her success and not made to feel ashamed of doing something "unfeminine." Unlike our own society where names like "tomboy" and "sissy" serve to make boys and girls play separately and avoid each other's activities, !Kung boys and girls play together and share most games.

In these memories, and in others not presented here, N≠isa portrays many of her childhood experiences as occurring away from the village. Memory 17 describes them following animal tracks far into the bush; memories 13–15 describe the children participating in sexual activities that would be disapproved of were adults present. These memories suggest that children either spend more time away from their parents' supervision than Draper observes (Chapter 9), or that the experiences they have at these times are among their most vividly remembered.

Part IV: Marriage[17]

(18) When adults talk to me, I listen. Once they told me that when a young woman grows up, she takes a husband. When they first talked to me about it, I said: "What? What kind of thing am I that I should take a husband? Me, when I grow up, I won't marry. I will just lie by myself. A man, if I married him, what would I think I would be doing it for?"

My father said: "N≠isa if you agree, you will marry a man and get food and give some to him, and he will eat it. I, I am old. I am your father and am old; your mother's old, too. You will get married, gather food and give it to your husband to eat. He also will do things for you—give you things you can wear. But if you refuse to take a husband, who will get food and give it to you to eat? Who will give you things that you shall have? Who will give you things that you will be able to wear?"

I said to my father and mother: "No. There's no question in my mind—I refuse a husband. I won't take one. What is it? Why should I take a husband? As I am now, I am still a child and won't marry. Why don't you marry the man you want for me and sit him down beside father? Then you'll have two husbands."

Mother said: "You're talking nonsense. I'm not going to marry him, you'll marry him. A husband, I want to give you. You say I should marry this other man? Why are you playing with me with this talk?"

I said: "Yes, that's what I am saying. Because you can see I am only a child, and yet you say I should get married. When I grow up and you tell me I should marry, then I will agree. But today I won't! I haven't passed through my childhood and I won't take a husband."

We continued to live and lived on and on and returned to just living. Then she talked about it again. "N≠isa, I should give you a husband. Which man shall I give you?"

I knew which man she wanted me to marry. I said, "I refuse that man."

She said, "Marry him. Won't you marry him?"

I said, "You marry him. Marry him and set him beside father."

I stopped talking. I felt ashamed and was silent. I said to myself, "What am I doing? Later I will still go back to mother. When I speak like that, am I not shitting on her?"

I thought that. Then we all went to sleep. We continued to live and just kept on living and more time passed.

(19)[18] Long ago my parents and I went to the village where old Kan//a and his son /"Tashay were living. My friend N!huka and I had gone to the water well to get water and he and his family were there, having just come back from the bush. When /"Tashay saw me, he decided he wanted to marry me. He called N!huka over and said, "N!huka, that young woman, that beautiful young woman . . . what is her name?"

N!huka told him my name was N≠isa, and he said, "That young woman . . . I'm going to tell mother and father about her. I'm going to ask them if I can marry her."

N!huka came back. We continued filling the water containers, then left and walked the long way back. When N!huka saw my mother she said, "N≠isa and I were getting water and while we were there, some people came to the well and filled their water containers, and a young man saw N≠isa and talked about marriage. He said his parents would ask you for N≠isa in marriage."

I was silent, just quiet. Because when you are a child and someone wants to marry you, you don't talk. At first my heart didn't agree to it. When they first talked about marriage, I didn't agree.

The next night there was a dance and we were singing and dancing, and he and his parents came from their camp and stayed with us at the dance. We danced and sang and danced and sang, and we didn't stop. N!huka and I sat together. /"Tashay came over to me and took my hand. I said: "What . . . what is it? What kind of person is this? What is he doing? This person . . . this person . . . how come I'm sitting here and he came and took hold of me?"

N!huka said, "That's your husband . . . your husband has taken hold of you, is that not so?"

I said, "Won't he take you? You're older, and he'll marry you."

She said, "What! Isn't he my uncle? I won't marry my uncle. Anyway, he is asking you to marry him."

His parents went to my mother and father. His father said: "We have come here, and now that the dancing is finished, I want to speak to you, to /Gau and Chu!ko, N≠isa's father and mother. I will speak with you. Give me your child, the child you gave birth to. Give her to me, and I will give her to my son. Yesterday, while we were at the well, he saw your child. When he returned he told me that in the name of what he felt, that I should today come and ask for her. Then I can give her to him. He said I should come for her."

My mother said: "Yes . . . but I didn't give birth to a woman, I bore a child. She doesn't think about marriage, she just doesn't think about the inside of her marriage hut."

Then my father said: "Yes, I conceived that child as well, and she is a person who doesn't think about marriage. When she marries a man, she leaves him and marries another man and leaves him and gets up and marries another man and leaves him. She refuses men completely. There were two men whom she already refused. So, when I look at N≠isa today, I say she is not a woman. There is even another man, Dem, his hut is over there, who is asking to marry her. Dem's first wife is giving her things. When Dem goes gathering and comes back, he gives things to his wife so she can give them to N≠isa. He asks N≠isa to sit with them. He wants her to stay and be a second wife. He wants her to take the food from his wife, so they can all eat together. But when his wife undoes the kaross and gives N≠isa food, she throws it down, ruins it in the sand, and kicks the kaross. It is because of that I say she is not a woman."

My father told that to /"Tashay's father. Then his father said: "Yes, I have listened to what you have said. That, of course, is the way of a child; it is a child's custom to do that. She gets married many times until one day she likes one man. Then they stay together. That is a child's way."

They talked about the marriage and agreed to it. All this time I was in my aunt's hut and couldn't see them, I could just hear their voices. Soon, I got up and went to my father's hut where they were talking. When I got there, /"Tashay was looking at me. I sat down. Then /"Tashay's mother said, "Ohhhh! How beautiful this person is! You are a young woman already. Why do they say that you don't want to get married?"

/"Tashay said, "Yes, she has just come in. I want you to take her and give her to me."

(20)[19] There were a lot of people there, everyone came. All of /"Tashay's friends were there, and when they saw me, they told him he was too old for me. Each one said he wanted to marry me himself. His younger brother and his nephew were sitting around talking that way.

I went into my mother's hut and sat there. I was wearing many beads and my hair was covered with ornaments. I went and sat beside mother. Another one of /"Tashay's friends came over and started talking as the others had, and I felt confused and couldn't understand why this was happening to me.

That night there was another dance and we danced and other people fell asleep and others kept dancing. In the morning they went back to their camp and we, to ours, and then we went to sleep. When the morning was late in the sky, his relatives came back. They stayed around and his parents told my aunt and my mother that they should all start building the marriage hut because they wanted to leave for another village. They began building the hut together, and everyone was talking and talking. There were a lot of people there. Then all the

young men went and brought /"Tashay to the marriage hut.
They stayed around the hut together near the fire. I was at
mother's hut. They told two of my friends to go get me and
bring me to the hut. I said to myself, "Oooooh . . . I'll run
away to the bush."

When they came for me they couldn't find me. I wasn't by
the fire.

"Where did N≠isa go? It's dark now, isn't it? Doesn't she
know that things may bite and kill her when it is dark like this?
Has she left?"

My father said, "Go tell N≠isa that if she behaves like that, I
will hit her, and she won't run away again. What's the matter
with her that she ran away into the bush?"

I had already gone. I stayed away a long time. I heard them
calling. "N≠isa——a! N≠isa——a!"

They were looking for me. I just sat, sat by the base of a
tree. I heard my friend, N!huka, call out. "N≠isa—e . . . N≠isa—e
. . . my friend . . . there are things there which will bite and kill
you. Now leave there and come back here."

They looked for me and looked and looked, and then N!huka
came and saw me. I ran away from her, and she ran after me and
chased me and then caught me. She called out to the others.
"People! N≠isa's here! Everyone come over here, come, take
her. N≠isa's here!"

They came and brought me back. Then they lay me down
inside the hut. I cried and cried, and people told me: "A man is
not something that kills you; he is someone who marries you,
and he becomes like your father or your older brother. He kills
animals and gives you things to eat. Even tomorrow; but because you are crying, when he kills an animal, he will eat it
himself and won't give you any. Beads, too. He will get some
beads, but he won't give them to you. Why are you afraid of
your husband and why are you crying?"

I listened and was quiet. Then he and I went and slept inside
the hut. He slept by the mouth of the hut, near the fire. He
came inside after he thought I was asleep. Then he lay down
and slept.

I woke while it was still dark and said to myself, "How am I
going to jump over him? How can I get out and go to mother's
hut?"

That's what I was thinking in the middle of the night. Then I
thought, "This person has married me . . . yes . . ." I lay there.
I lay there and thought some more. "Why did people give me
this man in marriage? The older people say he is a good person
and . . . ."

I lay there and didn't move. The rain came and beat down.

It fell and kept on falling and falling and then dawn broke. In the morning, he got up first and went and sat by the fire. I was frightened! I was afraid of him and lay there and didn't get up. I waited for him to go away from the hut and when he went to urinate, I left and went to mother's hut. I went there and sat down inside her hut.

That day all his relatives came to our new hut—his mother, his father, his brothers . . . everyone! They all came. They said, "Go tell N≠isa that she should come and her in-laws will put the marriage oil on her. Can you see her over there? Why isn't she coming out so we can put the oil on her in her new hut?"

I refused to go there. Then my older brother said, "No, no. N≠isa, if you continue like this, I'll hit you. Now get out there and go sit down Go over there and they will put the oil on you."

I still refused and just sat there. My older brother took a switch and came over to me. I got up because I was afraid of the switch. I followed him and walked to where the people were. My aunt put oil on /"Tashay, and his relatives put oil on me. Then they left, and it was just /"Tashay and me.

(21) We lived together and after a while /"Tashay lay with me. Afterward, my insides hurt. I took some leaves and tied them with a string around my stomach,[20] but it continued to hurt. The next morning I went gathering and collected some mongongo nuts and put them in my kaross. Meanwhile, I was thinking to myself, "Oooohhh . . . that man made my insides hurt. He made me feel pain today."

The next evening we lay down again. This time I took a leather strap, tied it around a piece of wood and then secured it to my genitals; I wanted to withhold my genitals. The two of us lay down and after a while he was looking for my genitals, and he felt the leather strap there. He said, "What . . . did another woman tell you to do this? Yesterday you lay with me so nicely when I came to you. Why are you today tying a piece of wood to your genitals? What are you holding back?"

I didn't answer. Then he said, "N≠isa . . . N≠isa . . . ."

I said, "What is it?"

He said, "What are you doing?"

I didn't answer him. I was quiet.

"What are you so afraid of that you tied your genitals with a piece of leather and with a branch?"

I said, "I'm not afraid of anything."

He said: "No, no. Tell me what you are afraid of. Why did you tie a branch to your genitals. In the name of what you did, I am asking you.

"What are you doing when you do something like that? You are lying with me as though you were lying with a Bantu, a stranger. Why did you tie a branch to your genitals?"

I said: "I refuse to lie down because if I do, you will take me. I refuse! I refuse your touching my genitals because when you lay with me yesterday, my insides hurt me. That's why I am refusing you today, and you won't have me."

273

He said: "You're not telling the truth, now untie the leather strap. Untie the strap from around your genitals. Do you see me as someone who kills other people? Am I going to eat you? Am I going to kill you? I'm not going to kill you. Instead, as I am now, I have married you and want to make love to you. Don't think I would marry you and not sleep with you. Would I have married you just to *live* with you? Have you seen any man who has married a woman and who just lives with her and doesn't have sex with her?"

I said, "No, I still refuse it! I refuse sex. Yesterday my insides hurt, that's why."

He said, "Mm. Today you will just lie there by yourself. But tomorrow I will take you."

I continued to refuse him and we just lay down. Before we went to sleep, he untied the strap and said, "I'm going to destroy it. If this is what use you put it to, I am going to untie it and destroy it in the fire."

Then we went to sleep and slept. He didn't take me, but he untied the strap because he was big and I was afraid of him. We went to sleep and got up the next morning. The men went out that day and then returned. That night /"Tashay and I entered the hut again and lay down together. I just lay there and after a while he touched my leg. I didn't move. I thought to myself, "Oh, what I did last night won't help me at all, because this man will hurt me. Then I'm going to give it to him, and he will have it. Some day it will no longer hurt me."

I said to him: "Today I'm going to lie here, and if you take me by force, you will have me. You will have me because today I'm just going to lie here. You are obviously looking for some 'food,' but I don't know if the 'food' I have is 'food' at all, because even if you have some, you won't be full."

Then I just lay down and he did his 'work.' Afterward he lay down.

(22) We lived together after that, but I ran away again and again. Once I ran away and slept in the bush and they found me in the morning. When my older brother said he was taking me back, I threatened to stick myself with a poison arrow. He got very angry and said: "If you try to stick yourself with an arrow,

then I'll beat you, and you'll understand what you were doing. As you stand here, you are talking very badly about what you are going to do to yourself. You are a person, a woman, and when you are alive, you don't say those things. When you are alive, you should be playing.

"All your friends have gotten married and N!huka, too, she is going to marry your uncle and sit beside him. Don't say you won't come back to the village, because you and N!huka will have your own huts. Will your friend have a hut, and you won't? That's all. As I am ≠Dau, your older brother, that's what I have to say."

I said: "Yes. This friend of mine has taken a husband, but surely she is older than I am. She is a grown woman. Me, I'm a child and don't think I should be married. Why have you come to ask me these things again?"

He said: "Put the *sha* roots you collected in your kaross and let's go. The person who sits here is your *husband!* He isn't anyone else's husband. He is the man we gave you. You will grow up with him, lay down with him, and give birth to children with him."

(23) When we returned to the village, I didn't go to my hut, but went and stayed at mother's hut. I went inside and rested. /"Tashay went to our hut and stayed there. He called to me. "N≠isa . . . N≠isa . . . ."

I asked him what he wanted and left my mother's hut and went over to him. He gave me some *sha* roots he had dug. I took them, gave some to mother and went back to her hut and stayed there. Late afternoon, when dusk was standing, I went back to our hut and roasted some food. I took the food out of the coals and gave him some and set mine aside to cool. When it was ready, I ate it.

I ran away a few more times. I used to cry when he lay with me and kept saying no. People talked to me about it. Let me tell you what they said.

My mother said, "A man . . . when you marry a man, he doesn't marry your body, he marries your genitals so he can have sex with you."

And my aunt told me, "A man marries you and has sex with you. Why are you holding back? Your genitals are right over there!"

I answered, "I am only a child. This person is an adult. When he enters and takes me, he tears my genitals apart."

We lived and lived, and soon I started to like him. After that I was a grown person and said to myself, "Yes, without doubt, a man sleeps with you. I thought maybe he didn't."

We lived on, and then I loved him and he loved me, and I

kept on loving him. When he wanted me, I didn't refuse and he slept with me. I thought, "Why have I been so concerned about my genitals? They are, after all, not so important. So why was I refusing them?"

I thought that and gave myself to him and gave and gave. I no longer refused. We lay with one another, and my breasts had grown very large. I had become a woman.

275

Discussion

Although the recent trend has been for !Kung women to marry when they are older, women of N≠isa's generation were occasionally married between the ages of thirteen and fifteen (Howell, Chapter 6). Parents are usually responsible for arranging the first marriage and later marriages if the couple is still young (see also L. Marshall 1959), but, as indicated in memory 18, their decision is not final. If the girl is strongly opposed to it, the marriage will not take place. When young girls do get married, it is usually to a man seven to fifteen years older. These first marriages are very unstable, and many break up within a short period of time (Lee 1974).

One of the questions raised by N≠isa's account of her marriage is why, if she experienced so much premarital sex play, was she anxious about marrying and having intercourse with her husband? The circumstances of the marriage suggest some possible explanations. Although she agreed to marry /"Tashay, she had hardly spoken to him before they were left together in the hut. The next morning, when the final ceremony was to be performed, she ran away, demonstrating her reluctance to leave her parents and her modesty in not accepting her new husband too easily (see also Marshall 1959). Her husband was probably some years older than she was and expected to sleep with her immediately. From the description of her discomfort after he had slept with her the first time, he must have been larger, genitally, than the boys she had had experience with. He threatened her with force. He also insisted that she sleep with him quite frequently. All these things, combined with the fear of having to eventually leave her parents for him, made her frightened of staying with him and appears to account for her repeated running away. The fact that she kept going back to him suggests her ambivalence rather than her dislike of him.

It could also be that she was generally frightened by any kind of new sexual experience. There is evidence for this in her first descriptions of learning to play sexual games with other children (Part III, 13). She described herself as always saying no, crying and running back to tell her mother, being frightened while most of the other children were participating, and needing a lot of encouragement before she could accept and finally enjoy this sexual play. Perhaps her fear of the unfamiliar is at work in both sets of memories.

By the last memory, N≠isa is still not a fully matured woman; she is only on the verge of menarche. But this memory presents her first successful efforts at staying with a man and her gradual moving away from her mother. She begins to accept a new person to take the place of her family.

Summary

N≠isa is an exceptionally articulate person, and much of her narrative is highly idiosyncratic; nevertheless, the events of her childhood, as she described them, resemble those of other !Kung women and touch upon a number of fundamental features of their life.

(1) Weaning from the breast, the birth of a sibling, and weaning from the back enforce on the !Kung child adjustments that are very difficult to make, and they spark off periods of intense unhappiness. N≠isa's descriptions confirm observations by Draper and Konner of the frustration children experience during these times. Looking back, adults see these events as having had a formative influence on their lives.

(2) Children are expected to share things with others even when they are very young. They discover, as N≠isa did, that giving and withholding things is a powerful vehicle through which anger, jealousy, and resentment, as well as love, can be expressed. This behavior is of great importance because it becomes the only means of distribution of goods in the adult economy.

(3) The general !Kung concern about, and pleasure in, food is already present in childhood. N≠isa's memories confirm Lee's observations that they express anxiety about their food supply in spite of the fact that they have enough to eat. (Lee 1968a).

(4) As reflected in N≠isa's confrontations with her parents, individualism is encouraged and strict obedience of parental authority is considered neither necessary nor desirable. This has the effect of ensuring a very wide range of personalities among the !Kung living in small, isolated groups. N≠isa's tales of physical punishment are puzzling, since it has not been observed by Draper or Konner. This contradiction should be resolved by further research.

(5) Children play in groups with other children much of the day. Because no formal teaching is done, it is in these groups that children acquire a good deal of the information, habits, and skills they need to survive in their environment and to become proper members of their culture. Unlike our own (middle-class) society, such groups

perform actual subsistence activities and actual sex play, including
sexual intercourse. In N≠isa's accounts children spend much of the
time away from adult supervision, although, as Draper points out
(Chapter 9), they are seldom far from adult help, if needed.

(6) N≠isa's memories of her early marriages show some of the
stresses involved when young girls marry men much older than themselves. Because young girls are in demand, due to the existence of a
small percentage of polygamous marriages, the girl's parents exercise
a good deal of control over their son-in-law and can afford to be
exacting. Early marriages are unstable (Lee 1972a, 1974; Howell,
Chapter 6).

(7) N≠isa's descriptions of the way girls learn about sex and of her
relationship with her husband /"Tashay suggest that relations between the sexes are not egalitarian, and that men, because of their
greater strength, have power and can exercise their will in relation to
women. This confirms Marshall's (1959) finding that men's status is
higher than women's. Still, it must be said that women have considerable voice in group affairs and considerable control over their
own lives (that is, in terminating an unsatisfactory marriage). In
these respects they may be more egalitarian than most other societies,
including our own.

While the factual confirmations and controversies raised by interviews such as these are important, the immediacy of feeling and
poetry that is contained in a person's account of his life is at least
equally important. Reading, "Look how I am today, I'm very small.
That's because people brought me up badly. I was too difficult for
them," is more informative than an ethnographer's guess as to the
effects of weaning in relation to a person's self-concept; reading,
"The rainy season came . . . My heart was so happy and I ate meat,
wagged my tail and imitated a dog. I laughed with my little tail and
laughed a little donkey's laugh . . . ," reveals more profoundly how
the !Kung feel about the beginning of the rainy season than a description of their concern about water availability. In an individual's
narrative expression of feeling, we can begin to grasp emotionally
what it may be like to be a !Kung.

This is important because all too often "primitive" people are
dismissed as being so different that it would be difficult to determine or identify with what they feel. This study has carried us beyond this prejudice by presenting the !Kung as *people:* reluctant to
leave friends, sometimes loving and sometimes angry with those
they love, sad and happy at the changes of the seasons, wanting to
live good lives. Underneath all the obvious differences, they are,
after all, not so very different from ourselves.

Further Studies to Part III

Draper's other work on hunter-gatherer childhood is found in Draper (1972a, 1973, and 1975). Studies of !Kung infancy and ethology can be found in Blurton Jones and Konner (1973), DeVore and Konner (1974), and in Konner (1971, 1972b, 1973a, 1973b, and 1973c). For a review of Spock's *Baby and Child Care* see Konner 1972a.

Man in trance

Education for Transcendence:

!Kia-Healing with the Kalahari !Kung

Richard Katz

San healer laying hands on a pregnant Herero woman

In the religions of the modern world there always seems an element which searches more intensely for contact with an ultimate level of being.[1] This element usually expresses itself in mystical approaches and spiritual disciplines, such as Zen Buddhism, ecstatic Christianity, Sufism, and Qabala. A central experience in this search is the experience of transcendence. The !Kung San are also engaged in a search for an ultimate level, which leads them to regularly experience heightened states of consciousness that certainly could be called transcendent. Despite all the obvious differences between the !Kung and the cultures in which the above mystical traditions and spiritual disciplines flourish, there is a fundamental similarity: in some frontier of human consciousness, persons seek an ultimate level of being beyond their individual selves.

This fundamental similarity in a variety of cultures has been described by others (see e.g., Eliade 1967). The !Kung, however, with their Stone Age-type existence, provide somewhat unique insights. We begin to understand how this search for an ultimate reality functions in a crucial yet poorly understood aspect of man's evolutionary sequence.

This paper is a beginning in the documentation of experiences of transcendence among the !Kung. The particular focus will be the !Kung's education for transcendence: how they learn to have, or better to accept transcendence.[2] Unless a !Kung is prepared to accept the experience of transcendence, it either does not come or comes in a form which he cannot experience, understand, or use. As with most cultures, the !Kung find that there must be a preparation or education for transcendence if that experience is to foster growth.

Transcendence and Growth

Altered states of consciousness are now receiving increased theoretical and empirical consideration in the social sciences. Ludwig (1969, pp. 9–10) has offered a definition of such altered states. He says they are:

> . . . any mental state(s) . . . which can be recognized . . . by the individual . . . or an objective observer . . . as representing a sufficient deviation in subjective experience or psychological functioning from general norms for that individual during alert, waking consciousness.

I find problems with this definition. For example, altered states of the more profound kind are more than "mental states;" the deviation which they represent is so fundamental that the person is at a different level of being than "subjective experience" or "psychological functioning." But Ludwig's definition suggests a typical and contemporary psychological starting point.

At the same time, social scientists are re-realizing that altered states of consciousness have been a perennial concern of man, and that there are deep roots for such study in ancient psychological, religious, philosophical, and spiritual disciplines. One particular altered state, very thoroughly considered in such ancient disciplines, is the experience of transcendence. This experience is especially important because, unlike certain other altered states, it has vast potential for increasing personal growth.

It is very important to remember that the experience of transcendence represents a special, unique level of being. Huston Smith (1969) has said:

> Transcendence should be defined neither quantitatively as "more of the same" nor qualitatively as "better than anything previously experienced" but in terms of the *kind* of value it designates. The effect of its appearance is to counter predicaments that are ingrained in the human situation. . . .

If we keep recognizing this noncomparative quality of transcendence, we will not confuse transcendence with ordinary psychological states, however intensified these psychological states may be.

The experience of transcendence has been approached from many perspectives (e.g., the essays in Richardson and Cutler 1969). Maslow (1962), for example, has offered a psychological perspective. He has described "peak experiences" in life during which " . . . many dichotomies, polarities and conflicts are fused, transcended or resolved." The emotional reaction during that state has a ". . . special flavor of . . . surrender before something great."

Among the more thoroughly described transcendent experiences within a spiritual perspective are the yogic state of *samadhi* and the Zen Buddhist state of *satori*. Suzuki (1956), for example, says that satori, or enlightenment, is an "intuitive looking into the nature of things" as opposed to an analytical or logical understanding of it. He quotes Zen masters as they speak of satori. Stressing the sense of the "beyond" in satori, one master says, "There is not a fragment of tile above my head, there is not an inch of earth beneath my feet." Another, stressing the spiritual revolution produced by satori, says, "The bottom of a pail is broken through."

There is always a tendency to rank these experiences of tran-

284

scendence according to their depth or purity or intensity. For example, Maslow's peak experiences may seem more a question of going beyond the ordinary self, while the experience of satori may seem more a question of participating in eternity. This difference in emphasis would lead one to place satori on a higher level.

And then sometimes Maslow writes about peak experiences in a way that suggests they do not even have that special, noncomparative quality of transcendence we discussed; and that instead of being transcendent experiences, peak experiences are merely intensifications of ordinary psychological processes. This presents still another problem.

But in this paper I would like to focus on experiences which are definitely transcendent; and on these transcendent experiences *in general,* rather than on the differences between them.

I have taken this approach because I want to consider issues in education which depend on the fact of transcendence, not its degree or level. A proper education can evoke a transcendent experience and transform it into an experience of growth. Certainly different experiences of transcendence have different implications for growth. Experiences of satori may produce spiritual revolutions, leading to the birth of a new man; on the other hand peak experiences may produce intense awe or joy or reflection, leading to a temporary change in emphasis or direction. I will not treat such different implications in this paper.

Central to any discussion of education for transcendence is the idea that man, or an aspect of man seeks something beyond himself. I am assuming such a need for transcendence. Huston Smith (1969) puts it this way: "Man lives forever on the verge, on the threshold of 'something more' than he can currently apprehend." He quotes Nietzsche's Zarathustra who says that "Man is a bridge and not an end."

Education for transcendence must deal directly with an experiential threshold. It must teach how one can cross the threshold of fear into the state of transcendence. This education must also bring transcendence into ordinary life, and ordinary life into transcendence, if personal growth is to occur (see Katz 1973 for a discussion of personal growth and transcendence).

!*Kia*-Healing with the !Kung

I want to describe the !Kung's !kia-healing[3] and their education for this !kia-healing (see Lee 1968b; and L. Marshall 1969 for other views of !kia; and Katz, in preparation, for a more extensive discussion of !kia and growth). The altered state of !kia is not a unitary concept. There are different levels and depths of !kia. I will focus on the deepest, most clearly transcendent !kia experiences.

285

I believe important insights into education for transcendence can emerge from this study of the !Kung. Many !Kung, approximately half the older adult males and one-third the adult women, learn to !kia.[4] During the !kia state, they heal and fulfill many religious functions. !Kia-healing is harmonious or synergistic with maintenance and growth on both the individual and cultural levels. The fact that large numbers of persons can experience transcendence in a way harmonious with their own and their culture's growth is somewhat unique and certainly significant.

Though the !Kung are in some senses remote from contemporary civilization, they seem completely contemporary in their education for transcendence. That process of education deals more with fundamental and enduring human characteristics than particular and transitory cultural settings.

San healing dance at dawn

The !Kia-Healing Dance

The primary structure for the occurrence of !kia is a dance which usually lasts from dusk to dawn, and may occur once or twice a week. The entire village comes to such dances, including children and old persons. The women gather around the fire, singing !kia songs and rhythmically clapping their hands. The men dance in a circle around the women, some working themselves into a !kia state.

!Kia, and its setting of the !kia dance, serves many functions. It is the !Kung's primary expression of a religious existence and a cosmological perspective. It provides healing and protection, being a magicomedical mode of coping with illnesses and misfortune. The !kia at the dance also increases social cohesion and solidarity. It allows for individual and communal release of hostility. Finally, the dance alters the consciousness of many members of this community. As individuals go into !kia, others at the dance, participating in various ways and to various degrees, themselves experience an alteration in their state of consciousness. An atmosphere develops at a dance whereby individual experiences of !kia can have a contagious effect on others.

Onset of !Kia

The !Kung say that !kia is due to the activation of an energy, which they call *n/um*. Those who have learned to !kia, are said to possess n/um and are called masters or owners of n/um. N/um resides in the pit of the stomach. As the master of n/um continues his energetic dance, becoming warm and sweating profusely, the n/um heats up and becomes a vapor. It then rises up the spine, to a point approximately at the base of the skull, at which time !kia results.

Bo[5] talks about the !kia experience:

> You dance, dance, dance, dance. Then n/um lifts you in your belly and lifts you in your back, and then you start to shiver. N/um makes you tremble; it's hot. Your eyes are open but you don't look around; you hold your eyes still and look straight ahead. But when you get into !kia, you're looking around because you see everything, because you see what's troubling everybody . . . Rapid shallow breathing, that's what draws n/um up . . . then n/um enters every part of your body, right to the tip of your feet and even your hair.

The action and ascent of n/um is described by Tsau:

In your backbone you feel a pointed something, and it works its way up. Then the base of your spine is tingling, tingling, tingling, tingling, tingling, tingling, tingling . . . and then it makes your thoughts nothing in your head.

This n/um is an energy which is held in awe and considered to be very powerful and mysterious. It is this same n/um that the master of n/um "puts into" somebody in attempting to heal him. So, once heated up, n/um can both induce !kia and combat illness.

!Kia as a Transcendent Experience

!Kia can be considered a state of transcendence because during !kia, a !Kung experiences himself as existing beyond his ordinary level of existence. !Kia itself is a very intense physical and emotional state. The body is straining against fatigue and struggling with convulsion-like tremors and heavy breathing. The emotions are aroused to an extraordinary level, whether they be fear or exhilaration or fervor. Also, a !Kung practices extraordinary activities during !kia. He performs cures, handles and walks on fire, claims x-ray vision, and at times says he sees over great distances. He does not even attempt such activities in his ordinary state.

Moreover, he can go beyond his ordinary self by becoming more himself, more essential, or by becoming more than himself. For example, there had not been a dance for a number of weeks at a particular waterhole. One of the important masters of n/um who lived there said he wanted to have a dance soon so that "I can really become myself again." I think he meant that he wanted to experience again what he felt was his more essential self. Tsau, a blind man who is one of the most respected n/um masters, describes his own transformation:

> . . . God keeps my eyeballs in a little cloth bag. When he first collected them, he got a little cloth bag and plucked my eyeballs out and put them into the bag and then he tied the eyeballs to his belt and went up to heaven. And now when I dance, on the nights when I dance, and the singing rises up, he comes down from heaven swinging the bag with the eyeballs above my head, and then he lowers the eyeballs to my eye level, and as the singing gets strong, he puts the eyeballs into my sockets, and they stay there and I heal. And then when the

women stop singing and separate out, he removes the eyeballs, puts them back in the cloth bag, and takes them up to heaven.

During the !kia state he becomes more than himself because he can now see, and he means that both figuratively and literally.

Through !kia, the !Kung participates in the religious dimension. Transcending himself, he is able to contact the supernatural, a realm where the ghosts of dead ancestors live. Sickness is a process in which these ghosts try to carry off a chosen one (the sick person) into their supernatural realm. The ghosts are strong but not invincible. Masters of n/um may struggle with the ghosts and may often win. While in !kia, a n/um master argues and contends with these ghosts. He carries on a sometimes heated dialogue: "Don't take this person yet, he's not ready to go." In his ordinary state, a !Kung is in awe of the supernatural and avoids talking about it; certainly he does not deal directly with it. If a person's n/um is strong, the ghosts will retreat; and the sick one will live. This struggle is at the heart of the n/um master's art, skill, and power.

!Kia can be viewed as an altered state of consciousness, altered to the degree and quality where it becomes a state of transcendence (see Tart 1969 for a survey of theory and research in this area). A !Kung's sense of self, time, and space are significantly altered. There is a feeling of ascent during !kia: a master of n/um says, "When I pick up n/um, it explodes and throws me up in the air, and I enter heaven and then fall down." During !kia others feel they are "bursting open, like a ripe pod" or "opening up" so that something more important can come out.

Educating for !Kia

In their struggle with illness, misfortune, and death, and in their search for contact with transcendent realms, the !Kung have the !kia-dance and n/um as their most important allies. Being fiercely egalitarian, the !Kung do not allow n/um to be monopolized or hoarded by a few religious specialists; rather they want to spread the teachings and n/um widely within the group. The !Kung see only increased benefits to the culture from increasing the number of n/um masters. Also, there are important benefits for the individual who learns to !kia—positive experiences such as being able to help others. Working against this desire for all to possess n/um is the fact that becoming a master of n/um is a long and painful process, fraught with danger. The education of a n/um master is a continuing resolution between these opposing forces.

Socialization for !Kia

One of the most striking things about !Kung education for !kia is
that it is very much a normal process of socialization. Every male
tries to become a master of n/um, though he may try more or less
hard. Many years before a person seriously tries to become a n/um
master, he is playing with !kia. A group of five- and six-year-olds
may perform a small !kia dance, imitating the structure of the dance,
the dance steps, and the !kia gestures, at times falling as if in !kia.
Through play, the child is modeling; as he grows up, he is learning
about !kia.

Furthermore, education for !kia occurs within the context of the
family, which, of course, is the major vehicle for socialization. The
primary source of information about !kia, as well as the experiential
teacher of !kia is likely to be one's father, perhaps one's uncle, or an
older brother.[6]

Seeking !Kia

But this strong and supportive context for !kia is not enough. A
!Kung must seek !kia—he must be willing and ready to receive n/um
which can evoke the experience of !kia. N/um is not "put into"
someone who cannot accept it. This seeking of !kia usually occurs
when a young man reaches twenty or so. He becomes a "student"[7]
and may express his search by going to as many dances as possible,
perhaps two or three a week; in a sense he is pushing himself to get
more experience with the !kia dance.

Predisposition for !Kia

Who is it that seeks n/um? And who finds it, or rather who is able
to accept n/um? Though approximately 50 percent of the adult
males do !kia and heal, 50 percent do not. There are several variables
which seem to increase the likelihood one would become a master
of n/um. First, !kia families seem to exist—if your father has n/um,
it is likely that you will get it.[8] Also, there are individual predisposing
factors.[9] For example, if you are very emotional, you are more
likely to become a n/um master. Experience with intense emotions
could be good preparation for the deeply emotional !kia experience.
Moreover, !Kung who have a richer fantasy life, who have more
access to their fantasies and are more able to accept them, are more
likely to become masters of n/um. Since fantasy is an altered state of
consciousness, these qualities could again be excellent preparation
for contacting and accepting another altered state, that of !kia.
Though I have no data on this, there might also be predisposing

characteristics of a more physiological and biochemical nature. Reaction to stress, brain-rhythm activity, and blood-sugar level are among the variables which can effect the appearance and nature of an altered state (Tart 1969).

The !Kia Experience

Socialization for !kia and seeking !kia are preparatory phases in education for !kia. At the heart of this educational process is the experience of !kia itself. There is consensual agreement and clarity about the concept of !kia and the action of n/um. Most !Kung, whether they !kia or not, can describe how n/um works and what it feels like to !kia. But during the !kia experience itself, these concepts and descriptions are not available. While there is conceptual clarity, there is experiential mystery. This is the case with one's first !kia experience; it is also, though usually to a lesser degree, the case with subsequent !kia. And when someone who has !kia over the years, experiences !kia with a new intensity or quality, the experiential mystery is again great. At its core, the education is a process of accepting a !kia *experience* for *oneself*. This is especially difficult because !kia is painful as well as unknown; it is a greatly feared experience.

Along with feelings of release and liberation, !kia also brings profound feelings of pain and fear. In describing the onset of !kia, n/um masters referred again and again to pain and fear. They describe searing pain in the area of the diaphragm and spleen, and at the pit of the stomach. A n/um master, recalling his first experience with n/um says, "N/um got into my stomach. It was hot and painful, like fire. I was surprised and I cried."

But as I thought about this pain and fear, I could not understand their depth and profundity only in physical terms; or put another way, the physical symptoms seemed also to be metaphors for other nonphysical processes. Finally, I talked with one of the two most knowledgeable and powerful healers. His description of !kia was both clear and subtle. He said that as a person enters !kia the fear is not only that he will lose himself, but also that he may never come back. To paraphrase it, the fear is of the experience of death without an experience of rebirth. This fear evokes its own special and profound pain. When the potential n/um master can accept the fact that he must die to himself *and* can also feel assured that he will be born again, then he can face the fear, overcome it, and break through to the !kia state.

One of the older masters of n/um describes this death and rebirth:

In !kia your heart stops, you're dead, your thoughts are nothing, you breathe with difficulty. You see things, n/um things; you see ghosts killing people, you smell burning, rotten flesh; then you heal, you pull sickness out. You heal, heal, heal, heal . . . then you live. Then your eyeballs clear and then you see people clearly.

Here we get some idea of why !kia remains an experiential mystery and why it is feared. We can say that to enter !kia, the !Kung must give up his familiar identity and assume a new !kia-identity. He gives up the familiar and enters the unknown. Looked at from another viewpoint, he must experience death before he can be reborn into !kia. This passage into the unknown is frightening for the !Kung as it has been for persons in every culture.

The Dance Structure

How do the !Kung educate for this critical passage into !kia? Of primary importance is that the person himself seeks !kia, and, if it comes to him, he must accept it. Various structures and techniques at the dance support his efforts and encourage them.

At any dance, the potential n/um master can receive support and encouragement from a number of people. First and foremost for the student is his teacher, who has agreed to train him and give him n/um. This teacher, perhaps with one or two other masters of n/um, will likely be the one who tries to put n/um into the student during a dance.

There are also a number of people who can become guardians. They may give the potential n/um master physical support when the onset of !kia makes him shaky and unstable, or hold him when he trembles during !kia, or lead him to others so he can heal them. The guardians serve another crucial function since the potential n/um master may do things which can be harmful to himself or others. For example, he may want to get closer to the fire to help his n/um boil up; but when he tries to put his head in the fire or throw hot coals in the air, someone at the dance will usually leap up and restrain him. These guardians, who are there to support and protect the potential n/um master, can be anyone at the dance.

Another supportive and at times inspirational group is the women who are singing and clapping the !kia-healing songs. Their singing and clapping stimulates the n/um to boil and rise up the spine. The intensity of their singing can help to determine and regulate the depth of one's !kia. Finally, there is the entire community that is present at the dance: friends, family, neighbors, all participating to some degree and by their physical presence offering support.

The Thermostatic Approach

As one continues to dance into the night, ever more seriously, one's n/um may begin to boil and !kia becomes imminent. At this point, another critical element in the educational process occurs. Almost as with a thermostat, the potential n/um master tries to regulate his condition. As he feels !kia coming on, he may involuntarily draw back from, and at times actively resist this transition to an extraordinary state. His teacher, the guardians, and the singing women, help him overcome this resistance. They try to help him master his fear of the intensifying, oncoming !kia. If his !kia is coming on so fast that his fear escalates and prevents him from experiencing the !kia, his teacher may make him stop dancing for a while, or drink some water, or lie down, all to "cool down" his too rapidly boiling n/um. The n/um must be hot enough to evoke !kia but not so hot that it provokes debilitating fear. Also, it is never a question of merely putting n/um into the student. The correct amount is critical. Experienced masters of n/um, for example, are encouraged to go as deeply into !kia as they can, provided they maintain enough control over the n/um to use it for healing.

Tsau tells what he does during a dance with someone who is learning to !kia:

> You must do the [student's spleen area] properly. You've got to fire arrows into that area; fire them in and fire them in and fire them in until these arrows of n/um, which are a lot like thorns, long thorns, are sticking out of the spleen and stomach area like a pin cushion, sticking out in all directions. So you see why we rub [the person's body] like we do, because the arrows are popping out of his body, and we're rubbing them back into his body. And that's why we take our sweat, and then we try to work the arrows around to the back. When we do that, his breath and soul return properly to his body; but if we don't do that, then he might die, he might die if we just left those things sticking out . . .

When the student is too fearful, Tsau ceases to focus the n/um inward and upward, and instead allows it to subside:

> If I come up to someone at the dance who is learning to !kia and he fears it, and he says, "please don't put your hands

on me because I might die," and he just says, "take your hands off me" then I leave him because he fears it . . . When a person says he is afraid, I remove the arrows I've put in.

Throughout this work at the dance, there is extensive physical contact between the potential n/um master and his teachers and guardians. Much of the sensitivity to these subtle thermostatic considerations comes from this intimate contact. Physical support complements the psychological support offered the potential n/um master.

Drugs are not used on any regular basis to induce !kia. There is, however, at least one indigenous drug which apparently is used infrequently and in a specialized manner.[10] If a student is having considerable difficulty learning to !kia, he may be given this drug at the beginning of a dance. The drug is offered as a training device, which may vault him over his intense fears as well as bringing him closer to the !kia state. The drug experience itself also becomes a preparation for !kia since both experiences are forms of altered states of consciousness. As with other techniques used at the dance, the dosage and time of ingestion of the drug are carefully regulated by the teacher. The drug is supposed to help the student over the barrier of fear and into !kia, not catapult him into yet another unknown and potentially frightening altered state.

There are specific and sometimes idiosyncratic signs that someone is approaching the threshold of fear and/or !kia. The signs must then be interpreted. Is the fear so intense that he must sit down? Or is the fear such that if he stays with it, he can overcome it and enter a !kia state? Some of the signs of fear and/or impending !kia are: is the body shaking? Does he have a glazed look? Are his eyes downcast? Is his face impassive? These are signs used not only by the person himself, but also by his teacher, guardians, and the women who are singing and clapping. If the women sense that someone is ready to go into !kia, they man intensify their singing and clapping to give him an extra push.

An example may describe the subtlety of this thermostatic idea. One young !Kung, who was new to !kia, had a look of tremendous fear as he was dancing. The singing and clapping, the dance in general, was at a high intensity. !Kia was threatening to overwhelm him. But instead of taking him away from the dance, two persons went to him, one holding him from the front, the other from behind, and physically brought him back to the dance. The three of them then continued dancing in that close physical contact, as the singing reached new levels of intensity and excitement. In a sense they brought him back to what he most feared, but now they were supporting him. He became able to go through his fear and into !kia. The approach to each potential n/um master depends on his particular history and present readiness for !kia.

As the person experiences the beginning of !kia, those who are reaching and working on him can confirm the validity of his experience. They can acknowledge his entrance into !kia.

!Kia Management

As !kia occurs at a dance, the atmosphere becomes more electric and the dance more focused. One person going into !kia is in a sense an incentive or stimulant for others to do likewise. At one dance, there were fifteen dancers, and twelve of them were potential n/um masters. I tried to imagine what would happen if all of them were to go into !kia at once. Certainly the process of education for !kia would be severely strained. But no more than two or three were in !kia at any one time. What happened was a process of !kia management. The more experienced n/um masters hold back their !kia until those who need more help are either under control or able to function in !kia. Rarely are there people in a state of !kia who need help and cannot get it.

The Teacher

The teacher is a !Kung who is a master of n/um. He remains an ordinary person during his non-!kia state, rather than an intimate of the gods or a chosen instrument. He does not demand obedience nor a long apprenticeship. The period of learning is focused during the dance itself. The emphasis is on experiential education. The core of the teaching is at those points when !kia is about to and does occur. The teacher is with the student at the threshold of the latter's fear and !kia, trying to help him over his fear and into !kia, and then guiding him to use that !kia for healing.

The blind, powerful n/um master Tsau said to me:

> . . . I ask God for n/um and put it into you. And I say to God, "Here's my child, give me some more n/um so I may put it into him" . . . Even today I'm going to put it into you, and you'll dance, dance, dance, dance. I'll put it into you . . . one of these days soon, when the women start singing, you'll start shivering . . . Let's dance tonight, let's dance tonight and . . . and dance tomorrow night and then I'm going to dance you again . . . I'll dance you tonight and dance you tomorrow night . . . I'm going to do you . . . and you will be trembling like

leaves in the winds . . . when I heal you, I will feel n/um trembling in your body, and then I'll say, "Oh, today this fellow has drunk n/um."

Though originally from the gods, n/um now passes regularly from man to man. Teaching is primarily by example. The teacher has been there before. He may be !kia at that particular time; certainly he has !kia many times before. He recognizes the student's progress, interprets his condition, and confirms that the student is !kia.

As he works with his student, the teacher combines many functions. He is likely to be a parent or close relative, and therefore he is responsible for the student's socialization in general. The teacher is a spiritual guide in that he initiates the student into the cultural mysteries, probing the nature of his existence. He is like a priest in that he has had contact with the ghosts and can guide the student to that realm. He is very much a therapist in that he tries to help the student accept his fear rather than be overcome by it. And he has been an academic teacher because very likely he taught the student the conceptual framework of !kia.

N/um as a Special Gift

The process of educating for !kia has consistent and constant features. For example, though n/um originally came from the gods, men now teach or give n/um to other men. Also, the !Kung usually get n/um in their mid-twenties, occasionally in their early twenties or early thirties. Certain exceptions to this usual educational process seem to stimulate the appearance of powerful n/um and to signify its continuing availability.

!Xəm is considered by other !Kung to be a powerful n/um master. He agrees. I asked him how other !Kung get their n/um; he said: "How do I know they got it? So they dance and do it; but do they *really* know what they're doing? I don't know. Maybe it's the singing of the women that does it." I then asked him whether he heals with the other masters of n/um in the village; he said, "What other masters of n/um? You think there are other n/um masters in the village?" !Xəm loves to joke but he nonetheless means what he says.

!Xəm's father had n/um, but did not give it to him. !Xəm received n/um directly from God. He describes it this way:

When I was about fourteen or fifteen, I was asleep, and God grabbed me by the legs and sent me out into the bush at night, and out there he gave me a small tortoise and told me, "This tortoise, leave it here and then in the morning, get your father

to degut it, and put n/um into it, and that will be your n/um."
And then God took me farther, and I was crying in the dark,
and my father came looking for me and found me crying, and
carried me back to the fireside. Then in the morning I said,
"Father, come and see this tortoise. Fix it for me and put
n/um in it, and give it to me because this is what God has given
me. Fix it and give it to me so I may keep it; so that when you
are dying, I can use it and I'll save you." But my father refused.
He just killed the tortoise, roasted it and ate it. Then the skin
of his throat parted and we could see his windpipe exposed.
Then God told me, "For what your father has done, I'm going
to kill him. The thing I gave to you that he ate is killing him."
And I refused and I said, "My father won't die." And I took
another tortoise with n/um in it, and dropped burning coals
into the shell. And then I put the shell to my father's lips, and
he drank the smoke, and the same day the skin above and the
skin below came together and closed, and he lived. Then God
said to me, "See what your father's arrogance has done to him.
You tell him to stop that and not to do it again or else I will
really kill him next time." And that's how I got what I have.
That's where I started it, and today I carry the people in the
different villages. If someone is sick, I go to them.

This vision and gift of n/um is both unusual and startling. So were
some of the immediate effects. !Xəm says, "I only danced after this
[vision] experience, and only began to !kia after this experience;
but *right* after!" He then says that twice after the vision, God took
him out to the bush alone, and he !kia. Initial !kia are almost always
times of especially strong fear, fear of the hot n/um and the unexpected intensity of the experience. But !Xəm's solo, God-induced
!kia were different. He says of these two experiences:

How could I be afraid during these !kia like the others are
afraid during their !kia? God killed my every thought. He
wiped me clean. Then he took my soul away whirling, my
thoughts whirled.

Tsau is considered an even more powerful n/um master, perhaps
one of the two most powerful ones in the area. And he also describes himself as such. He talked about how he got n/um:

When I was a tiny thing, sucking at my mother's breasts, I
took n/um, I drank n/um. It was n/um . . . it was at the breast,
I was about three or four years old. I would cry, and cry, and

cry. My mother would sing to me, and I would cry, and suck the breast, and cry. I just sat in my mother's lap and danced. I was afraid of the n/um. N/um was hot and hurt. . . That is my story. Others who !kia are much older than me, but they started their n/um later than me.

Other !Kung were understandably surprised at this early onset of !kia ability. As Tsau put it, people would say, "What's this youngster still at the breast doing?"

K"xau is a youngster of only eleven or twelve years. And yet already there is something special about his relation to !kia. He is an especially talented dancer, and dances more frequently than his peers. Most unusual, he seems already to have drunk n/um. In view of others, he has great possibilities for becoming a powerful n/um master. !Xəm describes a particular dance:

> I've looked at this kid, K"xau, and didn't see anything until recently. But a few months ago we had a dance in the bush, and the kid started crying and was carried around the dance crying by his playmates . . . He was witless . . . His father was away. I said, "This kid's already drunk n/um." Then I told the women, "Stop singing because this kid's father who is teaching him about n/um is far away, and I'm not going to work on him, and you're going to give this boy a lot of pain if you keep singing. Then the ladies stopped.

!Xəm then tried to figure out why K"xau is so special:

> . . . what is it that has made K"xau !kia while such a young boy? I'm trying to figure it out in my own mind what is it that sets him apart. . . When I see a little kid like that I say, "His heart is full, full of dancing" . . . it's his heart. He loves to dance. When the singing starts, he's not the least bit afraid of people, so he dances full out, and that's what helps him !kia.

Where others approach !kia with fear and caution, young K"xau's enthusiastic and devoted approach is striking.

!Kia in Context

The !Kung do not seek !kia for its own sake. They experience !kia in order to heal others. If they were just to !kia without healing, this would be seen as a misuse of these !kia-related powers. Also, !kia is not cultivated as a long-term state. A !Kung has to maintain his responsibilities as a member of a hunting and gathering group. He is a hunter and gatherer, who also happens to !kia. !Kia generally should occur within the period of a dance. One of the older and more experienced n/um masters did not come out of !kia when the dance ended the next morning. This extended !kia was not seen as a privilege, or an extra source of healing power; it was seen as a mistake. The n/um master himself was quite upset, and tried as hard as he could to come out of !kia. When he returned to his normal state later that morning, he was able to resume his ordinary, everyday responsibilities.

The intrinsically valuable experience of !kia remains thoroughly functional. !Kia always occurs in context. One way I have tried to describe this is with the concept of synergistic consciousness. !Kia-healing is a state of synergistic consciousness, harmonious with both individual and cultural levels of existence. !Kia supports the functioning and growth of the individual n/um master. It allows him to transcend himself and develop extraordinary powers during certain periods. It reaffirms his relationship with the supernatural and leaves him with a feeling of well-being. For a few of the most powerful healers, !kia also seems to raise their general level of being; their ordinary lives take on a special, spiritual quality. And !kia does not interrupt or disrupt the !Kung's carrying out his basic everyday responsibilities.

!Kia also supports the functioning and growth of the culture. When a !Kung becomes a master of n/um, everybody gains. With its religious, medical, and social dimensions, !kia is a major force in the culture. Also, there is no limit on n/um; no zero-sum game is involved. One !Kung becoming a master of n/um does not mean another !Kung cannot become one; often, especially if they know each other, it can mean just the opposite. N/um is an expandable substance. What is good for the individual is good for the culture is again good for the individual. This is a synergistic relationship.

Educating for Transcendence

Perhaps we can extract from the !Kung experience with !kia certain more general ideas about education for transcendence.

Beyond Transcendence

The experience of transcendence is momentary though in another sense timeless. The emphasis is not so much on having a transcendent experience but on what you do next—what effect this experience has on your life. The !Kung !kia in order to heal, and to participate in

the religious and spiritual dimension. !Kia has an integral place in the
ongoing life of the individual and his group. As documented so
vividly and so often, industrialized Westerners too easily place all the
emphasis on *achieving* the experience of transcendence (see the first-
person accounts in Kapleau 1967). They look harder and harder for
one transcendent experience, the breakthrough. The farther they
feel from that experience, the harder they look, the more desparate
they can become. If they are fortunate enough to stop grasping and
allow the experience to occur, then they are faced squarely with the
crux of the matter. For after the exhilaration and relief which can
follow the experience, there is often a letdown. And instead of
having found the answer, they are usually faced with a perplexing
question: what do I do now? Without a context, transcendence is a
transitory experience, with uncertain implications for personal growth.
The explorer of consciousness temporarily leaves himself and his
society. But after experiencing a truth, he returns to himself and to
his society, and attempts to live this truth with himself and others.

Certainly there have been dramatic instances where one transcendent experience changes the course of a life and begins a path
toward growth. Religious conversions, for example, do occur. But
there must be a fertile soil from which the experience can arise and
in which it can subsequently grow.

There is another aspect to this issue of transcendence in context.
What is an experience of transcendence for a particular person? How
does his life, as a context, affect the nature of that experience? Put
another way, is the !Kung experience of !kia analagous to other more
familiar experiences of transcendence—such as the Zen satori or the
mystical religious experience? My feeling at this point is that more
than likely they are similar. This does not deny the fact that *within*
any culture (or spiritual discipline), there are differences in degree or
level between experiences of transcendence.

I think that each culture transcends itself in a way specific and
organic to that culture. The mode and metaphors of transcendence
can be quite different, but I think the state is similar. For example,
one culture may have an *apparently* more sophisticated or elaborated
set of metaphors. But these may be merely a more literate representation of a universal experience of transcendence, and the emphasis
certainly belongs on the experience.

The Student Seeks

As was clear with !kia, the individual himself seeks the transcendent experience. But this seeking is not a grasping after !kia;
it is making oneself ready to receive n/um. This is in contrast to a

situation where someone sits back, waiting for it to happen *to* him, waiting for a teacher to *give* him an experience of transcendence. The saying that the teacher finds the student when the latter is ready can also be applied to the experience of transcendence. Transcendence grows in fertile soil.

An Experiential Passage

I have been talking about the experience, not the concept, of transcendence. Entering into a transcendent state is an experiential passage. Conceptual clarity about that state may give one a feeling of confidence or some comfort, but when it comes down to the moment of transcendence, it is of no help at all. In his book, *The Teachings of Don Juan,* Castaneda describes how his need for conceptual clarity about transcendence denies him the very experience of transcendence (Castaneda 1968).

But inevitably there is a strong desire to find out what will occur during a transcendent experience: "What will happen to me? How will I feel?" We all want to hold on to something—some "known"—when we face the unknown of a transcendent moment. But, just as inevitably, there can be no conceptual clarity in that moment because there are no concepts. The experience is transcendent because it has gone beyond concepts, beyond the mind.

Death and Rebirth

The !Kung describe a process of death and rebirth as critical to entering !kia. This is not surprising. There is a broad range of evidence suggesting this is the process which characterizes the entrance into a transcendent state. During an experience of death, you give up who you are, what you are accustomed to. And in the process of giving up your identity, you can enter the state of transcendence. The conviction that you will be reborn encourages you to enter this state. You can accept the fear; it is no longer immobilizing, as when you fear that you will become nothing or that you cannot come back again to yourself. Rebirth for the !Kung is being reborn into the !kia state; also, after the dance, being reborn as an ordinary, fully functioning !Kung. Having a conviction about rebirth is helpful. But the basic process is *being able to accept the unknown,* willingly going into fundamental mysteries. The hero's passage is a journey into the unknown. Facing the unknown, the boy becomes a man, the man a hero. (Campbell 1956 demonstrates the depth of man's commitment to this process.)

Today, particularly among young people, many are struggling to

establish a sense of their own identities. Many of them would recon-
ceptualize this struggle as an experience of transcendence. But often
the struggle is an expression of identity diffusion—a state of being at
loose ends, not particularly invested in anything—and identity diffusion is not equivalent to transcendence. You give up your identity
when you experience transcendence, but before you give up an
identity, you must first have one. The !Kung for the most part know
who they are and sense their place in their universe. They have an
identity which they can transcend.

The Teacher

I talked about the teacher of !kia as being someone who is there
at the crossroads, at the point of no return, who by his presence
encourages the student across fear into !kia. Although the emphasis
remains on the students being prepared for !kia, ready to receive
the n/um put into him, the !Kung teacher is initiating him into areas
the teacher has had experience with.

But the !Kung model is too rare today. There are many supposed
"teachers" of transcendence, but few who are encouraging others
toward a real transcendence they themselves have experienced. There
are few teachers who are relatively complete; who could, for example,
be both teacher and parent and be both responsibly. Also, many
"teachers" today operate without a context. The !Kung education
for !kia is effective primarily because it occurs within a context
which is actively interested in this education. When transcendence is
pursued in isolation of any cultural supports, if it is experienced, it
quickly dissipates, with very little effect on a person's daily behavior.
Transcendence needs to be educated toward growth.

Aspects of !Kung Folklore

Megan Biesele

Playing the musical bow

The purpose of this chapter is to explore in a general way !Kung
folklore and the light it sheds upon hunter-gatherer society. The
main outlines of the storytelling tradition will be delineated, and the
manner and extent of its appearance in the contemporary culture
will be discussed. Emphasis will be laid upon the somewhat exclusive
connection of old people with the stories, and reasons for this connection will be suggested. I will examine the types of tales found
among the !Kung and will present, by quoting or paraphrasing a few
of the more important stories, the central cast of tale characters
which revolves about a roguish God and his heroic daughter-in-law.
These stories will then be examined for structures, concerns, and
relationships which may illuminate further what we already know
about !Kung society. Basic themes, for instance, include some of the
fundamental problem points of living, such as marriage and sex, the
food quest, sharing, family relationships, the division of labor, birth
and death, murder, and blood vengeance. Other concerns include
the creation of the present world order and the relationship of
hunter-gatherers to peoples with more advanced economies. The outlines of a central !Kung tale cycle have begun to emerge around these
themes. It is with this central cycle that the chapter is primarily concerned.

The present !Kung collection was made in the course of field
work from 1970 to 1972. Before this time the only substantial collection of San oral texts was W.H.I. Bleek and L.C. Lloyd's *Specimens of Bushman Folklore.* This collection was made nearly one
hundred years ago, largely among the now extinct San of the Republic of South Africa. This valuable book consists mostly of fragments of ethnographic data, personal histories, and songs presented
as texts, but includes as well some twenty to thirty stories, roughly
divided into myths, fables, and legends. A further collection, also
made by Bleek and Lloyd in the 1870s, was published as *The Mantis
and His Friends,* and contains again about the same number of
stories. At about the same time J.M. Orpen was gathering stories
among the Maluti San of Basutoland. He published an article in the
Cape Monthly Magazine containing eight of them. In the early 1920s
Dr. Bleek's daughter Dorothea collected a number of Nharo tales at
Sandfontein on the border between Namibia and the then Bechuanaland Protectorate. Seven of these have appeared in *The Naron: A
Bushman Tribe of the Central Kalahari.*

Since that time, a few collections have been made among widely
spread groups of !Kung. In Namibia there appeared in 1952 a book
of *Märchen* adapted from !Kung tradition by Fritz Metzger and set

down in German under the title *Und Seither Lacht die Hyäne*. In the
1950s Manuel Viegas Guerreiro collected the material for his
Bochimanes !Khu de Angola, which includes several Portuguese
translations of !Kung stories from the region between Pereira d'Eça
and Serpa Pinto. Also in the 1950s collecting was done in Namibia
and in the Central Kalahari Reserve of Bechuanaland by Elizabeth
Marshall Thomas and Lorna Marshall. A few of their /Gwi stories
appeared in *The Harmless People* and more, perhaps eleven /Gwi and
fifteen !Kung, some in many versions, are in preparation. Four
!Kung stories and references to several more are included in Lorna
Marshall's "!Kung Bushman Religious Beliefs," *Africa* 32 (July 1962).
George Silberbauer includes a single /Gwi story in his 1965 *Bushman
Survey Report.* A Reverend Swanepoel is presently making a small
collection at Chum!kwe in Namibia, but he has as yet no publication
plans. The published !Kung collections thus represent rather a small
number of tales taken from all over the entire large !Kung area.

I felt that a comprehensive collection of the stories still being told
among the !Kung of Ngamiland would help to fill out our knowledge
of San oral traditions. Comparing such a collection with the earlier
ones would help us to know more about what (if anything) in these
traditions is common to different San groups widely distant from
each other in space and time.

I collected in Botswana from December 1970, to June 1972 a
total of seventy-five distinct stories, most in several different versions.
Of these, over fifty were gathered from !Kung of Kauri and of the
Dobe Area of Ngamiland.[1] The remaining stories were collected at
Ghanzi (thirty-two tales, of which nine are completely distinct from
Ngamiland !Kung stories) and from !Xō people at Takatshwane,
southeast of Ghanzi (twenty-two tales, of which thirteen are distinct).
It is my hope that these last collections, including as they do material
from the Central and Southern San language groups respectively,
will help to close a bit further the geographical gap between collections from northern Botswana and South Africa.

It should be emphasized, however, that this chapter does not
constitute an introduction to the folklore of the San in general. What
I have collected at Ghanzi and Takatshwane, and what I have read of
material coming from other parts of Botswana, from Angola, Namibia,
and the Republic of South Africa, present an extremely variegated
picture for San oral literature. Just as the ecological anthropologist
cannot answer the question "What do San hunter-gatherers eat?"
without reference to very localized and specific conditions, neither
can the student of folklore make many generalizations about their

oral traditions. The !Kung stories about Kauha the trickster god are very different from those of the /Gwikwe involving their god, Pisiboro, also a trickster. The long-ago Mantis god of the /Xəm people of the Cape, though he bears some resemblance to Kauha, has a whole cycle of adventures of his own. The Nharo, furthermore, have a genre of dramatic stories told to the accompaniment of a single *dəmagəri* bow played by up to five women at once. The whole genre is lacking among their neighbors the !Kung.

305

Yet there are fascinating connections to be found among some of the traditions (see M. Biesele, in press). There are also interesting comparisons to be made with traditions of some of the neighboring cultures, notably the Nama Hottentots (Khoi).

In all cases the stories were put on tape as they were told, with no interruptions for clarifications. They have been transcribed word for word in !Kung with the patient help of /Tuka of Dobe and others. In the case of the Nharo and !Xō stories, each taped story was followed immediately by a taped rendition in !Kung by Kan//ka of Ghanzi,

Story-telling at a meat distribution

who is trilingual and himself a competent storyteller. Nevertheless, the !Kung stories alone have pretensions to textual accuracy. They will be published later as texts with translations. In this introductory paper, however, only paraphrased summaries and a few translations appear.

The !Kung collection is also the only one which approaches comprehensive coverage of the available material. It includes as much as possible of the entire repertoires of eight good storytellers, five women and three men, as well as many scattered stories from a large number of other storytellers. I feel confident that this collection presents the main outline of !Kung tradition, and that few stories which would materially change this picture still remain to be found.

Though San oral literature contains a number of other forms, the bulk of what is repetitively performed consists of these *n≠wasi o n!osimasi,* "stories of the old people." These are without exception set in that long-ago time when God walked upon the earth, when animals were still people, and when many strange things occurred which do not occur in the world today. There are also hunting stories and historical stories in plenty, but these are just *n≠wasi* ("stories"). Synonyms for "stories of the old people" include *n≠wasi o n//ahamasi* ("stories of long ago") and *n≠wasi o k x'aishemasi* ("stories of the beginning"). To *n≠wa n!o* is to tell the old people's stories. Among the Ghanzi people it is to *n≠wa Huwesi* or *n//e Huwesi,* tell the doings of *Huwe* ("God") and all the people who were with him in the ancient time.

When I first went to Botswana, one of my main expectations was that I would find only a very small number of competent storytellers among the San. I imagined I would find expert raconteurs, in other words, individuals next to whom most people's narrative abilities would seem decidedly inferior. Second, I assumed that it would be the individual's way with words, rather than his knowledge of the items of lore, which would determine his status as a storyteller. I have been proved hasty in both suppositions.

I have been pleased to discover not only that the number of (non-farm) San who tell stories competently is quite large, but that virtually *every* old person (among !Kung every man or woman, around age forty-five or older, carries the appellation *"n!a"* (old) after his or her name) is able and usually willing to tell stories. In fact, of the many old people from whom I requested stories there were only a scant handful who could not tell stories of the old time with confidence and vigor.

On the other hand, a younger storyteller, a young or even middle-aged adult, is much rarer. These younger people, when asked for stories, will most often protest that they "have not grown old enough to have learned the things that old people know." I am satisfied that this observation holds even among groups still hunting and gathering in much the ancient way. Thus professed lack of knowledge among the young is not to be equated simply with changing times, though there is doubtless some correlation.

It seems, indeed, that there are definite social constraints reserving storytelling to older people. Even the hearing of the stories of the old days is peculiarly the province of age, in San society. I have seen very few instances of the stereotypical grandmother sitting by the fire telling tales to the small children. As Lorna Marshall has observed, !Kung seem to have little interest in teaching the lore of their forefathers to the children. The storytelling groups I observed consisted much more frequently of a small group of old people getting together for some real, grown-up enjoyment. The telling of stories among San is no watered-down nursery pastime but the substantial adult pleasure of old cronies over a bawdy or horrific or ridiculous tale. Children are not *barred* from listening to the stories, and they do wander in and out of a group of storytelling adults as freely as they do at a trance dance. They may listen with considerable interest for awhile. Younger adults are often present at these sessions too, and will listen attentively. Sometimes they too will tell stories, and tell them well. But there is usually a slight flavor of restraint in their participation—they seem to indicate by a respectful passivity that they are disclaiming primary knowledge of the things of ancient time. In a situation where no old people are present, younger people are more likely to tell stories forthrightly. Many of them do so with good command of detail. But the respect accorded to age in general seems also to be operative in their reticence before their elders.

Thus the group with strong and unabashed interest in hearing and learning the details of past doings is the old people. And most old people appear to feel as qualified as any other old person to retell them. Hence, though there is no special priestly or otherwise distinct group entrusted with the stories in San culture, the old people do, in effect, have something of a monopoly. It is a nonjealous guardianship, however: younger people who tell stories do exist and are welcomed by their elders. Yet there is a certain sense in which "stories of the old people" refers not only to those told about the ancients of long ago but also to those belonging to the ancients of today.

The most important factor linking this age-group exclusively with the tales is "factual" knowledge of the items of folklore. Many San,

308

of all ages, are more or less able to tell a good story if it concerns events through which they themselves have lived. It is the combination of the general verbal ability with the details of the early times usually known extensively only to the old, which produces a successful San storyteller. Broadly speaking, the old people do not have markedly superior narrative abilities, as far as I have been able to discover. Their storytelling seems to be a natural outgrowth and perfection of verbal activities they have been practicing all their lives.

Stylistically, it is hard to tell an ordinary narrative of a recent, actual event from a narrative of the olden times (though there do exist specific distinguishing features). It is rather the addition of knowledge, not secret knowledge but a large collection of items which takes a long time to accumulate, which results in competent storytelling. It is generally the case that by the time a person is a *zhu n!a* ("old person") he will have accumulated a good deal of this knowledge. An old woman I asked about the telling of stories said: *Zhu n!a n/wi /twa n//e, kum, kwara. Zhu !ke!ke'm ko ku n//e-'/na e ko Huwesi osi, te a n/i /twa //"xe twa te kwara ka. Te a n/i ku //"xe o kx'ai ka.* (The old person who does not tell stories just does not exist. Our forefathers related for us the doings of the people of long ago and anyone who doesn't know them doesn't have his head on straight. And anyone whose head is on straight knows them.)

All of this is not to say that there are not a few really excellent storytellers who stand out from this crowd of good talkers. In some cases they excel in verbal or dramatic abilities, in others by a gift for remembering and synthesizing fragmentary episodes into coherent cycles surrounding central figures. In a sense we do not begin to talk about verbal *art* until we analyze the special capacities such experts bring to bear on the body of traditional lore. At present, however, it is important mainly to emphasize the high degree of interest and participation in storytelling among the old. It is looked upon not as "something to do when you are old" but rather "something that you do when you are old."

Though there is keen enthusiasm over the performance of stories, their contents themselves are looked upon with scorn. The stories are heard with anything but awed reverence. Instead, amused indignation greets the outrageous or bumbling adventures of the long-ago people. !Kung have no explanation for why their ancestors related to them such absurdities. "Hey! The doings of the ancient times were foul (/"xau), I tell you!" was how Ti!kai n!a ended some of her stories. To know of these doings is the wisdom of the old people. But the happenings themselves are rarely considered of great account.

The !Kung make no distinction of genre among trickster-creation stories and animal-etiology stories. Nor is there a formal distinction between "sacred" stories and "profane" stories. No sort of story is considered to be "more true" than another. I tried in vain to find verbal equivalents for such categories as "stories which are considered true" and "stories which are considered false," or for "myths" versus "folktales." Even when people who also spoke Setswana or Herero were confronted with such distinctions in these languages, the reply was that *all* of these things, in San tradition, were *n≠wasi o n!osimasi.*

There is another reason too, I feel, why the animal stories are not taken as a separate class from the stories of God and his family. It is that, for the San, the animals were all people in the beginning. All stories dealing with animals, thus, deal with them in their character as human beings, though they already possess traits that will come to be synonymous with them when they become animals. The story which deals with the day on which all of them finally are given their animal shapes is in a sense the termination of the magical time in which the other stories take place. Since then animals have been animals and people, people. The situation in the tales, however, is very fluid, with animals sometimes taking parts that in other variants are taken by humans and supernatural figures.

For the purpose of introducing the body of these n≠wasi, we can ourselves make an informal separation of (1) the creation tales and those involving the trickster God, Kauha, and his relatives and animal associates from (2) the animal tales which are never found connected into longer cycles and usually have etiological endings. Of the fifty distinct !Kung tales in this collection approximately half fall into each category. Primarily represented in this paper is the first category.

This group is unified by a central cast of characters which binds the stories together like the links of a chain. The second group is devoid of such a focus, concentrating instead upon specific and apparently unconnected characters and incidents. But the former, taken as a whole, imparts strongly the flavor of a mythical time when all these personages were present in the same world and vitally connected with one another. The rest of this paper will introduce this first group of tales. The other group will be only briefly noted here.

In the Botswana !Kung stories centering around God at the time he was still upon the earth, he is referred to most often as "Kauha." This name is one of God's less potent ones, and it may be used publicly and in a normal tone of voice. (In fact, the word can also be used to refer to a human "master.") However, at times he is called

"Haishe," or "!Gara," or "Huwe," as well, and almost always
"Huwe" by the Ghanzi people. I concur with Melvin Konner (personal communication, February 1971) that a good case can be made
for translating his name in these tales as "God," since he is the same
personage who later ascended the sky and became divine. But since
the !Kung concept of "God" is not the same as any of the several
western concepts linked with that term, I feel it introduces less mis-
representation to keep to the actual !Kung word in transcription.

Kauha's family includes his wives, with whom he engages in endless trickery, his adventuring sons Kan//ka and !Xoma, and his
brother-in-law !Kõ!kõtsi/dasi, whose eyes are located on the insides
of his ankles. Perhaps the most interesting and enigmatic personage
in all the tales, however, is a lovely woman who may be Kauha's
daughter-in-law. Most of the time she is called !Xõ//kəmdima, an
extremely obscure name which may mean "beautiful antbear
maiden." An exact meaning for this name is very difficult to attain
and there are some possible alternative translations. Certainly her
antbear characteristics do not obtrude over her human ones. In some
versions, too, she is called !Kxodi or "elephant girl." At times she is
married to an elephant or hyena and at times to a human being who
may be one of Kauha's sons, the older brother of Kan//ka and
!Xoma. In some versions she is called merely !Keu!keua or !Keu-
!keuadi, references apparently to her little barking laugh. Then too,
there is some reason to identify her with the python. Finally, one
reliable informant told me she was not a person or an animal at all,
but an edible root called ≠dwa !kəma.

Around !Xõ//kəmdima revolves a huge, fascinating cycle touching
on the themes of marriage and marriage-service, murder and blood-
vengeance, birth and the origin of meat, and the balance of power
between men and women. Her story consists of a number of related
episodes which are often told separately but fit together with beautiful logic when told by a very good storyteller.

The story can be briefly paraphrased as follows. !Xõ//kəmdima's
husband is insulted (za) by his mother-in-law one day when the
mother-in-law and her granddaughter are out gathering bush food.
The mother-in-law sees a great number of chõ bulbs sticking out of
the ground, and she says, "Oh, is this where my son-in-law goes
hunting every day, that his balls have fallen 'kloh, kloh, kloh!' and
are scattered all over the place?" And the child hears. That evening,
when asked to carry a piece of fresh duiker meat from the carcass
her father is cutting up over to her grandmother, the little girl refuses,
saying, "Why should a person who insults my father receive any

meat?" The insult is related to the father, who pretends to forgive his mother-in-law and gives her the meat anyway. But instead he tricks her, and kills her by an axe-chop to the back of her neck. He props her up in a sitting position with a stick, however, so that she appears alive.

311

!Xõ//kəmdima, who has been out gathering elsewhere, returns with food. She offers some to her mother, who just sits there and does not answer. She discovers the death because of the trail of blood which has left the old woman's body and has flowed all the way to the fire. !Xõ//kəmdima sits by the fire and cries silently for her mother. She guesses that her husband is responsible for the murder, and she does not want to let on to him that she knows. Her husband asks why she is crying and she replies it is only the smoke in her eyes. Because of this ruse he is no longer watchful, so that she is able to leap upon him, crying, "Did my mother sound her death-rattle? Well then, so shall you!" and to plunge an awl into his throat.

Beyond this point there are many versions of how the husband's family tries to avenge his death. Here is a direct translation of one from Ghanzi which involves a motif well known to students of American Indian tradition, the Obstacle Flight (D672):

One day long ago Kan//ka and !Xoma went to the waterhole. They sat by the water with anger in their hearts against the person who had killed their older brother. They lay in wait for her there. The one who had killed their brother was the beautiful !Keu!keua. They waited for her by the waterhole.

After awhile, they heard someone coming down to the water. Kan//ka said to his younger brother, "Here she comes." But !Xoma contradicted him, saying, "Yo! When !Keu!keua comes down you'll know her by the sound of her approach. Do you think !Keu!keua is so poor that we will not hear the clinking of her bracelets and her anklets? There will be no doubt about it when she comes."

So they waited until they heard "n/enu, n/enu, n/enu, n/enu"; she came down with her bangles clinking. Kan//ka's heart leaped in fear and he said again, "Here she comes!" !Xoma scolded his brother and said, "Don't get excited, just stay down and wait. You're acting like a child. Even though I'm younger than you are, I'm not afraid. What's gotten into you?"

!Keu!keu came down and sat by the waterhole. The brothers got up and dipped some muddy water and gave it to her to drink. She refused it, saying: "Give me sweet, clean water. I've been walking a long way and am very thirsty. Let me drink. Anybody but you two would know enough to give me clean water." So they gave her clean water and she sat and was drinking it.

Now !Keu!keua had already warned her grandmother that morning, saying, "Grandma, when I go down to the waterhole today and don't return, and a little wind comes back to you, you'll know that I have died." Hearing the girl's words, her grandmother had already softened a gemsbok pouch in readiness, softened it and shook it out and laid it aside.

Meanwhile !Keu!keua was drinking the clean water, and as she drank, the spears of the two brothers met inside her body. And a little wind left her body as she died. The brothers tried to grab the wind but it got away. It went back to the village. There !Keu!keua's grandmother took the little thing and put it in the gemsbok pouch. It stayed and stayed in there and grew inside the pouch. The people continued to live at that place and it continued to grow. They kept on living there and eating there as long as there were things to eat.

Kan//ka and !Xoma finished their work at the waterhole and ran off to hide because they were afraid.

And the drops of !Keu!keua's blood that were in the little wind lay in the pouch and grew. And they grew and grew until they became a person. When the person was finished it came out; the grandmother spread out a skin, in the late afternoon she spread a skin and took out the girl and sat her upon it.

Then the other people of the village came around. And !Keu!keua laughed, *"!Keu !keu !keu !keu!"* Hearing her, her daughter said, "That's my mother laughing!" But another girl contradicted her, saying, "Face like a tsin-bean face! How can you have seen your mother? How can you talk like that when my older sister is dead, and my heart is so heavy with grief?" And another girl said "How can you talk this way when you know my aunt is dead, and my heart is heavy with grief?"

But they came and saw her sitting there, splendid and full-grown. Her daughter said, "There's my mother!" And !Keu-!keua's younger sister said, "There's my sister sitting there!" And they were happy together.

Then one day those two brothers who had killed !Keu!keua came to take her in marriage. They came again, came to the village and spent the night. In the morning, !Keu!keua packed her things as if to leave with them. She packed bowls full of morningstar thorns. She packed bowls of rain. She packed devil's-claw thorn bowls. She packed *!go≠tobe* thornbush, she packed whatever—*!ki* thornbush stumps. . . . Then !Keu!keua took her baby daughter, who was a guinea fowl, and put her

on her back in her kaross. But she turned the baby to face back-
wards, so that she could watch out for her mother's pursuers.

And !Keu!keua fled from the village with her daughter on
her back. And Kan//ka and !Xoma left the village in pursuit of
them. And they chased her and chased her and soon they were
catching up with her. So she began to strew morningstar thorns
in their path. She ran on and after while asked her daughter,
"Where are they now?" The baby answered, *"Zenenene!*
They're almost close enough to grab my forelock!" So !Keu-
!keua strewed more thorns. Kan//ka and !Xoma were caught
in the middle of the thorns, and it took them a long time to
make their way out. But finally they reached the end of the
thorns and began to pursue her again.

And soon they caught up with her a second time. !Keu!keua
didn't see them, so she asked her daughter, "Where have they
gone?" "Zenenene! They're very close now and are about to
grab my forelock!" This time, !Keu!keua strewed big devil's-
claw thorns.

After a long time, Kan//ka and !Xoma came through those
thorns too. Then they crept up e—e—ever so softly until they
were almost upon her! !Keu!keua said to her daughter, "Why
are you so quiet? Tell me where they are!" So the little guinea
fowl said, "Mother, look! They've caught up with us!" So
!Keu!keua began to strew !ki thorns, *n//ana* thorns (those little
acacias that grow thickly together), !ki stumps—she dropped
them all so they lay in the path.

Soon Kan//ka and !Xoma found themselves in the middle of
the thorns again. But they kept on following her anyway. They
followed her until !Keu!keua had dropped all her thorns and
had no more.

Next she tok out a little raincloud and hung it in the sky, a
raincloud full of hail. She shot it into the sky, where it stuck
fast. And Kan//ka and !Xoma ran on and on, and soon came to
where the cloud was hanging. !Keu!keua asked her daughter,
"Where are they now?" And the baby said, "They're very
close." So !Keu!keua commanded the cloud to come down.
And even though it was a little cloud it made everything so
dark that the two brothers couldn't see a thing. "Dzup!," the
cloud descended between !Keu!keua and her pursuers. Thus
they didn't see which way she went, didn't see that she went on
ahead where it was dry and no rain was falling.

And the little cloud began to drop hail. And the hail broke
the strings of Kan//ka and !Xoma's loincloths, so they just
stood there naked. And the bows and arrows they had, with
which they had been stalking her, just fell apart, beaten by the
hail and rain.

313

So the brothers and the rain went back to their village together. And there the rain danced with them and danced with
them and danced with them and made their things fall apart
and ruined everything they had.

!Keu!keua escaped and they did not know where she had
gone. (Translation from !Kung transcription, ≠Təbo n!a,
Ghanzi)

There are other versions of how the family of !Xō//kəmdima's
husband try to avenge his death. In some versions the shoes of the
dead husband and mother of !Xō//kəmdima are flung into the sky
and become vultures which lead the husband's younger brother(s)
to the scene of the crime. The younger brother, in some versions
miraculously born directly through his mother's stomach wall and
already speaking and running about, avenges his brother's death by
stabbing !Xō//kəmdima with an awl. She, as always, is reconstituted
from a bit of blood that flows away on the wind to lodge in her
grandmother's groin. The grandmother places this blood in succes-
sively larger receptacles until it has grown into a full-sized woman
again.

Meanwhile, !Xō//kəmdima's people in turn swear vengeance upon
her killer-suitors. The brothers escape her people (sometimes through
the agency of an anthill which cleaves itself), only to be vanquished
by the reconstituted !Xō//kəmdima herself with a magical gemsbok
horn given her by her grandmother. She blows the horn once and
flattens them and their entire village. In one version she ends by
turning triumphantly into a steenbok so that people may have meat.

The stories concerning the first knowledge of water sometimes
involve !Xō//kəmdima's elephant husband. He has sole knowledge
of the water, which he guards jealously from her and her people. But
the mud on his legs tips them off that he has been walking in a waterhole. After various altercations he is killed by the spears of
!Xō//kəmdima's brothers the !Gashehmsi, little black birds called
"the children of the rain."

Besides this !Xō//kəmdima, there is another beautiful female
heroine, the python, whose adventures I will paraphrase briefly.
Married to the kori bustard, the python is tricked by her younger
sister the jackal into climbing a tree after n≠a fruits. The branch of
the n≠a tree hangs out over a well, and the python girl falls in. Glee-
fully, the jackal puts on the python's discarded clothing and ornaments and struts off to alienate the affections of the handsome kori
bustard.

Back in the village, the kori bustard comes home from hunting and misses his wife. The graceless jackal, trying to imitate the smooth, regal step of the python girl so as to fool her husband, comes bouncing and clanking before him.

The kori bustard greets her as he is accustomed to greet his wife, by passing a wildebeest-tail whisk, dripping with fat, across her forehead. But the foolish jackal, unused to this courtesy exchanged between well-bred beings, becomes very excited: "Ooh! Fat is dripping! Fat is dripping!" She greedily licks the fat dripping onto her chops from her hairy forehead.

Thus the kori bustard knows that he has been tricked, and he schemes to do away with the jackal. As he is arranging their sleeping place for the night, he sets up rows of poisoned arrowheads in the sand under the skins where she is to sleep. She lies down, is pricked by the arrowheads, and cries out in protest. But the kori bustard says to her, "This is the same place you've slept ever since we got married; why do you suddenly begin to complain?"

So the jackal keeps quiet. By dawn she has died from the effects of the arrow poison. The kori bustard gets up and goes hunting, leaving her lying inside the house.

When the sun is well up and the jackal has not emerged, the old grandmother begins to worry whether the kori bustard's wife is sick. She sends the youngest child to investigate. The child finds the jackal dead in bed, with a dried clump of n≠a seeds protruding from her anus.

"Grandmother!" calls the child, *"N≠a !ko-!ko !kau-!kau !kwi-!kwi zi tsi-zi tsi!"* (a childish way of saying "n≠a seeds have dried in older sister's asshole!").

"What? Did you say I should put a leather pubic apron on her?" calls the grandmother, who is a little hard of hearing.

"N≠a !ko-!ko !kau-!kau !kwi-!kwi zi tsi-zi tsi!" shouts the child a bit louder.

"What? Did you say I should put a beaded pubic apron on her?"

At last grandmother is forced to come see for herself. She sees the dried clumps of seeds stuck in the jackal's anus, and she breaks off a piece and eats it. Then she and her granddaughter roast and eat the body of the treacherous jackal.

Meanwhile, the kori bustard goes to get his real wife out of the well. But the well beneath the n≠a tree is very deep, and the python is lying at the bottom. The kori bustard calls all the animals together to help him get her out. First the tortoise sticks in his leg to try to reach her, but it is far too short. Then the eland gives it a try, but

315

his leg only goes halfway. All the other animals, the kudu, the gemsbok, all of them, try to reach her and fail. At last the giraffe is called.
He puts his long leg in, down, down, down, all the way to the bottom.

"I can feel her . . . and I think she has given birth while she has
been down there!" The giraffe slowly pulls up his leg with the
python girl and all her children clinging to it.

The kori bustard, overjoyed to see his wife again, has skin mats
spread all the way from the well to the village. Then he walks proudly
back to their house on the trail of mats with the rescued python
girl. They sit happily on a skin there in the midst of their rejoicing
relatives.

There is another very important tale which concerns the kori
bustard as a kind of captain of the other animals. In this tale he is
identified as Kauha's servant. He uses his wings to fan the fire of
creation so that the animals may receive their distinctive markings
by branding. In some versions it is Kauha himself who does the
branding, and the kori bustard is absent.

> The kori bustard made a fire. In the fire he laid long irons.
> He used his big wings to blow upon the fire until the irons were
> red hot. Then he took up the irons and branded the horse and
> stood him aside, the bush horse, the one with stripes. The kori
> bustard created him; he made those stripes upon his hide with
> fire. And was done with him.
>
> He next took the eland and created the eland. And the eland
> was just dun colored. He went to the hartebeeste and did the
> same to him. Then he made the ostrich, he who says *"hom!"*
> And he gave the ostrich his wings, and the ostrich had wings.
>
> The kori bustard created all the animals in this way. He took
> the gemsbok, and the gemsbok calves, and made the stripes on
> their faces. Then he was finished with all of them. Duikers, all
> all the other animals, he created them too. And they were
> complete. . . (Direct translation from !Kung transcription,
> Tĩ!kai n!a, Kauri.)

God the Trickster

Most of the stories featuring Kauha before his ascent to the sky
have to do with the tricks he plays on his wives and has played on
him in turn. These stories are bawdy and scatological, and are cause
for great hilarity among the !Kung. Because of the tit-for-tat nature
of these stories, they are most often reeled off in rapid succession.

The storyteller becomes progressively more animated and the laughter more uproarious. As does the !Xõ//kəmdima cycle, these stories explore some of the fundamental problem points of living: sex, excrement, birth and death, hunting and gathering, sharing and cooking and eating food, the division of labor and the balance of power between men and women.

Here are a few of the things that take place between Kauha and his wives. One day he is out hunting and does not manage to kill anything. Fearing the hunger of his wives, he chops out his own anus and makes biltong of it. He brings home the biltong, and the wives start cooking it right away. But as soon as it gets hot, it leaps out of the pot and back into his asshole. "What kind of meat is this?" wonder the wives, and plot revenge.

The next day while Kauha is out hunting again, the wives cut off their labia and pound them up with *tama* melon seeds in a mortar. They set aside a dish of this food for their husband. When he comes home, he eats it with gusto. "What is this delicious meat you have pounded with the tama melon seeds?" he asks.

"We found the dried skin of a baby giraffe rolled up and stuck under the roof of a house in an abandoned camp," they reply. "Hunger defeated our scruples, and so we took it and pounded it up for food." Kauha goes to sleep satisfied, but later is awakened by the foul stench emanating from his own stomach and filling his nostrils. "What food is this?" he wonders, and schemes what he will do to them next.

The following day he hangs his balls up in a $n\neq ai$ tree, where they look like edible gum. The wives come along and eat the gum, but soon become aware of what it is and start yelling.

In another episode Kauha is looking for beautiful women to sleep with:

> Kauha wanted to get married. He asked one girl after another, but they all refused him. So he said to himself. "All right. Just let them wait and see what I'm going to do to them." Then he went off and turned himself into a springbok. Next he died, and lay down out in the bush somewhere.
>
> The women came that way gathering. They found the dead springbok lying in their path. "Ooh, ooh, ooh; I've found a springbok!" cried the girl that Kauha had especially wanted to marry. "Hey, everybody, I've found a springbok. Come here and let's pack it up to take home."
>
> All the girls ran up to see. "But since we have no string, how will we carry it? How can we possibly carry such a big thing over our shoulders?"

"Don't worry," replied the first girl, "We'll just carry it in a kaross. We'll carry it to the camp and then go borrow a knife from someone and skin it."

Now in the group of girls there was one that Kauha did not desire. This girl volunteered to carry the springbok first. She stowed it firmly in her kaross. The heavy meat rode high on her back, and she walked well. But as they walked, Kauha made himself very heavy. The kaross sagged, and in a short while the weight had completely defeated the girl. So she lay the bundle on the ground and called out to the first girl, "Come on, you found this meat—now you carry it."

The first girl said, "Who says I'm refusing? Give it to me and help me get it on my back." The girls continued walking. As they walked, Kauha slipped downwards in the kaross until he lay directly behind her buttocks. Then he began to do it to her—he was "marrying" her. He slid down right into her crotch, and she cried, "Ai! Why have you people placed this meat so it can slide down like it's doing? What am I doing wrong? Maybe I'm too short to carry this springbok. Maybe it's doing me this way because I'm too short."

The other girls said wearily, "Just push it back up and let's *go,* hey? We know it's heavy, but why should we be the only ones to carry it?" Nonetheless, they helped her out: another girl came to her and carried it for awhile. With her nothing happened, and they continued a long way along their path. When it was the first girl's turn again, she put the springbok back in her kaross. But as soon as she started to walk, Kauha slid down again and was "marrying" her. She would push him back up again, and he would slide back down again, and she would have to push him up again. "Hey!" she wondered. "What kind of meat is this?"

But she struggled on, and at last they arrived at the camp. The people were puzzled. "What meat is this that dies but is still alive like this seems to be?"

"It's meat we found lying in the bush. We've carried it home. But we don't know what this meat is up to: when some of us carry it, it's just fine. But when this girl tries to carry it, the meat does something awful to her. It's a terrible piece of meat."

"Can this be just a piece of regular old meat?" the people wondered. "Is it just a piece of regular old meat?" The people all sat around and talked it over. But at last they decided to skin it. When they skinned it, it turned out to have no blood and no guts. It was just a solid piece of meat, and it tasted bad. So they didn't eat it. "No," they said, "some terrible fever may have killed this animal. Something awful may have killed it, so that it tastes so foul. We just don't know about this meat."

So they threw it away. That's what they did with the meat those girls had found. (as told by !Kun/obe n!a)

In another story, Kauha is tricked by both the women and his brother-in-law !Kõ!kõtsi/dasi ("Eyes-on-his-Ankles"). Kauha is miffed one day because the women are eating roasted //xaru bulbs and only giving him raw ones to eat. So he takes his brother-in-law, and the two go out into the bush to gather their own //xaru so they can roast them. Kauha persuades !Kõ!kõtsi/dasi they should gather the //xaru with the tops still on. They gather a hunting-bag full and come home and lay it aside.

Now this brother-in-law's face is empty—he has no eyes. He and Kauha start playing ti (a game involving a row of holes in the sand and a tiny bead—good, quick eyesight wins it). !Kõ!kõtsi/dasi beats Kauha over and over. He continues to win because his eyes are on his ankles, close to the action! !Kõ!kõtsi/dasi keeps digging out the sand from the right holes all the time.

They play and play, and Kauha goes on losing. He begins to wonder how, if this guy has no eyes, he can win all the time. When they finish playing, !Kõ!kõtsi/dasi lies down to take a nap. When he is fast asleep, Kauha flicks sand in his face to see whether he will blink. Nothing happens. So he flicks sand on his neck. Nothing happens until he works his way down to the ankles. When these blink violently, Kauha makes a plan. "Tomorrow I will blind these eyes," he says to himself.

The next day he and !Kõ!kõtsi/dasi are roasting the //xaru bulbs. They build a fire and dig a great trench in the coals, a hole "like a porcupine burrow or an antbear burrow." They lay the //xaru in the coals but the tops stick out. So Kauha tells his brother-in-law to step on the tops to tamp them down into the hole. "When I rake the coals over them be sure to move your legs!" he says. !Kõ!kõtsi-/dasi wonders secretly to himself whether his eyes will get burned. And sure enough Kauha rakes the coals over his eyes! The eyeballs pop and hiss in the fire, singing *"Kho-Kho-Kho-Kho-Kho-tsuninini!"* Kauha mixes !Kõ!kõtsi/dasi up with the //xaru and roasts the lot. As he is being cooked, !Kõ!kõtsi/dasi sings:

Tsuninini! Come and eat me and your mouth will disappear!
Tsuninini! Come and eat me and your mouth will disappear!
Tsuninini! Come and eat me and your mouth will disappear!

Kauha's sons Kan//ka and !Xoma sit and listen to this song and wonder what it is their father is roasting. When they ask him, Kauha pooh-poohs his sons, saying it is their imagination. But they insist, "We're just telling what we heard." Then Kauha rakes the coals away and takes the //xaru out of the fire. He pops one into his mouth. Then he takes another one and peels it and eats it. But the next one he tries to eat hits against his mouth and drops to the ground. So does the next one! He tries again and again but the //xaru will not go into his mouth. Whatever has sung "tsuninini!" in the fire has already sewn his mouth closed! Sewn and sewn until it has disappeared.

Kauha is pretty surprised. He says to the people, "Sing for me so I can dance and cure myself and get my mouth back." They sing and dance. The women have all turned into birds. Kauha calls out "I want that bird with the long stomach way in the back there to come and dance in front of me!" But only other women come to him, never the one he wants. So he refuses them all and goes on dancing.

While he is dancing, the women steal the rest of the //xaru out of his hunting bag, and they eat it all up. They stuff the bag with wet sand to fool him, leaving a few //xaru at the mouth of the bag so it will appear full.

Kauha dances and dances, and eventually his mouth comes back. He goes to get more //xaru from the bag, and discovers he has been deceived. He calls again for the bird with the long stomach, the ≠təmsa bird, to dance with him, and refuses all other women. The ≠təmsa at last comes clapping and singing *"!Ka≠dē≠dē, !ka≠dē≠dē,"* dancing beautifully, unknowingly to her death. Kauha beats her long stomach that is full of //xaru until it becomes even longer, hanging down to the ground.

Kauha's sons Kan//ka and !Xoma appear again in another long story. In this story they are killed by lions. The lions bury them in the stomach contents from an eland kill. Kauha tracks them with the aid of the tortoise. He then causes lightning to come down and strike the lions dead in the midst of a dance. The ending of this story is an account of the origin of trancing.

Kauha and his sons figure as well in the story of the springhare. Here the springhare borrows Kan//ka's loincloth to dance in but fails to return it. Kauha, indignant, fashions the very first springhare hook to catch him, and flings wide springhare meat to all the world.

The last story I will mention that involves any of this central cast of characters deals with the origin of sex. Here Kauha, in this case called by another name, !Gara, is again portrayed as the innocent, bumbling fool bested by women and circumstances:

!Gara tried screwing his wife in the nostrils. Then he tried her ears. Finally, he screwed her nostrils again. He was getting nowhere.

His wife looked at him, and said, "Don't you know *anything*? What do you think you're doing in my nostrils and my ears? Can't you see that there's a much better place, here? *This* is what you 'eat,' you fool."

!Gara was a person who was really ignorant. He was definitely stupid and didn't know how things were. (as told by Kashe n!a)

Karã/'tuma: The Division of the Social World

This rambling list of stories has included the major adventures of Kauha and his family and of his servant the kori bustard and the kori bustard's wife, the python. Two other stories of prime importance in !Kung tradition involve quite distinct characters. The first is the well-known story of the origin of death, which involves an argument between the moon and the hare. There are as many versions of this story as there are tellers, but basically death comes to the world because the hare denies the moon's statement that men shall die but be forever reborn, just as the moon itself is (Motif A 1335.1, Origin of Death from Falsified Message):

When the moon died, it returned to life again, to pass again across the sky. "Everyone will do as I do," said the moon. When a person has died, don't think that he will just die and lie there and rot. Take need, follow what I, the moon do: I die and then live again, and die again only to live again. Everyone should do as I do."

But the hare contradicted the moon. "No! he said. "A person is born and he must die also. When he rots he will smell bad."

The moon argued with him, and said, "Watch me. I'm going to die and then I'll come alive again. Watch me and learn, and then we can both do it." But the hare refused. So the moon split his mouth open. The hare became the split-mouth hare that people chase.

The moon and the hare argued with each other, and harangued each other. The moon said, "Take my advice. . . . a person will die and yet return!" But the hare refused, so the moon took a hatchet and split his mouth. Then the hare scratched the moon's face in return. The two of them fought back and forth. The hare scratched the moon's face! That's why you can still see marks on the moon's face, because the hare scratched it and the scratches festered. When the hare had spoiled the moon's face, the two of them separated. They spent the next day separate, and the day after that. That's how their anger rose and they fought, chopping each others' mouths and clawing each other's faces. (as told by N//au n!a)

The second of these is the story of /'Tuma/'tuma, also called /'Tuma/'tumane or Karā/'túma. It deals with the division of the social world into hunter-gatherers and herder-farmers. Here is a direct translation:

We who were made first, have come to be last. And those who were created last, have come to be first. Even though they arrived later than we did, Europeans and Bantus have come to be ahead of us.

I refuse this thing, that we should have come to be the last of all. I fear this thing. It gives me pain. And I despise that old man of long ago who caused it to happen. I think that if I saw him today I would beat him. But he's dead and there's just nothing that can be done.

That old man who was responsible for all this was named /'Tuma/'tuma. He was also called Karā/túma. One day long ago Karā/túma was out hunting. And in the bush he discovered a cow. When he saw the cow, he said, "Is this a cow? Is this a buffalo?"

And the cow was not afraid of him; it did not run away. It just stood there. But Karā/'túma did not take it home with him to the village. Instead, he shot it. It just stood there, and he shot it. He never asked himself what is this creature that doesn't fear me, but merely shot it with his bow and arrow.

Then he went to tell the others. All the people gathered at the carcass of the cow to eat it.

Later Karā/'túma told the black people about the cow. (The black men were his younger brothers. For Karā/'túma's parents first bore him, then bore a black man, and last of all gave birth to a European. All of you Europeans here are small children compared to us.) He told a black man about the cows, and the black man said, "Let's go have a look at these things." So they went to see the cows. As soon as the black man saw that the cows didn't run away like other animals he said, "Ai! A thing like this which doesn't fear you, you certainly don't want to kill. Let's make a kraal, and drive them into it, and see what will happen."

So they chopped down thorn trees and made a kraal and drove the cows into it. One of the cows gave birth in the kraal.

So the black man took a thong and tied her hind legs, and she still just stood there. And he milked her, and brought the milk to Karā/'túma.

"You've helped me find this cow, and now let's drink the milk together." But Karā/'túma said, "Uh-uh, you eat first, and let me lick the pot!" That's what he said! "You eat first, and let me lick the pot!"

When I think about it, I want to kill him! It's a good thing he's already dead, because otherwise I'd be in jail for sure. If I had been there that day long ago, I would have killed him.

Well, the black man said, "Come on, let's eat! Lick the pot—what kind of talk is that?" But Karā/'túma persisted, saying, "No, you eat your fill first, and let me scrape what's left off the sides of the pot."

So the black man ate, and Karā/'túma licked the pot. When they were finished, Karā/'túma picked up a leather thong. But the black man came and grabbed the other end of it, and they tugged at the thong to see who could pull it out of the other's hands. Finally, the black man got the thong away from Karā/'túma. He gave Karā/'túma a piece of string instead, saying, "You can use string to do whatever you have to do; I need the thong for my cows. You have nothing you need to tie up with leather thongs."

Karā/'túma didn't refuse, but just took the string. Right there he should have put his foot down and fought the black man for the thong. But he didn't. He just took the string and started going about snaring animals with it. And the black man sat in comfort and milked his cows and drank the milk.

One day Karā/'túma came across a cultivated field, a field of sorghum. He tried some, and the husks burnt his skin, made him itch. So he went into the field and started a fire, and burned most of the field, leaving a few stalks standing. Then he went back to tell the black man what he had done. "I found some terrible things over there that burn your skin. So I set fire to them. But there are some left." And the black man said, "Let's go see." And when they got to the field, he said, "Are you crazy? This is sorghum; it's food, you fool. I'm going to take what's left home with me."

Thus Karā/'túma ruined us; that day he spoiled the chances of our people for all time. (Direct translation from !Kung transcription, !Kun/obe n!a, Kauri.)

Present space does not permit the discussion of the animal stories, or the other very interesting genres in !Kung and other San oral literature. The paper has limited itself to a preliminary exploration of the central cycle of !Kung stories. Further genres (songs, prayers, dialogues, and so forth), which hold at least as much interest as this one for the student of folklore, will be dealt with elsewhere.

It can be seen readily from this brief survey, however, that a collection of tales from living San presents material of very great interest to anthropology. In many cases social and ecological conditions dealt with in the stories are still observable in the present-day environment surrounding the storytellers. Structural analyses of the tales surely will help us to comprehend a few more of the cultural categories which have remained puzzling. Close attention to the tale variants may help us to know what degree of creative imagination is permissible within the bounds of !Kung tradition. And enjoyment of the stories for themselves may involve us personally in some of the less tangible aspects of !Kung life, things we rarely speak of but nevertheless strive to understand.

!Kung Knowledge of Animal Behavior

(or: The Proper Study of Mankind Is Animals)

Nicholas Blurton Jones and Melvin J. Konner

Dobe man bringing home a porcupine

The investigation reported here concerns !Kung knowledge of animal behavior (ethnoethology) and their methods of acquiring and organizing this knowledge. This chapter compares their data and methodology with the data and methodology of modern ethologists, as described for instance by Tinbergen (1963). The investigation came into being in the field as a result, in part, of a chance coincidence. An interest in animal behavior led to a question from Blurton Jones which aroused a lively response from some !Kung. This gave Konner the idea of investigating their interest further. The investigation had three other points of origin. (1) Levi-Strauss (1962) has argued that the competence of the mind of "savages" in particular fields is best evaluated by collaboration of anthropologists and "western" experts in the subject. (2) Washburn and Lancaster (1968), Laughlin (1968), and others have argued that the long period in human evolution during which man lived as a hunter and gatherer may be expected to have included a selection pressure on the human brain, such that man became interested in animal behavior and competent in finding out about it. Laughlin's observations on the Aleuts suggests that they indeed have great knowledge and interest in comparative anatomy and comparative behavior, and we might expect comparable knowledge among the !Kung. (3) Although it is commonplace among anthropologists to argue that *Homo sapiens,* of whatever race and culture, shows a uniformly high level of intellect, an opposite view is deeply ingrained in the mind of the layman and, as far as we can judge, in the minds of serious academic writers on the history of science and the achievements of western man. Variations in the use to which this intellect is put occur even within cultures, and this paper could be regarded as an attempt to see which variants in our culture compare most closely to the !Kung within the specific area of animal behavior. While we refer to some aspects of !Kung hunting procedure, we make no attempt to treat this subject systematically.

Methods and Procedures

In August and September 1970 Blurton Jones visited Melvin Konner and Marjorie Shostak during their field work. Besides investigating topics of mutual interest in child behavior, Blurton Jones and Konner held a series of discussion groups on animal behavior with five or six !Kung men at each group. In all we held six seminars in three villages, and they lasted two to three hours during the evenings. Before the meeting we would think of a general line of questioning, and during the meeting Blurton Jones would raise a question in animal behavior which Konner would translate to the !Kung. The !Kung, in turn, would then discuss the matter, one or more individuals might volunteer information. Konner would translate back to Blurton Jones, and both authors would enter replies in their notebooks. One seminar was completely tape-recorded. Once under way the discussions proceeded at a good pace, and it was notable that the participants found the exercise interesting and

Telling the hunt

showed little sign of tiring of the topic. The atmosphere was more like a lively seminar than an interview. As a precaution against misunderstanding, a !Kung man experienced in working with anthropologists and particularly with Konner and Shostak, participated in each meeting and, where necessary, retranslated from the idiosyncratic language of the older men into a more familiar !Kung.

In our questioning we concentrated on establishing how much the !Kung knew about animal behavior, with a view to checking this against existing knowledge of western scientists. Incidental to this, many hints came out about how they know and find out about behavior, and, to some extent, how they explain it. Consequently we can begin to make a comparison with modern ethology, a western science of the behavior of animals. In practice, the comparison with knowledge of western scientists is rendered quite as difficult as the comparison of methodology since the !Kung appear to know a good deal more about many subjects than do the scientists. Because of this we often cross-examined them on data that was new to us, and, in doing so, revealed interesting features of their methods for finding out about behavior and their attitudes toward observation and toward the nature of facts.

Comparisons with findings of western scientists was our main check against "tall stories." Blurton Jones's knowledge provided an immediate stimulus to cross-examine on any statement which contradicted or extended the better-known scientific findings. Some !Kung observations which we refused to believe were later proved correct when subsequently checked with ethologists who have worked in Africa.

Objectivity of Observations

It became evident fairly early in the study that the !Kung were very careful to discriminate data from theory and interpretation, and, even more so, to discriminate observed data from hearsay. But as data, along with directly observed behavior, goes behavior deduced from tracks. This seems to be regarded with confidence comparable to behavior that they have actually watched animals performing, but they always do distinguish the two data sources. A further distinction is made between, on the one hand, behavior that they have seen or reconstructed from tracks and, on the other hand, behavior that they think may happen, or that they have heard somebody say they have seen.

The features of the discussion which led us to believe that they

discriminate between observation and hearsay are of several kinds:
(1) They admit ignorance very readily. Often after a question there
would be a long silence, or a series of "I don't knows" from each
participant. This was distinct from a response to an unclearly phrased
or unclearly pronounced question, when always some attempt was
made to get a repetition of the question and to find out what was
being asked. Some remarks from the notes on the seminars support
this view: (a) One man said that he had heard of people who have
seen kudu fighting, but he himself never has. (b) When asked whether
newborn buffaloes (*Syncerus caffer*) stayed with their mothers or
were hidden, one man replied that because buffaloes are so dangerous, he had not looked to see where the babies were, "Since buffaloes kill you, you don't go after them." (c) And at another village
where they have on occasion gone after buffaloes, when asked
whether baby lions' eyes were open at birth, they laughed and said,
"If you go over there and look, won't you be dead?"

(2) They argue about generalizations based on scant data and will
disagree but will try to reach an answer. (a) On the subject of newborn buffaloes: one man suggested that buffaloes are like cows, so
would be unlikely to hide their babies; someone disagreed with this
suggestion, and a discussion ensued about what would really happen
with the buffalo. The discussion produced more observations; and,
eventually, once the problems of measuring time were resolved,
agreement was reached on the fact that the newborn buffalo follows
the mother from very early in its life. (b) Someone suggested that
lions spot and follow the tracks of their prey, and that they know
which animal they are following, whereupon others disagreed as to
whether the lion knows which track belongs to which prey. Although this is clearly not a field in which it would be easy to obtain
a correct answer, the fact that a guess at this is not acceptable is
some evidence of a distinction between fact and fiction. (It certainly
contrasts with the impression one has of 19th-century British gamekeepers, or the sort of countrymen among whom Gilbert White
(1789) had to attempt to discern the truth about the English coun-
tryside.) (c) After a disconcertingly complete demonstration of the
behavior of the honey guide (*Indicator spp.*) a man suggested that
the honey guide sometimes leads leopards to honey. This suggestion
was then qualified by the objective statement that if you are following the bird you sometimes see a leopard. The statement was taken
up immediately and negated by someone who claimed that the bird
leads people to leopards, not leopards to the honey. It would seem
to us very likely that, as the behavior of the honey guide is probably

329

based in part on a mobbing response to large animals, it may indeed
lead people to leopards by the same rather fortuitous way in which
it leads them to honey. In the same discussion the men said they did
not know whether the honey guide leads the honey badger (*Mellivora
capensis*) to honey, although the suggestion that this is so is widespread in the literature, and the !Kung knew that the honey badger
eats honey. In another discussion there was a striking rejoinder by
an elderly man that his colleagues should speak only if they have
seen things happen. This was provoked by a speculation that children
could be killed by fires.

(3) They are able to report new data and do so without pressure.
This again is markedly different from the average pet owner, or even
many countrymen, who must be really forced into saying what they
have seen. (a) We asked if lions ever eat elephants; this provoked
laughter until one elderly man said that they sometimes take baby
elephants, an observation which gained him many amazed and ad-
miring looks. He then proceeded to describe how he had seen the
body of a dead elephant baby, and the body of a dead lion, and sets
of tracks which had suggested to him that the lion had killed the
baby elephant, and the mother elephant had come and killed the
lion.[1] (b) During the questioning about kudu (*Tragelaphus strep-
siceros*) fighting, a young man described how he came across two
males with their horns interlocked, pushing at each other, and then
added that he shot them, they separated and died. Another man
imitated the sound of kudu fighting and described this as something
to listen for when stalking them for a kill. Someone else did an accurate imitation of the ungulate "flehmen" face, when describing
the courtship of eland. The frequent imitations, both accurate in
sound and convincing though not necessarily morphologically accurate in gesture, formed a large part of the descriptions (as, indeed,
in many ethological discussions!). In fact many of them seem to take
great delight in lengthy, detailed, and very gripping, even to the non-
!Kung speaker, descriptions of events they had seen. The nonverbal
arts of the story teller are very much in evidence, but as far as we
can see they did not take licence with the facts. These descriptions
also often include considerable detail, as illustrated, for example, by
a description of the method by which a leopard kills an animal: the
leopard sees the animal and, semiconcealed, crawls slowly toward it
until it is lying down four to five yards away; then it springs and
grabs the prey at the throat—its arms over the victim's shoulders and
legs around its waist. Then winding its tail around the back legs of
the animal (they say the leopard's tail is very strong), the leopard
bites the prey in the throat.

(4) They will disbelieve each other and on occasion seem to expect skepticism of each other. For example, when somebody said that he had heard that elephants bury their babies up to their neck in the sand, everybody laughed uproariously at his gullibility. A man who described once having seen tracks of ten leopards together at one gemsbok (*Oryx gazella*) kill said that he went back and brought people out to see the tracks because otherwise they would not have believed him. When they came to inspect the tracks themselves, they confirmed that he was correct in his interpretation.

(5) Their response to being asked how they know a particular fact is never defensive; it typically leads to a long and careful description of the observations or of the tracking evidence. For instance, we challenged a description of the hunting conduct of a pair of lions. A man had described how the lions approached together to a certain distance and then split up. One advanced directly a short way and then lay down to wait, while the other encircled the prey and then pounced on it, whereupon the waiting animal rushed up and joined in the attack. We questioned them on the evidence for the timing of the relative acts, and this question was met by careful description of the tracking evidence since nobody in this particular group had seen such an event. The tracking evidence for the paths taken by the two animals is clear enough; the evidence for relative timing of the attacks is that the subsequent tracks of the animal who lay down are not those of a lion stalking near to the prey nor of one about to leap at its prey, but were the tracks of a lion running leisurely in an erect posture.

We were anxious to follow up a description which we obtained in two separate villages from unrelated people of the way lions go about eating an animal they have killed. In particular, we were told that they do not eat the intestines but remove and bury them. This was such a surprise to us that we cross-examined them closely, only to find them obstinate in this view. There were two men who claimed to have watched lions doing this, and we found it hard simply to disbelieve them. We were also told, but now with some impatience, that people use this knowledge to get intestines which they, unlike lions, eat. We found people in both villages who had gone to the site after the lions had moved away and had dug up the intestines to take home.

Direct observations were also convincing for the immense amount of detail that was given, a point which we will return to when discussing the reasons for !Kung interest in animals. A further incredible elaboration of lions' fastidious feeding habits was also followed up: and although we cannot fault the !Kung's answers, at the same time we scarcely can bring outselves to believe the descriptions they gave us. They said that if during its careful dissection of the intestines from its prey, the lion breaks the intestines and lets their contents spill onto the carcass, it then will not eat the meat and often, indeed, will leave the entire carcass. They simply answered our general challenge by saying that if the lion has gone away, one is likely to see feces on the carcass; but, on the other hand, if the lion has removed intestines and is still there and one frightens it away, one never finds feces on the meat. Up to and excepting the abandonment of soiled carcasses, all these observations have been confirmed by ethologists' reports, either from the Serengeti in Tanzania (Schaller 1972, p. 271) or from the Wankie Reserve in Rhodesia (Douglas-Hamilton, personal communication to Blurton Jones, 1972), and by naturalists' reports from elsewhere (Guggisberg 1961; Stevenson-Hamilton 1954).

During descriptions of the calf-raising practices of various ungulates one man explained how the data for kudu could be obtained easily if one tracks the mother until finding the remnants of the birth. Then one observes the two pairs of tracks going together for a short time, which, in kudu, then divide in two directions. If one follows the baby tracks, one can find the baby hiding there.

(6) The only reports which went against our argument that the !Kung were quite reasonably objective in their reports of behavior are as follows: (a) A man said that the kudu infant is always hidden by the mother, and then said the mother hides it and goes off to eat until she has enough milk, whereupon she returns to feed the baby. The basic facts behind this description seem to be very clear, and this is, indeed, one common way in which ungulates care for their infants. However the confusion of observation of spaced feeding with the causal suggestion that she eats all this time to produce enough milk is different from most of the !Kung remarks and uncharacteristic of their usual distinction between observation and interpretation. (b) When somebody said that he had heard that elephants bury their babies up to their necks in the sand, although it led to general laughter, it did result in one man, again uncharacteristically, saying that he had seen this. On cross-examination it turned out that he had seen a pile of sand and a lot of tracks of elephants with babies, whereupon he wisely had given in to the !Kung view of elephants with infants and had run away without stopping to examine the pile of sand. (c) The discussion mentioned above of whether buffalo calf-raising resembled that of cows was also an example of !Kung nonobjectivity in that the person who suggested this possibility was at least speculating, though we felt that he regarded this as speculation and

not as a definitive statement on buffalo calf-raising. Indeed the examples which we quoted as giving rise to argument also seem to imply a failure in objectivity in the person who made the statement (see part 2 above).

333

We conclude from this summary of !Kung observational method that their efforts resemble the methods of modern-day western ethology; as regards (1) attention to detail, (2) distinguishing data from hearsay, and (3) general freedom from inference. In these respects their observations are superior to those of naturalists such as Gilbert White and Aristotle, and very sophisticated indeed when compared with the legions of animal behaviorists among western hunters, gamekeepers, and pet owners.

Explanations of Behavior

The general impression gained from these seminars is that !Kung are not particularly interested in explanations about behavior or theories about behavior, although this may have been influenced by our questioning; we focused on data and changed the line of questioning at certain points in a discussion to produce facts.

It was not possible to discriminate completely explanations from what were merely methods of reconstructing behavior from raw observations. For instance, the discussion of why one may see leopards while following a honey guide jointly concerns explaining this coincidence and reconstructing behavior of the honey guide; in fact, the behavior of the honey guide explains the likelihood of meeting leopards in this situation. Konner's observations of !Kung discussions during tracking indicate that they can generate hypotheses at a great rate, but these concerned behavior and condition of the animal that was giving rise to the spoor—that is, they are explaining the spoor. This is different from explaining why animals behave in ways in which they are found to behave, although in a tracking situation the theorizing consists of inducing the behavior from which it is possible to deduce the injury to the hunted animal, as well as the likely time until its death.

However, we may look at the seminars with a view to seeing traces of the distinction that ethologists make between causation of behavior, and functions, effects, or survival value of behavior. Ethologists hold these to be distinct kinds of subjects, distinct questions about why an animal behaves in the way it does, although many people (both laymen and nonzoologist students of behavior) are unaware of these possible distinctions. We may look at the !Kung's statements both to see whether they make this distinction and to see whether, within these particular fields, they show signs of explanations comparable with western biologists' explanations.

In the area of causation or motivation of behavior the !Kung seem to be very similar to the English laymen in that their motivation explanations mostly boil down to anthropomorphic statements. These usually can be reduced to the statement that an animal does something because it wants to, which is really no more than saying that it does it. When asked why lions' favorite prey was wildebeest (*Connochaetes taurinus*), the !Kung answered that it was because the meat tasted good. We asked whether people found it good; some said that it did, others that it did not, but they held to the suggestion that it tasted good to lions.

Other statements about motivation did not concern the goal. For instance, wild dogs (*Lycaon pictus*) are too frightened to attack people unless there are many dogs together, but in a group they are unafraid because there are many of them, just like people. This similarity to people was also mentioned when they told us that sometimes dogs kill lions, even adult lions, by ganging up on them (as spotted hyena (*Crocuta crocuta*) sometimes do: Kruuk 1972). It was explained that the dogs were not afraid because there were a lot of them, and that even people were not afraid if there were a lot of them. A similar kind of statement about motivation concerns animals who do or do not "have anger;" lions, leopards, and wild dogs were described by one man as the animals that have anger and therefore would take children if one lets them wander about. (Before contemporary scientists feel superior to these inadequate kinds of explanation, we might do well to consider the various forms of drive theory still prevalent in the behavioral sciences; see Hinde 1959).

Some explanations seem to be directly and ethnocentrically anthropomorphic. For example we found two pieces of behavior that were explained in terms of "withholding," a serious infraction against !Kung morality, and one for which great temptations may arise. When asked why lions should bury intestines which they are not going to eat, people answered that they did not know, but added that perhaps the lions were withholding meat from the vultures. One man also felt it was dangerous to take these buried intestines in case the lion felt that they were being "withheld" and took vengeance. (He claimed a dramatic instance of this.) Leopards, although they leave the intestines for the vultures to eat, wedge the ribs of their prey in a tree; but the !Kung say that they never return to eat them. When we asked why they hang things in trees, a man then said, "perhaps, I don't know, but they may be withholding from the brown hyena" (*Hyaena brunnea*). Another anthropomorphic drive explanation was the description of the baby eland (*Taurotragus oryx*) as lazy because it can be seen apart from its mother at an early age.

Moving on from the motivational field we come to a number of explanations that confuse, to greater or lesser degrees, motivation with function. Being told that leopards do not eat intestines we asked why; and someone, again saying first that he did not know, conjectured that perhaps they were like people in that they did not like eating feces, but unlike people in that they had no hands and could not get the feces out of the intestines. This is, on the face of it, a very reasonable, proposed, short-term justification for why leopards do not eat intestines. But to biologists the absence of hands is most interesting, not as a physical limitation of the leopard's behavior, but as a result of adaptation, or at least as something adaptively compatable with its behavior, especially feeding habits. This our !Kung informant had not taken into account.

That he is not alone among modern man becomes more evident when we discuss some explanations for features of ungulate calf-raising practices. The consensus of opinion seemed to be that on the first day a newborn buffalo calf is left by its mother, but subsequently it follows her except when the mother has to go far away to get water. When we asked why the mother leaves the baby when she goes for water, we were told that the baby can not walk because his feet are still soft. This may or may not be a correct explanation of the immediate causation of the separation, but it implies an error of explanation in terms of survival value which can be found readily in contemporary literature on mammalian development. Some contemporary writers, differentiating caching species from following species, explain this difference by reference to an assumed early state of development at birth of caching species. They assume that the young of such species are unable to walk, or, at least, to walk well enough to follow their mothers (Widdowson 1970). Apart from the clear incompatability of this interpretation with actual observations of the young of caching species (e.g., Walther 1969; and !Kung observations of kudu), this explanation is naive from the evolutionary point of view, since they assume the young of caching species must be born underdeveloped. Yet upon actual observation these writers would find that the underdeveloped state is in no way an explanation of the caching adaptation, and that even the reverse might be the case. Thus it seems that although the !Kung have no clear idea about evolution or the survival values of behavior, they are not as far behind some of their post-Darwinian contemporaries in this field as one might have expected.

The !Kung do seem to have some rudimentary views on ecology. The group sizes of kudu were held to depend entirely on the number of kudu in an area, and to be extremely variable with respect to season and locality. They argued that game tends to avoid areas where there are cows and people, although they explain this by their being frightened by cows rather than in terms of the lack of grass where cows graze. Indeed in the case of the kudu they may be justified because this species predominantly feeds on leaves (as the !Kung told us) and is one game species which has increased even during the recovery of cattle from the Rinderpest epidemic. It is also held that there used to be a good deal of game in the area, but there are fewer left. No very clear reason is given for this, and they could be referring to the particular area in which a village has not existed for a very long time. It seems to us more likely that any decrease in game is due to an increase in the range of cattle rather than to an increase in the number of people. The cattle denude the ground surface in an area of some miles' radius from each waterhole, which makes access to water difficult for the game—as does the fencing of the wells.

In the conversation that gave rise to these seminars we asked at one stage why the kudu had horns of the kind it has, and why it should have horns at all. Answers ranged from explanations of the shape in terms of the horns of combatant males interlocking (which coincides strikingly with recent biological work) to the statement that God gave him beautiful horns because he wanted the male kudu to be beautiful and to be different from female kudu so that he knew he was a male. (We were also given demonstrations and descriptions of the way that the kudu "cleans" its horns by scraping them in the sand.) God also enters into the discussions at other times, when, for example, he refuses to allow anyone to eat monkeys. And the old people say that monkey meat is bad so one does not eat it, and if one does, one dies. The word translated as "created" was used quite commonly in the discussions of resemblances and differences between animals.

Some discussions, like many a modern western ethology seminar, were rescued by a participant making the important point of discourse embodied in the following quote: "You were talking about its color; we are talking about its meat; if you want to talk about color, then this animal is different." (This remark incidentally capped a highly convincing demonstration that the !Kung were able to use a number of different classifications of animals and to move from one classification to another readily, an ability that is supposed to be little developed in "primitive" people. See Bruner et al. 1966.) In discussions of how carnivores hunt, and whether they do it like people, one man remarked that most carnivores hunt at night because they have noses and do not need to see far. (This is another reverse survival value explanation.) The lion's seeing with its nose was described during an account of a lion's hunt a little while later in the same seminar, and another man then added that a lion uses both its nose and its eyes.

The paucity of explanations alongside great richness of data about animal behavior makes an interesting contrast with the situation in animal behavior research in the west some sixty years ago when the literature was abundantly full of theory and empty of data. Our impression is that this has been true of animal behavior and psychology in other historical periods. The contrast of theory and data also can be seen in the difference between ethology and psychology; the latter has a greater concern for large scale theories and for testing hypotheses and a much smaller concern for amassing data (a lesser faith in human "inductive" ability?). Is it possible that there is in practice some incompatibility between a turn of mind geared to theorizing and a turn of mind geared to recording and discovering facts? What the !Kung seem really good at is working out what happens, not in explaining it or theorizing about it.

Why !Kung Study Behavior

The obvious answer to the question, that any people who hunt animals must know enough about them to catch them, can take several forms. In terms of natural selection it would seem to be irrefutable. But in terms of the resulting motivation the answer is not quite so clear. We would like to suggest four lines of evidence bearing on the motivation of !Kung interest in behavior. (1) First is the question of which species they know most about, whether they only know about their prey species and perhaps their possible predators or competitors, and know little and care little about other species. It is difficult for us to be confident about our conclusions on this question because our interests limited the issues we questioned. However we do have some idea of which animals the !Kung know most about.

(2) We have evidence that they sometimes observe animals more than is necessary for the purpose of the hunt in which they are in-

volved. For example, one man described courtship of a pair of gemsbok in great detail, adding that he was so involved in watching them that he forgot about shooting them, and they went out of sight before he was able to.

(3) Often during the seminars people would begin to discuss some point among themselves and recount observations to each other. This added to our very clear impression that they found the topic interesting for its own sake, and found the seminars highly absorbing. A strange feature of these discussions was that the participants seemed to gain a lot of new information, or at least heard about observations and generalizations concerning behavior which were quite new to them. This implied to us that the !Kung might not of their own accord discuss animal behavior very much, but what they do is to report at length and dramatically individual excursions and hunts.

(4) This gives rise to our fourth line of evidence about the reasons for knowledge of behavior. This is the immense amount of detail that they remember and, therefore, see when they are watching an animal. For example, we have mentioned their descriptions of the way a lion eats an animal it has killed. Admittedly this is a situation where if a !Kung sees it he can do little except watch; and he is interested in watching and waiting until he decides the time is right for lighting a fire to chase the lion away. But he need not observe or recall any details of this situation other than to note the responses of the lion to other lions or vultures or other creatures about, or to gain a very general impression of how much the animal has eaten. The amount of detail observed and remembered and the evident delight in recounting these observations suggest to us that natural selection has arranged for a greater interest in animal behavior than that aroused by the practicalities of any specific hunt. This provides a system in which a large store of information is accumulated and communicated, and which may or may not turn out to be of use in hunting. The motivation of these activities seems only indirectly related to hunting. Stories are told not because someone wants to go hunt a particular animal but because people are gathered around the fire, and someone has been on a hunt, or needs to entertain a visitor. This indirect adult communication of important information seems comparable to the indirect way young men acquire information about animals and technology, which appears to be quite simply a matter of watching and listening to other people and then trying for one's self. There is almost no direct teaching. Indeed Konner[2] witnessed an enlightening argument between some younger men who hunt very little and some

older and more active men. The inactive young men accused the older men of having neglected to teach them hunting. The older men countered that this was not something that one taught anybody, it was something that one just did. "You teach yourself"—a very common phrase among the !Kung—would be applicable here.

The evidence concerning the phylogenetic extent of their knowledge is difficult to evaluate. Most of our questioning was about ungulates because of Blurton Jones's interest in their maternal behavior, and much of the rest was about carnivores because of the !Kung's interest for survival and our interest in establishing whether carnivores were in any way a threat to children. They know a considerable amount about both these groups. And they appear to know more about lions from whom they scavenge than about other carnivores who seem to be of less importance as a source of food, or perhaps less difficult to chase away. They appear to know rather little about monkeys, probably because the only monkey found anywhere nearby was a vervet (*Cercopithecus aethiops*). It is perhaps relevant to remark that although they know about baboons and have occasionally seen them, most of the remarks about baboons came from one man's observations of a captive baboon that some white men had once had some miles away. But he was able to imitate and describe in enormous detail feeding behavior of this captive baboon and the foods it ate.

The seminars were occasionally interrupted if one of the participants got hold of our field guide to mammals. Once they were used to looking at the pictures (which took only a minute or two), these were a source of endless fascination; and, as far as we could see, any species was interesting. However, much of the fascination with the book was perhaps fascination in learning to see the pictures and a delight in being able to teach friends to do this. Another favorite evening occupation was to look at the Konners' color slides of familiar people or places. Although we asked very little about birds, unless sometimes trying to collect !Kung names for those illustrated in our books, their knowledge appeared to be extensive. An indicated above, they do describe accurately the mobbing behavior and inadvertent leading behavior of the honey guide, although without apparent grasp of the motivational issues involved. However, Konner did hold one seminar on bird behavior, with the help of Peter Jones, the Oxford-trained, Botswana government ornithologist. There was only one such seminar, and it focused on the behavior of passerines, especially quelea (*Quelea quelea*). But it did not generally inspire a level of confidence in !Kung knowledge comparable to what we were

accustomed in discussions of mammalian behavior. Still, one anec-
date is noteworthy.

Subsequent to the bird behavior seminar Konner, Shostak, and
Jones were traveling with two !Kung men by Land Rover. Knowing
of Jones's interest in quelea (he had been retained by the government
to explore possible solutions to the serious quelea pest problem), the
two men pointed out a low stand of thorn bushes which, at a distance, looked like any other but which, on close examination, proved
to have been stripped of leaves on the distal few inches of their
branches. The men said that this had been done by quelea, which
were in the habit of preparing bushes in this way and then returning
after a few days to rest on the ends of the branches. This observation, which was unknown to Jones, and which proved to be correct,
enabled him subsequently to improve greatly the efficiency of his
investigation and to collect at an early stage of the nesting cycle
specimens previously inaccessible to him (Peter Jones, personal communication).

We asked nothing about snakes, but we were told that one we dis-
turbed had to be killed, because although harmless, or at least not
poisonous, "it climbs up your legs and goes into your anus. . ." This
is in all likelihood a myth about the relatively unknown, comparable
to the giant baboon that lurks in the bush waiting for unsuspecting
women. However the snake in question fled up a small bush, and it
is quite conceivable that it sometimes mistakes peoples' legs for
trees, thus giving some substance to the legend.

Instances which provide evidence of the seriousness of their interest in behavior occurred when one night around midnight the seminar
was joined by four additional men who sat quietly behind the participants, listening with concentration and without fidgeting, talking,
or yawning despite the lateness. Also, during seminars people occasionally volunteered new information that we had not asked about,
and on one occasion a man volunteered new information about lion
hunting behavior and then moved on spontaneously to hunting behavior of wild dogs.

Evidence that knowledge of behavior is closely related to its applied value comes from many statements made during the seminars.
In discussing fighting of kudu, one man described the sound one
hears of their horns crashing, and how, if one hears the sound, one
can approach to shoot them. The same man, a very enthusiastic and
busy hunter also described how one tracks infant kudu, showing that
it sleeps away from its mother, and that one can follow it to where
it is hidden, and kill it by hitting it. In telling us how wildebeest

infants follow their mothers soon after birth, they said that one can not catch the infants because they follow their mothers so soon.[3] But in the same seminar people described the way in which the kudu mother returns and calls the fawn, which then runs out to join her to feed, and how the mother never goes to the place where the infant sleeps, a degree of detail which seems hardly necessary if one is simply trying to shoot mother or baby. Someone also described going again and again to the same place to examine sets of tracks of a mother which had been visiting an area repeatedly for several weeks. He found tracks going back and forth and failing to understand this, returned continually until he found tracks of the same animal with an infant. He then realized what was happening and, after this, tracked the pair and killed the infant. This whole procedure apparently took two months, and it seems hard to believe that the mystery of these repetitive tracks was not as great a motivation to make the man persist in his studies as was the slender possibility of catching up with the animal. Whichever his motivation, the man was clearly utilizing a long process to reconstruct from repeated observations of the tracks the behavior and the causal situation of that behavior.

The following observation indicates the practical value of knowing in detail the hunting behavior of competing predators. A !Kung man described how he and a lion were pursuing the same giraffe, or rather stalking it. The lion was the first to charge and climbed up the giraffe while fighting at it, but the !Kung and his companion frightened the lion away and shot an arrow into the giraffe. The giraffe ran off, and the man followed it for the rest of the day while it was still living. In the meantime, the lion was nowhere to be seen. The man went home, came out the next day to find the giraffe dead, and took the meat. During all this time the lion had failed to reach it. This may be a dramatic instance of the difference in the size of the home range of lions and people. !Kung hunts may cover enormous distances, but we have no information as to how much distance they cover geographically since their prey often turn back and go over the same ground again. But one man reported shooting a buffalo (which in itself is rather unusual), whereupon it ran away. What was unusual was that he shot it *before* it fled and claimed to have tracked it the next day for twenty miles, still failing to catch up with it. It must be noted that the !Kung method of killing requires extensive tracking *after* the first wound is made with the poisoned arrow, while the poison is taking effect. (Lion hunting procedure typically requires tracking, if any, only before the attack.)

We presume that much information is gained from descriptions of hunts and observations of others, but, as mentioned above, it seems to be mainly a matter of listening to people story-telling, and not a more highly ordered system of information transmission.

Whether the !Kung interest in animal behavior is of ultimate practical value in every case seems to us, finally, beside the point. The point is that evolution has produced in them an inquisitive turn of mind which leads them to explore problems and accumulate knowedge beyond what it is most immediately necessary for them to know. This turn of mind evidently proved more adaptive than a severely pragmatic approach, because evolution retained it.

In one seminar the !Kung listed four mental qualities essential in hunting: knowledge (*chi!ā*), sense (*kxai ≠n*), cleverness (*/xudi*), and alertness (*chiho*). Konner's observations of conversation during tracking reflect the sort of mental process that selection for hunting has retained. In effect, there is a set of problems to be solved by the hunters over the course of several hours or days, and these problems re-present themselves continually: Where is the animal now? Which way is it going, and how fast? Is it likely to stop or to reverse direction? Where and how seriously is it wounded? How long will it live? Answering these questions requires adducing evidence concerning time of year; time of day; heat; wind direction; terrain; depth, shape, and displacement of tracks; condition of feces; condition and displacement of grass, twigs, and shrubs along the spoor; amount, position, and color of blood on the ground, grass, and bushes; and the store of knowledge concerning the behavior of different prey species, especially when under attack, which we have demonstrated.

Some of this evidence is utilized in a simple way. For example, only gemsbok among antelope can be successfully hunted with dogs, because only they will consistently stand and fight the dogs, as opposed to fleeing. But most items of fact must be integrated in a complex way with all the other rapidly changing variables of the hunt. Typically, in the course of following an animal, a working hypothesis as to his position or condition will be advanced and then tested continually against the spoor. For example, Konner accompanied a man returning from an unsuccessful kudu hunt. It was early afternoon. They began following a gemsbok spoor which, the man said, was made the same morning. After about twenty minutes the man stopped and said, "No, it was made last night," and abandoned the spoor. Asked what made him change his mind, he indicated a single gemsbok hoofprint with a mouse track inside it, that is, superimposed on it. Since mice are nocturnal, the gemsbok print must have been left during the night.

If two or more men are hunting together, they will discuss, within the obvious noise restriction, the evidence bearing on the working hypotheses, and argue in a way not dissimilar to the discussions in the seminars. Konner observed a zebra hunt in which the working hypothesis, that the zebra was wounded high on the body, had to be abandoned when a man showed that grass, which had been bloodied near its high tip, had first been bent to the ground by the passing animal, bloodied by its foot, and then returned to the upright position after the animal passed. Thus the hypothesis of a wound in the foot was still sufficient to account for the data.

Such an intellective process is familiar to us from detective stories and indeed also from science itself. Evidently it is a basic feature of human mental life. It would be surprising indeed if repeated activation of hypotheses, trying them out against new data, integrating them with previously known facts, and rejecting ones which do not stand up, were habits of mind peculiar to western scientists and detectives. !Kung behavior indicates that, on the contrary, the very way of life for which the human brain evolved required them. That they are brought to impressive fruition by the technology of scientists and the leisure of novelists should not be allowed to persuade us that we invented them. Man is the only hunting mammal with so rudimentary a sense of smell, that he could only have come to successful hunting through intellectual evolution.

Nonscientific !Kung Beliefs about Animals

In order to avoid leaving the incorrect impression that all !Kung beliefs about animals are arrived at through strict induction, we mention briefly several nonrational beliefs:

Myths and the myth cycle: Stories are told (Biesele, Chapter 13), of an ancient time in which the identity of various animal species is closely enmeshed with that of mythic-heroic human figures. Some stories have the heroes turning into animals when they get into situations in which they need the animal's characteristics. These are told to account for the origin of some species (for example, the ant-bear, *Orycteropus afer*).

Baboon rapist: Women are warned not to walk in the bush alone at night lest they be attacked by a giant mythic baboon of remarkable sexual appetites. This possibility does not seem to dissuade them, though other, more realistic ones do at times.

Bird possession: Infants are sometimes said to be "possessed" (an unsatisfactory translation) by predatory birds which they see while sleeping. A parent recognizes that the infant has seen the bird because it clenches its fists at that moment in its sleep, like the bird closing its talons. After this an elaborate ritual must be performed daily to prevent the child's death, and some infant deaths are attributed to such possessions.

Others: As mentioned above, some harmless snakes are said to run up people's legs and enter their anuses. Millipedes are for some reason treated with utter revulsion and never touched under any circumstances, because of their alleged smell. A large caterpillar seen only in the rainy season is said to cause malaria.

Summary: A number of nonrational beliefs about animals may be enumerated, but these seem to play a small role in day-to-day !Kung life and in their interactions with animals. Bird possession is the only one people treat quite seriously. In other words, such beliefs do not interfere with the study of animal behavior. They seem to exist in a domain of the mind quite separate from ethno-ethological knowledge.

Conclusions

We regard our material as showing in summary:

(1) That !Kung have an advanced ability to observe and assemble facts about behavior and to discriminate facts from hearsay and interpretation. In this ability they surpass lay observers and many professionals in western society.

(2) Their explanations of animal behavior are, in contrast, not very notable. But it is important to remember that the faults in their interpretations that we have pointed out (theories of motivation which are tautologous, teleological, "survival value" explanations) are commonly found in western man, even among western scientists.

(3) Their motivation for acquiring knowledge about what animals do goes far beyond the immediate, momentary needs of hunting (beyond what is needed for successful hunting of the animal that they are observing). We suggest that this level of interest nonetheless may be of adaptive value. Knowledge is acquired when not needed, when the pressure is off, but it may well be useful at another time; or, collecting it may in some instances be "vacuum activity" in the strict ethological sense. In any case it is clear that the habits of mind involved will have been strongly selected for.

(4) There seems to be relatively little transmission of information from one man to another, even from old to young.

Perhaps verbal transmission of information is indirect, through people telling the story of their day's excursion as opposed to direct lecturing of old by young. Thus, as with (3) above, knowledge may be acquired mainly "out of context," in the relaxed social setting of the early evening, but it is then available when needed. One wonders if the trade-off for the rather patchy nature of the knowledge transmitted is a greater efficiency in the "filing" and retrieval of information stored in a system of the subject's own construction. This system is put to use when the subject wants to listen and when the story teller's art gives many pegs on which to hang the information, and is quite different from one where he would try to store in his head someone else's data filed on that person's system.

The explanation for the fact that knowledge gained "informally" is assimilated more easily and rapidly than knowledge gained under pressure or direct instruction lies somewhere common both to that psychological suggestion itself and to the fact that it usually *is* acquired this way in !Kung society. We have to ask why knowledge is acquired this way, and the answer to that may be also the answer to "why does memory work that way?" One suggestion, itself raising further questions, is in the adverse reaction many people have to direct instruction. Not only can they be intimidated and confused (Holt 1969), but Lee (1969b) and Gould (1969) indicate that !Kung and Yiwara Australian aborigines can be irritated by and can disapprove of people who tell other people what to do or in any way set themselves above anyone else. This presumably (and the people think so too) relates to very basic features of their society and its ecology such as food sharing. Since it is highly probable that successful exploitation of the social hunting niche depends on extensive food sharing, this is a powerful force among the selection pressures on hunter-gatherer behavior. It is not, perhaps, far-fetched to suggest that this force may have been strong enough for long enough to set constraints on the way that information was best transmitted from person to person and acquired by individuals. However, this is highly speculative, and we would claim to have demonstrated little beyond the importance of reexamining our ideas on the function of old people as teachers or libraries (we suggest they are not reference libraries but are dramatized documentary television) and of examining closely the ways that information about subsistence is acquired and transmitted in hunter-gatherer societies.

In the philosophy of science it is usually supposed that the purpose of a theory is to predict events in the future or in novel situations (though there are heretics among biologists who will comment that theories are a cover for ignorance, that theories and explanations always turn into descriptions when you really understand them). One might have thought then that there would be great survival value for the !Kung to have powerful theories about animal behavior. The perfect theory would allow one to predict even more of the behavior of every animal in every situation, and perhaps to contrive situations which maximize hunting success. But the !Kung with whom we talked did not seem to be great theorists. They simply loved to know about what animals do. There are several possible answers to this apparent paradox:

(1) There cannot be any grand universal theories of behavior; the nature of the data, primarily the diversity of species, forces on !Kung and biologist alike a greater respect for facts and for the diversity of life than for attempts to explain them in a simple way.

(2) The antipredator behavior of many species includes a highly adaptive random component—it is in part genuinely unpredictable (Driver and Humphries 1970; Humphries and Driver 1970). (But !Kung probably know when it becomes unpredictable and in what parameters it is unpredictable, for example, being ready for gemsbok at bay to charge or to run again.)

(3) The theory of behavior they use, an introspective, anthropomorphic interpretation, is adequate or even better than adequate. (We know cases where they emphasize a similarity to people—"Wild dogs are like people, if there are a few they are afraid, if there are many they are not afraid." So they are clearly aware that some animals react like people in some respects, but that others do not.)

Biologists do have one grand universal theory, the theory of evolution by natural selection. The !Kung do not have this theory, as far as we know. We should probe further about where animals come from and why they differ, before being totally confident about this. Besides the practical knowledge of animals that we have discussed, the !Kung have a rich mythology about animals, including stories of a mythical remote past. These were never referred to in our seminars, though on other occasions Konner discussed these matters with people, and Biesele (Chapter 13) has made a careful study of them. The two areas seem to be completely different compartments of intellectual life, and the existence of creation myths need not exclude an evolutionary theory. Indeed, the origin myths do accommodate biological change, holding as they do that all animals evolved from people; and the concept of adaptation does figure in them since the transformation often occurs when the animal's human progenitor has gotten himself, through mischief or stupidity, into a situation where he really needs some key adaptive feature of the animal. For example, the antbear "evolves" when its human ancestor tries to escape some pursuers by fleeing underground. In a short while his hands turn into antbear claws, more suitable for digging, a Lamarckian sort of change through adaptation. However, the references to God giving the male kudu horns is an indication of putting God and his motives in precisely the logical position of the theory of evolution by natural selection.

347

Answer (1) above seems to us the most likely. This is a subject that has been discussed fairly thoroughly in the biological literature (Lehrman 1953; Hinde 1966, or 2nd edition) with the conclusion that the diversity of animals is such as to make the possibility of a general theory of motivation and behavioral mechanism highly unlikely. It seems as if the !Kung would do best simply to know a lot about each animal. Though this would not preclude a pay-off for predicting from a well-known species to a little-known species through some kind of taxonomy, they are clearly aware of and act according to *species* difference. "Look out, it's a gemsbok not a kudu, you know." (Gemsbok charge, kudu do not.)

It is tempting to suggest that the history of "grand unifying theories of behavior" in animal behavior has a parallel, if not actually more than one, in the possibility that if one's main concern is animal behavior, one's main problem is variety and the initial strategy is to acquire factual knowledge; whereas if one's main concern is human behavior, one's main strategy is to apply an introspection-based theory. The latter may work very well on humans, but it cannot be extended far into the variety of animals.

In discussion of our results we are, perhaps, handicapped by being practicing scientists rather than full-time students of the history of science. Nonetheless we should attempt now to evaluate two of the points we raised in the introduction. Man's evolution in a hunter-gatherer niche should have meant that there was selection pressure on the human brain such that man became interested in animal behavior and competent about finding out about it. We can say that the !Kung are clearly interested in animals and animal behavior; the extent of their enthusiasm is hard to convey. They are also clearly very competent in finding out about animal behavior *from nature*—from the animals themselves and their tracks. In contrast they seem to acquire less from each other than we might expect. They distinguish sharply between observed behavior and hearsay and interpretation. In this respect they have an ability and an approach which is also one of the basic features of the scientific method and which has most sharply distinguished science from other intellectual pursuits. They are able to and they believe it important to distinguish reports of observation from other kinds of statement.

This brings us to the second point: the narrow perspective of some writers on the history of science and the intellectual achievements of urban man. We must concede that the !Kung show no use of mathematics, and on the whole do little experimentation (also true of the majority of western man). But it seems equally clear that the !Kung have, and use in their profession, some of the intellectual requirements of modern science.

Every contributor to this volume could hammer his or her own nails into the coffin of western man's dramatizations of his intellectual rise from the Stone Age. We found our animal behavior seminars chastening at many levels. The sheer volume of knowledge is breathtaking. They laughed to hear that there are people who think that the spotted hyena only scavenges; they know that lions sometimes scavenge from hyena kills; and so on and on. The accuracy of observation, the patience, and the experiences of wildlife they have had and appreciate are enviable. The sheer, elegant logic of deductions from tracks would satiate the most avid crossword fan or reader of detective stories. The objectivity is also enviable to scientists who believe that they can identify it and that the progress of science is totally dependent upon it. Even the poor theorization of our !Kung left one uneasy; their "errors," the errors of "Stone Age savages," are exactly those still made today by many highly educated western scientists (tautological theories of motivation, inadequate application of natural selection theory). We have gained little or nothing in ability or intellectual brilliance since the Stone Age; our gains have all been in the accumulation of records of our intellectual achievements. We climb on each other's backs; we know more and understand more, but our intellects are no better. It is an error to equate the documented history of intellectual achievement with a history of intellect. It is an error to assume that changes in about 7,000 years of urban civilization represent a final stage in a progress which can be extrapolated downwards into our preurban past. Just as primitive life no longer can be characterized as nasty, brutish, and short, no longer can it be characterized as stupid, ignorant, or superstition-dominated.

15

Sharing, Talking, and Giving:
Relief of Social Tensions among the !Kung

Lorna Marshall

People sitting close together

This chapter describes customs practiced by the !Kung which help them to avoid situations that are likely to arouse ill will and hostility among individuals within bands and between bands. My observations were made among !Kung in the Nyae Nyae area in Namibia (South West Africa). Two customs which I consider to be especially important and which I describe in detail are meat-sharing and gift-giving. I discuss also the ways in which mannerliness, the custom of talking out grievances, the customs of borrowing and lending and of not stealing function to prevent tension from building up dangerously between members of a group and help to bring about peaceful relationships.

The common human needs for cooperation and companionship are particularly apparent among the !Kung. An individual never lives alone nor does a single nuclear family live alone. All live in bands composed of several families joined by consanguineous or affinal bonds. The arduous hunting-gathering life would be insupportable for a single person or a single nuclear family without the cooperation and companionship of the larger group. Moreover, in this society, the ownership of the resources of plant foods and waterholes and the utilization of them are organized through the band structure, and individuals have rights to the resources through their band affiliation.[1] Thus, the !Kung are dependent for their living on belonging to a band. They must belong; they can live no other way. They are also extremely dependent emotionally on the sense of belonging and on companionship. Separation and loneliness are unendurable to them. I believe their wanting to belong and be near is actually visible in the way families cluster together in an encampment and in the way they sit huddled together, often touching someone, shoulder against shoulder, ankle across ankle. Security and comfort for them lie in their belonging to their group, free from the threat of rejection and hostility.

Their security and comfort must be achieved side-by-side with self-interest and much jealous watchfulness. Altruism, kindness, sympathy, or genuine generosity were not qualities that I observed often in their behavior. However, these qualities were not entirely lacking, especially between parents and offspring, between siblings, and between spouses. One mother carried her sick adult daughter on her back for three days in searing summer heat for us to give her medicine. N/haka carried her lame son, Lame ≠Gau, for years. Gau clucked and fussed over his second wife, Hwan//ka, when she was sick. When !'Ku had a baby, her sister, /Ti!kai, gathered food for her for five days. On the other hand, people do not generally help each other. They laugh when the lame man, !Xəm, falls down and do not help him up. !'Ku's jealous eyes were like those of a viper when we gave more attention to her husband, ≠Toma, than to her on one occasion because he was much more ill than she. And, in the extreme, there was a report from the 1958 Marshall expedition of an instance of apparently callous indifference in one band on the part of some young relatives to a dying, old, childless woman, an old aunt, when her sister with whom she lived had died.

351

Occasions when tempers have got out of control are remembered with awe. The deadly poisoned arrows are always at hand. Men have killed each other with them in quarrels—though rarely—and the !Kung fear fighting with a conscious and active fear. They speak about it often. Any expression of discord ("bad words") makes them uneasy. Their desire to avoid both hostility and rejection leads them to conform in high degree to the unspoken social laws. I think that most !Kung cannot bear the sense of rejection that even mild disapproval makes them feel. If they do deviate, they usually yield readily to expressed group opinion and reform their ways. They also conform strictly to certain specific useful customs that are instruments for avoiding discord.

Talking and Talks

I mention talking as an aid to peaceful social relations because it is so very much a part of the daily experience of the !Kung, and because I believe it usefully serves three particular functions. It keeps up good, open communication among the members of the band; through its constantly flowing expression it is a salutary outlet for emotions; and it serves as the principal sanction in social discipline. Songs are also used for social discipline. The !Kung say that a song composed specifically about someone's behavior and sung to express disapproval, perhaps from the deepest shadow of the encampment at night, is a very effective means of bringing people who deviate back into the pattern of approved behavior. Nevertheless, during our observations, songs were not used as much as talking. If people disapprove of an individual's behavior, they may criticize him or her directly, usually putting a question, "Why do you do that?", or they may gossip a bit or make oblique hints. In the more intense instances what I call a talk may ensue.

The !Kung are the most loquacious people I know. Conversation in a !Kung encampment is a constant sound like the sound of a brook, and as low and lapping, except for shrieks of laughter. People cluster together in little groups during the day, talking, perhaps making artifacts at the same time. At night, families talk late by their fires, or visit at other family fires with their children between their knees or in their arms if the wind is cold.

There always seems to be plenty to talk about. People tell about events with much detail and repetition and discuss the comings and goings of their relatives and friends and make plans. Their greatest preoccupation and the subject they talk about most often, I think, is food. The men's imaginations turn to hunting. They converse musingly, as though enjoying a sort of daydream together, about past hunts, telling over and over where game was found and who killed it. They wonder where the game is at present, and say what fat bucks they hope to kill. They also plan their next hunts with practicality. Women (who, incidentally, do not seem to me to talk as much as men in !Kung society) gave me the impression of talking more about who gave or did not give them food and their anxieties about not having food. They spoke to me about women who were remembered for being especially quick and able gatherers, but they did not have pleasurable satisfaction in remembering their hot, monotonous, arduous days of digging and picking and trudging home with their heavy loads.

Another frequent subject of conversation is gift-giving. Men and women speak of the persons to whom they have given or propose to give gifts. They express satisfaction or dissatisfaction with what they have received. If someone has delayed unexpectedly long in making a return gift, the people discuss this. One man was excused by his friends because his wife, they said, had got things into her hands and made him poor, so that he now had nothing suitable to give. Sometimes, on the other hand, people were blamed for being ungenerous ("far-hearted") or not very capable in managing their lives, and no one defended them for these defects or asked others to have patience with them. The experiences of daily life are a further topic of conversation. While a person speaks, the listeners are in vibrant response, repeating the phrases and interposing a contrapuntal "eh." "Yesterday," "eh," "at Deboragu," "eh," "I saw Old /"Xashe." "You saw Old /"Xashe," "eh, eh." "He said that he had seen the great python under the bank." "EH!" "The python!" "He wants us," "eh, eh, eh," "to help him catch it." The "ehs" overlap and coincide with the phrase, and the people so often all talk at once that one wonders how anyone knows what the speaker has said.

Bursts of laughter accompany the conversations. Sometimes the !Kung laugh mildly with what we would call a sense of humor about

people and events; often they shriek and howl as though laughter
were an outlet for tension. They laugh at mishaps that happen to
other people, like the lions eating up someone else's meat, and
shriek over particularly telling and insulting sexual sallies in the
joking relationships. Individual singing of lyrical songs accompanied
by the //gwashi (pluriarc), snatches of ritual music, the playing of
rhythmical games, or the ritual curing dances occupy the evenings
as well, but mostly the evening hours are spent in talk.

353

As far as we know, only two general subjects are avoided in conversation. Men and women do not discuss sexual matters openly
together except as they make jokes in the joking relationship. The
!Kung avoid speaking the names of the gods aloud and do not converse about the gods for fear of attracting their attention and perhaps
their displeasure.

A talk differs from a conversation or an arranged, purposeful discussion. It flares spontaneously, I believe from stress, when something is going on in which people are seriously concerned and in
disagreement. I think that no formalities regulate it. Anyone who
has something he wants to say joins in. People take sides and express
opinions, accusing and denying, or defending persons involved. I
witnessed one such talk only, in 1952. It occurred over a gift-giving
episode at the time of N!ai's betrothal and involved persons in Bands
1 and 2 who were settled near together at the time. Hwan//ka, the
mother of /"Xontah, N!ai's betrothed, had diverted a gift—a knife—
that people thought was making its way to K"xau, the present husband of N!ai's mother. Instead of giving it to him at the time when
an exchange of gifts was in order, she gave it to one of her relatives.
N!ai's mother's sister, !'Ku, sitting at her own fire, began the talk.
She let it be known what she thought of Hwan//ka, in a loud voice,
a startling contrast to the usual low flow of talk. /Ti!kai, N'ai's
mother, sitting with her shoulder pressed against her sister's, joined
in. People went to sit at each other's fires, forming little groups who
agreed and supported each other. From where they sat, but not all at
once and not in an excited babble, they made their remarks clearly,
with quite long pauses between. Some expressed themselves in agreement with !'Ku as she recounted Hwan//ka's faults and deviations,
past and present. Hwan//ka's family and friends, who had moved to
sit near her, denied the accusations from time to time, but did not
talk as much or as loudly as !'Ku. Hwan//ka muttered or was silent.
!'Ku said she disapproved of her sister's daughter marrying the son of
such a woman but would reconsider her position if Hwan//ka gave
the expected gift to K"xau. The talk lasted about twenty minutes.

At that point Hwan//ka got up and walked away, and the talk subsided to !'Ku's mutterings and others' low conversation. In a few
days Hwan//ka gave K"xau a present, not the gift in question, but
one which satisfied K"xau, and, as they said, "they all started again
in peace."

There is a third form of verbal expression which might be called
a "shout" rather than a "talk," but as far as I know the !Kung have
no special name for it. It is a verbal explosion. Fate receives the heat
of the remarks in a "shout."

We were present on two such occasions, one in 1952, the other in
1953. Both occurred in response to the burning of shelters. In both
instances little children, whose mothers had taken their eyes off
them for a few minutes had picked up burning sticks from the fire,
had dropped them on the soft, dry, bedding grass in the shelters and,
at the first burst of flame, had sensibly run outside unscathed. On
the first occasion, the two children, who were about three years old,
were frightened and were soothed and comforted by their mothers
and other relatives. They were not scolded. On the second occasion,
Hwan//ka, the two-year-old granddaughter of Old ≠Toma and /Təm,
had set fire to her grandparents' shelter. She was not apparently
frightened at all and was found placidly chewing her grandfather's
well-toasted sandal. She was not scolded either.

What was especially interesting was the behavior of the people.
On both occasions they rushed to the burning shelters, emitting all
at once, in extremely loud, excited voices, volcanic eruptions of
words. The men made most of the noise, but the women were also
talking excitedly. No one tried to do anything, nor could they, for
the grass shelters burned like the fiery furnace. I asked the interpreters to stand close to one person at a time and try to hear what
he said. People were telling where they had been when the fire
started, why they had not got there sooner. They shouted that
mothers should not take their eyes off their children, that the children might have been burned. They lamented the objects which had
been destroyed—all in the greatest din I have ever heard humans produce out of themselves. It went on for about eight or ten minutes
in bursts, then tapered off for another ten. While Old ≠Toma's
shelter was burning, he and his wife, /Təm, the great maker of beads,
sat on one side weeping. After the shouting had subsided, a dozen or
more people set about looking for Old ≠Toma's knife blade and
arrow points and picking up what beads they could find for /Təm in
the cooling ashes. The two instances of "shouts" provided examples
of the vehemence which vocal expression can have and vividly illustrated the !Kung way of venting emotion in words.

There is still another kind of talk, not conversation, that I consider to be an outlet for tension and anxiety. We happened to hear it only in relation to anxiety about food and do not know if other concerns sometimes find expression in this way. It occurs in varying degrees of intensity. It is a repeating of something over and over and over again. For instance, whether it is actually so or not, someone may be reiterating that he has no food or that no one has given him food. The remarks are made in the presence of other individuals, but the other individuals do not respond in the manner of a discussion or conversation. In an extreme instance we saw a woman visitor go into a sort of trance and say over and over for perhaps half an hour or so in ≠Toma's presence that he had not given her as much meat as was her due. It was not said like an accusation. It was said as though he were not there. I had the eerie feeling that I was present in someone else's dream. ≠Toma did not argue or oppose her. He continued doing whatever he was doing and let her go on.

All these ways of talking, I believe, aid the !Kung in maintaining their peaceful social relations. Getting things out in words keeps everyone in touch with what others are thinking and feeling, releases tensions, and prevents pressures from building up until they burst out in aggressive acts.

Aspects of Good Manners

In !Kung society good manners require that, when !Kung meet other !Kung who are strangers, all the men should lay down their weapons and approach each other unarmed. The first time ≠Toma approached us, he paused about thirty or forty feet away from us, laid down his bow, arrows, and assegai (spear) on the ground, and walked toward us unarmed. After we were accepted and given !Kung names, we were no longer strangers and we never observed the practice again.

Good manners require that visitors be received courteously and asked to sit by the fire. The woman whose fire it is may welcome the visitor by taking a pinch of the sweet smelling *sā* powder, which she carries in a little tortoise shell hung from her neck, and sprinkling it on the visitor's head in a line from the top of the head to the forehead.

Good manners in eating express restraint. A person does not reveal eagerness or take more than a modest share. When a visitor comes to the fire of a family which is preparing food or eating, he should sit at a little distance, not to seem importunate, and wait to be asked to share. On several occasions we gave small gifts of corned beef to be shared with a group. The person who received the food from us would take only a mouthful. Once an old man who received the meat first only licked his fingers. The lump of food would be passed from one to another. Each would take a modest bite. The last person often got the most. I found it moving to see so much restraint about taking food among people who are all thin and often hungry, for whom food is a source of constant anxiety. We observed no unmannerly behavior and no cheating and no encroachment about food. Although informants said that quarrels had occurred occasionally in the past between members of a band over the time to go to gather certain plant foods, and although we observed expressions of dissatisfaction, no quarrels of any kind arose over food during our observations.

The polite way to receive food, or any gift, is to hold out both hands and have the food or other gift placed in them. To reach out with one hand suggests grabbing to the !Kung. Food may be placed also in front of the person who is to receive it.

Good manners in general should be inoffensive. Any behavior which is likely to stir up trouble is regarded with apprehension and disapproval by the !Kung. In view of this, the joking relationship has its interesting side. Men and women who have the joking relationship insult each other in a facetious way and also point out actual faults or remark on actual episodes which embarrass a person. Everyone joins in the uproarious, derisive laughter. All this is joking and one should not take offense. The !Kung say this teaches young persons to keep their tempers.

In contrast to the joking is their care in other aspects of conduct to avoid giving offense. ≠Toma said, for instance, that if he were forming a hunting party and a man whom he did not want asked to join him, he would be careful to refuse indirectly by making some excuse and would try not to offend the man.

Gossip which can stir up trouble is discouraged. People do gossip but usually discreetly, in low voices, with near and trusted relatives and friends. It is best to mind one's own business, they say.

People are expected to control their tempers, and they do so to a remarkable degree. If they are angry, aggrieved, or frustrated, they tend to mope rather than to become aggressive, expressing their feelings in low mutters to their close relatives and friends. ≠Toma told us that he had lost his temper twice when he was a young man and on one occasion had knocked his father down. On the other he had pushed his wife into hot ashes. It had so frightened him to realize that he could lose control of himself and behave in this violent way that, he said, he had not lost his temper since.

Meat-sharing

The !Kung custom of sharing meat helps to keep stress and hostility over food at a low intensity. The practical value of using up the meat when it is fresh is-obvious to all, and the !Kung are fully aware of the enormous social value of the sharing custom. The fear of hunger is mitigated: the person with whom one shares will share in turn when he gets meat; people are sustained by a web of mutual obligation. If there is hunger, it is commonly shared. There are no distinct haves and have-nots. One is not alone.

To have a concept of the potential stress and jealousy that meat-sharing mitigates in !Kung society, one has only to imagine one family eating meat and others not, when they are settled only ten or fifteen feet apart in a firelit encampment, and there are no walls for privacy. The desert does not hide secret killing and eating because actions are printed in its sands for all to read. The idea of eating alone and not sharing is shocking to the !Kung. It makes them shriek with an uneasy laughter. Lions could do that, they say, not men.

Small animals, the size of duikers or smaller, and birds belong to the man who shoots or snares them. Tortoises, lizards, grasshoppers, and snakes are picked up incidentally and belong to the person who picks them up. That person may share his find only with his or her immediate family or with others as he or she chooses, in the way plant foods are shared. ≠Toma says that if he has only a small creature, he and his family eat a meal and give a little to anyone who happens to be nearby at the time.

The custom of meat-sharing applies to the big animals which are deliberately hunted by hunting parties. In the Nyae Nyae area they were eland, kudu, gemsbok, wildebeest, hartebeest, springbok, warthog, and ostrich. Buffalo were found less commonly. The Nyae Nyae hunters sometimes managed to shoot the wary giraffe but only occasionally. All the above-mentioned animals weigh hundreds of pounds; a large bull eland may weigh a ton. It is the meat of these animals that is distributed according to custom and is shared by all present in the encampment.

The composition of the hunting party is not a matter of strict convention or of anxious concern. Whoever the hunters are, the meat is shared and everyone profits. The men are free to organize their hunting parties as they like. No categories of consanguineous kin or affines are prohibited from hunting together, whether or not they have the joking relationship or practice the sitting and speaking avoidances. Men from different bands may hunt together.

A father has authority over his sons and sons-in-law and could ask them to go hunting or to accompany him and would expect them to obey. Otherwise, participation in a hunting party is voluntary. Any man may instigate a hunt and may ask others to join. No one is formally in command of a party unless he is the father with his sons or sons-in-law, but often an informal kind of leadership develops out of skill and judgment. The men fall in with the plans and suggestions of the best hunter or reach agreement among themselves somehow.

Hunting parties are usually composed of from two to four or five men. One hunter alone would be at a disadvantage in many ways. Ordinarily, the !Kung do not form large parties. Small parties hunting in different directions have much more chance of finding game than one large single party has.

When the kill is made, the hunters have the prerogative of eating the liver on the spot and may eat more of the meat until their hunger is satisfied. If they are far from the band, they may eat the parts that are especially perishable or most awkward to carry, like the head, and they sometimes eat the cherished marrow. They then carry the animal to the band in its parts, bones and all, or, if the animal is very big, they leave most of the bones and cut the meat into strips. The strips dry to biltong quickly and thus are preserved before they decay, and they can be hung on carrying-sticks[2] and transported more easily than big chunks. The blood is carried in bags made of the stomach or bladder.

The gall bladder and testicles are discarded at the kill. Eventually the picked bones and horns are thrown away. (The !Kung make only a few artifacts of bone and horn; the artifacts last a long time and seldom need replacing.) Sinews are kept for making cord. The hide would be skinned off whole and tanned, if it were suitable for a kaross and someone wanted a new kaross at the time. Otherwise, the hide is dried, pounded up, and eaten. Hides are actually quite tasty. Feet are picked of very tissue; gristle is dried and pounded. Soft parts, such as the fetus, udder, heart, lungs, brains, and blood, are often given to old people with poor teeth. Intestines are enjoyed and desired by all. The meat of the rump, back, chest, and neck is highly appreciated. Nothing is wasted; all is distributed.

The owner of the animal is the owner of the first arrow to be effectively shot into the animal so that it penetrates enough for its poison to work. That person is responsible for the distribution. The owner may or may not be one of the hunters.

Hunters have arrows which they acquire in three different ways. Each man makes arrows for himself, shaping the points (usually now of metal, but still possibly of bone or wood) with some slight distinction so that he will know them from the arrows of other men. Secondly, arrows are given as gifts. The man, who made the arrow or had himself acquired it as a gift, may give it to someone else, either a man or a woman, consanguineous kin, affine, or friend. Thirdly, people lend arrows to one another. The status of the arrow plays its part in the distribution of the animal killed with it. There is much giving and lending of arrows. The society seems to want to extinguish in every way possible the concept of the meat belonging to the hunter.

A hunter chooses which arrow he will use. The owner of the arrow —who ipso facto owns the animal—may therefore be the hunter himself, who has chosen to use an arrow he made or one that was given him, or he may be a person who lent the arrow to the hunter.

There may be several hunters in the hunting party and several arrows in the animal, but this seems to cause no confusion or conflict. Every arrow is known, of course. The hunters see which first penetrates effectively so that its poison could account for the kill. But I think that often it is arranged beforehand who will own the animal. A man asking another to accompany him might say, "Come and help me get a buck." Or "Old Gau lent me an arrow and asked me to hunt for him. You come too."

I think there is little or no dissension as to who owned the animal because it is not a cause for great stress; each hunter gets a share of the meat anyway. I think also that a man wants sometimes to be the owner of the meat in order to start the distribution off in the direction of his own relatives, but that one is also content sometimes not to have the onus of the main distribution.

If the animal is large, the hunters cut it up at the kill. If the whole animal is to be cut up in the encampment, any of the men may participate in the butchering. They cut the animal in a customary way each time—all know how to do it, all are skilled. If the owner of the animal is a man, he would probably work at butchering himself; and the hunters would probably help, but not necessarily so. Others might do this work. Women do not participate in butchering an animal, and we did not see any assist in carrying the meat around in the distribution even though we saw women carry meat at other times.

The first distribution the owner makes is to the hunters and to the giver of the arrow, if the arrow was not one the owner made himself. The meat, always uncooked in the first distribution, is given on the bone unless the animal is so large that the meat has been cut into strips at the kill.

In a second distribution, the several persons who got meat in the first distribution cut up their shares and distribute them further. This meat also is given uncooked. The amounts depend on the number of persons involved, but should be as much as the giver can manage. In the second distribution, close kinship is the factor that sets the pattern of the giving. Certain obligations are compulsory. A man's first obligation at this point, we were told, is to give to his wife's parents. He must give to them the best he has in as generous portions as he can, while still fulfilling other primary obligations, which are to his own parents, his spouse, and his offspring. He keeps a portion for himself at this time and from it gives to his siblings, to his wife's siblings if they are present, and to other relatives and friends who are there; possibly he gives only in small quantities by then.

Everyone who receives meat gives again, in another wave of sharing, to his or her parents, parents-in-law, spouse, offspring, siblings, and others. The meat may be cooked and the quantities small.

Visitors, even though they are not close relatives, are given meat by the people whom they are visiting. This social rule is strongly felt. Visitors may receive small quantities of cooked meat, which is like being asked to dinner.

Name-relatives often receive generous portions of meat because they have the same name as the giver or because their names associate them with his close kin, but this seems to be more a favor than an absolute rule. ≠Toma said there were far too many men named ≠Toma for him to give them special consideration.

The result of the distribution is that everybody gets some meat.

In the later waves of sharing, when the primary distribution and primary kinship obligations have been fulfilled, the giving of meat from one's own portion has the quality of gift-giving. !Kung society requires at this point only that a person should give with reasonable generosity in proportion to what he has received and not keep more than an equitable amount for himself. Then the person who has received a gift of meat must give a reciprocal gift some time in the future. Band affiliation imposes no pattern on this giving. Except that the hunters are customarily given a forequarter or a hindquarter, no rule prescribes that any particular part of the animal must be given to any particular person or to any category of kin or affine. People give different parts of the meat and different amounts, this time to some, next time to others, more generously or less generously according to their own reasons. We are certain that the motives are

the same as in gift-giving in general: to measure up to what is expected of them, to make friendly gestures, to win favor, to repay
past favors and obligations, and to enmesh others in future obligation. I am sure that when feelings of genuine generosity and real
friendliness exist, they would also be expressed by giving.

The distribution of an eland which was killed by K''xau Beard
of Band 2 will serve as an example of the way meat was shared on
one occasion. (On every occasion, the amounts given and the parts
given would differ, and the first recipients would vary.) More than a
hundred !Kung were present at /Gausha at the time of the hunt.
Both /Gausha bands (Bands 1 and 2) were present. Bands 3, 4, and
7, and a sprinkling of people from other bands were visiting.

The hunting party was composed of four men: K''xau Beard, with
//Kau, his first wife's brother, and /Twi, his own brother, both of
whom lived with him in Band 2. N!aishe, his brother-in-law, who was
visiting at the time, joined the party.

The party had hunted for eight days without success in heat so
exhausting that they had to lie covered with sand through the middle
part of the day.

/Twi was the first to see the eland. It was a huge one. As /Twi had
been asked by his brother to come and help on the hunt, he told his
brother where the eland was and did not shoot at it himself.

Two boys joined the men to track the eland after it was shot. The
party tracked it for three days and then found it dead from the
poison. They cut up the meat and brought it to the encampment at
/Gausha, which was two days' travel away. The hunt had lasted
thirteen days in all.

K''xau Beard was himself the owner of the arrow. The arrow had
been given by one person to another five times. /Gau Music of Band
1, who had made it, gave it to his sister, /''Xoishe, who gave it to her
husband, ≠Gau of Band 3. He gave it to his brother, K''xau, also of
Band 3, who gave it to his wife, Tï'!kai. Tï'!kai gave it to K''xau
Beard, her brother, who shot the eland with it and who was responsible for the distribution of the meat.

K''xau Beard first gave meat to the hunters who helped him, as
was the custom. To N!aishe he gave a forequarter and to //Kau a
forequarter and the head. (The hunters usually received a forequarter
or hindquarter or an equivalent amount. The head was an extra gift.)
The two boys who helped track got nothing because their fathers
would give them some, we were told. To our astonishment, /Twi
was given nothing. K''xau Beard explained that his brother would

eat from his pot. (Actually he might eat more in this way as he would not have to share the cooked meat with anyone but his wife and child.)

K''xau Beard's sister, /Ti!kai, who had given him the arrow, received the meat of the back and throat and the intestines.

K''xau Beard kept the meat of the neck for himself. Continuing the distribution he gave the rest of the meat as follows:

To his first wife, //Kushe, he gave both hindquarters, the meat of the chest, the lungs, part of the liver, and one hind foot. To his mother he gave the meat of the belly and one hind foot. To his sister, //Kushe, and to /Tasa, the wife of his brother, /Twi, he gave one front foot each.

The amount given to his first wife was enormous. In addition to giving to her co-wife, also named //Kushe, and to her children and her co-wife's children, she gave a large portion of meat to her parents who lived with them in Band 2. (On other occasions the man had given directly to his wife's parents—not through his wife.) When the meat was cut up, //Kushe gave to her father, Old ≠Toma, four bundles of strips of boneless raw meat (it was somewhat dried by then). There were about ten or twelve strips to a bundle, about 76 cm to 92 cm long. We guessed the weight of this gift to be about 27 to 32 kg. She gave meat also to her two younger brothers, /Gau and /''Xontah. (Her other brother, //Kau, who had been one of the hunters, had got his share from K''xau Beard.) She gave to her co-wife's father, ≠Gau of Band 4, and to old /''Xashe of Band 4, her co-wife's MoFa. She then gave to six other persons, all in Band 1. They were: her cousin, Old Gau (her FaSiSo); his two daughters; two other cousins (FaSiDas), /Ti!kai and !'Ku; and !'Ku's husband, ≠Toma.

The giving of raw meat went on. Old ≠Toma gave to eighteen people: his wife; six affines; three consanguineous kin; two name-relatives (that is, a visitor whose father's name was ≠Toma, and Old /Gasa, whose deceased husband's name was ≠Toma); and six other persons. Telling us the reasons for giving to the last six, whose consanguineous or affinal connections (if any) with Old ≠Toma were so remote we did not bother to trace them, he said of one, "He is an old man whom I like in my heart," and of another, "He was hungry for meat." In the end Old ≠Toma gave some of the meat back to his daughter, //Kushe.

/Ti!kai of Band 3, the giver of the arrow, gave raw meat to six persons: her husband's mother; his brother and his two sisters (all in

Band 2); a visitor who was her HuSiHuBr; and her mother's brother in the visiting Band 7.

Persons who had by this time received substantial amounts of raw meat began giving to others. We recorded sixty-three gifts of raw meat. Doubtless there were more. After the raw meat was given, individuals shared their portions, cooked or raw, with parents, off-spring, spouses, and others.

Meat is not habitually cooked and eaten as a family meal among the !Kung. When an individual receives a portion of meat, he owns it outright for himself. He may give and share it further as he wishes, but it never becomes family or group property. The men, women, and children may cook their pieces when and as they wish, often roasting bits in the coals and hot ashes and eating them alone at odd times. Or someone may start a big pot boiling, and several people will bring their pieces to put into it at the same time, each taking his own piece out when it is cooked.

The sense of possessing one's own piece personally is, I believe, very important to the !Kung. It gives one the responsibility of choosing when to eat one's meat and struggling with hunger as best one can when it is finished, without occasion or excuse for blaming others for eating more than their share.

It has often been reported that when San have plenty of meat, they gorge themselves until they can hardly walk. We have seen the Nyae Nyae !Kung eat hearty meals of meat when they have been long without, but nothing more than we considered a normal amount. They hang meat in the bushes to dry and can keep it for some time. It is not uncommon for them to eat quite sparingly and save bits for a coming journey or against a future day of hunger.

The !Kung are quite conscious of the value of meat-sharing and they talk about it, especially about the benefit of the mutual obligation it entails. The idea of sharing is deeply implanted and very successfully imposes its restraints. To keep meat without sharing is one of the things that just is not done.

Gift-giving

The custom of gift-giving, in my opinion, comes second only to meat-sharing in aiding the !Kung to avoid jealousy and ill will and to develop friendly relations. !Kung society puts considerable emphasis on gift-giving. Almost everything a person has may have been given to him and may be passed on to others in time. The !Kung make their artifacts, on the whole, of durable material and take good care of them. The objects may last for generations, moving in a slow current among the people. The dealings in gift-giving are only between individuals, but they are numerous and provide occasion, perhaps more than any one other activity does, for visits which bring groups of people together.

We gave cowrie shells as parting gifts in 1951 to the women in Band 1, the band which first sponsored us and with which we stayed on each expedition wherever they were. When providing ourselves with gifts for the !Kung on our first expedition, we had had to guess as best we could what would appeal to them. The idea of cowrie shells came from seeing in museums so many West African objects encrusted with the shells. We thought the !Kung might like them as a novelty and bought a supply from a New York shell dealer. They came from the Pacific, and we amused ourselves imagining future archaeologists finding them in !Kung sites in the Kalahari, to their bewilderment. We carefully observed that there were no cowrie shells among the !Kung ornaments before we gave them. We gave to each woman enough for a short necklace, one large brown shell and twenty smaller gray ones. In 1952, there was hardly a cowrie shell to be found in Band 1. They had been given to relatives and friends, and they appeared not as whole necklaces but in ones and twos in people's ornaments to the edges of the area.

The !Kung have not developed special objects to use as gifts. Nor have they invested ordinary objects with special gift significance. What they give each other are the common artifacts and materials of everyday life. However, among those, some are more highly valued than others, as one would expect. I gathered that relative scarcity of material was a factor and that objects were appreciated for their beauty, workmanship, and appropriate size (a wide headband is better than a narrow one). People took an interest in remembering to whom an object had been given in the recent past, but the !Kung, who are present-oriented, do not place special value upon antiquity as such or systematically hold the distant past in mind.

The !Kung decorate their artifacts very little. (They have developed music and dancing but not the plastic or pictorial arts.) However, they delight in ornaments with which to adorn themselves. The most highly valued are the traditional ornaments of ostrich-eggshell beads, especially the wide headbands and the necklaces of five or six strings of beads that reach to the navel—the measurement of a good necklace. The creamy white of the shells is particularly becoming to the yellow-brown skin of the !Kung and is a relief from the monotonous gray-brown of the karosses that the women wear. The !Kung also like ornaments made with European beads of all colors, though white is preferred. They like all beads, any beads, we were told; K"xau Beard said that the only thing they do not like about beads is scarcity of them.

They value artifacts that take time and care to make: the musical instrument (pluriarc) called //gwashi; a well-shaped wooden bowl; a long string of dance rattles. They also value metal implements and pots; these they obtain by trade.

The !Kung do not trade among themselves. They consider the procedure undignified and avoid it because it is too likely to stir up bad feelings. They trade with the Bantu, however, in the border country settlements of western Botswana. The !Kung offer well-tanned antelope hides and ostrich-eggshell beads. For these they obtain tobacco; beads; knives; axes; malleable metal for making arrowpoints and assegai blades; and occasional files and chisels, fire-strikers, and pots.

The odds are with the Bantu in the trading. Big, agressive, and determined to have what they want, they easily intimidate the !Kung. Several !Kung informants said that they tried not to trade with Herero if it was possible to avoid it because, although the Tawana were hard bargainers, the Herero were worse. /Twi of Band 1, a mild man, said he had been forced by a Herero, one whom he was afraid to anger, to trade the shirt and pants we had given him as a parting gift in 1952 for a small enamel pan and a little cup. /Ti!kai had more gumption. A Herero at the beginning of a negotiation with him brought out a good-sized pile of tobacco but took from it only a pinch when it was time to pay. /Ti!kai picked up the object he was trading and ran off. ≠Toma said with amused exaggeration that "a very good Herero, a respectable one, will give a handful of tobacco for five cured steinbok skins. A bad Herero will give a pipeful" (he showed the size of his fingernail) "for three skins." The Tawana values are a little better. A well-tanned gemsbok hide brings a pile of tobacco about 36 cm in diameter and about 10 cm high. The values vary. Some that were reported to us were three duiker or steinbok skins for a good-sized knife, five strings of ostrich-eggshell beads for an assegai.

The !Kung have become dependent on metal, especially knives, axes, and arrowpoints. They have been able to trade enough for every man to have these implements. They could, however, exist without them and do still use a few bone and wood arrowpoints, as it is poison, not penetrating power, that makes their arrows deadly.

The pots are Ovambo or Okavango pottery (the !Kung make no pottery themselves) or European ironware. The !Kung like to have a pot around to borrow sometimes; not everyone wants to carry one. They cook mostly in hot ashes. More for their novelty, I thought, than for their worth, the !Kung trade also for old oddments of cloth garments (they weave neither cloth nor mats), pieces of blankets, basins, and so forth—things they do not really need but like to have.

Tobacco they need "to make the heart feel better." Oddly enough for these passionate smokers, tobacco is not given as much emphasis in gift-giving as one might expect. They do make gifts of tobacco, but when anyone lights a pipe he passes it around anyway; all present drag smoke into their lungs until they almost faint, and it does not seem to matter much who owned the tobacco.

Eland fat is a very highly valued gift. An eland provides so much fat that people can afford to be a little luxurious. They rub it on themselves and on their implements, and they eat it. ≠Toma said that when he had eland fat to give, he took shrewd note of certain objects he might like to have and gave their owners especially generous gifts of fat.

Real property and the resources of plant foods and waterholes are not owned by individuals and cannot be given away. However, meat, once it is distributed after the hunt, and plant foods, once they are gathered, become private property and may be given. Artifacts are privately owned by the individual man, woman, or child, as outrightly owned if received as a gift as if made by the individual. The !Kung borrow and lend a great deal—in itself this is one of the ways they support each other and aid themselves in maintaining social solidarity—but this does not blur the clarity of ownership. Each object acquires some markings of its own from the maker and from usage. It is easy for the !Kung, with their highly developed powers of observation and visual memory, to keep track of the commonest objects, know the ownership, and remember the history of the gifts.

As far as we know, no rules of avoidance govern the objects given to any category of person. For instance, although women, especially when menstruating, should not touch hunting weapons lest the hunter's powers be weakened, they may own arrows that are given to them.

The gifts vary in quantity. One which /Ti!kai gave to ≠Toma was considered generous. It was a fine ostrich-eggshell headband, three ostrich eggshells, and a well-tanned duiker skin as soft as suede. Another generous gift consisted of a knife, an assegai, and a triple string of traded white European beads. Often gifts were less. The feelings persons have for each other, the degree of their past indebtedness, what they happen to possess and can give determine the generosity of the gift.

The acquisition, per se, of the objects is seldom, I believe, of primary importance to most individuals in gift-giving—that is, if the objects are their own artifacts. As the !Kung come into more contact with Europeans—and this is already happening—they will feel sharply the lack of our things and will need and want more. It makes them feel inferior to be without clothes when they stand among strangers who are clothed. But in their own life and with their own artifacts, they are comparatively free from both material want and pressures to acquire. Except for food and water (important exceptions!) with which the Nyae Nyae !Kung are in balance, but I believe barely so, they all had what they needed, or they could make what they needed. Every man can and does make the things that men make, and every woman the things that women make. No one was dependent upon acquiring objects by gift-giving.

The !Kung live in a kind of material plenty because they have adapted the tools of their living to materials which lie in abundance around them and are free for anyone to take (wood, reeds, bone for weapons and implements; fibers for cordage; grass for shelters), or to materials which are at least sufficient in quantity to satisfy the needs of the population. The Nyae Nyae !Kung have hides enough for garments and bags; they keep extra hides for when they need them for new garments or when they want them for trade; otherwise they eat them. The !Kung can always use more ostrich eggshells for beads to wear or trade, but enough are found, at least, for every woman to have eight or ten shells for water-containers—all she can carry—and a goodly number of bead ornaments.

In their nomadic hunting-gathering life, traveling from one source of food to another through the seasons, always going back and forth between food and water, they carry their young children and all their belongings. With plenty of most materials at hand to replace artifacts as required, the !Kung have not needed or wanted to encumber themselves with duplicates or surpluses. They do not even want to carry one of everything. They borrow what they do not own. I believe for these reasons they have not developed permanent storage, have not hoarded, and the accumulation of objects has not become associated with admirable status. Instead of keeping things, they use them as gifts to express generosity and friendly intent, and to put people under obligation to make return tokens of friendship.

Even more specifically in my opinion, they mitigate jealousy and envy, to which the !Kung are prone, by passing on to others objects that might be coveted.

Except, as ≠Toma said, that it would be surprising to see a man give a present to a woman who was not related to him (and vice versa I imagine), anyone may give to anyone. Degree or kind of consanguinity or affinity, having the joking relationship or lacking it, impose no requirements or restrictions. We did hear people say, however, that the *k"xau n!a* of a band may feel that he should lean well to the generous side in his giving, for this position focuses a little extra attention on him, and he wants whatever attention he attracts not to be envious. Someone remarked that this could keep such a man poor.

The times of giving are determined almost entirely by the individual's convenience. The !Kung do not know their birthdays or anniversaries and have no special days of the year which they mark by giving gifts. Gifts are required by convention on only three ritual occasions. The type or quantity of the gift is not patterned, but the gift should be generous. The occasions are (1) betrothals and (2) weddings, when the parents exchange gifts and give to the young couple, and (3) the ritual of a baby's first haircut, when the *!ku n!a,* the person for whom the baby is named, should give him a fine present.

Relatives give to young people with the idea of setting them up in life. K"xau Beard gave an assegai and a kaross to his FaSiSo, saying it was his duty to see that the boy got some things because among the boy's relatives he was the most able to do so. The boy's father was very old, he explained, and did not have many possessions. People expect to wait a long time for young people to make return gifts.

The two rigid requirements in gift-giving are that one must not refuse a proffered gift and that one must give in return. Demi said that even if he might prefer not to be obligated to someone, he would accept and prepare to make his return gift. If a gift were to be refused, he continued, the giver would be terribly angry. He would say, "Something is very wrong here." This could involve whole groups in tensions, bad words, taking sides—even a talk might occur —just what the !Kung do not want. Demi said it does not happen: a !Kung never refuses a gift. (I thought of our Christmas giving and how one would feel it one's Christmas gift were refused.) And a !Kung does not fail to give in return. ≠Toma said that would be "neglecting friendship." A person would know that others thought him "far-hearted" and "this would worry him."

In reciprocating, one does not give the same object back again but something of comparable value. The interval of time between receiving and reciprocating varies from a few weeks to a few years. Propriety requires that there be no unseemly haste. The giving must not look like trading.

Incidentally, we were not included by the !Kung in their gift-giving patterns. They gave us a few things spontaneously which they thought we would enjoy—python meat for instance—but did not feel obligated to reciprocate for every gift we gave them.

Asking for a first-time gift or asking that a return gift be made after due time has elapsed is within the rules of propriety. People prefer that others give in return without being asked, but ≠Toma says he does not hesitate to ask if a gift is long overdue. If a person wants a particular object, he may ask for it. Asking is also a means by which people play upon each other's feelings. One can test a friendship in this way. One can give vent to jealousy or satisfy it by acquiring some object. And one can make someone else uncomfortable. I thought that /Ti!kai (an intelligent man, but very touchy, self-centered and—with us—uncooperative) used to ask for gifts in order to play with anger, arousing it for the sake of feeling it, as children do with fear, playing witches in the dark. His remarks one day indicated a mingling of feelings and purposes. He told us that one may ask for anything. He did, he said. He would go to a person's fire and sit and ask. (I could imagine him with his black, glancing eyes, sitting and asking!) He would ask usually for only one or two things, but if a person had a lot, he might ask for more. He said he was almost never refused. However, if a man had only one pot and /Ti!kai asked for it, the man might say "I am not refusing but it is the only pot I have. If I get another, you may come for this one. I am very sorry but this is the only pot I have." /Ti!kai said this would not make him angry unless he were refused too many times. To be refused too many times would make a person very angry. But, said /Ti!kai, he himself did not tire of people asking him for gifts. Asking, he claimed, "formed a love" between people. It meant "he still loves me, that is why he is asking." At least it formed a communication of some sort between people, I thought.

I have stressed the mitigation of envy and jealousy as the important value of gift-giving. !Kung informants stressed more the value of making a friendly gesture even if it is only a token gesture. It puts people under the obligation of making a friendly gesture in return. People are quite conscious of this and speak about it. Demi said, "The worst thing is not giving gifts. If people do not like each other, but one gives a gift, and the other must accept; this brings a peace between them. We give to one another always. We give what we have. This is the way we live together."

Absence of Stealing

One day, when I wanted to talk with a group of informants about what the !Kung considered to be a wrongdoing, I began with /Ti!kai. He said promptly, "making crooked arrows and fighting," but could not think of anything else that was a wrongdoing. Informants had previously said that not sharing food would be the worst thing they could think of. Others had mentioned that the breaking of the incest and menstruation prohibitions would be very wrong, and that girls should not sit in immodest postures. No one seemed to think lying was very serious wrongdoing, and no one mentioned stealing. I finally asked directly and K"xau replied meditatively they had not thought to mention stealing because they did not steal.

We had heard of a man who took honey from a tree, honey which had been found and marked and was therefore owned by someone else. He was killed for it by the furious owner. That was the only episode of stealing that we discovered.

The !Kung stole nothing from us. Even when we went away on trips leaving several bands of !Kung settled around our camp site, we left our supplies and equipment unlocked, in the open or in our tents, with confidence that nothing would be stolen. Things that we lost or forgot in the !Kung encampment were returned to us, even two cigarettes in a crumpled package.

Stealing without being discovered is practically impossible in !Kung life because the !Kung know everybody's footprints and every object. Respect for ownership is strong. But, apart from that, /Ti!kai said, "Stealing would cause nothing but trouble. It might cause fighting."

Conclusion

During seventeen and a half months of field work with the Nyae Nyae !Kung (with Bands 1 and 2 and many visitors, usually about sixty to seventy-five persons), I personally saw only four flare-ups of discord and heard about three others which occurred in neighboring bands during that period. All were resolved before they became serious quarrels. Of the seven, four were flare-ups of sexual jealousy. Another was the talk about Hwan//ka's gift. Two were minor disagreements about going somewhere. On one occasion, K"xau Beard coerced his young second wife into going with him when she wanted to stay visiting her parents. He coerced her swiftly and decisively by snatching her baby from her arms and walking off with him. In a flash the wife ran a few steps and hit him on the head with her digging stick, then she went around in a circle, stamping her feet in great, high stamps like an enraged samurai in a Japanese print, then she followed her husband. On another occasion, /Ti!kai gave his brother a shove for refusing to accompany him. None of the conflicts concerned food.

On a later expedition, in another year, John Marshall witnessed three serious quarrels.[3] Anger flared more hotly than in the episodes I saw. One of those quarrels was about food. It was a dispute about the possession of an animal that had been killed. Another was about a marital matter, another about the failure of a curer to come to cure a sick child when he was asked. All three quarrels were resolved by talks. Vehement talking it was, but it stopped short of physical fighting.

I consider that the incidence of quarrels is low among the !Kung, that they manage very well to avoid physical violence when tensions are high and anger flares, and that they also manage well to keep tension from reaching the point of breaking into open hostility. They avoid arousing envy, jealousy, and ill will; and, to a notable extent, they cohere and achieve the comfort and security which they so desire in human relations.

Further Studies to Part IV

Although much of the project's work on behavior and belief remains to be published, several studies have already appeared. Katz deals with the !Kung trance in his recent book, *Preludes to Growth* (1973). Previous work on the trance dance has been published by Lee (1967, 1968b) and by Marshall (1962, 1969). John Marshall made a short informative film on the trance entitled "Num chai" (1971), see also Marshall and Biesele (1974). Biesele's studies of !Kung folklore include Biesele (1972b, 1972d, 1972e, and in press). Previous studies include Lorna Marshall's (1962) and Bleek and Lloyd (1911, 1923).

Long before the current project was organized, Lorna Marshall was publishing a distinguished series of papers on the ethnography of the Nyae Nyae !Kung (1957, 1957b, 1959, 1960, 1961, 1962, 1965, and 1969). The Nyae Nyae !Kung are also documented in a series of films by John Marshall including "The Hunters" (1956) and a number of others available from Documentary Educational Resources, 24 Dane Street, Somerville, Massachusetts.

Contributors Bibliography Notes Index

Contributors

Megan Biesele was trained in literature and anthropology at the University of Michigan, and completed her Ph.D. dissertation at Harvard in 1975. Biesele conducted fieldwork in northwestern Botswana in 1970–72 and 1975–76 and has written a number of articles and reviews on !Kung folklore and culture change.

Nicholas Blurton Jones heads the Developmental Ethology Section of the Institute of Child Health at the University of London. He has studied the ethology of birds and mammals as well as the behavior of preschool children. He carried out San fieldwork in 1970 in collaboration with Melvin J. Konner.

Irven DeVore is a Professor of Anthropology at Harvard University. He received his Ph.D. in Anthropology from the University of Chicago in 1962. In addition to his field trips to the Dobe Area San in 1963, 1964, and 1967–68, he has made intensive studies of baboon behavior and ecology in East Africa. His books include *Primate Behavior* (1965), *Primates* (with S. Eimerl, 1965), and *Man the Hunter* (with R. Lee, 1968).

Patricia Draper received her Ph.D. in Anthropology from Harvard in 1972. She carried out fieldwork on child socialization among nomadic and sedentary !Kung in 1968–69 and 1975. She has written articles on !Kung childhood and adult sex roles as well as reviews of the socialization literature. She is currently Assistant Professor of Anthropology at the University of New Mexico.

Mathias G. Guenther has a Ph.D. in Anthropology from the University of Toronto (1973). He worked among the acculturated San of the Ghanzi farms from 1968 to 1970 and again in 1974. He holds an appointment in anthropology at Wilfred Laurier University, Waterloo, Canada.

John D.L. Hansen, M.B., Ch.B., M.D., has made extensive medical and nutritional studies of children in South Africa. He is currently Professor and Head, Department of Paediatrics, University of the Witwatersrand, Johannesburg, South Africa.

Henry Harpending has taught at Harvard and Yale Universities and is currently an Assistant Professor of Anthropology at the University of New Mexico. He carried out genetic and demographic fieldwork among the San in 1968–69 and 1975. He received his Ph.D. in Anthropology from Harvard in 1971. He is the author of a number of articles on hunter-gatherer population structure and related topics.

Nancy Howell received her Ph.D. in Sociology from Harvard University in 1968. She carried out extensive fieldwork on the demography of the hunting and gathering San in 1967–69. Currently she is an Associate Professor of Sociology at the University of Toronto. She is the author of *The Search for an Abortionist* (1969) and several articles on the demography of small populations.

Richard Katz is a research psychologist at the Massachusetts Mental Health Center studying community mental health and is a lecturer on Psychology at Harvard Medical School. He has a Ph.D. in Psychology from Harvard (1965) and has taught at Brandeis University. He is the author of *Preludes to Growth* (1973). He did fieldwork with the !Kung in 1968 in collaboration with Richard Lee.

Melvin J. Konner received his Ph.D. in Anthropology from Harvard in 1973, and he is now Lecturer and Research Fellow (Foundations' Fund for Research in Psychiatry) at the same institution. Konner did fieldwork on infant development among the !Kung in 1969–71 and 1975. He is the author of several articles and reviews in the areas of child development and ethology.

Richard B. Lee received his Ph.D. in Anthropology from the University of California at Berkeley in 1965. He has taught at Harvard and Rutgers and is currently an Associate Professor of Anthropology at the University of Toronto. Lee carried out fieldwork on !Kung ecology and social organization in 1963–64, 1967–69, and 1973. His works include *Man the Hunter* (with I. DeVore, 1968), *The New Native Resistance* (with J. Jorgensen, 1974), and numerous articles on the !Kung.

Lorna Marshall was educated at Radcliffe College and made several field trips to the !Kung of the Nyae Nyae Area of Namibia during the 1950s and 1960s. She is the author of a number of major articles on !Kung ethnography and a monograph on her research will shortly be published by Harvard University Press.

Marjorie Shostak studied English Literature and Music at Brooklyn College and Columbia University. She collected the life histories of eight !Kung women in the field in 1969–71 and 1975, and she also studied !Kung music and art. She is a Fellow at the Radcliffe Institute and author of *Nisa: The Life and Words of a !Kung Woman*.

Jiro Tanaka received his Ph.D. in Anthropology from Kyoto University. He has carried out fieldwork among the /Gwi and //Gana of Central Botswana in 1967–68 and 1970–72 and is the author of a monograph on the /Gwi (in Japanese) and several articles on San ecology. He is now an Associate Professor in the Department of Primate Ecology at the Primate Research Institute, Kyoto University.

A. Stewart Truswell, M.B., Ch.B., M.D., has conducted nutritional and medical research in England and southern Africa. He has made field trips to the Dobe Area in 1967, 1968, and 1969. Currently he is Professor of Nutrition and Dietetics and head of the Department of Nutrition and Food Science, Queen Elizabeth College, University of London.

Sherwood L. Washburn is Professor of Anthropology at the University of California, Berkeley and past president of the American Anthropological Association. He is the author of numerous articles and monographs on problems in the evolution of human behavior.

John E. Yellen, an archaeologist, received his Ph.D. from Harvard University in 1974. He carried out fieldwork in ethnoarchaeology and conducted excavations in the Dobe Area in 1968–70 and 1975–76. Currently a Research Associate at the Smithsonian Institution, Washington, D.C., he is the author of several articles on the archaeology of hunter-gatherers.

Bibliography

(An asterisk denotes publications of the Harvard Kalahari Research Group.)

377

Ainsworth, M.D.S. 1962. *Deprivation of Maternal Care.* Geneva: World Health Organization.
—— 1967. *Infancy in Uganda.* Baltimore: Johns Hopkins University Press.
—— S.M. Bell and D.J. Stayton. 1972. Individual differences in the development of some attachment behaviors. *Merrill-Palmer Quarterly* 18:123–144.
Albrink, M.J., J.W. Meigs, and M.A. Granoff. 1962. Weight gain and serum triglycerides in normal men. *New England J. Med.* 266:484.
de Almeida, A. 1965 *Bushmen and Other Non-Bantu Peoples of Angola.* Publication of the Institute for the Study of Man in Africa, vol. 1. Johannesburg. Witwatersrand University Press.
Ascher, R. 1961. Analogy in archaeological interpretation. *Southwestern J. of Anth.* 17:317–325.
Ask-Upmark, E. 1967. *A Primer of High Blood Pressure.* Stockholm, Sweden: Svenska Bokförlaget.
Balikci, A. 1964. Development of basic socio-economic units in two Eskimo communities. *Bull. Nat. Mus. Can.* 202.
Bayley, N. 1969. *Manual for the Bayley Scales of Infant Development.* New York: Psychological Corporation.
Bechuanaland Protectorate. 1964. *Report on the Census of the Bechuanaland Protectorate, 1964.* Gaberones: Ministry of Home Affairs, Government Printer.
Ben Shaul, D.M. 1962. The composition of the milk of wild animals. *Int. Zoo Year Book* 4:300–332.
Berndt, R.M. 1970. Comment on Birdsell (1970). *Current Anthropology* 11: 132–133.
*Biesele, M. 1972a. Hunting in semi-arid areas—the Kalahari Bushman today. Special edition of *Botswana Notes and Records.*
*—— 1972b. The black-backed jackal and the brown hyena a !Kung Bushman folktale. *Botswana Notes and Records* 4.
*—— 1972c. To whom it may concern (English translation of an open letter to the chiefs of Botswana from a !Kung woman). *Kutlwano* August.
*—— 1972d. *A Contemporary Bushman's Comments on the Brandberg Paintings.* (MS).
*—— 1972e. *Song texts by the Master of Tricks, Kalahari San Thumb Piano Music.* (MS).
*—— 1975. Folklore and Ritual of !Kung Hunter-gatherers. Ph.D. dissertation, Harvard University, Cambridge, Mass.
*—— In press. Religion and folklore. In P.V. Tobias, ed., *The Bushman.* Cape Town: H. & Rousseau Publishers.
Binford, L.R. 1962. Archaeology as anthropology. *American Antiquity* 28(2): 217–225.

—— 1968a. Methodological considerations of the archaeological use of ethnographic data. In R.B..Lee and I. DeVore, eds., *Man the Hunter.* Chicago: Aldine.

—— 1968b. Post-pleistocene adaptations. In S.R. and L.R. Binford, eds., *New Perspectives in Archeology.* Chicago: Aldine.

—— 1971. Interassemblage variability—the Mousterian and the "functional" argument. Paper presented at Research Seminar on Archaeology and Related Subjects, December 14-16, Sheffield.

—— and S.R. Binford. 1966. A preliminary analysis of functional variability in the Mousterian of Levallois facies. *Amer. Anth.* 68(2):238-295.

Birch, H.G., and J.D. Gussow. 1970. *Disadvantaged Children: Health Nutrition and School Failure.* New York and London: Grune and Stratton.

Birdsell, J.B. 1970. Local group composition among the Australian aborigines: a critique of the evidence from fieldwork conducted since 1930. *Current Anthropology* 11(a):115-142.

Biss, K., K.J. Ho, B. Mikkelson, L. Lewis, and C.B. Taylor. 1971. Some unique biologic characteristics of the Masai of East Africa. *New England J. Med.* 284:694.

Bleek, D.F. 1928a. *The Naron: A Bushman Tribe of the Central Kalahari.* Cambridge: Cambridge University Press.

—— 1928b. Bushmen of Central Angola. *Bantu Stud.* 3:105-125.

—— 1929. *Comparative Vocabularies of Bushman Languages.* Cambridge: Cambridge University Press.

Bleek, W.H.I. 1869. The Bushman Language. In R. Noble, ed., *The Cape and its People.* Cape Town: Juta.

Bleek, W.H.I., and L. Lloyd. 1911. *Specimens of Bushman Folklore.* London: George Allen & Co., Ltd.

—— and —— 1923. *The Mantis and His Friends.* Cape Town: T. Maskew Miller.

*Blurton Jones, N.G. 1971. An experiment on eyebrow-raising and visual searching in children. *J. Child Psychol. Psychiat.* 11:233-240.

*—— 1972. Comparative aspects of mother-child contact. In N.G. Blurton Jones, ed., *Ethological Studies of Child Behavior.* Cambridge: Cambridge University Press.

*—— and M.J. Konner. 1973. Sex differences in the behavior of Bushman and London two- to five-year-olds. In J. Crook and R. Michael, eds., *Comparative Ecology and Behavior of Primates.* New York: Academic Press.

Boas, F. 1888. The central Eskimo. *Bur. Amer. Ethnol. Ann. Rep.* 6:399-699. Washington: Smithsonian Institution.

Botswana Government, National Archives. *Papers on the settlement of the Ghanzi District.* Nos. Hc. 140/7; s.5/1; s.182/5; s.469/1/1-4.

Bower, T., J. Broughton, and M. Moore. 1970. Infants responses to approaching objects: an indicator of response to distal variables. *Perception and Psychophysics* 9:193-196.

Bowlby, J. 1952. *Maternal Care and Mental Health.* Geneva: World Health Organization.

—— 1969. *Attachment and Loss,* vol. 1: *Attachment.* London: Hogarth.

Brain, C.K. 1967. Bone weathering and the problem of bone pseudo-tools. *So. Afr. J. Sci.* 63:97-99.

—— 1969. The contribution of Namib Desert Hottentots to an understanding of Australopithecine bone accumulations. *Scientific Papers of the Namib Research Station,* no. 39: 13-22.

378

Bronte-Stewart, B., A. Keys, J.F. Brock, A.D. Moodie, M.H. Keys, and A. Antonis. 1955. Serum cholesterol, diet and coronary heart disease: an inter-racial survey in the Cape Peninsula. *Lancet* 2:1103.

—— O.E. Budtz-Olsen, J.M. Hickley, and J.F. Brock. 1960. The health and nutritional status of the !Kung Bushmen of South West Africa. *S. Afr. J. Lab. Clin. Med.* 6:188–216.

Bruner, J. 1968. Processes of cognitive growth in infancy. *Heinz Werner Lectures.* Cambridge, Mass.: Clark University.

—— R. Olver, and P. Greenfield. 1966. *Studies in Cognitive Growth.* New York: John Wiley & Sons.

Burchell, W.J. 1822. *Travels in the Interior of Southern Africa.* London: Longman, Hurst et al.

Campbell, J. 1815. *Travels in South Africa.* London: Black and Perry.

—— 1837. *A Journey to Lattakoo.* London: The Rel. Tract Soc.

Campbell, J. 1956. *Hero with a Thousand Faces.* Cleveland: The World Publishing Co., Meridan Books.

—— 1969. *The Masks of God,* vols. 1–4. New York: Viking Press, Compass Books.

Carlson, L.A., L. Levi, and L. Orö. 1968. Plasma lipids and urinary excretion of catecholamines in man during experimentally induced emotional stress, and their modification by nicotinic acid. *J. Clin. Invest.* 47:1795.

Carstens, W.P. 1966. *The Social Structure of a Cape Coloured Reserve.* Cape Town: Oxford University Press.

Castaneda, C. 1968. *The Teachings of Don Juan.* New York: Ballentine Books.

Cavalli-Sforza, L.L. 1973. Pygmies, an example of hunter-gatherers, and genetic consequences for man of domestication of plants and animals. In *Proc. IVth Internat. Congr. Human Genet.,* in press.

Chagnon, N.A. 1968. *Yanamano: The Fierce People.* New York: Holt, Rinehart & Winston.

Chang, K.C. 1967a. Major aspects of the interrelationship of archaeology and ethnology. *Current Anthropology* 8:227–243.

—— 1967b. *Rethinking Archaeology.* New York: Random House.

Chisholm, M.J., and C.Y. Hopkins. 1966. Kamlolenic acid and other conjugated fatty acids in certain seed oils. *Amer. Oil Chemists Soc. J.* 43:390.

Clark, J.D. 1970. *The Prehistory of Africa.* New York: Praeger.

Coale, A.J., and P. Demeny. 1966. *Regional Model Life Tables and Stable Populations.* Princeton: Princeton University Press.

Coles, J.M. and E.S. Higgs. 1969. *The Archaeology of Early Man.* New York: Praeger.

Cook, G.C. 1973. Incidence and clinical features of specific hypolactasia in adult man. In Börgstron, B., Dahlqvist, A., and Hambreus, L., eds., "Intestinal Enzymes Deficiencies and their Nutritional Implications," *Symposia of the Swedish Nutrition Foundation,* 11. Uppsala: Almqvist and Wiksell.

Cooke, H.B.S. 1964. The pleistocene environment of southern Africa. In D.H.S. Davis, ed., *Ecological Studies in Southern Africa.* Monographie Biologicae, vol. 14, 1–23.

Corman, H., and S. Escalona. 1970. *Stages of sensori-motor development: a replication study.* Dept. of Psychiat., Albert Einstein School of Med. (MS).

Crawford, M.A. 1968. Fatty-acid ratios in free-living and domestic animals: possible implications for atheroma. *Lancet* 1:1329.

—— 1969. Dietary prevention of atherosclerosis. *Lancet* 2:1419.

379

Damas, D. 1969. Characteristics of central Eskimo band structure. In D. Damas, ed., Contributions to anthropology: band societies. *Nat. Mus. Can. Bull.* 228:116–138.

Dart, R.A. 1937. The physical characteristics of the /zauni–≠Khomani Bushmen. *Bantu Stud.* 11:175–246.

—— 1957a. The Makapansgat Australopithecine Osteodontokeratic culture. *Proc. IIIrd Pan-Africa Congr. Prehist.,* pp. 161–171.

—— 1957b. The Osteodontokeratic culture of Australopithecus prometheus. *Transvaal Mus. Memoir,* no. 10.

DeVore, I. 1963. Mother-infant relations in baboons. In H. Rheingold, ed., *Maternal Behavior in Mammals.* New York: Wiley & Sons.

*—— 1970. The ways of primates. In *Science Year 1971.* Chicago: Field Enterprises Educational Corp.

*—— 1971. The evolution of human society. In J.F. Eisenberg and W.S. Dillon, eds., *Man and Beast: Comparative Social Behavior.* Washington: Smithsonian Institution Press.

*—— 1972. Quest for the roots of society. In P. Marler, ed., *The Marvels of Animal Behavior.* Washington: National Geographic Society.

*—— and M.J. Konner. 1974. Infancy in hunter-gatherer life: an ethological perspective. In N.F. White, ed., *Ethology and Psychiatry.* Toronto: University of Toronto Press.

Dice, L.R. 1952. *Natural Communities.* Ann Arbor: University of Michigan Press.

Diem, K., ed. 1962. *Documents Geigy Scientific Tables.* 6th ed. Basle, Switzerland: Geigy.

Dornan, S.S. 1917. The Tati Bushmen (Masarwa) and their language. *J. Roy. Anthrop. Inst.* 47:37–113.

*Draper, P. 1972a. !Kung Bushman Childhood. Ph.D. dissertation, Harvard University, Cambridge, Mass.

*—— 1972b. *Crowding among living hunter-gatherers: comments on the concept of density and its relationship to pathology in humans.* (MS).

*—— 1973. Crowding among hunter-gatherers: the !Kung Bushmen. Science 182:301–303.

*—— 1975. !Kung women: contrasts in sexual egalitarianism in the foraging and sedentary contexts. In R. Reiter, ed., *Toward an Anthropology of Women.* New York: Monthly Review Press.

*—— *!Kung subsistence work at /Du/da: variation in adult work effort among the !Kung,* forthcoming.

Driver, P.M., and D.A. Humphries. 1970. Protean displays as inducers of conflict. *Nature* 226:968–969.

Drucker, P. 1955. *Indians of the Northwest Coast.* Garden City, N.Y.: Natural History Press.

Dunn, F. 1968. Epidemiological factors: health and disease in hunter-gatherers. In R. Lee and I. DeVore, eds. *Man the Hunter.* Chicago: Aldine, pp. 221–228.

Durkheim, E. 1912. *The Elementary Forms of the Religious Life.* Translated by J.W. Swain (1961). Collier Books Edition. New York: Collier Books.

Editorial. 1968a. Serum-lipids in Bushmen. *Lancet* 2:395.

Editorial. 1968b. Systolic murmurs in the elderly. *Brit. Med. J.* 4:530.

Eliade, M. 1967. *From Primitives to Zen.* New York: Harper & Row.

Elton, C. 1927. *Animal Ecology.* New York: The Macmillan Co.

Engelter, C., and A.S. Wehmeyer. 1970. Fatty acid composition of oils of some edible seeds of wild plants. *Agric. Food Chem.* 18:25.

Escalona, S. et al. 1969. *The Einstein scales of sensori-motor development.* Dept. of Psychiat., Albert Einstein School of Med. (MS).

FAO Nutritional Studies, no. 15. 1957. *Calorie requirements.* Report of the Second Committee on Calorie Requirements. Rome: FAO.

Fitzsimons, V.F. 1962. *Snakes of Southern Africa.* Cape Town: Purnell & Sons, Ltd.

Fowler, W. 1972. A developmental learning approach to infant care in a group setting. *Merrill-Palmer Quarterly* 18:145–175.

Fox, F.W. 1966. *Studies on the Chemical Composition of Foods Commonly Used in Southern Africa.* Johannesburg: South African Institute for Medical Research.

Freeman, L.G., Jr. 1968. A theoretical framework for interpreting archeological materials. In R.B. Lee and I. DeVore, eds., *Man the Hunter.* Chicago: Aldine.

Geber, M., and R.F.A. Dean. 1967. Precocious development of newborn African infants. 2nd ed. in Y. Brackbill and G.G. Thompson, eds., *Behavior in Infancy and Early Childhood.* New York: The Free Press.

Geldenhuys, P.J., A.F. Hallet, P.S. Visser, and A.C. Malcolm. 1967. Bilharzia survey in the Eastern Caprivi, Northern Bechuanaland and Northern South West Africa. *S. Afr. Med. J.* 41:767.

Gillet, S. 1969. Notes on the settlement in the Ghanzi district. *Botswana Notes and Records* 2:52–55.

Goldrick, R.B., P.F. Sinnett, and H.M. Whyte. 1970. An assessment of coronary heart disease and coronary risk factors in a New Guinea highland population. In R.J. Jones, ed., *Atheroslcerosis, Proc. IInd Symp.* New York: Springer-Verlag.

Gould, R.A. 1969. Subsistence behavior among the western desert aborigines of Australia. *Oceania* 39:253–274.

—— 1971. The lithic assemblage of the western desert aborigines of Australia. *American Antiquity* 36:149–169.

Grove, A.T. 1969. Landforms and climatic change in the Kalahari and Ngamiland. *Geographical Journal* 135:191–212.

Gsell, D., and J. Mayer, 1962. Low blood cholesterol associated with high calorie, high saturated fat intakes in a Swiss alpine village population. *Amer. J. Clin. Nutrition* 10:471.

Guenther, M. 1971. Kalahari Bushmen in transition. *Rotunda* 4:8–16.

Guerreiro, M. V. 1968. *Bochimanes !Khu de Angola.* Lisboa: Instituto de Investigação Científica de Angola.

Guggisberg, C. 1961. *Simba.* Capetown: Howard Timmius.

Hahn, T. 1881. *Tsuni-//Goam, the Supreme Being of the Khoi-Khoi.* London.

Haith, M., ed. 1972. Symposium on smiling. *Merrill-Palmer Quarterly of Behavior and Development* 18:321–367.

Hamilton, M., G.W. Pickering, J.A.F. Roberts, and G.S.C. Sowry. 1954. The aetiology of essential hypertension. 1. The arterial pressure in the general population. *Clin. Sci.* 13:11.

Hammel, H.T. 1964. Terrestrial animals in cold: recent studies of primitive man. In D.B. Dill, ed., *Handbook of Physiology* 4. Amer. Physiol. Soc.

*Hansen, J.D.L., A.S. Truswell, C. Freeseman, and B. MacHutchon. 1969. The children of hunting and gathering Bushmen. *S. Afr. Med. J.* 43:1158.

Harlow, H.F. 1958. The nature of love. *Amer. Psychol.* 13:673–685.

*Harpending, H.C. 1971. !Kung Hunter-Gatherer Population Structure. Ph.D. dissertation, Harvard University, Cambridge, Mass.

*—— and T. Jenkins. 1973a. !Kung population structure. In J.F. Crow, ed., *Genetic Distance.* New York: Plenum, in press.

*—— and —— 1973b. Genetic distance among Southern African populations. In M. Crawford and P. Workman, eds., *Method and Theory in Anthropological Genetics.* Albuquerque: University of New Mexico Press, in press.

Harper, L. 1972. Early maternal handling and preschool behavior of human children. *Develop. Psychobiol.* 5:1–5.

Hart, C.W.N., and A.R. Pilling. 1965. *The Tiwi of North Australia.* New York: Holt, Rinehart & Winston.

Hawthorne, V.M., C.R. Gillis, A.R. Lorimer, F.R. Calvert; and T.J. Walker. 1969. Blood pressure in a Scottish island community. *Brit. Med. J.* 4:651.

Hegsted, D.M., R.G. McGandy, M.L. Myers, and F.J. Stare. 1965. Quantitative effects of dietary fat on serum cholesterol in man. *Amer. J. Clin. Nutrition* 17:281.

Heinz, H.J. 1961. Factors governing the survival of Bushmen worm parasites in the Kalahari. *South Afr. J. Sci.* 57:207–213.

—— 1963. *The future of the Bushmen of the Kalahari; a plea report by request of the Bechuanaland Government,* limited circulation.

—— 1965. *Die Zukunft der Buschmanner der Kalahari.* Afrika Heute.

—— 1966. Social Organization of the !Ko Bushmen. Master's thesis, University of South Africa, Pretoria.

—— 1968. An Investigation of Social Relations of Bushmen on a Ghanzi Farm. Unpublished paper on a report prepared for the Ghanzi District Commissioner.

—— 1970. Experiences gained in a Bushmen pilot settlement scheme. *First Interim Report, Occasional Paper.* Johannesburg: University of Witwatersrand.

—— 1971. Experiences gained in a Bushman pilot settlement scheme. *Second Interim Report, Occasional Paper.* Johannesburg: University of Witwatersrand.

Helm, J. 1965. Bilaterality in the socio-territorial organization of the Arctic drainage Dene. *Ethnology* 4:361–385.

Hepburn, J.D. 1895. *Twenty Years in Khama's Country.* London: Hodder and Stoughton.

Hiatt, L.R. 1962. Local organization among the Australian aborigines. *Oceania* 32:276–286.

—— 1965. *Kinship and Conflict: A study of an Aboriginal Community in Northern Arnhem Land.* Canberra: ANU Press.

—— 1966. The lost horde. *Oceania* 37:81–92.

—— 1968. Ownership and use of land among the Australian aborigines. In R.B. Lee and I. DeVore, eds., *Man the Hunter.* Chicago: Aldine.

Higgs, E.S., C. Vita-Finzi, D. Harris, and A. Fagg. 1967. The climate, environment and industries of Stone Age Greece, Part III. *Proc. Prehist. Soc.* 33(1).

Hinde, R. 1959. Unitary drives. *Animal Behavior.* 7:130–141.

—— 1966. *Animal Behaviour.* London and New York: McGraw-Hill.

Hinde, R., and Y. Spencer-Booth. 1967. The effect of social companions on mother-infant relations in rhesus monkeys. In D. Morris, ed., *Primate Ethology*. Chicago: Aldine.

—— and —— 1968. The study of mother-infant interaction in captive group-living rhesus monkeys. *Proc. Roy Soc.* B.169:177–201.

—— and —— 1971. Effects of brief separations from the mother on rhesus monkeys. *Science* 173:111–118.

Hinshaw, R., P. Pyeatt, and J.P. Habicht. 1972. Environmental effects on child-spacing and population increase in highland Guatemala. *Current Anthropology*. 13:216–230.

Holt, J. 1969. *How Children Fail*. Hamondsworth: Penguin Books.

Howell, F.C. 1965. Early man. In *Life Nature Library*. New York: Time, Inc.

*Howell, N. n.d. *Demographic Studies of the !Kung Bushmen of the Dobe Area of Botswana: A Preliminary Report*. Princeton: Office of Population Research, Princeton University. (MS).

*—— n.d. *Estimating Absolute Age in a Remote and Nonliterate Population: A Method for Assigning Ages to Individuals of the !Kung Bushmen of the Dobe Area of Botswana*. Princeton: Office of Population Research, Princeton University. (MS).

*—— 1973. The feasibility of demographic studies in "anthropological" populations. In M. Crawford and P. Workman, eds., *Method and Theory in Anthropological Genetics*. Albuquerque: University of New Mexico Press.

*—— 1974. An empirical perspective on simulation models of human population. In J. MacCluer and B. Dyke, eds., *Computer Simulation of Human Populations*. New York: Academic Press.

*—— *Kinship as Connectivity*, in preparation.

Humphrey, T. 1965. The embryologic differentiation of the vestibular nuclei in man correlated with functional development. *Int. Symp. Vestibular and Oculomotor Problems*, Tokyo.

Humphries, D.A., and P.M. Driver. 1970. Protean defence by prey animals. *Oecologia* 5:285–302.

Imanishi, K. 1968. *Jinrui no Tanjo*. Tokyo. In Japanese.

Interdepartmental Committee on Nutrition for National Defense. (I.C.N.N.D.). 1963. *Manual for Nutrition Surveys*. 2nd ed. Washington, D.C.: U.S. Government Printing Office.

Itani, J. 1966. Chimpanzee no shakai kozo. *Shizen* 21(8). In Japanese.

—— and A. Suzuki. 1967. The Social unit of chimpanzees. *Primates* 8.

Jackson, W.P.U. 1964. *On Diabetes Mellitus*. Springfield, Ill: C.C. Thomas.

Jarrett, R.J., I.A. Baker, H. Keen, and N.W. Oakley. 1972. Diurnal variation in oral glucose tolerance: blood sugar and plasma insulin levels morning, afternoon and evening. *Brit. Med. J.* i:199.

Jarvis, J.F., and H.G. van Heerden. 1967. The acuity of hearing in the Kalahari Bushmen. A pilot survey. *J. Laryngol. Otol.* 81:63.

Jay, P. 1963. Mother-infant relations in langurs. In H. Rheingold, ed., *Maternal Behavior in Mammals*. New York: Wiley & Sons.

Jelliffe, D.B. 1966. *The assessment of the nutritional status of the community*. W.H.O. Monograph Series, no. 53. Geneva: World Health Organization.

*Jenkins, T. 1973. Red-Blood-cell adenosine deaminase deficiency in a "healthy" !Kung individual. *Lancet* (Sept. 29), 736.

—— H. Lehmann, and G.T. Nurse. 1974. Public health and genetic constitution of the San ("Bushmen"): carbohydrate metabolism and acetylator status of the !Kung of Tsumkwe in the North-western Kalahari. *Brit. Med. J.* 2:23–26.

*—— H. Harpending, H. Gordon, M. Keraan, and S. Johnston. 1971. Red-cell-enzyme polymorphisms in the Khoisan peoples of Southern Africa. *Amer. J. Human Genetics* 25:513–532.

Jensen, G.D., R.A. Bobbitt, and B.N. Gordon, 1968. Sex differences in the development of independence of infant monkeys. *Behaviour* 30:1–14.

Jersky, J., and R.H. Kinsley. 1967. Lactase deficiency in the South African Bantu. *S. Afr. Med. J.* 41:1194.

Joffe, B.I., W.P.U. Jackson, M.E. Thomas, M.G. Toyer, P. Keller; B.L. Pimstone, and R. Zamit. 1971. Metabolic responses to oral glucose in the Kalahari Bushmen. *Brit. Med. J.* 4:206–208.

Kaminer, B., and W.P.W. Lutz. 1960. Blood pressure in Bushmen of the Kalahari Desert. *Circulation* 22:289.

Kannel, W.B., N. Brand, J.J. Skinner, Jr., T.R. Dawber, and P.M. McNamara. 1967. The relation of adiposity to blood pressure and development of hypertension. *Ann. Int. Med.* 67:48.

—— W.P. Castelli, T. Gordon, and P.M. McNamara. 1971. Serum cholesterol, lipoproteins, and the risk of coronary heart disease. The Framingham study. *Ann. Int. Med.* 74:1.

Kaplan, J. 1972. Differences in the mother-infant relations of squirrel monkeys housed in social and restricted environments. *Devel. Psychobiol.* 5:43–52.

—— and R. Schusterman. 1972. Social preferences of mother and infant squirrel monkeys following different rearing experiences. *Devel. Psychobiol.* 5:53–60.

Kapleau, P. 1967. *Three Pillars of Zen.* Boston: Beacon Press.

*Katz, R. 1973. *Preludes to Growth: An Experiental Approach.* New York: The Free Press.

*—— *Boiling Energy: Community Healing among the Zhu/twasi,* in preparation.

Keay, R.W.J., ed. 1959. *Vegetation Map of Africa South of the Tropic of Cancer.* London.

*Kennelly, B.M., A.S. Truswell, and V. Schrire. 1972. A clinical and electro-cardiographic study of !Kung Bushmen. *S. Afr. Med. J.* 46:1093–1097.

Kessen, V., M.M. Haith, and P.H. Salapatek. 1970. Human infancy: a bibliography and guide. In P. Mussen, ed., *Manual of Child Psychology.* New York: Wiley & Sons.

Keys, A., ed. 1970. Coronary disease in seven countries. *Circulation* 41 and 42, suppl. 1.

—— J. Brozek, A. Henschel, O. Mickelson, and H.L. Taylor. 1950. *The Biology of Human Starvation,* vol. 1. Minneapolis: University of Minnesota Press.

—— et al. 1958. Lessons from serum cholesterol studies in Japan, Hawaii and Los Angeles. *Ann. Int. Med.,* 48:83.

Khosla, T., and C.R. Lowe. 1968. Height and weight of British men. *Lancet* 1:742.

Kokernot, R., E. Szlamp, J. Levitt, and B. McIntosh. 1965. Survey for antibodies against arthropod-borne viruses in the sera of indigenous residents of the Caprivi Strip and Bechuanaland Protectorate. *Trans. Roy. Soc. Trop. Med. and Hygiene* 59:553–562.

*Konner, M.J. 1971. Infants of a foraging people. *Mulch* 1:44–73.

*—— 1972a. Review of Baby and Child Care, Benjamin Spock, M.D. *Mulch* 2:70–78.

*—— 1972b. Aspects of the developmental ethology of a foraging people. In N.G. Blurton Jones, ed., *Ethological Studies of Child Behaviour,* Cambridge: Cambridge University Press.

*—— 1973a. Newborn walking: additional data. *Science* 179:307.

*—— 1973b. Infants of a Foraging People. Ph.D. dissertation, Harvard University, Cambridge, Mass.

*—— in press. Infancy among the Kalahari Desert San. In P.H. Leiderman and S. Tulkin, eds., *Cultural and Social Influences in Infancy and Early Childhood.* Stanford: Stanford University Press.

Korner, A. 1972. State as variable, as obstacle, and as mediator of stimulation in infant research. *Merrill-Palmer Quarterly* 18:77–94.

Korner, A., and R. Grobstein, 1966. Visual alertness as related to soothing in neonates. implications for maternal stimulation and early deprivation. *Child Develop.* 37:867–876.

Korner, A., and E. Thoman. 1970. Visual alertness in neonates as evoked by maternal care. *J. Exper. Child Psych.* 10:67–78.

Kruuk, H. 1972. *The Spotted Hyena.* Chicago: University of Chicago Press.

Kuper, A. 1970. *Kalahari Village Politics: An African Democracy.* Cambridge: Cambridge University Press.

Lalouel, J. 1973. *Topology of population structure.* In N.E. Morton, ed., Population Genetics Monographs, vol. 3. Honolulu: University of Hawaii Press.

Lancaster, J. 1971. Play-mothering: the relations between juvenile females and young infants among free-ranging vervet monkeys *(Cercopithecus aethiops). Folia Primat.* 15:161–182.

Langworthy, O. 1933. Development of behavior patterns and myelinization of the nervous system in the human fetus and infant. *Carnegie Institution of Washington, Contributions to Embryology* 24:1–57.

Lanternari, V. 1963. *The Religion of the Oppressed.* New York: Mentor.

Laughlin, W. 1968. Hunting: An integrating biobehavior system and its evolutionary importance. In R.B. Lee and I. DeVore, ed., *Man the Hunter.* Chicago: Aldine.

Leacock, E. 1955. Matrilocality in a simple hunting economy (Montagnais-Naskapi). *Southwestern J. of Anth.* 11:31–47.

—— 1969. The Montagnais-Naskapi band. In D. Damas, ed., Contributions to anthropology: band societies. *Bull. Nat. Mus. Can.* 228:1–17.

*Lee, R.B. 1965. Subsistence ecology of !Kung Bushmen. Ph.D. dissertation, University of California, Berkeley.

*—— 1966a. (Review of) Bushmen and other non-Bantu Peoples of Angola by Antonio de Almeida. *African Studies* 25(3):164–165.

*—— 1966b. (Review of) Report to the Government of Bechuanaland on the Bushman Survey by George B. Silberbauer. *American Anth.* 68:1040–1043.

*—— 1967. Trance cure of the !Kung Bushmen. *Natural History* (November), pp. 30–37.

*—— 1968a. What hunters do for a living, or how to make-out on scarce resources. In R.B. Lee and I. DeVore, eds., *Man the Hunter,* pp. 30–48. Chicago: Aldine.

*—— 1968b. The sociology of !Kung Bushman trance performances. In R. Prince, ed., *Trance and Possession States.* Second Annual Conference, R.M. Bucke Memorial Society, March 1966, pp. 35–54.

*—— 1969a. !Kung bushmen subsistence: an input-output analysis. In A.P. Vayda, ed., *Environment and Cultural Behavior,* pp. 47–79. New York: Natural History Press.

*—— 1969b. Eating Christmas in the Kalahari. *Natural History* (December), pp. 14–22, 60–63.

*—— 1969c. !Kung Bushmen (letter). *S. Afr. Med. J.* 43:47.

*—— 1971a. The Bushmen of the Kalahari Desert (Record and Filmstrip). In *Studying Societies: Patterns in Human History.* New York: Macmillan.

*—— 1971b. Kalahari-1 Site and Its Contents. In *The Origins of Humanness: Patterns in Human History.* New York: Macmillan.

*—— 1972a. The !Kung Bushmen of Botswana. In M. Bicchieri, ed., *Hunters and Gatherers Today,* pp. 327–368. New York: Holt, Rinehart & Winston.

·*—— 1972b. Work effort, group structure and land use in contemporary hunter-gatherers. In P.J. Ucko et al., eds., *Man, Settlement, and Urbanism,* pp. 177–185. London: Duckworth.

*—— 1972c. The intensification of social life among the !Kung Bushmen. In B. Spooner, ed., *Population Growth: Anthropological Implications,* pp. 343–350. Cambridge: MIT Press.

*—— 1972d. Population growth and the beginnings of sedentary life among the !Kung Bushmen. In Brian Spooner, ed., *Population Growth: Anthropological Implications,* pp. 329–342. Cambridge: MIT Press.

*—— 1972e. !Kung spatial organization: an ecological and historical perspective. *Human Ecology* 1(2):125–147.

*—— 1973a. The evolution of technical civilizations. In C. Sagan, ed., *Communication with Extra-Terrestial Intelligence: CETI,* pp. 85–94. Cambridge: MIT Press.

*—— 1973b. Mongongo: The ethnography of a major wild food resource. *Ecology of Food and Nutrition* 2:307–321.

*—— 1974. Male-female residence arrangements and political power in human hunter-gatherers. *Archives of Sexual Behavior* 3:167–173. Original from a paper presented at the workshop "Male-Female Behavior Patterns in Primate Societies" at the IV International Congress of Primatology (honoring Sherwood L. Washburn), Portland, Oregon, August 1972.

*—— *Kung Ecology,* in preparation.

*Lee, R.B., and DeVore, I., eds. 1968. *Man the Hunter.* Chicago: Aldine.

*—— and —— 1970. Ngamiland !Kung Bushmen: research in progress. *Botswana Notes and Records* 2:122–125.

Lehrman, D. 1953. A critique of Konrad Lorenz's theory of instinctive behaviour. *Quart. Rev. Biol.* 28:337–363.

Leistner, C.A. 1967. *The plant ecology of the southern Kalahari.* Botanical Survey of South Africa Memoir 38, Pretoria.

LeVine, R. 1970. Cross-cultural study in child psychology. In P. Mussen, ed., *Manual of Child Psychology.* New York: Wiley & Sons.

Levi-Strauss, C. 1962. *The Savage Mind.* London: Weidenfeld and Nicolson.

Longacre, W.A., and J.E. Ayres. 1968. Archaeological lessons from an Apache wickiup. In S.R. and L.R. Binford, eds., *New Perspectives in Archeology.* Chicago: Aldine.

Ludwig, A. 1969. Altered states of consciousness. In Tart, ed., *Altered States of Consciousness.* New York: Wiley & Sons.

Maccoby, E., and J. Masters. 1970. Attachment and dependency. In P. Mussen, ed., *Manual of Child Psychology.* New York: Wiley & Sons.

McGraw, M. 1963. *The Neuromuscular Maturation of the Human Infant.* 2nd ed. New York: Hafner.

McGregor, I.A., W.Z. Billewicz, and A.M. Thomson. 1961. Growth and mortality in an African village. *Brit. Med. J.* 2:1.

Maguire, B. n.d. *A report on the food plants ('veldkos') of the !Kung Bushmen of the Gautsha pan and Cigarette areas of northeastern South West Africa,* based on collections and observations made from mid-December 1952 until February 1953 in collaboration with the Harvard-Peabody Anthropological Expedition to South West Africa. (MS, circa 1954).

Mann, J.I., A.S. Truswell, D. Hendricks, and E. Manning. 1970. Effects on serum lipids in normal men of reducing dietary sucrose or starch for five months. *Lancet* 1:870.

Marais, J.S. 1939. *The Cape Coloured People, 1652-1937.* London: Longmans, Green and Co.

Marks, A.E. 1971. Settlement patterns and intrasite variability in the Central Negev, Israel. *Amer. Anth.* 73(5):1237–1244.

Marks, S. 1972. Khoisan Resistance to the Dutch in the Seventeenth and Eighteenth Centuries. *J. Afr. Hist.* 13:55–80.

Marshall, J. 1956. *The Hunters.* Somerville, Mass.: (Film) Center for Documentary Anthropology.

—— 1957. Ecology of the !Kung Bushmen of the Kalahari. Senior honors thesis in Anthropology, Harvard University, Cambridge, Mass.

—— 1958. Man as a hunter, parts 1 and 2. *Natural History* 67(6):291–309; 67(7):376–395.

Marshall, L. 1957a. The kin terminology system of the !Kung Bushmen. *Africa* 27(1):1–25.

—— 1957b. N!ow. *Africa* 27(3):232–240.

—— 1959. Marriage among the !Kung Bushmen. *Africa* 29:335–365.

—— 1960. !Kung Bushman bands. *Africa* 30:325–355.

—— 1961. Sharing, talking and giving: relief of social tensions among !Kung Bushmen. *Africa* 31:231–249.

—— 1962. !Kung Bushman religious beliefs. *Africa* 32(3):221–225.

—— 1965. The !Kung Bushmen of the Kalahari Desert. In J. Gibbs, ed., *Peoples of Africa.* New York: Holt, Rinehart & Winston.

—— 1968. Discussion. In R.B. Lee and I. DeVore, eds., *Man the Hunter,* Chicago: Aldine.

—— 1969. The medicine dance of the !Kung Bushmen. *Africa* 39(4):347–381.

*—— and M. Biesele. 1974. *N/um Tchai: The Ceremonial Dance of the !Kung Bushmen.* A Study Guide. Somerville, Mass: Documentary Educational Resources.

387

Maslow, A. 1962. *Toward a Psychology of Being.* Princeton: Van Nostrand Co.

Mason, R. 1962. The Prehistory of the Transvaal. Johannesburg: University of the Witwatersrand Press.

Mauss, M. 1906. Essai sur les variations saisonieres des sociétés eskimos: étude de morphologie sociale. *L'Année Sociologique* 9:39–132.

Meggitt, M.J. 1962. *Desert People: A study of the Walbiri Aborigines of Central Australia.* Sydney: Angus & Robertson.

*Metz, J., D. Hart, and H.C. Harpending. 1971. Iron, folate and vitamin B$_{12}$ nutrition in a hunter-gatherer people: a study of the !Kung Bushmen. *Amer. J. Clinical Nutrition* 24:229–242.

Metzger, F. 1952. *Und Seither Lacht die Hyäne.* Windhock: John Meinert.

Michel, P. 1967. Les grandes étapes de la morphogenèse dans les bassins des fleuves Sénégal et Gambie pendant le Quaternaire. Paper for 6th Pan African Congress on Prehistory in Dakar. Mimeographed.

Miller, D.C., S.S. Spencer, and P.D. White. 1962. Survey of cardiovascular disease among Africans in the vicinity of the Albert Schweitzer Hospital in 1960. *Amer J. Cardiol.* 10:432.

Miller, K., A. Rubenstein, A., and P.O. Astrand. 1968. Lipid values in Kalahari Bushmen. *Arch. Int. Med.* 121:414.

Monod, T. 1958. Majabat al Koubra. Contribution a l'etude de l'Empty Quarter ouest-Saharien. *Inst. Fr. d'Afr., Noire* no. 52.

Moodie, D. 1839. *The Record.* Cape Town.

Morton, N.E. 1964. Genetic studies of northeastern Brazil. *Cold Spring Harbor Symposia on Quantitative Biology* 29:69–79.

—— 1969. Human population structure. *Ann. Review of Genetics* 3:53–74.

Movius, H.L., Jr. 1965. Upper Périgordian and Aurignacian hearths at the Abri Pataud, Les Eyzies (Dordogne). *Miscelanea en Homenaje al Abate Henri Breuil* 2:181–189.

—— 1966. The hearths of the Upper Périgordian and Aurignacian Horizons at the Abri Pataud, Les Eyzies (Dordogne), and their possible significance. *Amer. Anth.* 68(2):296–325.

Murray, J.F., M.L. Freedman, H.I. Lurie, and A.M. Merriweather. 1957. 1 Witkop: a synonym for favus. *S. Afr. Med. J.* 31:657.

Neel, J.V., and N.A. Chagnon. 1968. The demography of two tribes of primitive, relatively unacculturated American Indians. *Proc. Natl. Academy of Sci.* 59:680–689.

Neeld, J.B. Jr., and W.N. Pearson. 1963. Macro and micromethods for the determination of serum vitamin A using trifluoracetic acid. *J. of Nutrition* 79:454–462.

Oken, D., and H.A. Heath. 1963. The law of initial values: some further considerations. *Psychosomatic Medicine* 25:3–12.

Orpen, J.M. 1874. A glimpse into the mythology of the Maluti Bushmen. *Cape Monthly Magazine.*

Paolucci, A.M., M.A. Spadoni, V. Pennetti, and L.L. Cavalli-Sforza. 1969. Serum free amino acid pattern in a Babinga pygmy adult population. *Amer. J. Clin. Nutrition* 22:1652.

—— M.A. Spadoni, and V. Pennetti. 1973. Modifications of serum-free amino acid patterns of Babinga adult pygmies after short-term feeding of a balanced diet. *Amer. J. Clin. Nutrition* 26:429–434.

Parkinson, C.E., and I. Gal. 1972. Factors affecting the laboratory management of human serum and liver vitamin A analyses. *Clin. Chim. Acta* 40:83–90.

Pettifor, J.M., and J.D.L. Hansen. 1974. Lactose intolerance in San populations. *Brit. Med. J.* 3:173.

Piaget, J. 1954. *The Construction of Reality in the Child*. New York: Basic Books.

—— 1962. *The Origins of Intelligence in Children*. New York: Norton.

Piddocke, S. 1965. The potlatch system of the southern Kwakiutl: a new perspective. *Southwestern J. of Anth.* 21:244–264.

Polgar, S. 1972. Population history and population policies from an anthropological perspective. *Current Anthropology* 13(2):203–211.

Prechtl, H. 1965. Problems of behavioral studies in the newborn infant. In *Advances in the Study of Behavior*, vol. 1. New York: Academic Press.

Prechtl, H.F.R., and D. Beintema. 1964. *The Neurological Assessment of the Full-Term Newborn Infant*. London: Heinemann.

Prechtl, H., and H. Lenard. 1968. Verhaltensphysiologie des Neugeborenen. In *Fortschritte der Pädologie*. Berlin: Springer-Verlag.

Radcliffe-Brown, A.R. 1930. The social organization of Australian tribes, part 1. *Oceania* 1:34–63.

Rasmussen, K. 1931. *The Netsilik Eskimos: social life and spiritual culture*. Report of the Fifth Thule Expedition, 1921–24, vol. 8, nos. 1–2. Copenhagen: Gyldendalske Boghandel.

Ratcliffe, J.D. 1967. The most primitive man on earth. *Reader's Digest*, p. 129.

Rheingold, H. 1960. The measurement of maternal care. *Child Develop.* 31:565–575.

Richards, M., and J. Bernal. 1972. An observational study of mother-infant interaction. In N.G. Blurton Jones, ed., *Ethological Studies of Child Behavior*. Cambridge/New York: Cambridge University Press.

—— and —— n.d. *Neuromotor development scale (based on McGraw 1963)*. Unit for Research on Medical Applications of Psychology. Cambridge University, Cambridge. (MS).

Richardson, H., and D. Cutler, eds. 1969. *Transcendence*. Boston: Beacon Press.

Roberts, A. 1957. *Birds of South Africa*. Cape Town: Cape Times Ltd.

Robinson, H.B., and N.M. Robinson. 1971. Longitudinal development of very young children in a comprehensive day care program: the first two years. *Child Develop.* 42:1673–1684.

Rose, F.G.G. 1960. *Kinship Age Structure and Marriage of Groote Eylandt*. Berlin: Academia-Verlag.

Saunders, S.J., A.S. Truswell, G.O. Barbezat, W. Wittmann, and J.D.L. Hansen. 1967. Plasma free amino acid pattern in protein-calorie malnutrition. Reappraisal of its diagnostic value. *Lancet* 2:795.

Schaller, G.B. 1972. *The Serengeti Lion*. Chicago: University of Chicago Press.

Schapera, I. 1930. *The Khoisan Peoples of South Africa: Bushmen and Hottentots*. London: Routledge and Kegan Paul, Ltd.

—— 1952. *The Ethnic Composition of Tswana Tribes*. Monographs on Social Anthropology, no. 11. London: London School of Economics.

—— 1956. *Government and Politics in Tribal Societies*. London: Watts.

389

Schrire, C. (formerly C. White). 1972. The ethno-archaeology of subsistence behaviour in Arnhem Land. In D.L. Clarke, ed., *Models of Archaeology.* London: Methuen.

Selous, F.C. 1893. *Travel and Adventure in South-East Africa.* London: Rowland Ward & Co.

Service, E.R. 1962. *Primitive Social Organization: An Evolutionary Perspective.* New York: Random House.

Service, E.R. 1966. *The Hunters.* Englewood Cliffs: Prentice-Hall.

Silberbauer, G.B. 1963. Marriage and the girl's puberty ceremony of the G/wi Bushmen. *Africa* 33(3).

—— 1965. *Bushman Survey Report.* Gaborone: Bechuanaland Government.

—— 1972. The G/wi Bushmen. In M.G. Bicchieri, ed., *Hunters and Gatherers Today.* New York: Holt, Rinehart & Winston.

—— and A. Kuper. 1966. Kgalagari masters and Bushman serfs: some observations. *African Studies* 25(4):171–179.

Smith, H. 1969. The reach and the grasp: transcendence today. In H. Richardson and D. Cutler, eds., *Transcendence.* Boston: Beacon Press.

Smithers, R.H.N. 1966. *The Mammals of Rhodesia, Zambia and Malawi.* London: Collins Clear-Type Press.

—— 1968. *A Checklist and Atlas of the Mammals of Botswana.* Salisbury: Trustees of the National Museums of Rhodesia.

Spencer, B., and F. Gillen, 1899. *The Native Tribes of Central Australia.* London: Macmillan.

—— and —— 1904. *The Northern Tribes of Central Australia.* London: Macmillan.

Spencer, R. 1959. The north Alaskan Eskimo: a study in ecology and society. *Bur. Amer. Ethnol. Bull.* 171.

Spock, B. 1968. *Baby and Child Care.* Revised edition. New York: Pocket Books.

Stanner, W.E.H. 1965. Aboriginal territorial organization: estate, range, domain, and regime. *Oceania* 36:1–26.

Stevenson-Hamilton, J. 1954. *Wildlife in South Africa.* London: Cassell.

Steward, J.H. 1936. The economic and social basis of primitive bands. In R.H. Lowie, ed. *Essays in Anthropology Presented to A.L. Kroeber.* Berkeley: University of California Press.

—— 1938. Basin-plateau aboriginal socio-political groups. *Bur. Amer. Ethnol. Bull.* 120.

—— 1955. *Theory of Culture Change: The Methodology of Multilinear Evolution.* Urbana: University of Illinois Press.

*Steinberg, A., T. Jenkins, H. Harpending, and G. Nurse. in press. Immunoglobin genetics in Kalahari peoples. *Amer. J. Human Genetics.*

Story, R. 1958. *Some plants used by the Bushmen in obtaining food and water.*m Botanical Survey of South Africa, Memoir no. 30. Pretoria.

Strehlow, T.G.H. 1947. *Aranda Traditions.* Melbourne: Melbourne University Press.

Sundkler, B. 1948. *Bantu Prophets in South Africa.* Cambridge: Cambridge University Press.

Suttles, W. 1960. Affinal ties, subsistence, and prestige among the coast Salish. *Amer. Anth.* 62:296–305.

—— 1962. Variations in habitat and culture on the Northwest Coast. *Acts of the 34th International Congress of Americanists, Vienna 1960.*

—— 1968. Coping with abundance: subsistence on the Northwest Coast. In R.B. Lee and I. DeVore, eds., *Man the Hunter.* Chicago: Aldine.

Suzuki, D.T. 1956. *Zen Buddhism: Selected Writings of D.T. Suzuki.* Edited by Barrett. Garden City, N.Y.: Anchor Books.

Taggart, P., and R. Carruthers. 1971. Endogenous hyperlipidaemia induced by emotional stress of racing driving. *Lancet* 1:363.

*Tanaka, J. 1969. The ecology and social structure of Central Kalahari Bushmen. In T. Umesao, ed., *African Studies III.* Kyoto: Kyoto University.

*—— 1971. *The Bushmen.* English translation by D.W. Highes and G.L. Barnes; Dept. of Anthropology, Univ. of Michigan, Ann Arbor. Tokyo: Shisakusha.

Tanner, J.M. 1964. *The Physique of the Olympic Athlete.* London.

—— and R.H. Whitehouse. 1962. Standards for subcutaneous fat in British children. *Brit. Med. J.* 1:446.

Tart, Charles, ed. 1969. *Altered States of Consciousness.* New York: John Wiley.

Thomas, E.M. 1959. *The Harmless People.* New York: Alfred A. Knopf, Inc.

Thomas, E.W. 1950. *Bushman Stories.* London: Oxford University Press.

Thomson, D. 1939. The seasonal factor in human culture. *Proc. Prehist. Soc.,* n.s.5:209–221.

Tinbergen, N. 1963. On the aims and methods of ethology. *Z. Tierpsychol.* 20:410–433.

Tinley, K.L. 1966. An ecological reconnaissance of the Moremi Wildlife Reserve, Botswana. Johannesburg: Okovango Wildlife Society.

Tobias, P.V. 1956a. On the survival of the Bushmen. *Africa* 26:174–186.

—— 1956b. The Evolution of the Bushmen. *Amer. J. Phys. Anthrop.* 14:384.

—— 1962a. On the increasing stature of the Bushmen. *Anthropos* 57:801.

—— 1962b. Early members of the Genus Homo in Africa. In G. Kurth, ed., *Evolution and Hominisation.* Stuttgart.

—— 1964. Bushman hunter-gatherers: a study in human ecology. In D.H.S. Davis, ed., *Ecological Studies in Southern Africa.* The Hague: W. Junk.

—— 1966 The peoples of Africa south of the Sahara. In P.T. Baker and J.S. Weiner, eds., *The Biology of Human Adaptability.* London: Oxford University Press.

—— 1970. Puberty, growth, malnutrition and the weaker sex and two new measures of environmental betterment. *The Leech* 40:101.

—— 1971. The stronger sex. *University of Witwatersrand Convocation Commentary, April.*

Tomita, K. 1966. The sources of food of the Hadzapi tribe: the life of a hunting tribe in East Africa. In K. Imanishi, ed., *University African Studies I,* Kyoto.

Traill, A. 1973. The compleat Guide to the Koon, Mineographed. Department of Linguistics, University of the Witwatersrand, Johannesburg.

*Truswell, A.S. 1972. Human nutritional problems at four stages of technical development. Inaugural Lecture delivered at Queen Elizabeth College, May, University of London.

*—— 1972. Nutritional status of Bushmen in N.W. Botswana. Paper read at 9th International Congress of Nutrition, September, Mexico City.

*—— and J.D.L. Hansen. 1968a. Medical and nutritional studies of !Kung Bushmen in Northwest Botswana: a preliminary report. *S. Afr. Med. J.* 42:1338.

*—— and —— 1968b. Serum-lipids in Bushmen. *Lancet* 2:684.

*—— and J.I. Mann. 1972. Epidemiology of serum lipids in southern Africa. *Atherosclerosis* 16:15–29.

*—— J.D.L. Hansen, P. Wannenburg, and E. Sellmeyer. 1969. Nutritional status of adult Bushmen in the northern Kalahari, Botswana. *S. Afr. Med. J.* 43:1157.

*—— B.M. Kennelly, J.D.L. Hansen, and R.B. Lee. 1972. Blood pressures of !Kung Bushmen in northern Botswana. *Amer. Heart J.* 84:5–12.

Tulkin, S.R. 1970 Mother-infant interaction in the first year of life: An inquiry into the influences of social class. Ph.D. dissertation, Harvard University, Cambridge, Mass.

—— 1971. Infants' reactions to mother's voice and stranger's voice: social class differences in the first year of life. Paper presented at the 1971 meeting of Society for Research in Child Development.

—— and J. Kagan. 1972. Mother-child interaction in the first year of life. *Child Develop.* 43:31–42.

Turnbull, C. 1965. *Wayward Servants: The Two Worlds of the African Pygmies.* Garden City: Natural History Press.

—— 1968. The importance of flux in two hunting societies. In R.B. Lee and I. Devore, *Man the Hunter.* Chicago: Aldine.

Van Reenen, J.F. 1966. Dental features of a low-caries primitive population. *J. Dental Res.* 45:703.

Vayda, A.P. 1961. A re-examination of Northwest Coast economic systems. *Trans. N.Y. Acad. Sci.,* ser. 2 23:618–624.

Vogt, E.Z. 1961. Some aspects of Zinacantan settlement patterns and ceremonial organization. *Estudios de Cultura Maya, I.* Mexico.

Walker, A.R.P., and B.F. Walker. 1969. The bearing of race, sex, age and nutritional state on the precordial electrocardiograms of young South African Bantu and Caucasian subjects. *Amer. Heart J.* 77:441.

Wallace, A. 1972. Shifts in Conditions of Anthropological practice. *Newsletter of the Amer. Anthrop. Assoc.* 13(1):10–11.

Walther, F. 1969. Flight behaviour and avoidance of predators in Thomason's gazelle. *Behaviour* 34:184–221.

—— 1972. African infant precocity. *Psychol. Bull.* 78(5):353–367.

Warren, N. 1971. *African infancy and early childhood.* Department of Psychology, University of Sussex. (MS).

Washburn, S., and C. Lancaster. 1968. The evolution of hunting. In R.B. Lee and I. DeVore, eds. *Man the Hunter.* Chicago: Aldine.

Watermeyer, G.S., J.I. Mann, and A.S. Truswell. 1972. Serum lipids in Ovambos. *S. Afr. Med. J.* 46:1390.

Watson, P.J., S.A. LeBlanc, and C.L. Redman. 1971. *Explanation in Archeology.* New York: Columbia University Press.

Weare, P., and A. Yalala. 1971. Provisional vegetation map of Botswana (first revision). *Botswana Notes and Records* 3:131–147.

Wehmeyer, A.S. 1966. The nutrient composition of some edible wild fruits found in the Transvaal. *S. Afr. Med. J.* 40:1102.

*—— R.B. Lee, and M. Whiting, 1969. The nutrient composition and dietary

importance of some vegetable foods eaten by the !Kung Bushmen. *S. Afr. Med. J.* 43:1529.

Wellington, J.H. 1955. *Southern Africa,* vol. 1. Cambridge: Cambridge University Press.

—— 1964. *South West Africa and Its Human Issues.* London: Oxford University Press.

Westphal, E.O.J. 1962. On classifying Bushman and Hottentot languages. *Afr. Lang. Stud.* 3:30–48.

—— 1963. The linguistic prehistory of Southern Africa: Bush, Kwadi, Hottentot and Bantu linguistic relationships. *Africa* 33:237–265.

White, B.L., and P.W. Castle. 1964. Visual exploratory behavior following postnatal handling of human infants. *Perceptual and Motor Skills* 18:497–502.

—— and R. Held. 1967. Plasticity of sensorimotor development. In J. Hellmut, ed., *Exceptional Infant,* vol. 1, *The Normal Infant.* Seattle: Special Child Publications.

White, C. 1971. Man and environment in Northwest Arnhem land. In D.J. Mulvaney and J. Golson, eds., *Aboriginal Man and Environment in Australia.* Canberra: Australian National University Press.

—— (see also Schrire), and N. Peterson. 1969. Ethnographic interpretations of the prehistory of western Arnhem Land. *Southwestern J. of Anth.* 25.45–67.

White, Gilbert. 1789. *The Natural History of Selbourne.* Edited and introduction by James Fisher. London: The Cresset Press, 1947.

Whiting, B. ed. 1974. *Six Cultures: Studies of Child-rearing.* New York: J. Wiley and Sons.

Whiting, J. 1971. Causes and consequences of the amount of body contact between mother and infant. Paper read at the American Anthropological Association Annual Meetings, New York.

—— and I. Child. 1953. *Child Training and Personality.* New Haven: Yale University Press.

Widdowson, E.M. 1970. Harmony of growth. *Lancet* 901–905.

Wiessner, P. 1972. *The Use of Ethnographic Data in Archaeological Investigation.* (MS).

Willey, G.R. 1953. Prehistoric settlement patterns in the Viru Valley, Peru. *Bur. of Amer. Ethnology Bull.* no. 155. Washington: Smithsonian Institution.

Williams, B.J. 1968. The Birhor of India and some comments on band organization. In R.B. Lee and I. DeVore, eds., *Man the Hunter.* Chicago: Aldine.

Wilmsen, E.N. 1972. *Interaction, Spacing Behavior and the Organization of Hunting Bands.* (MS).

Wilson, M., and L. Thompson. 1969. *The Oxford History of South Africa.* London: Oxford University Press.

Wolfheim, J.H., G.D. Jensen, and R.A. Bobbitt. 1970. Effects of group environment on the mother-infant relationship in pigtailed monkeys *(Macaca nemestrina). Primates* 11:119–124.

Wood, P. 1956. *Diseases of the Heart and Circulation,* 2nd ed. London: Eyre and Spottiswoode.

Woodburn, J. 1968a. Stability and flexibility in Hadza residential groupings. In R.B. Lee and I. DeVore, *Man the Hunter.* Chicago: Aldine.

—— 1968b. An introduction to Hadza ecology. In R.B. Lee and I. DeVore, eds., *Man the Hunter*. Chicago: Aldine.

Worsley, P. 1957. *The Trumpet Shall Sound*. London: MacGibbon.

Wyndham, C.H., J.F. Morrison, J.S. Ward, G.A.G. Bredell, M.J.E. von Rahden, L.D. Holdsworth, H.G. Wenzel, and A. Munro. 1964. Physiological reactions to cold of Bushmen, Bantu and Caucasian males. *J. Appl. Physiol.* 19:868.

*Yellen, J.E. 1971. Archaeological excavations in Western Ngamiland. *Botswana Notes and Records* 3:276.

*—— 1972. *Animals*. Cambridge: Educational Development Center.

*—— 1974. A Study of Cultural Variation in Middle and Late Stone Age Assemblages in Western Ngamiland, Botswana. Ph.D. dissertation, Harvard University, Cambridge, Mass.

*—— Cultural patterning in faunal remains: evidence from the !Kung Bushmen. In J. Yellen and D.W. Ingersoll, eds., *Experimental Archaeology*. New York: Columbia University Press, in press.

*—— and H.C. Harpending. 1972. Hunter-gatherer populations and archaeological inference. *World Archaeology* 4(2):244–253.

Zelazo, P.R., N.A. Zelazo, and S. Kolb. 1972. "Walking" in the newborn. *Science* 176:314–315.

Notes

1. The Dobe-/Du/da Environment: Background to a Hunting and Gathering Way of Life

1. The environmental topics in this chapter are more fully covered in previous publications. See Lee 1965; 1969; 1972a and b.

2. The question of climatic successions in the Kalahari is intriguing and largely unanswered. Grove (1969) postulates at least one wetter period prior to the formation of the alab dunes and a second one postdating the dune formation. Given that small shifts in the southern and westernmost extension of the ITF can result in extremely marked changes in rainfall, it seems likely that the northern Kalahari experienced numerous and pronounced climatic changes which will prove extremely difficult to disentangle in the geological record.

2. Settlement Patterns of the !Kung: An Archaeological Perspective

1. Following Willey (1953) two types of analogy may be distinguished: "specific historical," and "general comparative": The latter type is considered below.

2. This follows, basically, Chang's distinction between ecologically and sociologically oriented behaviors (1967b). While Chang uses the term "settlement pattern" to describe the former, and "community pattern" for the latter, I am following more common usage by subsuming both variables under the single heading "settlement pattern."

3. This aspect of !Kung spatial organization is considered in great detail in Chapter 3, as well as Lee (1965, 1972e) and Yellen and Harpending (1972).

4. I wish to express my gratitude to Polly Wiessner who drafted and undertook a great deal of the analysis on the settlement plans which I collected.

5. In Binford's terms (1971) the !Kung have a "curated" technology, which means that they save their tools. The reason for this is evident: iron tools are extremely difficult to obtain and they last for a long time. Thus the !Kung take them from camp to camp.

6. This sample includes all camps occupied in the N!abesha, /Tanagaba, and the Hwanasi areas. At N/on/oni ≠toa, camp 29, occupied for fifty man-hours, was eliminated in an attempt to keep the man-hours as nearly equal as possible in the three areas.

7. It is also interesting to note Gould's statement that among the Western Desert aborigines: "The trimming of stone adze flakes is done mainly in the habitation area *(ngura)* of the campsite, with each man performing the work around his own hearth." (1971, p. 152)

3. !Kung Spatial Organization: An Ecological and Historical Perspective

1. I would like to thank Sa//gai, /Ti!kai, ≠Toma !kom !gowsi, /"Xashe, //Kaihan!a, and K"xau!koma for their patience in describing past land-use patterns in the /Xai/xai-/Gem areas, and for many fruitful suggestions. Mark Dornstreich, Pat Draper, Michael Harner, Henry Harpending, June Helm, Nancy Howell, Patricia Koten, Eleanor Leacock, and John Yellen have made helpful comments on earlier versions of the paper. R.J. Andersson and the officers of the Botswana Weather Office kindly provided the raw data on Maun and Ghanzi rainfall. Lois Johnson drew the figures. The material for this paper was collected during three years of field work with the !Kung in 1963 to 1964 and 1967 to 1969. A version of this paper also appeared in *Human Ecology* 2:125–147 (1972).

4. Subsistence Ecology of Central Kalahari San

1. As it is specific for a dry river in the Kalahari with a shallow and flat bed, I have used the word "molapo" in its Tswana sense, "dry river."
2. "Pan" is a dry lake seen in the bushveld of Southern Africa and has a shallow and flat bed like a frying pan.
3. *The Ecology and Social Structure of Central Kalahari Bushman: A Preliminary Report* (1968) describes the general features of San economic life and social life.
4. Most of the ≠Kade San food items cannot be preserved. Storage of these two beans is an exceptional case together with the occasional preservation of dry meat for a few days. Significant quantities of stored food are, however, restricted because of frequent migration.
5. The field work upon which this study is based was supported by the Kyoto University Scientific Expedition for Africa (July 1967–March 1968) and the United States National Institute for Mental Health (May 1971–June 1972).

I am grateful to Dr. J. Itani of Kyoto University and Dr. Irven DeVore of Harvard University for their encouragement and support.

The Government of Botswana kindly gave permission for the work in the Central Kalahari Game Reserve to be undertaken.

5. From Hunters to Squatters: Social and Cultural Change among the Farm San of Ghanzi, Botswana

1. J. Marshall 1958; L. Marshall 1960; 1962, 1965. Lee 1965; 1968a and b.
2. For a few examples see Tobias 1964; Silberbauer 1965, pp. 114–132; Silberbauer and Kuper 1966; Heinz 1968.
3. Field research was carried out between September 1968 and April 1970, financed by Canada Council and Province of Ontario Fellowships. I gratefully acknowledge my debt to these organizations.
4. Colored (or, in Afrikaans, *Kleurling*) is the racial category whose members have, or have had in previous generations, one parent who is a full or mixed European. Most of the Colored of South Africa live in Cape Province and are the

offspring of early Hottentot, Malay, slave, and European settlers who intermarried. Their language, values, and life style is that of Europeans, albeit poor Europeans. Most of the Ghanzi Colored are immigrants from South Africa or Namibia who entered the area over the last decades. There are also some local Colored who are the offspring of racial intermixture between European settlers and San or African women.

5. There are only a few dozen Hottentots in the district. They are Nama (who call themselves *Gei/khana*), and it appears that they were once numerous in Ghanzi and well-organized politically. Possibly they were immigrants from Great and Little Namaqualand. Today not a trace is left of their previous "empire" (see Silberbauer 1965, p. 114).

6. In the southern villages the processes of acculturation are somewhat different from the ones dealt with in this paper, as the contacting people are primarily Africans. Information on San-African interaction in the area can be found in Silberbauer and Kuper 1966; Kuper 1970, 45 ff.; Silberbauer 1965, pp. 127-135; Lee 1965, pp. 20-38.

7. Information on these treaties is found in the National Archives, Gaborone, in the papers on "Settlement of the Ghanzi District" (number HC. 140/7).

8. It is important to keep in mind that these are stereotypes. The alleged depredations, past and present, of Africans against San that are described in the following two paragraphs are all aspects of this negative stereotype conceptualized by some farm San. There are very few early records to confirm whether the San were, in fact, regularly raided by the Tawana in the past (see Selous 1893, pp. 101, 105, 110, Hepburn 1895, p. 78; and Dornan 1917). Likewise, there are no recent cases of Africans killing or enslaving San nor, do I expect, will there be any in the future, Botswana being a progressive, independent country.

9. This is one of the two general categories of classifying animals. The other one is *'ko/wa* ("meat animal") which consists of all the edible creatures that are harmless to man. *N/ie /wa* are all the creatures that are inedible and harmful to man—the predators, crocodiles, scorpions, and Africans, as well as some Europeans.

10. This information on disease is based on the carefully kept clinical records at the San mission clinic where my wife, who was in charge, treated almost 10,000 patients during field work. Another source is the report on a medical survey of the Ghanzi district carried out in 1969 by the American Peace Corps physician, Dr. J. Thaler.

11. It is noteworthy that D.F. Bleek (1928a, p. 46) reports that over forty years ago the Nharo west of Ghanzi (in Sandfontein at the Namibian border) already used this term of self-reference. Bleek translates *k' 'amka* as "weak" and it would seem a plausible speculation that it has since acquired the meaning of "stupid" in the Ghanzi area due to the pressures of the marginal situation in which the farm San finds himself.

12. See D.F. Bleek 1928, p. 28; L. Marshall 1965, p 271; and Lee 1968b, p. 51.

13. These developments of large, social political gatherings of San consisting of many groups might shed light on the early accounts of the San which depict them as living in relatively large (100-200 members) predatory groups led by autocratic "captains" (e.g., Burchell 1822, pp. 162-164; or Campbell 1815, pp. 348-349; 1837, p. 198). This nontraditional picture of San social organization might be explained by processes of acculturation similar to those in Ghanzi.

6. The Population of the Dobe Area !Kung

1. The research on which this paper was based was carried out both in the field and at the Office of Population Research, Princeton University. I would like to acknowledge the contribution made to this research by Ansley Coale, Director of the Office of Population Research, through critical and constructive readings of drafts of the work reported here, through my demographic training, and through the provision of a stimulating and pleasant work environment. Jane Menken of OPR also contributed substantially to this work.

7. Regional Variation in !Kung Populations

1. This work was supported by NIMH grant MH 13611 to Irven DeVore and Richard Lee and by the research allocations committee of the University of New Mexico.

8. Medical Research among the !Kung

1. When some of these data were presented at the XI International Congress of Nutrition in Mexico on 1972, D.S. McLaren pointed out that during frozen storage the apparent value of vitamin A, by the method we used (Neeld and Pearson, 1963), can go up. Parkinson and Gal (1972) illustrate an example of this phenomenon. Serum vitamin A's were measured within 4 weeks of our return from Botswana (exact dates can no longer be found) and one of the author's sera (taken in the field) was included at the second visit as a control.

9. Social and Economic Constraints on Child Life among the !Kung

1. This characteristic noncompetitiveness was predicted for hunting and gathering societies as a whole by John W.M. Whiting in his comments during the Man the Hunter Conference (Lee and DeVore 1968, p. 339): "Although I know of no data on the subject, I would be very surprised if there were many competitive team sports among the hunters and gatherers—another reason for the emphasis on individual achievement rather than group responsibility."

2. Konner has pointed out that older children are likely to be doing some informal, nondirective child tending of their own—just by being on the premises as are the adults. I agree with this qualification and that the attention shown by an older child to a child of the 2½- to 5-year-old age group is generally voluntary, spontaneous, and quite erratic. Older children are not imbued with a sense of responsibility for young children.

10. Maternal Care, Infant Behavior and Development among the !Kung

1. I am grateful to Irven DeVore, Jerome Kagan, and N.G. Blurton Jones for all forms of support and friendship from the inception of this work to the present, and to Marjorie Shostak for her assistance and companionship through-

out. Financial support has come from the National Science Foundation (G.S.-2603), the National Institutes of Health (5-RO1-MH-13611), the Milton Fund, and the Foundations' Fund for Research in Psychiatry.

2. This technique emerged from a study (Chapter 14) by Blurton Jones and Konner of !Kung knowledge of animal behavior. It consisted of group interview and discussion.

11. A !Kung Woman's Memories of Childhood

1. Memories 1 and 2 probably took place when N≠isa was three or four years old; memories 3, 4, 5, and 6 when she was about six or seven.

2. Insults making reference to the genitals are common and are given either in jest or in anger. Even when expressed angrily, they are not very serious.

3. "Stinge": the word *"kxung,"* to be stingy, or to withhold, is repeatedly used as a verb throughout the narrative, "Stinge" seemed to me the closest possible English rendering.

4. The bush is a general term referring to all land beyond the village camp boundary.

5. N≠isa was probably between the ages of five and seven in memories 7, 8, 9, and 10.

6. "Ruin": the !Kung word *k"xwia* meaning general disruptiveness.

7. The !Kung believe that the expression of intense anger is sometimes followed by sickness in the person to whom the anger was directed.

8. Thumb piano: a musical instrument now very popular among !Kung children. It is questionable whether this is actually the instrument she played because the thumb piano is believed to have been introduced more recently.

9. "Homa": fictitious village name.

10. The caterpillars eaten by the !Kung are about two inches long and have smooth skins. They are considered a great delicacy.

11. N≠isa was from six to twelve years old during the episodes in this section.

12. The expression "tchi" literally means sexual intercourse, but in reference to children it only means experimental sexual play without actual intromission.

13. The !Kung word *"//"xwasi -"* literally means "to work" and is used humorously in this context.

14. The kaross *chikn!a* is a skin worn by women. When it is tied around the waist and neck, a pouch is formed in which children and food are carried.

15. Trance dance: see Katz (Chapter 11).

16. *" Xai, kow-a-di "*: cried out during the trance dance by a man in trance and in the act of curing.

17. N≠isa was probably about thirteen years old in memory 18 and fifteen years old in memories 19, 20, 21, 22, and 23.

18. N≠isa was married five times in all. At the time of the interviews, she was living with her fifth husband. /"Tashay, whom she meets and married in memories 22–26, was her third husband. She was about thirteen years old the first time she married. This marriage lasted only a few days because her husband, who was much older, had an affair with an older woman. Traditionally, when a grown man marries a young girl, an older woman is asked to spend the first few nights with the couple. This gives the girl a sense of protection and helps her adjust to her new situation. In N≠isa's case, however, the older woman contributed to the

break-up of the marriage. The woman, one of N≠isa's relatives, had been N≠isa's husband's lover prior to the marriage. During the first few nights, they engaged in sexual relations in the hut. N≠isa told her parents about it, and they dissolved the marriage.

N≠isa's next marriage, begun about a year later, lasted a few months and ended in a dispute about food. Because there is an imposed scarcity of women of marriageable age (due to polygamy), a son-in-law has to prove himself worthy of his wife (L. Marshall 1959; Lee 1974). In N≠isa's father's eyes, her second husband did not fulfill his responsibilities. They quarreled over some meat that the son-in-law had brought with him from his parents' village. Her father asked for a portion, and her husband said he would give it to him in the morning. When her father then pressed him for a share, her husband refused. Her father took this refusal as an insult and said it showed he would not take care of his daughter and her family in the future. Much to N≠isa's delight (she still did not feel ready to be married), her father told him the marriage was finished and that he should leave.

N≠isa married her third husband, /"Tashay, when she was about fifteen. Her breasts had begun to develop, but she had not yet reached menarche. In the marriage negotiations described in memory 19, N≠isa's father blames her for having left her previous husbands and accuses her of being fickle, although he and his wife had actually terminated both previous marriages. When parents discuss marriage plans with their daughter's prospective parents-in-law, it is usual for them to deprecate her. This is in keeping with the general !Kung concern to avoid being thought of as acting "proud."

19. The !Kung have a simple marriage ceremony which takes place over a two-day period. When both sets of parents have agreed to the marriage, the two mothers work together and build a marriage hut for the couple. The !Kung believe that the sun is death-giving because it dries up all the water, and consequently, during this day, the girl keeps a covering over her head so that the sun will not shine on her. Once the sun has set, a firebrand from the fire of each set of parents is brought over to light the fire in front of the marriage hut. Women friends and girlfriends go to where the girl has been waiting, pick her up so that her feet do not touch the ground, and carry her to the marriage hut. They leave her inside, and she lays down with the cover still over her. Male friends escort the boy, and he sits down outside the hut with his friends. Boys and girls sit by the couple's fire and have a good time: they sing, play music, and eat whatever they have. Neither the couple nor their parents joins them in these activities. Late in the night the boy goes into the hut to sleep, but not to make love. The next morning oil and red powder are rubbed over the bodies of the couple by female relatives of both. This marks the end of the formal ceremony (L. Marshall 1959).

20. The !Kung, when they are sick, sometimes tie a piece of rope or leather around the body part that ails them.

12. Education for Transcendence: !Kia-Healing with the Kalahari !Kung

1. Revision of a chapter appearing in Richard Katz, *Preludes to Growth: An Experiential Approach* (Free Press, 1973). Copyright 1973, Transpersonal Insti-

tute, 2637 Marshall Drive, Palo Alto, California 94303. Reprinted by permission with slight editing from Volume 5, Number 2 of the *Journal of Transpersonal Psychology.*

2. In future writings I plan to present research findings on other aspects of this experience of transcendence: the dance structure in which the experience occurs, the phenomenology and psychology of the experience, the healing which results from the experience, characteristics of those who have the experience, and the effects of this experience on individual and cultural maintenance and growth. See Katz (in preparation) for a presentation of many of these findings.

3. The following sections are based on field work I did while living with the !Kung in the Kalahari Desert in northwest Botswana, Africa. My research was supported by NIMH grant #MH 13611.

I am indebted to Richard Lee, who was my colleague, collaborator, and interpreter in the field. His help continues to be invaluable. The !Kung accepted me and gave me a sense of home. Several !Kung made a special effort to teach me some things about !kia. I feel an enduring gratitude toward them; and out of respect, they shall remain anonymous.

I have decided to retain certain !Kung words such as *!kia* and *n/um.* These words are central to an understanding of their experiences of transcendence, and they are not easily translated. Certain translations have already been offered in the literature; !kia has been translated as trance, and n/um as medicine. But these English words are vague and possibly inaccurate. I hope that a more complete and accurate understanding of the !Kung words can emerge from considering what the *!Kung* say about the *experiences* the words refer to. For the sake of simplicity, I will use !kia and !kia-healing interchangeably, though there are other !kia states not connected with healing.

4. I will not be talking here specifically about !Kung women. But the *process* of educating for !kia is fundamentally similar for men and women.

5. A pseudonym, as are all other !Kung personal names used in the text.

6. Of those who have n/um, 57 percent were taught to !kia, i.e., received n/um, from their kin (19 percent were taught by their fathers); 25 percent were taught by nonkin; 9 percent received n/um from God; 2 percent were self-taught; and 7 percent did not specify their source of n/um. These percentages are derived from interview data collected by Richard Lee.

7. I am using the term "student" to signify someone who has yet to !kia and who is seeking n/um. I also use the term "potential n/um master." It signifies someone who, at a particular dance in which he participates, will !kia. It is a more inclusive term, including students who for the first time will get n/um during that dance, as well as persons of varying experience in !kia.

8. Richard Lee has collected data which show a significant relationship between a father's having n/um and his son's getting n/um, whether or not the father actually teaches the son. Could there be some inheritability of a predisposition toward !kia?

9. See Katz (in preparation) for a more complete description of the data on these individual predisposing factors.

10. The drug is awaiting botanical identification and analysis. It appears to be a psychoactive substance which has not yet been reported in the literature. I never observed the use of this drug during any of the !kia-healing dances I attended.

13. Aspects of !Kung Folklore

1. Kauri is a small collection of semipermanent villages near the southeast extremity of !Kung territory. It lies twelve miles west of the Tswana village of Tsau, between toteng and Nokaneng. Tsaukwe and Nharo speakers are frequent visitors there, as are the Dobe !Kung.

14. !Kung Knowledge of Animal Behavior (or: The Proper Study of Mankind Is Animals)

1. Schaller (1972) describes a not dissimilar occurrence, and Douglas-Hamilton (personal communication) has found fairly significant predation by lions on elephants around Lake Manyara in Tanzania.

2. This discussion took place early in Konner's stay and was interpreted with the assistance of Henry Harpending.

3. Incidentally this bears on one of Lee's (1968a) statements about the source of food at one time of year. In a table in his paper he lists running down fawns, a note suggesting that perhaps only fawns of caching species are taken, where it may be possible to catch them before they begin to run.

15. Sharing, Talking, and Giving: Relief of Social Tensions among the !Kung

1. This chapter was originally published in *Africa* 31:3 (July 1961), 231–249. It is republished here with the kind permission of the International African Institute.

The second paragraph of the essay is partially rewritten for greater clarity. The sentence marked with this note is especially changed. It formerly read: "Moreover, in this society the ownership of resources of food and water is organized through the headmen of bands and individuals have rights to these resources by being members of a band connected to the headman by some near or remote kin or affinal bond." I feel that the statement needs explanation, especially the word headman. However, since this paragraph is not the place to explain it, I prefer to take the sentence out to make instead the more general statement that the ownership of resources is organized through the band structure, and to give brief explanation of the former sentence in this note. The head of a band is called *k"xau n!a,* "big owner." He does not own the resources personally or exclusively as !Kung own their artifacts. He symbolizes the ownership for the band and gives the ownership continuity.

2. Slabs of meat are cut into strips in the following manner: an incision is made across the slab from the edge, say the right edge, an inch or two down from the top of the slab; the incision is stopped shortly before it reaches the left edge. An inch or two below it another incision is begun, this time at the left edge; it is stopped shortly before it reaches the right edge; and so on. Held at the top, the slab cut in this way unfolds into a zigzag strip, about one to two inches wide.

3. This paragraph, mentioning the three additional quarrels that John Marshall witnessed and filmed, is an addition to the paper.

Index

INDEX

408